MAIMONIDES' CONFRONTATION
WITH MYSTICISM

THE LITTMAN LIBRARY OF
JEWISH CIVILIZATION

Maimonides' Confrontation with Mysticism

MENACHEM KELLNER

London

The Littman Library of Jewish Civilization
in association with Liverpool University Press

The Littman Library of Jewish Civilization
Registered office: 4th floor, 7–10 Chandos Street, London WIG 9DQ

in association with Liverpool University Press
4 Cambridge Street, Liverpool L69 7ZU, UK
www.liverpooluniversitypress.co.uk/littman

Managing Editor: Connie Webber

Distributed in North America by
Oxford University Press Inc., 198 Madison Avenue,
New York, NY 10016, USA

First published in hardback 2006
First published in paperback 2010

Catalogue records for this book are available from the
British Library and the Library of Congress

ISBN 978-1-906764-15-9

Publishing co-ordinator: Janet Moth
Copy-editing: Lindsey Taylor-Guthartz
Proof-reading: Philippa Claiden
Index: Menachem Kellner
Design: Pete Russell, Faringdon, Oxon.
Typeset by Hope Services (Abingdon) Ltd.

Printed and bound in Great Britain by
CPI Group (UK) Ltd., Croydon, CRO 4YY

Foreword

❦

MOSHE IDEL

MANY BOOKS on Maimonides have been written and still more will appear. Most are written by scholars of Maimonides, themselves often open or hidden Maimonideans. Menachem Kellner's book is written by a scholar who does not necessarily wish to be identified as a religious or intellectual follower of his subject. Not that Professor Kellner has anything against Maimonides; on the contrary, he would like to have the best of him consonant with modern sensibilities. His book presents the Great Eagle in the relativity of his greatness. This means that he believes that, in order to understand Maimonides and his achievement, it is necessary to encounter the various religious versions of Judaism that existed before Maimonides. This necessitates a relativizing approach, since Maimonides' views should be understood, not so much as the expression of a 'true' Judaism, but as the fascinating alternative he offered to other forms of the religion.

Less a philosopher than a religious thinker, Maimonides is presented here against the religious background that informed his many innovative and influential choices. The book is thus not only an analysis of the thought of the great religious thinker but a complex survey of what was actually available on the horizon of the many contemporary Jewish literatures, with which he engaged in a dialogue that was often critical. The discussions that serve as the background and foil to Maimonides' thought reiterate the lack of a Jewish orthodoxy before him, a leitmotiv of one of Professor Kellner's earlier books. In a way, Maimonides himself was not an orthodox thinker, since there was no established orthodoxy before his time, but he strove to establish an orthodoxy and indeed succeeded in doing so. Thus, while Maimonides' religious outlook serves as a clear centre for the entire enterprise, Professor Kellner tells a story that is much more complex than a simplistic portrait of the Great Eagle as the opponent to the elusive Sabians, or as a religious leader dealing with unpleasant characteristics of earlier Judaism. In order to do this, he has had to engage a huge bibliography—the only reliable way of evaluating the originality of Maimonides' thought. Maimonides did the same; he confessed to having read two hundred books of magic, perhaps more than many of the scholars of magic in academia today.

Professor Kellner surmises the pre-Maimonidean existence of Jewish world-views that he calls proto-kabbalistic (similar to the thought of Rabbi Judah Halevi), which, in different ways, constituted the trigger for Maimonides' rethinking of Judaism. This rethinking process is the core of the original contribution of the present book, which deals with a religious reform. The best way to understand the gist of Maimonides' project would be to present him as a reformer, not unlike Martin Luther with his reform of Catholic Christianity. However, while the Protestant Reformation was basically fideistic, the Maimonidean one was naturalistic. What was the essence of this reform? Professor Kellner would formulate it as follows: Maimonides thoroughly depersonalized proto-kabbalistic Judaism, including the concept of divinity, angelic terminology, the Divine Presence (*Shekhinah*), the Glory (*kavod*), demons, and, finally, man himself, who is ideally reduced to his mental capacity. In reaction to this intellectualist reform of many elements in Jewish proto-kabbalism, a counter-reformation led by the younger generation of Maimonides' contemporaries created the historical forms of kabbalism. This was perhaps the deepest restructuring of Judaism since Rabbi Yohanan ben Zakai.

The main assertion that emerges from Professor Kellner's book is that Maimonides was a religious thinker who attempted, as Kellner formulates it, to disenchant Judaism. As presented by Judah Halevi, Nahmanides, or the vast majority of kabbalists, Judaism presents the concepts of purity, commandments, or the process of halakhic decision-making as parts of an enchanted universe, with complex ontologies and occult affinities that predetermine much of religious life. Endowing religious man with choices and great freedom, Maimonides created a new, if highly elitist, Judaism, thus undercutting one of the most characteristic features of the two major forms (biblical and rabbinic) of earlier Judaism: the democratic structure of religious knowledge as envisioned in both biblical and rabbinic Judaism. Elitism is irrevocably related to esotericism, as Professor Kellner suggests, and this immediately necessitates a certain type of exclusive religion. The secrecy that enwraps the ideals—and perhaps the beliefs—of this new form of Judaism represents not a continuation of the modest discussions of the 'secrets of the Torah' found in rabbinic or Heikhalot literature, but, rather, the infusion of a new form of esotericism of Platonic origin, which has as its main audience the community no less than the canonical book. The secrets are dangerous, not because they misrepresent Torah but because they are potentially damaging to the masses and may destabilize communal solidity. In a way Maimonides, who shuns particularistic strands which ontologize the Jew, arrives at an elitist position that creates a new community of thinkers—à la al-Farabi—to wit, non-Jewish Jews. Shifting the centre of gravity of the halakhocentric rabbinic system from specific deeds to specific thoughts engenders an intrinsic state of tension in the superiority of the mental over the performative.

A more historical remark on the margin of this book: it is quite optimistic. To believe that one person was able to reform so many aspects of rabbinic Judaism single-handedly, to enrich it by importing such dramatically different concepts, shows that the profound structures of this religion are flexible enough to allow the emergence and success of astonishing reforms. The fact that, great as Maimonides was, he did not overcome the traditional forms of proto-kabbalism shows that the dynamic of religion is much more complex than subscribing to authorities, however widely accepted. Tradition, inertia, nostalgia, and a deep involvement with the classical texts were strong antidotes against the magical power of Maimonides' persuasion. In fact, I believe that in order to succeed in such a dramatic reform, one must be a great magician of language.

The great irony of the later development of Judaism is found in its most widespread and used text: the prayer-book. Maimonides formulated the 'Thirteen Principles', which (in a more poetic version) became the credo of traditional Jews, included in the liturgy and recited every day. This would seem to be maximum canonization de facto. However, exactly this achievement was paralleled by potential opponents of Maimonides' views. The proto-kabbalists are represented in the prayer-book by the Aleinu prayer, with its Heikhalot terminology and anti-Christian overtones, while the full-fledged kabbalists who wrote the Zohar and the arch-kabbalist Rabbi Isaac Luria received the same accolade: their Aramaic texts and poems also became an accepted part of the traditional liturgy, part of the generally prevailing peaceful coexistence between strikingly divergent forms of thought. This unacknowledged, implicit, and eclectic theological pluralism is far removed from Maimonides' theological strictures. If Judaism is to be defined or described by its practice more than by its beliefs, the prayer-book—the most widespread and influential Jewish document—tells us a story that can be summarized as follows: Maimonides the theological thinker, who offers an abstract orthodoxy, is complemented by poetic pieces replete with mysticism, whose theosophy is quite different from his. Coherence is not a matter of a commonly accepted theology—people who think together about the nature of God as part of their worship—but is performative in nature, achieved by people reciting the same texts synchronically speaking together. This sonorous ambience, important in rabbinic Judaism, remained important after the intellectualist reform. If, for Maimonides, Jews are those who think correctly about God and reality, then it is Halevi who prevailed in the liturgical emphasis on Hebrew, pronunciation, and togetherness. While Maimonides would have some problems with the content and the form of prayer in some hasidic *shtiblakh*, he would nevertheless be quite welcome among those mystical enthusiasts. Particularistic as they are, they are nevertheless more tolerant than the universalistic Maimonides.

In one of his generous remarks, Professor Kellner argues that Maimonides would agree with my approach. I wish, and have my reasons to assume, that Maimonides would agree with Kellner's.

Preface

THE MAIMONIDES presented in this book will seem to many readers to be so far out of the mainstream of Judaism as to have left it altogether. Traditionalist Judaism today is often understood by its practitioners and presented by its exponents and interpreters as if the crucial element in Jewish religious identity is ethnic, determined by descent from Abraham, Isaac, and Jacob. Such Jews, influenced by the thought of Rabbi Judah Halevi (d. 1141) and the ontological essentialism of kabbalah, in effect see the crucial event in Jewish religious history as being the Covenant of the Pieces between God and Abraham. Maimonides sees the crucial event in Jewish religious history as the revelation at Sinai, when the descendants of Abraham, Isaac, and Jacob converted to Judaism.

This point must be fleshed out. Thinkers like Judah Halevi, the authors of the Zohar, Maharal of Prague (c.1525–1609), Rabbi Shneur Zalman of Lyady (1745–1813), and Rabbi Abraham Isaac Kook (1865–1935) were all convinced that Jews are distinguished from non-Jews by some essential characteristic which made them ontologically distinct and superior. This view has no source in the Hebrew Bible at all and very few clear-cut sources in rabbinic literature, but it came to dominate medieval and post-medieval Judaism. (This is hardly surprising, given the way in which the non-Jewish world threatened the Jews for much of this period.)

Maimonides, as I will make clear below, did not express himself unambiguously on these issues; as is well known, he wrote esoterically. If he contradicts himself on the issue of universalism and particularism, why not see his universalist statements as exoteric window-dressing, which do not reflect his true views? Another way of putting this is to ask why one should insist, as I will be doing in this book, on taking his universalist statements as basic and reading his particularist statements in their light? Why not do the reverse? After all, that is the way in which Maimonides has been read by many of his students over the centuries (a reading, I might add, which allows him to remain an authoritative figure in rabbinic circles).

One ought to adopt the following methodology. First, it is crucial to read what Maimonides actually said, not what he should have said (according to the reader's preconceptions). What Maimonides actually says in very many contexts is surprisingly universalist.

Second, one must examine what options were really open to Maimonides—that is, what ideas were really available to him. These options include not only the tradition of Greek–Arabic philosophy (with its implicit universalist thrust), but a tradition of Jewish biblical and rabbinic universalism as well.

Third, one ought to adopt a method proposed by the philosopher Susan Haack (in the context of an argument against epistemological relativism) and see Maimonides' writings as a kind of crossword puzzle. At any given point in filling out a crossword puzzle, a number of different solutions might satisfy any given hint. But that does not make all solutions equally reasonable. As Haack notes, 'How reasonable a crossword entry is depends on how well it is supported by its clue and any already completed entries; how reasonable these other entries are, independent of the entry in question; and how much of the crossword has been completed.'[1] Reading Maimonides as a particularist demands the revision of a great many already completed entries in the Maimonidean crossword.

[1] Haack, 'Staying for an Answer', 12.

Acknowledgements

THE BOOK you hold in your hands has been gestating for quite some time. As with so many other good things in my life, it began with a conversation with my wife, Jolene S. Kellner. I had made some comment or other about the deleterious impact of kabbalah upon Judaism; Jolene wanted me to back up the comment with facts. This book is not what she asked for, but without her it would not have come to be.

Four colleagues read the manuscript in its entirety, and I am deeply grateful to them for their time and sage counsel: James Diamond, Moshe Idel, Charles Manekin, and Kenneth Seeskin. Moshe Idel further honoured me by agreeing to write the foreword. Many other colleagues have been extremely helpful in reading parts of the book in its various reincarnations (how inappropriate a word!); I here record my thanks to Ya'akov Blidstein, J. H. Chajes, Shai Cherry, Gad Freudenthal, Joshua Golding, Warren Zev Harvey, Raphael Jospe, Avi (Seth) Kadish, Daniel J. Lasker, Berel Dov Lerner, Diana Lobel, Avram Montag, Gedaliah Oren, Marc Shapiro, Josef Stern, and Alan Yuter. Over the years I have had the privilege of teaching many of the texts analysed here to classes at the University of Haifa. The input of many students has helped me refine my understanding of the texts and issues examined in this book. In particular, I record my gratitude to Yisrael Ben-Simon, Nurit Feinstein, Oded Horetzky, Liron Hoch, Hayim Shahal, Yisrael Stockman, and Eliezer Zitronenbaum. Over the many enjoyable years I have been at the University of Haifa, I benefited from the sage counsel of my friend and colleague, Mordechai Pachter, on many subjects, not just kabbalah, though I have certainly learned much from him on this subject as well. During a recent sabbatical I attended his stimulating lectures and gained immensely thereby. The influence upon me of Steven S. Schwarzschild, who died in 1989, increases with each passing year—an indication, I hope, of growing wisdom on my part. *Tsadikim afilu bemitatam nikra'im ḥayim* (which may be paraphrased as 'The righteous live on after their death').

Texts from the *Guide of the Perplexed* are quoted from the translation of Shlomo Pines (Chicago: University of Chicago Press, 1963). Texts from Judah Halevi's *Kuzari* are quoted from the forthcoming translation of Barry

Kogan and the late Larry V. Berman (Yale Judaica Series, in press). I thank Professor Kogan for his great kindness and for providing me with an advance copy of this translation.

The Littman Library has once again outdone itself. At every step of the way Connie Webber, Ludo Craddock, Janet Moth, and Lindsey Taylor-Guthartz have been exemplars of everything an author can look for in a publishing team. They are also fun to work with. I would also like to thank Pete Russell for the striking cover illustration.

Portions of this work have appeared in the following articles. In every case I have reworked, revised, and expanded the earlier versions. Grateful appreciation is here expressed for permission to reprint the following:

Portions of Chapter 3, from 'Spiritual Life', in Kenneth Seeskin (ed.), *Cambridge Companion to Maimonides* (New York, 2005), 273–99.

An earlier version of Chapter 4, from 'Maimonides on the Nature of Ritual Purity and Impurity', *Da'at*, 50–2 (2003), 1–30; a portion of this chapter (which did not appear in the *Da'at* article) is translated from 'The Moral Significance of the Laws of Ritual Purity and Impurity: A Maimonidean Study' (Heb.), *Sha'anan*, 9 (2004), 213–21.

An earlier version of Chapter 5, from 'Maimonides on the "Normality" of Hebrew', in Jonathan Malino (ed.), *Judaism and Modernity: The Religious Philosophy of David Hartman* (Aldershot, 2004), 413–44.

Portions of Chapter 7, from 'Steven Schwarzschild, Moses Maimonides, and "Jewish Non-Jews"', in Görge K. Hasselhoff and Otfried Fraisse (eds.), *Moses Maimonides (1138–1204): His Religious, Scientific, and Philosophical Wirkungsgeschichte in Different Cultural Contexts* (Würzburg, 2004), 587–606, and from 'Was Maimonides Truly Universalist?', *Trumah: Beitraege zur juedischen Philosophie*, 11 (Festgabe zum 80. Geburtstag von Ze'ev Levy) (2001), 3–15.

Several paragraphs from the Afterword are translated from 'Rabbis in Politics: A Study in Medieval and Modern Jewish Political Theory' (Heb.), *Hevrah umedinah*, 3 (2003), 673–98.

Contents

❧

Note on Transliteration and Conventions Used in the Text

THE transliteration of Hebrew in this book reflects consideration of the type of book it is, in terms of its content, purpose, and readership. The system adopted therefore reflects a broad approach to transcription, rather than the narrower approaches found in the *Encyclopaedia Judaica* or other systems developed for text-based or linguistic studies. The aim has been to reflect the pronunciation prescribed for modern Hebrew, rather than the spelling or Hebrew word structure, and to do so using conventions that are generally familiar to the English-speaking reader.

In accordance with this approach, no attempt is made to indicate the distinctions between *alef* and *ayin*, *tet* and *taf*, *kaf* and *kuf*, *sin* and *samekh*, since these are not relevant to pronunciation; likewise, the *dagesh* is not indicated except where it affects pronunciation. Following the principle of using conventions familiar to the majority of readers, however, transcriptions that are well established have been retained even when they are not fully consistent with the transliteration system adopted. On similar grounds, the *tsadi* is rendered by 'tz' in such familiar words as barmitzvah, mitzvot, and so on. Likewise, the distinction between *het* and *khaf* has been retained, using *ḥ* for the former and *kh* for the latter; the associated forms are generally familiar to readers, even if the distinction is not actually borne out in pronunciation, and for the same reason the final *heh* is indicated too. As in Hebrew, no capital letters are used, except that an initial capital has been retained in transliterating titles of published works (for example, *Shulḥan arukh*).

Since no distinction is made between *alef* and *ayin*, they are indicated by an apostrophe only in intervocalic positions where a failure to do so could lead an English-speaking reader to pronounce the vowel-cluster as a diphthong—as, for example, in *ha'ir*—or otherwise mispronounce the word.

The *sheva na* is indicated by an *e*—*perikat ol*, *reshut*—except, again, when established convention dictates otherwise.

The *yod* is represented by *i* when it occurs as a vowel (*bereshit*), by *y* when it occurs as a consonant (*yesodot*), and by *yi* when it occurs as both (*yisra'el*).

Names have generally been left in their familiar forms, even when this is inconsistent with the overall system.

Guide of the Perplexed

References in the text and notes to Maimonides' *Guide of the Perplexed* are to part and chapter, followed by the page number in the Pines translation.

ONE

Maimonides' Critique of the Jewish Culture of his Day

༖

Introduction

MOSES MAIMONIDES (1138–1204) expressed a vision of Judaism as a remarkably naturalist religion of radical responsibility.[1] His Judaism is a religion in which concrete behaviour serves the needs of abstract thought; that abstract thought is the deepest layer of the Torah and, at least in Maimonides' day, could be most clearly and accurately expressed in the vocabulary of the Neoplatonized Aristotelianism which Maimonides accepted as one of the highest expressions of the human spirit. This Judaism was simultaneously deeply elitist and profoundly universalist.[2] Maimonides crystallized and expressed his vision of Judaism because the Jewish world in his day was, in his view, debased and paganized.[3]

In terms of his contribution to the Jewish tradition, Maimonides may be fairly characterized as one of the most influential Jews who ever lived. Aside from the first Moses and Rabbi Judah the Prince, it is hard to think of any individual whose career had such a dramatic influence on the

---

[1] I realize that the term 'Judaism' would have meant little to Maimonides; I use it here as shorthand for something like 'the body of doctrines and teachings set forth in the Written and Oral Torahs and accepted as authoritative by Maimonides'.

[2] I am, in general, leery of using expressions to describe aspects of Judaism for which no Hebrew equivalent exists (since that seems a pretty good indication that the concept named is not native to the Jewish tradition). But in this case, there is no way around it; Maimonides' vision of Judaism *was* profoundly universalist. The precise meaning of this claim will become clear as we proceed.

[3] For an excellent description of the world against which Maimonides struggled, see Hayman, 'Monotheism' and, with special reference to a contemporary critic of Maimonides, Langermann, 'Letter', esp. p. 56. Relevant here is the following comment in Shaked, '"Peace Be Upon You, Exalted Angels"', 207: 'In the medieval period, as we can see from the Geniza material, a measure of harmony was achieved between *Hekhalot*, liturgy, and the magic texts.' It is against that 'harmony' that Maimonides struggled.

history of Judaism as a body of laws and traditions. His law code, the *Mishneh torah*, had a profoundly 'democratizing' effect upon Judaism (giving direct and relatively easy access to the entire body of Jewish law to anyone who could read the extremely clear Hebrew in which the book was written), and made possible the composition of subsequent codes, pre-eminently the *Shulḥan arukh* of Joseph Karo (1488–1575). As a philosopher, Maimonides' closest competitor for prominence is Judah Halevi (d. 1141), but Maimonides has been influential in all generations and in all circles, whereas Halevi's influence, while very deep in certain sectors, was barely felt in others, and was certainly intermittent.[4] If we consider Maimonides the halakhist and Maimonides the philosopher as one individual (as we should), then the oft-repeated saying, 'from Moses to Moses there arose none like Moses', looks less like popular hagiographa and more like a restrained evaluation of the facts.[5]

However, despite this, not long after his death a composition appeared which, for contrary impact and influence in the realms of thought and prac-tice, can be seen as a worthy competitor to the works of Maimonides. I refer, of course, to the Zohar. The world of the Zohar is so unlike that of Maimonides that at times it appears impossible that it and Maimonides' *Guide of the Perplexed* should both be accepted as authoritative in the same religious tradition. It is to one aspect of the complex relationship between the worlds of the Zohar and of the *Guide* that I intend to devote this study. That aspect was well summarized by the late Isadore Twersky, who, apro-pos Maimonides' unusual views concerning the nature of the Hebrew lan-guage, noted that 'Maimonides' desacralization of language should be seen as an expression of his consistent opposition to hypostasized entities endowed with intrinsic sanctity.'[6]

Twersky is surely correct. Among the entities which Maimonides seeks to 'de-hypostasize' are the property of holiness, the Hebrew language, the Land of Israel, the people of Israel, the divine glory (*kavod*), the divine pres-ence (*shekhinah*), angels, and sin.[7] Consistent with this approach, he seeks

---

[4]   See Shear, 'Later History'.

[5]   On the early stages of Maimonides' reputation, see Twersky, 'Maimonides' Image'. Note is rarely taken of the remarkable fact that this popular expression of respect for Maimonides seems to echo Deut. 34: 10, 'Never again did there arise in Israel a prophet like Moses, whom the Lord singled out face to face.' In the popular imagination of the Jewish people, Moses ben Maimon seemed to give the lie to that verse.

[6]   *Introduction*, 324 n.

[7]   Gad Freudenthal pointed out to me that I am misusing the word 'dehypostasize'

to present distinctions fundamental to Judaism, such as holy/profane, ritually pure/ritually impure, permissible/impermissible, and, especially, Jew/non-Jew as institutional, sociological, and historical issues, and not as ontological matters.[8] These distinctions, Maimonides held, do not reflect the presence or absence of actual properties in the entities under discussion, but, rather, the ways in which the Torah commands Jews to behave with respect to these entities.

In each of these issues Maimonides implicitly (and sometimes explicitly) criticizes important elements of the dominant Jewish culture of his day.[9] Focusing our attention on that critique allows us to understand that his overall aim in his writings was not only the harmonization of philosophy and Torah, as is often thought to be the case, but, also, the use of philosophy to purify a corrupted and paganized Torah.

Attending to the historiography of Moshe Idel will make this point clearer. Idel, as I will explain below, has argued persuasively that kabbalah crystallized out of pre-existing materials in response to the challenge posed by Maimonides. He has also noted that Maimonides' views themselves crystallized in response to what I call 'proto-kabbalistic' elements in Judaism. The Maimonides who emerges from this interpretation is thus

here, since, strictly, one can only hypostasize or dehypostasize notions, not entities. But that is precisely my point: Maimonides was convinced that certain notions had been illegitimately hypostasized. He sought to correct that state of affairs by showing that these matters were 'only' notions, not entities.

[8] Relevant too is the fact that, according to Maimonides' view, the narratives and commandments of the Torah appear to be historically conditioned, not absolute. This point will be developed below, in Ch. 2 (on halakhah), Ch. 3 (on holiness), and in Ch. 4 (on ritual purity and impurity).

[9] Maimonides presents what might be called a statement of the main textual components of the normative rabbinic culture of his day towards the end of his introduction to the *Mishneh torah*, where he lists the books summarized in his own work: geonic commentaries, halakhic monographs and responsa, as well as the following talmudic works: the Babylonian and the Jerusalem Talmuds, *Sifra*, *Sifrei*, and the Tosefta. However, in addition to these sources, I hope that the present work will show that, in order fully to understand Maimonides, we must also take note of less formal aspects of the Jewish culture of his day: *piyutim* (liturgical poetry), Heikhalot literature, the writings of such figures as Judah Halevi, and even magical writings. Scholars have typically sought to understand Maimonides against the background of 'high' culture, be it of the rabbis or of the Muslim philosophers. A fuller picture of Maimonides demands that we pay attention to the 'low' culture (often shared by members of the rabbinic elite of his day) against which he struggled.

something of a tragic figure: seeking to purify Judaism from 'proto-kabbalah', what he actually succeeded in doing was to force these currents of thought from the subterranean depths in which they had hitherto flowed up to the bright light of day. In that light they flourished, grew, and ultimately became dominant. Kabbalah has long since become the mainstream of Judaism, relegating Maimonideanism to the status of a largely ignored backwater.

Maimonides was a religious reformer, but he was also a proud and loyal Jew. He realized that, were he to formulate his vision of Judaism as a series of theses and nail them onto the synagogue door in Fustat, he would either be ignored or foment schism, neither of which would accomplish his ends.[10] He therefore decided to express his vision of Judaism in a way that would not harm those incapable of accepting it, while helping those who were capable.[11] With very few exceptions, Maimonides does not openly attack Jewish positions which he rejects. He ignores the opposition wherever he can, stating, or at least, hinting at the truth as he sees it. This may have been a matter of personality or a matter of policy, or both, but it certainly seems to be a consistent mode of operation throughout his writings.[12]

[10] Maimonides consistently sought to avoid controversies which might divide the Jewish people or threaten the stability of Jewish society. On this, see Blidstein, *Prayer in Maimonidean Halakhah*, 138–43; id., *Authority and Dissent*, 149–50. Ratson Arussi cites many examples of Maimonides' attempts to avoid controversy in his 'Unity and Separatism'.

[11] A good example of this approach is Maimonides' famous statement in the preface to his *Eight Chapters* which form the introduction to his commentary on Mishnah *Avot*: 'Know that the things about which we shall speak in these chapters and in what will come in the commentary are not matters invented on my own nor explanations I have originated. Indeed, they are matters gathered from the discourse of the Sages in the Midrash, the Talmud, and other compositions of theirs, as well as from the discourse of both the ancient and modern philosophers and from the compositions of many men. Hear the truth from whoever says it. Sometimes I have taken a complete passage from the text of a famous book. Now there is nothing wrong with that, for I do not attribute to myself what someone who preceded me said. We hereby acknowledge this and shall not indicate that "so and so said" and "so and so said", since that would be useless prolixity. *Moreover, the name of such an individual might make the passage offensive to someone without experience and make him think it has an evil inner meaning of which he is not aware. Consequently, I saw fit to omit the author's name, since my goal is to be useful to the reader.* We shall explain to him the hidden meanings in this tractate.' I cite the text as it is translated in Maimonides, *Ethical Writings*, 60 (emphasis added).

[12] With respect to Maimonides' apparent propensity to fight positions without specifying what he is fighting against, Ivry, 'Isma'ili Theology', 271–99, argues that part of

Maimonides did not wait till he wrote the *Guide of the Perplexed* in order to express his vision of Judaism. All of his writings express this vision to one extent or another. In writings addressed to ordinary Jews *and* their rabbis he subtly refashions the Judaism of his readers into one closer to the austere and demanding faith which he believed was revealed at Sinai.[13]

The Judaism Maimonides Opposed

In order to see how he does this, we shall have to embark upon a short tour of elements of the Judaism Maimonides found in North Africa and in Egypt when his family was forced to flee its ancestral Andalusia. This tour

Maimonides' motivation in writing the *Guide* was to counter teachings of Isma'ilism. His response was not direct, but 'oblique' (p. 280). 'A good deal of the *Guide of the Perplexed*', Ivry argues, 'should thus be seen as a response to, and implicit rebuttal of, various Isma'ili themes and assertions, as well as a qualified, tacit endorsement of others' (p. 282). Ivry goes on to comment, importantly for our purposes here: 'Accordingly, Maimonides may be seen, in much of the first part of the Guide, and elsewhere, as engaged in a prolonged struggle not merely or even essentially with a primitive Jewish fundamentalism, but rather with a highly imaginative theosophy. This theosophical approach, while nourished by earlier Jewish sources, could well have been encouraged by certain parallel religious formulations in Shi'i literature . . . It may well be that Maimonides is inveighing against a traditional but growing religious fashion in his day, one current among Jews and Muslims alike; a fashion that was temporarily stalled with the political defeat of the Fatimids and with the success of Maimonides' own efforts, but which, in the form of Kabbalah and later Persian theosophy, was not to be denied much longer in either faith' (p. 285). Another example of fighting a position without specifying what he was fighting against may be found in Maimonides' comment on Mishnah *Ḥag.* 2: 1. The Mishnah clearly saw *ma'aseh bereshit* and *ma'aseh merkavah* as esoteric subjects. Maimonides proposes a 'new' content for them without ever mentioning the other contents which he clearly knew had been associated with these terms in the past. This may reflect a strategy of quietly replacing 'proto-kabbalistic' materials with philosophically (and hence for Maimonides, more Jewishly) appropriate contents. (This idea was suggested to me by my reading of Sirat, 'Study of *Ma'aseh Bereshit*'.) Compare further Maimonides' explanation of the purpose of *ḥukim* as fighting an undeclared war against idolatry. For details, see J. Stern, *Problems and Parables*, esp. pp. 109–60. Compare also Idel, 'Jewish Thought in Medieval Spain', 264, commenting on Maimonides' 'silent polemic' against *Sefer yetsirah*.

[13] See Kellner, 'Literary Character of the *Mishneh Torah*'. For a valuable study of Maimonides' 'art of writing', see Henshke, 'On the Question of Unity'. I do not mean to imply that Maimonides never changed his mind about substantive issues; rather, I take no stand on the matter here. For a recent discussion, see Langermann, 'Maimonides and Miracles'.

will enable us to discover that there are underlying unities in Maimonides' religious and philosophical thought, deeper than those detected in the past. He was convinced that the Judaism of his native Andalusia was vastly more sophisticated and true to the actual teachings of the Torah than was much of the Judaism to which he was exposed when he settled in Fostat, in Egypt. In the *Guide* (i. 71; pp. 176–7) he goes so far as to say that, unlike 'the scanty bit of argument' that one finds in the writing of 'some *gaonim*', who took over many Kalam ideas,

the Andalusians among the people of our nation, all of them cling to the affirmations of the philosophers[14] and incline to their opinions, in so far as these do not ruin the foundation of the Law. You will not find them in any way taking the paths of the Mutakallimun. In many things concerning the scanty matter of which the later ones among them had knowledge,[15] they have therefore approximately the same doctrine that we set forth in this Treatise.

In this passage Maimonides, the refugee intellectual, thinks back fondly (and innacurately) of the lost land of his youth. As Herbert Davidson notes on this text, 'The notion that all the Jews living [in Andalusia] were adherents of the philosophers . . . is hyperbole brought to a dizzying height.'[16] Hyperbole or no, it expresses Maimonides' attitude towards the Jewish culture in which he was raised and that in which he found himself during his maturity.[17] The point of this book is to show that the Jewish culture of the Muslim East was deficient in Maimonides' eyes not only

[14] By which Maimonides means the Arab Aristotelians. On this, and the whole passage quoted here, see H. A. Wolfson, *Repercussions*, 168.

[15] In his translation, Pines notes: 'Literally: the scanty matters found among the later ones of them. This apparently refers to the passages of the Talmud and the Midrashim that, as Maimonides states in the beginning of this chapter, belong to the old esoteric tradition.'　　　[16] H. A. Davidson, *Moses Maimonides*, 90.

[17] On Maimonides' pride in his Andalusian background and concomitant reservations about the Judaism he found in North Africa and Egypt, see Blau, '"At Our Place in al-Andalus"'; id., 'Maimonides, al-Andalus'; Kraemer, 'Maimonides and the Spanish Aristotelian School'; and id., 'Life of Moses ben Maimon'. Bortz, 'El mas insignificante', collects a large number of texts in which Maimonides makes proud reference to his Andalusian background. The issue is also addressed in Friedman, *Maimonides, the Yemenite Messiah, and Apostasy*, 51, 67–8. For the role played by Andalusia in Muslim and Christian, as well as Jewish, self-understanding, see Menocal, *Ornament of the World*. For Maimonidean reservations concerning the level of Jewish learning and understanding in contemporary Babylonia, see the introduction to Stroumsa, *On the Beginnings*, and Langermann, 'Letter'. Maimonides also peppers his writings with uncomplimentary comments about the level of true understanding of Torah displayed by his rabbinic

because so many of its thinkers adhered to the Kalam, but also because so many of its thinkers, rabbis, and laity considered as Torah doctrines and teachings which Maimonides was sure had no place there.

As noted just above, Moshe Idel has propounded a two-part thesis concerning the relationship of Maimonides and the kabbalah. According to Idel, Maimonides crystallized his views in reaction to what we may call 'proto-kabbalistic' tendencies in pre-Maimonidean Judaism. By unearthing an ancient tradition, Idel argues, Maimonides 'implicitly indicated that any existing strain of Jewish esotericism consisted of distortions of ancient esoteric truth . . . [this was] an attempt to change the prevalent understanding of the ultimate essence of Judaism . . . instead of an overt confrontation, he chose a silent opposition.'[18] Maimonides' opposition was not actually 'silent', something Idel himself notes in a fuller statement of his position:

Maimonides' conception of the history of the *Sitre Torah* [lit. 'secrets of the Torah'] and their content is, in my opinion, revolutionary. According to him, the peculiar meaning of *Ma'aseh Bereshit* and *Ma'aseh Merkavah* was lost soon after the Tannaitic period. Maimonides implicitly discredited the corpus of mystical literature which included, inter alia, long discussions concerning the nature of these two subjects. Even treatises overtly entitled *Beraita de-Ma'aseh Bereshit* or *Ma'aseh Merkavah* passed unmentioned by him. No one who is aware of Maimonides' wide range of Jewish knowledge can imagine that Maimonides was ignorant of this brand of literature. Moreover, another important treatise belonging to the *Hekhalot* corpus, *Sefer Shiur Komah*, was openly rejected by Maimonides, who regarded it as a Jewish Byzantine forgery. It seems that he was the first important Jewish theologian who dared oppose most ancient types of Jewish mystical theology, either by ignoring their existence, or by an overt attack.[19]

Thus far the first prong of Idel's account of Maimonides and kabbalah: Maimonides was aware of proto-kabbalistic elements in Judaism and formulated his vision of Judaism in conscious opposition to them.

contemporaries. For some examples, see Kellner, *Maimonides on the 'Decline of the Generations'*, 37–54. See further Kreisel, 'Torah Commentary', 33, who notes that Maimonides 'did not hide his negative opinion of most of the rabbinic scholars of his generation due to their ignorance of the truths of philosophy'. Kreisel cites as representative sources *Guide* ii. 6 (Pines, p. 263), the parable of the palace in *Guide* iii. 51 (on which see Kellner, *Maimonides on Human Perfection*, ch. 3), and the opening of Maimonides, *Essay on Resurrection*. Compare further below, p. 118.

[18] Idel, '*Sitre 'Arayot* in Maimonides' Thought', 86.
[19] Id., 'Maimonides and Kabbalah', 34. The *Shiur komah* will be discussed below.

The second, and better-known, prong of Idel's thesis maintains that, in an ironic twist of fate, it was Maimonides' struggle against what I have called proto-kabbalah that called forth kabbalah itself:

Kabbalah emerged in the late twelfth and early thirteenth centuries as a sort of reaction to the dismissal of earlier mystical traditions by Maimonides' audacious reinterpretation of Jewish esotericism and his attempt to replace the mystical traditions with a philosophical understanding. Kabbalah can be viewed as part of a restructuring of those aspects of rabbinic thought that were denied authenticity by Maimonides' system. Far from being a total innovation, historical Kabbalah represented an ongoing effort to systematize existing elements of Jewish theurgy, myth, and mysticism into a full-fledged response to the rationalistic challenge. Indeed, we can consider Kabbalah as part of a silent controversy between the rationalistic and mystical facets of Judaism. It was 'silent' in that the main organon of the Kabbalistic response took the form not of open attacks on Maimonides — an extremely rare phenomenon in early Kabbalah — but of an ongoing building of an alternative to his system on the basis of earlier materials.[20]

The two prongs are summarized in the following statement:

But just as the purification of Jewish literature caused a relocation of the mysterious, mystical, or magical elements in midrash, so the rationalistic reconstructions of Judaism prompted, in turn, a powerful reaction wherein an amalgam of older traditions, including the same mystical, mythical, and magical elements, came to the surface in more overt and crystallized forms.[21]

The first part of Idel's thesis depends upon the existence of 'proto-kabbalistic' elements in pre-Maimonidean Judaism. Much of his book *Kabbalah: New Perspectives* is devoted to providing evidence of such elements. Idel has been criticized over the nature of the evidence he adduced in that book.[22] It is not my place to involve myself in that dispute, nor am I particularly competent to do so. What I do want to argue, however, is that Maimonides agrees with Idel. To put the point in historically more accept-

[20] Idel, *Kabbalah: New Perspectives*, 253. As Idel notes, Heinrich Graetz was the first scholar to express this idea. For further discussion, see Scholem, *Origins of the Kabbalah*, 7.

[21] Idel, 'Infinities of Torah', 143. This is further argued convincingly by Idel, '*Sitre 'Arayot* in Maimonides' Thought', 86; id., 'Maimonides and Kabbalah', 34; and id., *Kabbalah: New Perspectives*, 253. For a parallel view, see J. Stern, *Problems and Parables*, 160: 'Maimonides' explanation of the ḥuqqim attempted to bring about the fall of myth in Judaism. Instead it led, through its formative influence on Nahmanides just one generation later, to the resuscitation of the same myths.'

[22] See e.g. Alter, 'Jewish Mysticism in Dispute'.

able terms, reading Maimonides as if he agrees with Idel enables us to understand the entire Maimonidean corpus in a new, integrative fashion. This is the burden of what I will be trying to do in this book. To the extent that I succeed, I will not only be making claims about Maimonides but will also provide important support for Idel's position.[23]

Idel's view that Maimonides was fighting a battle against important spiritual trends in the Judaism of his day should be contrasted with that of Harry Austryn Wolfson:

In point of time, Halevi preceded Maimonides. Yet in comparing them we must treat Halevi as the critic of the tendency which Maimonides represented, the tendency which began long before Halevi and reached its climax in Maimonides. Maimonides may be considered as swimming with the stream, he was the expression of his age; Halevi was swimming against the stream, he was the insurgent, the utterer of paradoxes.[24]

Wolfson, I believe, misunderstood what Maimonides was doing, largely because he was unaware of the materials unearthed by scholars such as Gershom Scholem, Idel, and their colleagues. Maimonides was confronted

---

[23] Serving as a catalyst for kabbalah is not the only ironic consequence of Maimonides' work. David Berger notes that Maimonides' rationalist messianism may have sparked messianic movements which would clearly have been very much not to his liking; see Berger, 'On Some Ironic Consequences'. In this context, one wonders what Maimonides would have made of the use made of him by contemporary religious Zionists (on which, see Kellner, 'Messianic Postures') and by contemporary Habad hasidim. Maimonides was (guardedly) critical of poetry; several scholars have noted the irony in the fact that many poems were composed in his honour, in opposition to him, and by way of summarizing his Principles of Faith. With respect to the former, see the references to Maimonides in the index to Alharizi, *Book of Taḥkemoni* and the list of sixty-nine poems about him in Steinschneider, 'Indications'. This irony has been noted; see Schirmann, 'Maimonides and Hebrew Poetry', 436, and Friedman, *Maimonides, the Yemenite Messiah, and Apostasy*, 5, 136, 198. For poems based upon the Principles of Faith, see Marx, 'List of Poems'. For poems written in opposition to Maimonides, see Einbinder, *Beautiful Death*, 84, 88. Joel Kraemer, it should be noted, has pointed out that Maimonides' view of poetry was actually more nuanced than is often thought to be the case. See his 'Maimonides and the Spanish Aristotelian School', 42–5. Mark Verman notes another possible ironic consequence of Maimonides' career. The notion of *gilgul*, transmigration of souls, he opines, 'was an outgrowth of the intense speculation about the afterlife that was stimulated by the Maimonidean controversy and facilitated by the dissemination of philosophical writings about the soul in the middle and late twelfth century'. See Verman, 'Reincarnation', 426.

[24] H. A. Wolfson, 'Maimonides and Halevi', 129–30.

with a form of Judaism which found, perhaps, its most sophisticated theoretical exponents in Judah Halevi, who preceded Maimonides,[25] and in Moses Nahmanides (1194–1270), who followed him.[26] *Pace* Wolfson, the Judaism of Halevi and Nahmanides dominated the Jewish world before

[25] Kreisel convincingly argues for the position that Maimonides was familiar with Halevi's work; see his 'Judah Halevi's Influence on Maimonides'. Joel Kraemer takes it as given that Maimonides knew the *Kuzari*, and cites texts which prove that Maimonides was also familiar with some of Halevi's poetry; see id., 'Six Unpublished Maimonides Letters', 82. Pines, 'Parallels', 251, writes: 'The foregoing observations assume that Maimonides, having read the *Kuzari*, adapted various texts in that work—those discussed above and perhaps also others—for his own purposes. The hypothesis that he and Judah Halevi had a common source is, of course, also possible. But it is unnecessary, given the practical certainty that Maimonides was familiar with the *Kuzari*; an important apologetic and theological work written by a celebrated member of the Jewish community of Spain would hardly have escaped his notice.' See further Pines, 'On the Term *Ruḥaniyut*'; on p. 533 Pines takes it as obvious that Maimonides knew Halevi's work well. Most recently, Gil and Fleischer, *Judah Halevi*, 199–203, discuss Halevi's prominence in Egypt in the generation before Maimonides. Indeed, the poet Elazar Hakohen ben Halfon lived long enough to write poems of praise for both Halevi and Maimonides. Given the excitement among Egyptian Jewish intellectuals at Halevi's visits to Alexandria and Cairo in 1140–1, it seems hardly credible that Maimonides, who reached Egypt in 1165 or thereabouts, was unfamiliar with the man and his work. Note also that Schirmann, 'Maimonides and Hebrew Poetry', 433, cites a letter to Samuel ibn Tibbon in which Maimonides quotes a line of poetry (which he says was 'written by the ancients') which has been attributed to Halevi. See Kraemer, 'Maimonides and the Spanish Aristotelian School', 42.

[26] By citing Halevi and Nahmanides together I mean only to imply that much of what they hold in common distinguishes them sharply from Maimonides. See Novak, *Theology of Nahmanides*, 34–5 and Idel, 'Abulafia's Secrets', 516: '[Nahmanides was] quite critical, though only rarely mentioning names, toward allegorical exegesis and philosophical intellectualism, he is much more in concert with those forms of thought found in some of the Jewish philosophers who preceded Maimonides, like Yehudah ha-Levi or Abraham bar Ḥiyya, for example. He was more open toward magic and had a positive view of the perception of Hebrew as a natural language. Maimonides' stand on this issue consists, however, in weakening the importance of the sacred language by attenuating its special status.' For more on the connection between Halevi and Nahmanides, compare Isadore Twersky's comment: 'In many respects, R. Judah Halevi, Nahmanides, and the Maharal constitute a special strand of Jewish thought—threefold, yet unified' ('Maimonides and Eretz Israel', 261 n.). On Halevi's influence on Nahmanides, see the studies listed in Kanarfogel, 'On the Assessment', 78. Nahmanides cites 'the author of the *Kuzari*' at least once in his commentary on the Torah, at Deut. 11: 22.

and after Maimonides and continues to dominate it today.[27] If anyone was swimming against the stream, it was Maimonides, not Halevi.

The Philosophical Basis of Maimonides' Opposition

Maimonides was forced to swim against the mainstream of important elements in the regnant rabbinic culture of his day because of two foundational philosophical positions. These are his consistent rejection of the idea that species and other universals exist outside the mind and his insistence on the absolute transcendence of God. With respect to the first, he writes:

After what I have stated about providence singling out the human species alone among all the species of animals, I say that it is known that no species exists outside the mind, but that the species and the other universals are, as you know, mental notions and that every existent outside the mind is an individual or group of individuals.[28]

---

[27] I deliberately ignore Abraham Ibn Ezra (b. 1089); despite Twersky's best efforts, there seems to be no convincing proof that Maimonides was familiar with his work. See Twersky, 'Did R. Abraham Ibn Ezra Influence Maimonides?'. Sara Stroumsa would disagree; see her 'Sabians of Haran', 287. For some parallels between Maimonides and Ibn Ezra, see H. A. Davidson, *Moses Maimonides*, 117 (with references to earlier literature), 375, and 404.

[28] *Guide* iii. 18 (p. 474). Maimonides repeats the point at the end of the same chapter (p. 476): 'It would not be proper for us to say that providence watches over the species and not the individuals, as is the well-known opinion of some philosophic schools. For outside the mind nothing exists except the individuals; it is to these individuals that the divine intellect is united. Consequently providence watches only over these individuals.' Maimonides immediately continues: 'Consider this chapter as it ought to be considered; for through it all the fundamental principles of the Law will become safe for you and conformable for you to speculative philosophic opinions; disgraceful views will be abolished.' Elisheva Oberman and Josef Stern first drew my attention to these passages. Alfred Ivry comments perceptively: 'Maimonides, as a good Aristotelian and would-be nominalist, would like to "save the phenomena" and not add to them immaterial entities of a conjectural and ultimately redundant sort' ('Strategies of Interpretation', 116). In the notes to his Hebrew translation of this passage, Michael Schwartz draws attention to a helpful discussion in H. A. Wolfson, *Repercussions*, 33–5. *Pace* Wolfson, in a note on this passage, also cited by Schwartz, Eliezer Goldman calls Maimonides' position 'conceptualist' as opposed to 'nominalist'. For our purposes the distinction between these two interpretations can be ignored. See Goldman, *Research and Studies*, 101 n. 38. Maimonides' nominalism affects other aspects of his thought; see Silman, 'Halakhic Determinations'. Maimonides' nominalism is connected, I might note, to a thoroughgoing Aristotelian empiricism. See e.g. the following comment in *Guide* iii. 21 (p. 485): 'For we know all that we know only through looking at [existent] beings.'

Maimonides here adopts a variant of a position later to be called 'nominalism' and to be made famous by William of Ockham (d. 1347) and his famous 'razor': one ought not multiply entities beyond necessity. I do not want to involve Maimonides in a later scholastic debate. Let us simply say here that for reasons of economy and elegance (and thus following Aristotle as he understood him), Maimonides sought for a universe with as few entities as possible. Indeed, as he says in the second chapter of the *Mishneh torah*, everything in the created universe can be resolved into one of three classes of entities: those composed of matter and form and subject to generation and corruption, those composed of matter and form and not subject to generation and corruption, and those composed of form only. This tripartite division leaves no room for the multifarious denizens of the universe so beloved of ancient Jewish mysticism: angels and demons, forces, powers, occult properties (*segulot*), all those aspects of the cosmos which we today would lump together under the rubric 'supernatural'. For Maimonides there is God and nature and nothing else.[29]

Thus we see that Maimonides' economical universe is not simply a matter of philosophical temper (Aristotelian and Ockhamite); rather, it is an important religious position as well. Judaism, Maimonides was convinced, 'depopulated the heavens',[30] and he was committed to battling efforts to repopulate them. But not just the heavens; Maimonides fought against a tendency to attribute existence on some objective ontological plane to notions which, he was convinced (as I will demonstrate in what follows), were best understood as names, not entities. The implications of this position are far-reaching. Intrinsic holiness cannot inhere in the people of Israel, for example, since there is no such thing as the people of Israel, there are only individual Jews. Furthermore, there can be no such thing as sanctity as such; at most there can be sacred objects, places, times, and perhaps individuals. Nor can there be ritual purity as such, only ritually pure or impure objects, places, and individuals. Sanctity and purity are not properties which inhere in objects, places, times, and individuals; rather,

[29] When I use the term 'nominalism' below, I mean it as shorthand for the ideas expressed in this paragraph, and nothing beyond that.

[30] I borrow the phrase from the English critic Anthony Julius; see his *Idolizing Pictures*, 33. This claim might strike some readers as odd, given that Maimonides included in his heavens at least ten and perhaps as many as fifty separate intellects (on which see below, Ch. 8). However, given the science of his day, the existence of these intellects (as disembodied movers of the heavenly spheres and bodies) is scientifically necessary. Their existence is in no way 'uneconomical'.

they are names the Torah gives to certain forms of behaviour. Just as God may be characterized by attributes of action, never of essence (*Guide* i. 51–2), matters ordained by God are defined in terms of behaviour, not of essence.

Thus, Maimonides combines philosophical nominalism with religious nominalism: halakhic entities and distinctions are precisely that, halakhic. Halakhah, for Maimonides, as will be demonstrated below in Chapter 2, does not *describe* an antecedently existing reality; rather, it *constitutes* or *constructs* a social reality. This point is important for Maimonides since it assists him in protecting God's transcendence.[31] The Torah, for example, obligates Jews to be holy, because God is holy (Lev. 19: 2). Were that interpreted to mean that Jews (or sacred objects, times, and places) are or can be essentially holy, we would be saying that God and certain created entities share the characteristic or property of holiness, an approach which Maimonides repeatedly disallows.[32] Holiness, for anything but God, must be *institutional*, a matter of halakhic definition, but not essential and somehow actually in the world.

The connection between Maimonides' nominalism and his emphasis on the transcendence of God may be made clearer by taking advantage of an insight of Mary Douglas'. At the beginning of *Leviticus as Literature* Douglas emphasized the radical nature of biblical monotheism, writing:

All the other religions were polytheistic in one sense or another, only Israel's religion was severely monotheistic. There were no subsidiary or rival deities at all, only one true God who forbade any cult to be paid to any others. This does not mean that the existence of other spirits was denied. In fact the Bible has a role for angels as messengers of God or as manifestations of God; Satan figures as an independent agent in Zechariah, the angel of God appears in the Book of Numbers to rebuke Balaam. The wicked thing was to pay cult to the spiritual beings around.[33] Only the one God has any power,[34] and it is pointless to apply to lesser spiritual beings, as well as an unpardonable insult to the majesty of the one God.

---

[31] By 'transcendent' here I mean that God, as creator, is wholly unlike all created entities. God is one, but also unique.

[32] See the second and third of Maimonides' Thirteen Principles, *MT* 'Laws of the Foundations of the Torah', 1: 8, and *Guide* i. 55 (p. 128).

[33] Compare Maimonides' natural history of idolatry in *MT* 'Laws of Idolatry', ch. 1, discussed below in Ch. 2.

[34] Compare the fifth of Maimonides' Thirteen Principles, in which this point is emphasized.

Everything else flows from this. It is hard to realize how completely their strict monolatry separated the religion of Israel from the others in the region.[35]

The last sentence of this otherwise very Maimonidean paragraph helps us to understand what Maimonides is all about: biblical Judaism surely can appear as monolatry (the worship of one god, where other gods may be presumed to exist), and in Maimonides' day, there were many texts circulating, attributed to talmudic rabbis, which clearly lent themselves to this interpretation (to put the matter mildly). But true Judaism, Maimonides was convinced, was absolute and pure monotheism, not monolatry.

The purer the monotheism, the more transcendent is God. But the more God is understood as transcendent, the greater the need and impulse to posit quasi-divine intermediaries to bridge the gap between God and ourselves. However, such intermediaries turn monotheism into monolatry. There is ample evidence that much of the Judaism which Maimonides knew had succumbed to this dangerous impulse. Maimonides was faced with an exquisitely difficult dilemma: he had to protect the absolutely unique and hence wholly transcendent God of true Judaism from all attempts at humanization and personification, while at the same time not making God's transencendence so blatant as to invite the positing of intermediaries.[36]

Maimonides' nominalism and emphasis on divine transcendence led him to adopt positions which today would be called universalist,[37] and which were certainly unusual in his day. In his view, all human beings are created

[35] Douglas, *Leviticus as Literature*, 2–3. The notes in this paragraph are mine, not Douglas's.

[36] Gershom Scholem notes: 'In opposition to the pantheistic unity of God, cosmos, and man in myth, in opposition to the nature myths of the Near-Eastern religions, Judaism aimed at a radical separation of the three realms; and above all, the gulf between the Creator and His creatures was regarded as fundamentally unbridgeable' (*On the Kabbalah and its Symbolism*, 88). In a comment relevant to the Maimonidean dilemma posited here, Scholem notes: 'The price of God's purity is the loss of His living reality.' Maimonides, it appears, was acutely aware of this problem, which helps to explain the reticent way in which he expressed his ideas.

[37] In *Maimonides on Judaism and the Jewish People* I argue that Maimonides maintained that Jews as such were in no way intrinsically different from any other people. I did not connect that issue to his nominalism, as I do here. I hope to issue a revised and greatly expanded Hebrew translation of my book, in which the point made here will be taken up at much greater length. In the meantime, see my articles 'On Universalism and Particularism in Judaism', 'Chosenness, Not Chauvinism', 'Overcoming Chosenness', and 'Was Maimonides Truly Universalist?'.

with the same general potential; there is nothing inherent which distinguishes Jews from non-Jews. The processes leading to human perfection must thus be open in principle to all human beings—Maimonides cannot (nor does he wish to) make it impossible for non-Jews to achieve perfection without the Torah.[38]

Esotericism and Elitism

As demonstrated by his esotericism, Maimonides clearly realized that his vision of Judaism was not widely accepted in his day.[39] Indeed, it might be fair to say that his great Iberian predecessor, Judah Halevi, wrote his *Kuzari* precisely in order to refute the kind of Judaism which was soon to find its classic expression in the works of Maimonides.[40] However, while Maimonides realized that his views were unusual, he was also convinced that they were correct. Judaism, he thought, was in desperate need of reform in order to return to its pristine purity. The question facing him was how best to effect that reform.

The *Guide of the Perplexed* is an avowedly esoteric work, i.e. a work containing a secret teaching, not meant for every reader to comprehend. By its very nature, an esoteric work is one addressed to more than one audience at a time. In that sense, I am convinced that all, or almost all, of Maimonides' writings must be understood as esoteric, addressed simultaneously to several audiences. That does not mean that works other than the *Guide* contain contradictions or that any of his works contained teachings which Maimonides thought were Jewishly heterodox. He was convinced,

[38] This claim depends upon an interpretation of *MT* 'Laws of Kings', 8: 11, which I present and defend at greater length below, in Ch. 7.

[39] Maimonides was an esoteric writer for a number of reasons. There were some matters that could not in principle be expressed clearly—they could only be apprehended intuitively. There were other matters about which he could not make up his mind. There were yet other matters that were too dangerous to reveal clearly. I do not believe that he was motivated by fear of danger to himself, but, rather, by fear of endangering the simple faith of non-philosophical Jews. For more on this sort of esotericism, see Kellner, 'Literary Character of the *Mishneh Torah*'. For a valuable studies of the whole issue, see Klein-Braslavi, *King Solomon*, and Seeskin, *Searching for a Distant God*, 177–88. Herbert Davidson has subjected Leo Strauss's esoteric reading of Maimonides to a devastating critique in *Moses Maimonides*, 393–402.

[40] I hope I may be permitted the following conceit: Maimonides struggled against 'proto-kabbalah', the most elite (and perhaps therefore dangerous) expression of which was Halevi's *Kuzari*; that book itself, in turn, was written in reaction to 'proto-Maimonideanism'.

however, that his writings contained teachings which many of his contemporaries would find to be Jewishly heterodox.

To my mind, Maimonides' esotericism is directly linked to his elitism.[41] Convinced that he and very few like him truly understood the truths taught by Judaism, he chose to hide this truth from the masses. He may have done this out of disdain for the masses, out of fear of persecution or—and this, I think, is the truth—out of a sense of *noblesse oblige*. Revealing the truths of the Torah to people incapable of or unwilling to accept them would benefit no one. Rather, Maimonides chose to write in such a way that his true opinions could be teased out of his writings, but not by everyone.[42] He did this so well that his writings to this day function as a kind of Rorschach test: people very often see in them what they expect to find in them.[43]

Let us grant, for the sake of argument, that the interpretation of Maimonides presented here is correct. Why did he not make his points

[41] For examples of Maimonides' elitism, see the end of his introduction to the *Guide*, before the list of contradictions (p. 16). For another emphatic example, see *Guide* ii. 36 (p. 372). See also his comments in his introduction to *Ḥelek*, the tenth chapter of Mishnah *Sanhedrin*, where he speaks of a group whose 'members are so few in number that it is hardly appropriate to call them a group'. I cite the translation from Twersky, *Maimonides Reader*, 408. *MT* 'Laws of the Foundations of the Torah', 4: 11, would be another good example, as is Maimonides' comment on Mishnah *Ḥag*. 2: 1. For an English translation, see Kellner, 'Maimonides' Commentary'. Twersky notes the exoteric character of Maimonides' elitism; see the many sources cited in his *Introduction*, 468–71.

[42] On this style of writing in the *Mishneh torah* see Kellner, 'Literary Character of the *Mishneh Torah*'.

[43] I owe this arresting image to Jolene S. Kellner. Perhaps the clearest example of this phenomenon is the way in which kabbalists, such as Abraham Abulafia (b. 1240), 'kabbalized' the *Guide*. On this phenomenon, see Idel, 'Maimonides' *Guide of the Perplexed*' and his other studies cited there. I do not pretend that I am immune to this myself, although I have made great efforts to avoid falling into this trap. The late R. Joseph Kafih (1917–2002) made a similar comment in a letter to the latest translator of the *Guide* into Hebrew, Michael Schwartz: 'For Maimonides in my opinion is like a mirror. Everyone who stands opposite him sees his own reflection; Maimonides thus has many faces, and everyone finds his taste in him.' R. Kafih here was expressing approval for Schwartz's project of retranslating the *Guide of the Perplexed* into Hebrew. I doubt that he meant to say that it is in principle impossible to understand Maimonides, to one degree or another, as he understood himself. (Of course, in this interpretation of his words, I may be simply confirming R. Kafih's point!) See Schwartz's translation, ii. 752. Probably without realizing it, R. Kafih mirrored the following comment of Twersky's (*Introduction*, 358): 'To a great extent the study of Maimonides is a story of "self mirroring".'

clearly and directly? Why did he write so that his ideas have to be teased out of texts scattered throughout his writings?

Maimonides announces to his readers that he wrote the *Guide of the Perplexed* esoterically. At the end of his introduction, he discusses seven causes of the contradictions which may be found in books. The fifth relates to pedagogical necessity. Concerning the seventh he writes:

In speaking about very obscure matters it is necessary to conceal some parts and disclose others. Sometimes in the case of certain dicta this necessity requires that the discussion proceed on the basis of a certain premise, whereas in another place necessity requires that the discussion proceed on the basis of another premise contradicting the first one. In such cases the vulgar must in no way be aware of the contradiction; the author accordingly uses some device to conceal it by all means.[44]

At the very end of this introduction, Maimonides wrote a sentence which gave birth to probably thousands of pages of commentary: 'Divergences that are to be found in this Treatise are due to the fifth cause and the seventh. Know this, grasp its true meaning, and remember it very well so as not to become perplexed by some of its chapters' (p. 20).

Maimonides' Failure

The Jewish world in which Maimonides lived was uncongenial to the austere, abstract, demanding vision of Torah which he preached. Evidence from a wide variety of sources shows that Jews in Maimonides' day—common folk and scholars alike—accepted astrology, the magical use of divine names, appeals to angels, etc.[45] Eschewing approaches like that of Luther, which generated schism, Maimonides chose, not to attack Judaism as practised and understood in his milieu, but to offer an alternative, carefully presented so as to arouse the least possible opposition and resentment.

In one sense, he failed in his attempt. This is evidenced by the controversies which swirled around his writings both during his lifetime and for centuries after his death.[46] But the very existence of these controversies shows that he had supporters, who were certainly emboldened by his example to defend their vision of Torah. However, this is at best an indication of only

[44] *Guide* i, Introd. (p. 18).

[45] On the persistence of these matters in post-Maimonidean thought, see Schwartz, *Amulets*.

[46] For a recent study, with references to some of the voluminous earlier literature on the subject, see W. Z. Harvey, 'Levi ben Abraham'.

modest success. Maimonides' failure to purify Judaism is, ironically, further demonstrated by the fact that it was his project which apparently brought about the crystallization of everything which he opposed in the form of kabbalah.

Elements of Proto-Kabbalah

Maimonides would have agreed with Moshe Idel: many views which were later systematized, crystallized, and made prominent in kabbalah were prevalent in the Judaism of his own day. In staking out his positions, Maimonides seems to be taking clear issue with the dominant understanding of the Jewish tradition as it had developed to his day, and certainly as it found expression in the views of thinkers like Judah Halevi before him and Nahmanides after him. In what follows I shall speak interchangeably of 'proto-kabbalistic' elements in Judaism and of the 'Halevi–Nahmanides' view of Judaism. Many important distinctions can be drawn here, of course, but for our purposes they may be safely ignored.

Aside from the writings of Halevi, with what aspects of proto-kabbalah was Maimonides familiar?[47] There is one such work which strongly influenced Halevi and, it appears certain, was known to Maimonides; thus it makes sense to begin our survey with the strange and short composition known as *Sefer yetsirah*. Maimonides' opposition to the doctrines found in that book appears most clearly in his views concerning the nature of the Hebrew language (discussed below, in Chapter 5). Jewish thinkers attached special significance to the Hebrew language and saw in it a tool which not only reflects reality at its deepest level, but creates realities as well.[48] This is

[47] See Maimonides' comment in his 'Letter on Astrology' to the effect that he did not think that a single Arabic language text on idolatry had escaped his notice; see Maimonides, *Letters*, trans. Sheilat, ii. 481. Compare statements in the same vein in *Guide* iii. 29 (p. 518), and iii. 49 (p. 612). In his comment on Mishnah *AZ* 3: 3 he reports a conversation he had with an expert on astral magic (concerning the shape of a 'dragon' amulet); compare also his extended comment on *AZ* 4: 7. The apparent inconsistency between Maimonides' erudition in idolatrous writings and his statement in *MT* 'Laws of Idolatry', 2: 2 that God has forbidden the reading of such books has generated considerable discussion. See e.g. L. Kaplan and Berger, 'On Freedom of Inquiry'. One assumes that, if Maimonides made a special study of Arabic language texts on idolatry, it is likely that he was familiar with (what were surely in his eyes) idolatrous texts written by Jews in Hebrew and Aramaic.

[48] On the status of Hebrew in *Sefer yetsirah*, see Altmann, 'Saadya's Theory of Revelation'; Dan, 'Religious Meaning'; Idel, 'Midrashic versus Other Forms of Jewish

certainly the view of *Sefer yetsirah*, as Idel notes: *Sefer yetsirah* 'contributed the theory that the letters of the Hebrew alphabet entered the process of creation not only as creative forces but as the elements of its material structure'.[49] *Sefer yetsirah* was seen as a legitimate expression of talmudic Judaism by most of Maimonides' philosophic predecessors and successors.

1. *Sefer yetsirah*

Sefer yetsirah is both influential and enigmatic. Though it is traditionally attributed to the patriarch Abraham, scholars are deeply divided over the question of its place and time of composition.[50] In some ways, it is hard even to call it a book, since it has reached our hands in three different recensions.[51] There are dramatic differences of opinion concerning the very nature of the book. Sa'adiah Gaon (882–942) saw it as a scientific work,[52] while Halevi emphasized its teachings concerning what may be called Hebrew language mysticism.[53] It has been treated as an astrological

Hermeneutics'. It is surely worthy of note that, while Halevi included a commentary on *Sefer yetsirah* in the *Kuzari* (iv. 25), Maimonides, so far as is known to us, never mentioned the work. It is hardly credible that he never heard of it. On this Idel comments: 'The fact that Maimonides totally ignored the existence of [*Sefer yetsirah*] can be taken as a silent polemic [against it]' ('Jewish Thought in Medieval Spain', 264). Langermann, 'On Some Passages', 226–7, points to places in Maimonides' writings where he appears to be reacting to passages in *Sefer yetsirah*. Liebes, *Ars Poetica*, 94 and 298, affirms that Maimonides knew *Sefer yetsirah*, used some of its language in some places, and reacted to it in others. For more on *Sefer yetsirah*'s attitude towards Hebrew, see below, Ch. 5 n. 32.

[49] Idel, 'Reification of Language', 47.

[50] For discussions of the issue, see Alloni, 'Date of the Composition' and, more recently, Wasserstrom, 'Sefer Yesira and Early Islam' and Dan, 'Three Phases'.

[51] See Hayman, 'The "Original Text"', and Langermann, 'New Redaction'. For the book itself, see Gruenwald, 'Preliminary Critical Edition'. See now the French translation (with introduction and notes) of Fenton, *Sefer Yesirah*. Aryeh Kaplan's traditionalist translation and commentary may be consulted with great profit.

[52] See Jospe, 'Early Philosophical Commentaries'; Pines, 'Quotations from Saadya's Commentary'; Sirat, *History of Jewish Philosophy*; and Zwiep, *Mother of Reason*, 54. See also Altmann, 'Saadya's Theory of Revelation'. In 'Saadya's Goal', Haggai Ben-Shammai argues that in his commentary, Sa'adiah sought to detach *Sefer yetsirah* from mythical, mystical, and magical interpretations proposed by earlier interpreters of the book.

[53] Halevi's view has recently been championed by Zwiep, *Mother of Reason*, 54. In this, Zwiep follows Idel; see Idel, 'Reification of Language' and id., 'Midrashic versus Other Forms of Jewish Hermeneutics'.

treatise,[54] and as having astronomical import;[55] others have connected it to Jewish magic.[56] It was read by Hasidei Ashkenaz, the German mystics of the twelfth and thirteenth centuries, as a mystical text, and many scholars have traced the source of the kabbalistic doctrine of the *sefirot* to this work.[57] Three prominent students of Jewish mysticism have recently proposed three very different views of *Sefer yetsirah*: Joseph Dan harks back to a variant of Sa'adiah's view, and sees its author as primarily a scientist, who was also a mystic.[58] Moshe Idel finds in *Sefer yetsirah* guidance for the creation of a *golem*, an artificial human.[59] Yehudah Liebes has recently devoted an entire book to the work, in which he argues that it is fundamentally a meditation on creativity, divine and human.[60]

Maimonides, it is safe to say, knew *Sefer yetsirah*. Shlomo Pines has given good grounds for this assertion,[61] and Y. Tzvi Langermann has recently supported this view in a convincing fashion.[62] If this is so, why does Maimonides never mention the book in any of his extant writings? Idel is convinced that he deliberately ignored *Sefer yetsirah*.[63] It appears to be a good example of Maimonides' penchant for attacking objectionable texts and positions from the flanks, rather than frontally.

However we interpret *Sefer yetsirah*, it is clear that the doctrine of language it contains must have appeared dangerous to Maimonides. Helpful in this regard is the following comment of the historian of magic and science Brian Vickers, who notes that one of the ways of distinguishing the occult from the scientific is the

[54] Kiener, 'Astrology in Jewish Mysticism'.

[55] Langermann, 'Hebrew Astronomy'.

[56] See P. Hyman, 'Was God a Magician?'.

[57] See e.g. E. R. Wolfson, 'Theosophy of Shabbetai Donnolo'.

[58] Dan, 'Religious Meaning'.

[59] Idel, *Golem*, 9–26. Idel's thesis is criticized by Schäfer in 'Magic of the Golem'.

[60] Liebes, *Ars Poetica*. For critiques, see Langermann, 'On the Beginnings', and Wasserstrom, 'Further Thoughts'. (Wasserstrom argues for a 9th-cent. origin for *Sefer yetsirah*, as opposed to Liebes' 2nd-cent. dating.) Wasserstrom's late dating is supported by Fleischer in 'On the Antiquity', who thinks that the later dating should be seriously considered.

[61] Pines, 'Quotations from Saadya's Commentary'.

[62] Langermann, 'On Some Passages'. See also Liebes, *Ars Poetica*, 94, who finds traces of *Sefer yetsirah* in Maimonides' language in *MT* 'Laws of the Foundation of the Torah', 2: 10.

[63] See Idel, 'Maimonides and Kabbalah', 34, and id., 'Jewish Thought in Medieval Spain', 264. Dan, 'Three Phases', cites other examples of figures who ignored *Sefer yetsirah*.

relationship between language and reality. In the scientific tradition, I hold, a clear distinction is made between words and things and between literal and metaphorical language. The occult tradition does not recognize this distinction: Words are treated as if they are equivalent to things and can be substituted for them. Manipulate the one, and you manipulate the other.[64]

Maimonides' approach to the nature of Hebrew is but a reflection of his deeper adherence to the scientific culture of his day, and of his rejection of the occult. But more than that, attributing objective power to the Hebrew language, maintaining that its letters are the elements out of which the cosmos was created, etc., are all ways, Maimonides seems to have held, of limiting the power and aweful uniqueness and transcendence of God.[65] Seeing Hebrew in this fashion is also, I might add, inconsistent with Maimonides' unswerving universalism. If Hebrew has special and important religious properties, it follows that anyone seeking to approach God using any other language is condemned to remain at a distance.

2. Heikhalot Literature

Sefer yetsirah is connected in some fashion with a body of literature called, by contemporary scholars, if not by the authors of these writings themselves, 'Heikhalot literature' (after the heavenly palaces, *heikhalot*, often described therein). The main texts of this body of literature have been collected and published synoptically by Peter Schäfer.[66]

One of the best-known texts associated with the Heikhalot literature is a short disquisition on the size and shape of God's body, *Shiur komah*. This

[64] See Vickers, 'Analogy vs Identity', 95. For another concise statement of the worldview rejected by Maimonides see Johnson, *In the Palaces of Memory*, 97: 'it was long assumed that there was some intimate connection between a man and his name, between the word and the thing it stood for. Viewed this way, texts were not just representational, a string of symbols to be decoded. If words and names were magic, then a scripture or an incantation had power to change things in the world. A man could be cursed, quite literally, by plugging his name into the proper spell.'

[65] According to this view, not only God but all who know how to manipulate Hebrew have power over the universe.

[66] Schäfer, *Synopse zur Hekhalot-Literatur*. For a discussion of different scholarly views on Heikhalot literature, see E. R. Wolfson, *Through a Speculum that Shines*, 74–81. It is important to note that most of the MSS in our possession today which contain these texts originated in the circle of the German pietists (12th–13th cents.); see Ta-Shema, 'Library of the Ashkenaz Sages', and Schäfer, 'Idea of Piety'. Very few of these texts have appeared in careful English translations. The one major exception is the text known today as *Ma'aseh merkavah*, translated and analysed in Janowitz, *Poetics of Ascent*.

highly anthropomorphic text[67] was actually cited by Maimonides in his *Commentary on the Mishnah*; later in life he denounced it as a 'Byzantine forgery', and angrily denied that he had ever thought that it was a normative Jewish text. It cannot be doubted, in any event, that he was at least aware of the book and that in his maturity he rejected it as un-Jewish.[68]

Prominent in the Heikhalot literature are the issues of the manipulation of God's name[69] and the use of amulets and charms, either to ward off evil or to promote some desired end. The writing of amulets containing holy names and the manipulation of divine names (*shemot* in Hebrew, *al-shemot* in Maimonides' Judaeo-Arabic) were common forms of magical praxis in antiquity, widely accepted among the Jews.[70] Maimonides gives short shrift to these practices.[71]

Seeing God's name as something powerful which may be used is not only typical of clearly magical works like the *Ḥarva demosheh* (Sword of

---

[67] Some have interpreted the book as an attack on anthropomorphism. That may or may not be the case, but on the level of *peshat* (simple meaning), the book is a description of God's body. For discussion, see Schäfer, *Hidden and Manifest God*, 99–103, 149, and Deutsch, *Gnostic Imagination*, 80–99, 140–4. Deutsch surveys the views of contemporary scholarship on the nature of *Shiur komah*. For the text itself and a lengthy discussion of issues surrounding it, see M. S. Cohen, *Shi'ur Qomah: Liturgy and Theurgy*, which contains an English translation of the text, and id., *Shi'ur Qomah: Texts and Recensions*. Asi Farber-Ginat emphasizes the liturgical character of *Shiur komah* in id., 'Studies in *Sefer Shiur Komah*'. This important study contains an extensive bibliography of studies on the *Shiur komah*.

[68] On the apparent change in Maimonides' attitude towards *Shiur komah* (from regarding it as an authoritative text to viewing it as a forgery), see Kafih, 'Fragment', and the comments in Lieberman, 'Appendix D'. For an exhaustive survey of the whole issue, see Jospe, 'Maimonides and *Shiur Komah*'.

[69] For studies, see Groezinger, 'Names of God'; Elior, 'Concept of God'; ead., 'Mysticism, Magic, and Angelology'; ead., *Three Temples*, 246–7; Janowitz, *Poetics of Ascent*; Lesses, *Ritual Practices to Gain Power*; Scholem, 'Name of God'; Swartz, *Mystical Prayer*, 3–20; id., *Scholastic Magic*, 19, 120; and E. R. Wolfson, 'Theosophy of Shabbetai Donnolo'.

[70] The question of how best to define 'magic' has become a major issue in recent scholarship. For a recent discussion, see Harari, 'Religion, Magic, and Adjurations'. For our purposes, the behaviours forbidden by Maimonides in *MT* 'Laws of Idolatry', 11, can serve to delimit the parameters of magical praxis. See also *Guide* iii. 37 and the discussion of that text in Schwartz, *Astrology and Magic*, 108–10.

[71] That he knew about them cannot be doubted. Altmann, 'Maimonides' Attitude', 207, notes that *Guide* i. 26 shows that Maimonides 'was acquainted with the mystical writings about the permutations of the Divine Name'.

Moses),[72] but also has rabbinic sources.[73] The apparent orthodoxy of the notion may explain the fervour with which Maimonides attacks it in *Guide of the Perplexed* i. 61–2 (discussed in Chapter 5 below).[74]

Many readers today will have a hard time understanding Maimonides in this connection, since few are aware of the extent to which magic infiltrated the very warp and woof of Jewish life in antiquity. This may become clearer if we note another example of the sort of writing Maimonides attacks: *Sefer harazim* (Book of Mysteries). This book is a compilation of magical texts, including many bizarre names meant to be invoked in magical formulae, which, according to Ithamar Gruenwald, was compiled in the sixth or seventh centuries out of much earlier elements, not all of which were understood by the compiler.[75] Lee I. Levine dates the work to the fourth century, and characterizes it as a 'Jewish handbook of popular magic that was heavily indebted to popular pagan (later Christian traditions) and practices that were ubiquitous throughout the ambient Roman-Byzantine world'.[76] Baruch Levine dates the book even earlier, suggesting that it may have been written in the first century.[77] The work was reconstructed on the basis of Genizah texts and published in its entirety for the first time by

---

[72] See Harari's edition of the *Ḥarva demosheh* and the critical comments in Bar-Ilan, 'Review'. The 'sword' in this book is a list of holy names that can be used for magical purposes. Harari (p. 52) shows that the work was known to Hai Gaon (939–1038), while Bar-Ilan, 'Review', 140, argues that it goes back to the 6th cent. There is no evidence that Maimonides knew this work, but it was hardly atypical. *Ḥarva demosheh* was originally edited by Gaster in *Studies and Texts*, iii. 69–103. Gaster's translation of the text appears in vol. i, pp. 312–37; he comments on the text on pp. 288–311.

[73] See e.g. BT *Kid. 71a*, *Mak. 11a*, *Men. 29b*, and *Pes. 50a*.

[74] Maimonides' comments in *MT* 'Laws of *Tefilin*', 5: 4, are relevant here too: 'It is customary to write the word *shadai* [one of the names of God] on the outside of the *mezuzah*, opposite the space between the paragraphs. Since it is on the outside, it is not objectionable. But those who write the names of angels, holy names, verses, or special shapes on the *mezuzah* are included in the category of those who have no share in the world to come, since these fools not only cancel the commandment, but make of a great commandment, the unification of the name of the Holy One, blessed be He, His love, and His worship, a charm for their own benefit since they, in their stupidity, think that this is a matter which benefits them concerning worldly vanities.' See also ibid. 6: 13. For background, see Jansson, 'Magic of the Mezuzah', Lichtenstein, 'Mezuzah as an Amulet', and Gordon, 'Mezuzah'.

[75] Gruenwald, *Apocalyptic and Merkavah Mysticism*, 225–34.

[76] L. I. Levine, *Judaism and Hellenism in Antiquity*, 10.

[77] See B. Levine, 'Appendix', 344.

Mordecai Margolioth in 1967.[78] The book is representative of a great number of similar books,[79] and represents a kind of literature with important connections to the world of the Talmud.[80] For our purposes it is important not only because it is representative of a large class of similar works, and not only because—its heterodoxy notwithstanding[81]—it was a work widely accepted as normative in Jewish antiquity,[82] but because it was apparently known to Maimonides. As Margolioth points out in the introduction to his edition of the work (p. 40), Maimonides makes reference in *MT* 'Laws of Idolatry', 6: 1, to the custom of holding a sceptre made of myrtle. This, according to Margolioth, is a detail of magical praxis found only in *Sefer harazim*.

The question of the nature of the connections between the Heikhalot literature and the world of the Talmud, in particular, and of the place of magic in rabbinic culture in general, is hotly disputed.[83] With respect to *Sefer harazim*, Margolioth sees it as entirely outside the rabbinic mainstream. P. S. Alexander, on the other hand, holds that 'there is good evidence to suggest that such [magical] material circulated at the very heart of rabbinic society'.[84] Alexander is supported by Peter Schäfer, who holds that 'the Talmud is more lenient towards magic than Margolioth, and *Sefer harazim* is a wonderful example of how plain magic could well be integrated into the theological framework of rabbinic Judaism'.[85] The

---

[78] Margolioth, *Sefer harazim*. On this edition, see Dan, 'Margolioth's Edition'. The work is translated into English in Morgan, *Sepher ha-Razim*.

[79] On this, see Gruenwald, *Apocalyptic and Merkavah Mysticism*, 225 and, importantly, the discussion in Scholem, *Jewish Gnosticism*, 10, 66–74, 81–4, and 94–100.

[80] Dan, 'Margolioth's Edition', 212; Schäfer, 'Jewish Magic Literature'.

[81] See Gruenwald, *Apocalyptic and Merkavah Mysticism*, 230: 'conjuration of the angels is frequently connected with ritual performances which, according to traditional standards, are downright idolatry. One is expected to offer libations to the angels and incense to the astral bodies. In one case one even has to sacrifice a white cock to the moon and stars. Most surprising is the prayer to Helios, which one has to say if one desires to see the sun rising in its chariot.'

[82] Margolioth, *Sefer harazim*, 41.

[83] For a survey of the positions, see Swartz, 'Book and Tradition'. Swartz's own position (pp. 227–8) is that the authors of the Heikhalot texts were neither members of the rabbinic elite nor anti-rabbinic *amei ha'arets*, but, rather, literate Jews connected to, but not actually members of, the core rabbinic elite.

[84] See Alexander, 'Incantations and Books of Magic', 349.

[85] See Schäfer, 'Magic and Religion', 38.

connections between *Sefer harazim* and Heikhalot literature are also obscure.[86]

Sefer harazim and works like it may explain the fervour of Maimonides' statements in *Guide* i. 61–2, and surely explain why he found it of such pressing importance to undermine the theory of Hebrew which makes these works possible.[87]

Was Maimonides familiar with this literature? It stretches credulity to think that he was not. The vast amount of this material found in the Cairo Genizah, for one thing, makes it likely that he knew it. Furthermore, he claims to have read every idolatrous text he could find;[88] is it possible that he read non-Jewish idolatrous texts and ignored Jewish ones? Moreover, we have seen that he himself mentions at least one Heikhalot text, *Shiur komah*, and there is indirect evidence that he was familiar with *Sefer harazim*. Several scholars have also found indications of his familiarity with Heikhalot themes and texts in his writings.[89]

Maimonides' Opposition to the World of Proto-Kabbalah

Up to this point I have tried to outline the main contours of the Jewish world against which Maimonides struggled. It is this struggle to which the body of this book is dedicated, which proves that the normative Jewish

[86] See Elior, 'Mysticism, Magic, and Angelology', 41. For more on *Sefer harazim*, see Goldin, 'Magic of Magic', 353–5.

[87] For background on the magical and theurgic uses of Hebrew in rabbinic texts and culture, see Gruenwald, '*Haketav, Hamikhtav*, and the Articulated Name'. For evidence that the magical and theurgic uses of divine names were widespread in the generations immediately after Maimonides, see the text by Abraham Abulafia cited in Idel, 'Judaism, Jewish Mysticism, and Magic', 35–56. [88] See above, n. 47.

[89] In a cleverly argued discussion, S. Harvey suggests 'the possible influence of merkavah terminology and symbolism on Maimonides': see id., 'Maimonides in the Sultan's Palace', 64. Gruenwald, 'Maimonides' Quest', 142, notes that 'there are good reasons for believing that Maimonides was familiar with some of the mystical writings of the *merkavah* mystics'. Fishbane, 'Some Forms', argues that some of Maimonides' religious language is derived from texts of 'mystical theosophy'. The point I am urging here is different from that made by Harvey and Fishbane: not only did Maimonides use language and symbolism derived from *merkavah* texts, but he purposefully did so in order quietly to undermine the teachings of those texts and replace them with what was in his mind a more refined and truer version of Judaism. Compare Ivry, 'Isma'ili Theology', 285.

world of Maimonides' day was indeed suffused with proto-kabbalistic elements.

One way of drawing a sharp line between Maimonides' spiritual world and that which he attacked is by attending to a point made by Y. Tzvi Langermann. Langermann refers to what he calls Judah Halevi's 'hyper-realism', which he defines as 'the tendency to view geometrical constructs not as useful devices for organizing knowledge, not as arbitrary (though not lacking some rationale) conveniences but rather as real and important elements of the universe'. He further comments that hyperrealism 'has become typical of a certain type of Jewish religious thinker (especially those of a kabbalistic bent)'.[90] Maimonides, in stark if unstated opposition to the world of 'proto-kabbalah' as found in Heikhalot literature, and in equally stark if rather clearer opposition to the worlds of Judah Halevi before him and of Nahmanides after him (and here I paraphrase Langermann), viewed halakhic distinctions and entities as devices ordained by God for organizing our lives, not as elements of God's universe with some sort of independent existence. Another way of putting this is to say that Maimonides was a religious and not just a philosophical nominalist (in the informal sense of the word as we are using it in this chapter).

Another way of understanding Maimonides' divergences from the world of proto-kabbalah (i.e. the Jewish world he found in North Africa, Egypt, Babylonia, and Yemen, so different to him from the Jewish world he had left behind in Andalusia) is to examine his understanding of the nature of halakhah (the subject of Chapter 2 below). Does halakhah reflect an antecedently existing ontological reality, or does it constitute a social, institutional reality? If the former, halakhah could not be other than it is; if the latter, halakhah could have been different. If the former, the this-worldly consequences of sin can be seen as objective and actual; if the latter, the this-worldly consequences of sin can only be in the social realm. Connected to this is the interesting fact that, for Maimonides, the consequences of mistakes made with respect to halakhic matters are relatively benign, while those made with respect to some metaphysical matters are fatal and final.[91]

For Maimonides, holiness consists in the fulfilment of the commandments. In Chapter 3 I analyse Maimonides' approach to the holiness of persons, of the people of Israel, of the Land of Israel and Jerusalem, of

[90] Langermann, 'Science and the *Kuzari*', 508–9.

[91] The distinctions hinted at here have interesting implications for questions of rabbinic authority; I take these up in detail in my article 'Rabbis in Politics' and more briefly below in the Afterword.

Torah scrolls, *tefilin*, and *mezuzot*, and of special times (sabbath and holy days). In each case Maimonides was faced with three different possibilities. The holiness of persons, nations, places, objects, and times could be something with ontological standing which inheres in them from the time of creation, something with ontological standing which was attached to them at some point in history, or a name for their institutional standing within the halakhic framework.[92]

Before explaining further this tripartite distinction, an introductory comment is necessary. The question of what holiness is has been very rarely asked of Jewish texts, perhaps because the notion of holiness is so pervasive in Judaism that asking Jewish texts about the nature of holiness is like asking fish about the nature of water.[93] Thus, with the exception of the *Kuzari*, it is hard to pinpoint pre-Maimonidean texts which take a stand, explicitly or implicitly, on this issue.[94]

The first two conceptions of holiness outlined above have in common the idea that, however it *becomes* holy, a holy place, person, nation, time, or object is, once holy, objectively different from profane places, persons, nations, times, and objects. According to both these views, sanctity is real, it inheres in sacred places etc., it is intrinsic to them; it is, one might say, part of their metaphysical make-up; it has ontological standing. Holy places, persons, nations, times, and objects are ontologically distinct from (and religiously superior to) profane places, persons, nations, times, and objects. This distinction is part of the universe, whether from the time of creation or, say, from Sinai.

Let me try to make this point clearer with an analogy. Radioactivity existed before Geiger discovered a way to measure it. Similarly, holiness can be thought objectively to inhere in holy places, persons, nations, times, and objects, even though there is no way for us (presently) to measure it. It is

[92] I am deeply grateful to Joshua Golding for helping me to think through this issue; he is no way responsible for the use to which I put his insights here.

[93] Compare Jacobs, 'Holy Places', 4, who points to 'the absence of anything like a systematic treatment of the topic [of holiness in Judaism]'. My claim here is well illustrated in a fascinating study by Peters, *Jerusalem and Mecca*. The question of how Judaism and Islam understand the nature of holiness is nowhere addressed in this important book.

[94] Even Halevi, who clearly sees the distinctions between the Land of Israel and all other lands, and between the Jewish people and other peoples, as reflecting something real in the universe (i.e. as having what I have been calling here ontological standing), nowhere speaks clearly and explicitly about the nature of holiness in and of itself.

'out there', a feature of the objectively real world, even if not part of the world susceptible to laboratory examination. Of course, radioactivity relates to the material universe, and holiness to the spiritual universe, but the analogy should be helpful all the same.

I find a different, third view of holiness in the thought of Maimonides. According to his view holiness cannot be characterized as ontological or essentialist, since holy places, persons, nations, times, and objects are in no objective way distinct from profane places, persons, nations, times, and objects; holiness is a status, not a quality or property. It is a challenge, not a given; normative, not descriptive. It is institutional (in the sense of being part of a system of laws and determined by those laws) and hence contingent. This sort of holiness does not reflect objective reality, it helps constitute social reality. According to this view, holy places, persons, times, and objects are indubitably holy, and must be treated with all due respect, but they are, in and of themselves, like all other places, persons, times, and objects. What is different about them is the way in which the Torah commands that they be treated. Holy places, persons, nations, times, and objects derive their sanctity from the roles they play, the uses to which they are put.[95]

Maimonides could not adopt any variant of the ontological, essentialist interpretation of holiness: the Torah obligates Jews to be holy, because God is holy (Lev. 19: 2). Were that interpreted to mean that Jews (or sacred objects, times, and places) are or can be essentially holy, we would be saying that God and certain created entities share a characteristic, namely, the characteristic of holiness. This is something which, as noted above, Maimonides repeatedly disallows. Holiness, it follows, must be *institutional*, a matter of halakhic definition, not ontological, somehow actually in the universe.[96]

---

[95] A good example of the ambiguity on the subject of holiness in pre-Maimonidean Judaism may be found in the language of the opening formula of blessings ordinarily recited before the fulfilment of any positive commandment: 'Blessed are You, Lord our God, Who has sanctified us with His commandments and commanded us to . . .'. One can understand this language as affirming that the imposition of the commandments has made Israel essentially holy, or, on the other hand, as affirming, as I claim Maimonides does, that holiness is a consequence of fulfilling the commandments and that it means nothing more than that.

[96] My thinking on holiness was greatly helped by W. Z. Harvey, 'Holiness'; Seeskin, 'Holiness as an Ethical Ideal'; Silman, 'Commandments and Transgressions'; and id., 'Introduction'. For useful studies of some of the many texts that express a distinctly non-Maimonidean understanding of holiness, see the studies collected in Dan, *On Holiness*.

With respect to the issue of holiness, it takes an intricate and extended argument to demonstrate Maimonides' position, and it is hard to point out definite texts to which he may have been responding. But with respect to an issue intimately related to the nature of holiness, that of ritual purity and impurity, the situation is very different. Biblical and rabbinic texts, when taken together, allow for a wide variety of approaches to the meaning of ritual purity and impurity (*toharah* and *tumah*). In Chapter 4 below I will focus on two such approaches. Maimonides was familiar with them both; he adopted one and consciously rejected the other.

Given the letter and language mysticism which characterized Jewish mysticism in its various historical manifestations, Maimonides' understanding of the nature of the Hebrew language is an obvious subject of analysis in this study, forming the subject of Chapter 5. For Maimonides, Hebrew is a language like all other languages, possessing no special qualities and no special powers. Its letters are certainly not the elements out of which the cosmos was created.

Ancient Jewish mysticism, so strongly influenced by Neoplatonism, loved to hypostasize biblical and rabbinic notions; among the most important of these was the notion of God's presence (*kavod*, *shekhinah*). Maimonides, as I prove in Chapter 6, took every opportunity afforded him to intepret such terms in a non-ontological fashion.

In what way are Jews distinct from non-Jews? It is a central teaching of Judah Halevi that the distinction between Jews and non-Jews resides in some level of existence which even full conversion cannot modify. Maimonides' radical rejection of this approach is a further expression of his unwillingness to grant ontological status to halakhic entities and distinctions.

Maimonides' depersonification of angels seems to be a clear attempt to distance himself from the dominant Jewish culture of his day, i.e. the Judaism apparently taught as normative by many, perhaps all, of his rabbinic colleagues in North Africa and the Middle East.[97]

I do not mean to imply that one should connect every aspect of Jewish culture which Maimonides criticized to proto-kabbalah. Thus, I think that his well-known (if usually overstated) aversion to non-liturgical poetry has nothing to do with proto-kabbalah.[98] On the other hand, Maimonides'

---

[97] If Maimonides was unenthusiastic about angels, it is hardly surprising that he seems to have been hostile to demons. See below, Ch. 8 n. 79.

[98] On his attitude towards non-liturgical poetry, see Schirmann, 'Maimonides and Hebrew Poetry', and Yahalom, 'Maimonides and Hebrew Poetry'. With specific reference

critique of liturgical poetry, *piyutim*, is usually linked to strictly halakhic issues.[99] Examination of the content of these hymns, however, will show that they are suffused with proto-kabbalistic motifs. Maimonides had plenty of extra-halakhic reasons for trying to ban their recitation in the synagogue.

❧

Many of Maimonides' Jewishly unusual positions can be understood as consequences of his philosophical and religious nominalism and of his insistence on the absolute transcendence of God. In tracing the Jewish consequences of his positions, he was forced to make (often implicit, but none the less emphatic) criticisms of the Judaism of his day. Examining that Judaism through the prism of Maimonides' reaction to it, as I seek to do in this book, will give us a new, fuller, picture of what he was trying to accomplish.

In scholarly circles, Maimonides is often depicted as if he should be understood primarily against the background of Greek, Hellenist, and Arabic philosophy. Lawrence V. Berman summarized this view in the title of his classic article, 'Maimonides, the Disciple of Alfarabi'. In traditionalist Jewish circles, by contrast, Maimonides is often depicted as if he should be understood exclusively in the context of the Jewish tradition, as it existed before him and as it continued to exist after him. For the last twenty-five years, following the lead of scholars such as Isadore Twersky and David Hartman, I have sought to argue that Maimonides is best understood against both these backgrounds and that he stood at the intersection of two vectors, one beginning with the first Moses and the second beginning with Plato.

It now appears to me that in searching for rabbinic and philosophical antecedents to his thought, I have paid too little attention to the Judaism against which Maimonides was reacting. True, much of what he wrote

to his discussion of poetry in his comment on Mishnah *Avot* 1: 15 see Kraemer, 'Influence of Islamic Law', 232, and Yahalom, '"Sayeth Tuviyah ben Tsidkiyah"'. I might note that, given the importance of poetry in the cultural arsenal of Andalusian scholars, it makes little sense to see Maimonides as an out-and-out opponent of it. For helpful studies in this regard, see Brann, 'Arabized Jews'; Kozodoy, 'Reading Medieval Hebrew Love Poetry'; Scheindlin, 'Merchants and Intellectuals'; and id., *Wine, Women, and Death*. See also below, the very end of Ch. 4.

[99] For an accessible discussion, see Kadish, *Kavvana*, 398–9.

appears to have been written as if he were trying to refute Judah Halevi, but it is the way in which Halevi is representative of the Jewish culture of his day which has been insufficiently noted.[100]

Maimonides did not simply sift through the rabbinic and philosophical literature available to him in order to find raw materials for his highly naturalistic account of Judaism. He also studied the proto-kabbalistic literature attributed to the talmudic rabbis and the allied literature written by their successors, in order to pinpoint elements which needed to be refined or even rejected altogether.

Excursus: Terminology

What can one call that which distinguishes holy from profane persons, nations, places, times, and objects (according to the view of those who hold that there is really something 'out there' in virtue of which the holy person, nation, place, time, or object is holy)? I have toyed with terms such as ontological, essential, real, inherent, intrinsic, actual, concrete, tangible, genuine, existent, substantial. In the end, I have chosen to remain with the first two, using them interchangeably. Explaining why will make my point clearer.

For Maimonides, ontological distinctions are rooted in form (as opposed to matter). On the level of form, nothing distinguishes a kosher (and hence very holy) Torah scroll from one that was written, say, by a heretical scribe (and which must be burned); or, on the level of form, nothing distinguishes between two identical spoons, one dedicated to use in the Temple (and hence holy) and one dedicated for use in the home (and thus profane). Another way of putting this general point is that Maimonides definitely believes in essences in the sense of natural divisions: human beings are *essentially* different from apes. What he denies is that such distinctions hold between holy and profane persons, nations, places, times, and objects. In terms of essence, for example, there is no distinction between Mount Moriah and Mount Carmel; both are simply mountains. That the Temple was built on one and that I live on the other are important (at least to me) facts in historical, institutional, halakhic terms; the former is holy and the latter is not. But 'all' that means is that Jews are commanded to treat them differently, not that they are in any sense distinct in any but geographical, historical, institutional, or halakhic terms.

[100] Diamond, *Maimonides and the Hermeneutics of Concealment*, 159–61, paints a picture of the Maimonidean project similar to the one I advance here.

While the word 'substantial' would make sense in a strictly philosophical context to express this point, in common usage it has taken on the connotations of solidity and size and would probably be misleading. 'Existent' also would mislead, thanks to its connotation of concreteness. While Maimonides certainly denies that there is any 'inherent' (i.e. permanently characteristic) difference between holy and profane entities, some of his opponents would agree, since they hold that entities can *become* holy. Similarly, he and some of his opponents could agree that holiness is not necessarily 'intrinsic', in the sense of belonging naturally to the holy entity. Words such as 'concrete' and 'tangible' do an injustice to Maimonides' opponents since none of them think that holiness is something that can be detected in the physical world. A term such as 'actual' does a disservice to Maimonides, since he thinks that a holy person, nation, place, time, or object is actually holy and in an important sense different from a similar but profane person, nation, place, time, or object. The difference is on the plane of halakhic institutions and social relations, but that does not make it not actual or unimportant. The same holds true for 'genuine'. Using 'real' is awkward for the same reason: I do not want to give the impression that the distinction between holy and profane is ephemeral in Maimonides' eyes. I thus remain with 'ontological' or 'essential' as best expressing the notion I try to analyse here.

TWO

The Institutional Character of Halakhah

৵

Introduction

RABBENU NISSIM BEN REUVEN GERONDI (*c.*1310–76) raises a question concerning a well-known midrashic comment on Deuteronomy 17: 11. The verse reads: 'You shall act in accordance with the instructions given you and the ruling handed down to you; you must not deviate from the verdict that they announce to you either to the right or to the left.' On this last expression, *Sifrei* on Deuteronomy (paragraph 154) comments: 'Even if they tell you that right is left, and left is right.' Rabbenu Nissim asks:

There is place here for further investigation, to wit: it is fitting that this [position] follow from the view of those who think that there are no reasons for the commandments of the Torah at all and that all of them are consequences exclusively of [God's] will alone. According to this, the thing itself is neither ritually impure nor ritually pure, for example, but what makes it ritually impure or pure is a consequence of [God's] will alone.[1]

Were this the case, Rabbenu Nissim points out, and since the Torah commands that we follow the decision of the sages of each generation, no damage could occur to the soul of the person who follows the decision of the sages of his generation, even if they *mistakenly* tell him that right is left, or left is right, or, more to the point, that it is permissible to eat something which, in fact, is actually not kosher. Rabbenu Nissim rejects this position:

But . . . we choose not to adopt this position, but believe that all that the Torah forbids us harms us and leaves an evil impression in our souls, even if we do not know its cause. According to this view, then, if the sages were to agree concerning an impure thing that it was pure, what will be? For that thing will harm us and cause what is in its nature to cause, even though the sages agreed that it is pure. (p. 437)

[1] Nissim ben Reuven Gerondi, *Derashot haran*, Sermon 11, p. 436. My thanks to Seth Kadish for drawing my attention to Rabbenu Nissim's text.

Ingesting something unkosher actually harms the Jew. The forbidden food is forbidden *because* it is in itself harmful (at least to Jews). It is not forbidden because it is unhygienic, or to make a point about the nature of the universe, or to instil discipline, or to keep Jews away from morally or religious offensive ideas; it is forbidden because eating it leaves an evil impression on the soul of the Jew who eats it.

Rabbenu Nissim emphasizes the point in the following analogy:

Similarly, if physicians were to agree that a particular medicine is lukewarm, while, for example, it is [really] warm to the fourth degree, there is no doubt that the medicine will not have the effect in the body expected by the physicians, but will work according to its nature. Similarly, that which the Torah has forbidden us since it harms the soul, how will its nature be changed [just] because the sages haves agreed that it is permitted? (p. 437)

There is objective harm in (a Jew's) eating something not kosher, or touching something ritually impure. Similarly, the benefit obtained by properly offering a sacrifice, or wearing *tefilin* that have been prepared according to law, is real. By analogy, if an expert physician prescribes the wrong medicine, it will not function as the physician expected, but as its nature determines.[2]

The continuation of Rabbenu Nissim's discussion is interesting but not relevant to my concerns here. We have read enough to see that he recognizes two positions on the nature of the commandments of the Torah. According to one position, the commandments reflect nothing other than the inscrutable will of God. This is halakhic positivism with a vengeance. Rabbenu Nissim rejects this view and adopts another one, most clearly expressed in the Middle Ages by Judah Halevi, according to which the commandments of the Torah were laid down by God because something about the nature of the universe causes a benefit to the Jew who fulfils them, just as the prohibitions of the Torah were laid down because their violation causes some harm to the Jewish violator.

In the present chapter I will show that Maimonides adopts a third position. For him the commandments of the Torah are not purely positivist (in the sense that in most cases God could just as easily have commanded

---

[2] It is a safe bet that this is a veiled reference to *Kuzari* i. 79. For a view at odds with that of Rabbenu Nissim, see *Sefer haḥinukh*, no. 496. The author of *Sefer haḥinukh* (who is often thought to reflect a Maimonidean sensibility) accepts with relative equanimity that rabbis might err in their halakhic decisions, arguing that it is better to accept a mistaken halakhic decision than encourage the development of competing Torahs.

something else), but they do not reflect anything about the metaphysical nature of the universe either. Rather, the commandments of the Torah are wise and beneficial, but in many cases reflect specific historical realities; had these realities been different (and they could have been), then many of the commandments would have been different. To summarize the points I will prove in what follows, for Maimonides the commandments of the Torah are historically conditioned, they do not reflect an antecedent metaphysical reality but, rather, constitute a new institutional, social reality. Without being purely positivist, they could have been different; but, once commanded, they must be obeyed.

Two Opposing Views

I shall address here a question about the nature of halakhah which is rarely, if ever, addressed by halakhists, but which has profound implications for our understanding of what halakhah is meant to be, and important ramifications for the question of what Torah is, and how it is meant to relate to the world.[3] I will delineate two fundamentally opposed conceptions of what halakhah is; Maimonides, it will turn out, holds one view, while his opponents (Judah Halevi and other 'proto-kabbalists' before him; Nahmanides and the kabbalists after him[4]) hold a conflicting view. I will first state and explain the two views, and then show that they are indeed held by the thinkers to whom I attribute them.[5] Maimonides' view, as I

[3] I address some of those ramifications in my article 'Rabbis in Politics' and below in the Afterword.

[4] See Idel, 'On Some Forms of Order in Kabbalah', p. xxxviii: 'Unlike the rabbinic treatment of the mitzvot as basically non-constellated, namely as ungoverned by metaphysical structures, most of the kabbalists subordinated them to supernal entities and processes, thus creating more comprehensive frameworks.'

[5] In three valuable articles Yochanan Silman addresses many of the issues raised here, and my discussion is indebted to him. See (in order of publication): 'Halakhic Determinations', 'Commandments and Transgressions', and 'Introduction'. Where I use the opposition 'institutional' (following Blidstein; see below, n. 7) vs. 'ontological', Silman uses the opposition 'nominalist' vs. 'realist'. Silman's discussions are particularly valuable for showing the concrete halakhic implications of these 'meta-halakhic' issues. His book, *The Voice Heard at Sinai*, is not directly relevant to the issues addressed here. In it Silman traces two conceptions of Torah: as the product of an all-inclusive revelation given once for all time at Sinai or as an ongoing process involving human agency. The first position has obvious affinities to the realist/ontological conception of halakhah (see ibid. 19) but is logically independent of it.

explicate it here, is part and parcel of his opposition to the 'hyperrealism'[6] of what I call 'proto-kabbalah'.

Does halakhah *reflect* an antecedently existing ontological reality, or does it *constitute* a social, institutional reality? According to the first view, halakhic distinctions, such as permitted and forbidden, kosher and unkosher, ritually pure and ritually impure, and holy and profane, reflect actual distinctions in the universe. These distinctions may not be observable but are none the less real. It is an expression of God's special love for the Jewish people that he makes these distinctions known to them through the Torah. This is the position held by thinkers such as Judah Halevi, Nahmanides, and the authors of the Zohar. It is probably the view held unconsciously by most Jews since the medieval acceptance of the Zohar as a normative Jewish text, and it appears to be the view held by almost all Jews today who observe halakhah.

In opposition to this view, halakhah may be understood, not as reflecting any ontologically real if physically unobservable distinctions in the universe, but as constituting or creating a social reality in the world in which humans live and interact.[7] Understood in this fashion, halakhah is nothing other than an expression of God's will, which could in principle have been expressed differently.[8] To adopt a modern idiom, 'halakhah' is the name

---

[6] I borrow this term from Y. Tzvi Langermann; see his 'Science and the *Kuzari*'. In this book I use the term 'ontological' where Langermann uses 'hyperrealism'. In private correspondence, Gad Freudenthal (who suggested the term 'hyperrealism' to Langermann) used the term 'conventional' where I use 'institutional'.

[7] Ya'akov (Gerald) Blidstein is the author of a series of important studies on what might be called Maimonides' 'meta-halakhah' in which this point is elucidated. Among the most relevant for our purposes here are the following, listed in order of publication: 'Tradition and Institutional Authority', 'Oral Law', 'Maimonidean Structures', ' "Even if He Tells You Right is Left" ', and *Authority and Dissent*. Another scholar whose studies are important in this context is David Henshke, especially his article 'The Basis of Maimonides' Concept of Halakhah'. My interpretation of Maimonides is interestingly supported from a slightly different angle by Sinclair, 'Legal Thinking'. The perceptive studies of Yochanan Silman on the nature of halakhah (above, n. 5) are clearly relevant in this context.

[8] I originally wrote that halakhah was 'arbitrary'—not in the sense of being capricious, but in the sense that it was not necessary that it be expressed as in fact it was. Kenneth Seeskin convinced me that the term would cause more confusion than it would clear up. He suggested the term 'contingent', but that strikes me as even worse, implying that God's will as expressed in the commandments is dependent upon something outside God. I have thus been forced to adopt variants of the inelegant but precise

given to a set of rules which create an institution called 'Judaism'. These rules could in principle have been different, without thereby being any the less expressions of God's wisdom and benevolence (as is shown, for example, by Maimonides' explanation of why God commanded the Jews to bring sacrifices[9]). These rules could have been different, but that does not mean that they are unreasonable, that they fail to embody important teachings, or that they are morally neutral. For example, the specific

expression, 'could in principle have been different'. Here is Professor Seeskin's communication to me on this subject: 'Consider three classes of things: 1. Something that is truly arbitrary; in other words, no possible reason could be given for preferring one alternative to the other. The standard medieval example is that of a thirsty man placed between two equal glasses of water. In this case, it is arbitrary which one he picks. 2. Something that could be otherwise but is superior to its alternatives, e.g. the design of the human body. According to Maimonides, other designs were possible but this is the simplest and most elegant. 3. Something that is necessary and could not be otherwise, e.g. the truths of metaphysics. In regard to causality, the Mutakallimun argue that everything belongs in class 1, the emanationist that everything belongs in class 3. I read Maimonides as trying to defend a middle ground. If the Mutakallimun were right, God would not accomplish anything by making choices. If the alternatives are truly arbitrary, nothing is gained by doing things this way rather than that. *Guide of the Perplexed*, iii. 25 tells us that God never does anything futile, frivolous, or in vain. If the emanationists were right, there would be logical reasons for why everything is the case. But there are many things for which no reason is available. Therefore Maimonides thinks there are things that belong in class 2 and that God does exercise free choice. I submit the same is true of the commandments. Though they could be otherwise, it is still the case that God had reasons for picking this rather than that. Hence they are contingent but not arbitrary.'

I must thank Professor Seeskin for saving me from an egregiously bad choice of terminology. At the end of his *Book of Commandments* (Negative Commandment 365), Maimonides emphatically insists that every single commandment has a reason and a cause; see also *Guide* iii. 25 and the text from *Guide* iii. 26 (p. 507), cited below on p. 148. Using the term 'arbitrary' (even in the arbitrary sense in which I had planned to use it) would have been inexcusable.

[9] For Maimonides' historical explanation of the sacrificial cult, see *Guide* iii. 32 (p. 526). For a recent and thorough discussion, see J. Stern, *Problems and Parables*, 23–35 and 140–50. Maimonides presents the entire sacrificial cult as a concession to the primitive character of the Jews in Egypt. Considering how many biblical commandments relate directly to the sacrificial cult (including all the commandments concerning the Tabernacle and all the commandments concerning ritual purity and impurity), this is quite a remarkable claim. Stern examines Nahmanides' outraged rejection of Maimonides' position. For the wider context, see Benin, *Footprints of God*. The relevant texts are cited and analysed below, in Ch. 4.

commandments regulating incest could have been different (after all, some relations permitted by Rabbanites are forbidden by Karaites). Once given, however, they are definitely normative.[10] Violations of these rules can have serious consequences on a psychosocial level, leading up to and including the death penalty,[11] but have no direct consequences on an ontological level. Obedience to the commandments in and of itself does not gain one entry to the world to come.

There are interesting and important consequences which follow from these views. According to the first (essentialist or ontological) view, halakhah could not be other than it is. A place, object, time, or person is holy, for example, because there is some actually existent property called 'holiness' which in some sense inheres in that place, object, time, or person. A particular item is ritually impure, not because it satisfies or fails to satisfy certain criteria which could in principle have been different, but because it really is ritually impure on some level of reality beyond any accessible to human senses or sensing devices.

According to the latter, Maimonidean view (i.e. the view which I will shortly show was held by Maimonides), halakhah could have been different. Indeed, many of the commandments of the Torah, Maimonides maintains, reflect actual historical events which did not have to occur; had history worked out differently, many Torah ceremonials would be different.

According to the essentialist view the consequences of sin are objective and actual; sinning harms the sinner, dimishes her, stains her, changes the nature of her soul. For Maimonides, sinning is bad for the sinner 'only' in the Platonic sense that doing evil harms the doer no less (if not more) than

[10] Maimonides, it is very important to emphasize, was neither an antinomian nor an Asharite (who, as Maimonides explains in *Guide* iii. 17, held that God rules the world with a divine will divorced from wisdom and morality).

[11] Halakhah constitutes reality in an institutional, but not ontological, sense. This halakhic reality can be very important and have grave consequences. If an unmarried man and an unmarried woman have intimate relations, for example, the halakhic consequences of the act are almost non-existent. If on the same day the woman should marry another man, and after the wedding have relations again with the first, both are guilty of a capital offence. All that has changed is the woman's marital status, but that change is enough to cost her and her paramour their lives. Unless one holds that the ceremony of marriage somehow effected a change in the woman's ontological status, that after the wedding she was different in some metaphysically significant sense, and not 'just' in terms of social, religious, and legal status, then what we have here is an example of how change in halakhic status can have profound implications even with respect to matters of life and death, even though it does not affect extra-social reality at all.

the one to whom evil is done. For an essentialist, such as Judah Halevi, performing the commandments properly brings about changes in the world (and for some kabbalists, in the divine *sefirot* as well);[12] it is not surprising that according to this view, such behaviour leads one to a share in the world to come, while halakhic malfeasance can cut one off from the world to come. Maimonides, on the other hand, as we shall see, explicitly teaches that the commandments are instruments for the creation of morally (and ultimately, intellectually) improved individuals and societies; he teaches implicitly that obedience to the commandments *per se* does not guarantee one a share in the world to come, unless it be coupled with at least a minimal degree of intellectual perfection.

For essentialists, mistakes concerning halakhic matters can be costly; mistakes in matters of dogma unfortunate, and in matters of science, uninteresting. For Maimonides, the consequences of mistakes made with respect to halakhic matters are relatively benign, while those made with respect to some dogmatic issues are fatal and final; since, for Maimonides, matters of dogma and science (i.e. physics and metaphysics) overlap, mistakes in these areas can be as dangerous as mistakes in matters of dogma.

Perhaps one useful way of understanding the difference I am trying to point out, between Maimonides on the one hand and essentialist thinkers such as Halevi and Nahmanides on the other, is to recall the opposed views of Émile Durkheim and Rudolph Otto. For Durkheim, religion expresses and satisfies social needs,[13] while for Otto it reflects

[12] The point at issue is well stated by Jacob Katz (referring to a different, but similar, context): 'The major impact of the kabbala on the national plane is to be seen not in the Sabbatean deviation, but in a general shift in religious values—a shift that, beginning in the latter part of the seventeenth century, went hand in hand with the social changes then becoming manifest. The shift was reflected in the new significance attached to performance of the practical commandments. While halakhic and ethical literature of the time saw observance of the commandments as, first and foremost, obedience to the will of the lawgiver, the kabbalist viewed such observance as a sort of mechanism for setting the machinery of the upper spheres in motion. Each tiny particular of each commandment was linked, in this scheme, to a specific point in the divine system, and anyone who performed that commandment was thereby directing the operation of that system. This in turn determined not only the fate and reward of the individual, but also the advancement or retarding of the perfection of the whole world' (*Tradition and Crisis*, 190).

[13] See Durkheim, *Elementary Forms*, 327: 'Religious forces are in fact only transfigured collective forces, that is, moral forces; they are made of ideas and feelings that the spectacle of society wakens in us, not of sensations that come to us from the

metaphysical realities.[14] Maimonides, it may be said, adopts a Durkheimian rather than an Ottonian perspective on fundamental distinctions in Judaism. For Maimonides, these distinctions are God-given and create social *realities*, without reflecting metaphysical realities. Among other things, it is the point of this book to prove that this is indeed Maimonides' position.

Maimonides' View

For Maimonides, one studies halakhah in order to learn how God commands that Jews should behave. One studies metaphysics (the secrets of the Torah)[15] in order to understand the very nature of the world which God created. It must be emphasized that both kinds of study have the same actional consequence: the imitation of God.[16]

Metaphysics is not a social institution, could not be different, and expresses a truth of an entirely different kind from the 'truth' expressed in halakhah. The world is as it is and, it would seem, on some level, as it must be. Not only does God not play dice with the universe, but God, even though the author of the principles according to which nature works, is unwilling ever (or almost ever) to suspend them. Apprehending metaphysical truths is not to play a game right; it is to look into the mind of God, so to speak, and, perhaps, to become God-like in the sense that one thereby becomes eternal.[17]

It follows, then, that for Maimonides Torah could have been different while nature could not be other than it is. Could that be? I think the way

physical world?' Durkheim's translator, Karen Fields, well summarizes his position as follows: 'Sacredness . . . is a quality that objects acquire . . . when they are set apart and forbidden. They are made sacred by groups of people who set them apart and keep them bounded by specific actions; they remain sacred only so long as groups continue to do this' (pp. xlv–xlvi).

[14] See Otto, *Idea of the Holy*, 11: 'The numinous is thus felt as objective and outside the self.' Otto's translator, John Harvey, comments that with respect to numinous feeling, 'it is Otto's purpose to emphasize that this is an objective reality, not merely a subjective feeling in the mind' (p. xvi).

[15] On metaphysics as embodying the secrets of the Torah, see below, section 4, in the discussion of Maimonides, *Commentary on the Mishnah*, Ḥag. 2: 1. Relevant studies include Idel, '*Sitre 'Arayot* in Maimonides' Thought' and Kellner, 'Maimonides' Allegiances'.

[16] I argue for this interpretation in *Maimonides on Human Perfection*.

[17] For a discussion of Maimonidean texts on immortality, see ibid. 1–5 and Kellner, 'Is Maimonides' Ideal Person Austerely Rationalist?'.

to look at it is as follows: God is 'author' of both the world and of nature.[18] God could have made the world differently,[19] but once that it is made, it works as it is made. As will be shown below, Torah clearly could have been given differently; but once the commandments are given, they are to be obeyed as given.[20]

There is another parallel here: we learn about God by looking at nature; we can also learn about humans by looking at God's commandments concerning them. The commandments reflect God's deep understanding of human nature, which does not really change. Thus, the concrete historical stimulus may no longer be valid, but the insight into human nature found in the law remains valid.[21] Thus Maimonides can hold that, even though the circumstances which brought about the promulgation of laws will change, this does not mean that the laws themselves will ever be abrogated.

This point needs to be made clearer. The need for moral law, political law, and ritual law reflects the fact that post-Adamic human beings are not governed by intellect.[22] In that sense, such laws are a necessary aspect of the human condition. But the specific details of the laws of the Torah reflect what might be called historical accident. Since Abraham chose God more than God chose Abraham (at least according to Maimonides),[23] and because the Torah was given to the descendants of Abraham only because they were his descendants[24] (and not because of any intrinsic characteristics of theirs), it follows that the Torah could have been different. Had Abraham, for example, been a Navajo and not a Hebrew, the Torah would have been written in the Navajo language and the specific histories, laws,

[18] For a remarkable expression of this motif by a Maimonidean, if not by Maimonides himself, see the comment on Exod. 32: 32 by Gersonides (1288–1344).

[19] Perhaps; but since God would certainly have created the best of all possible worlds, it may be that God could not have made the world differently. The issue is surely interesting, but of no direct relevance to our discussion.

[20] On this issue see the illuminating discussion in Henshke, 'On the Question of Unity'.

[21] For an interesting discussions of this point, see Rabinovitch, 'Maimonides, Science, and *Ta'amei ha-Mitzvot*', and Seeskin, *No Other Gods*. See also n. 125 below, Ch. 4 n. 57, and Ch. 7 n. 63.

[22] See *Guide* i. 1; Berman, 'Maimonides on the Fall of Man'; and W. Z. Harvey, 'How to Begin to Study'.

[23] See *MT* 'Laws Concerning Idolatry', 1: 3, which will be discussed in detail at the end of this chapter.

[24] See Lerner, 'Winged Words to Yemen', 482; for a representative text, see below, n. 115.

customs, and ceremonials would have reflected Navajo, not Hebrew, realities. Furthermore, since, according to Maimonides, many specific cere- monials were instituted in order to make Jews as unlike idolaters as possible, had the Sabian idolaters of Moses' time practised their idolatry differently, Judaism would be practised differently.[25] In this sense, the laws of Judaism are as they are because of historical circumstance, but they could have been different.[26]

[25] The Sabians were a pre-Islamic sect that played an important role in Maimonides' history of religion. According to his account, Abraham's mission was directed against the Sabians, and many Mosaic laws were promulgated to uproot Sabian ideas and prac- tices. For a recent study on the Sabians, with references to earlier literature, see Peters, 'Hermes and Harran', esp. pp. 188, 193–206. See also Kraemer, *Humanism in the Renaissance of Islam*, 84; in n. 176 Kraemer cites many other studies on the Sabians. Tamara Green has recently devoted a whole book, *City of the Moon God*, to the histori- cal and religious world of the Sabians. See also De Blois, '"Sabians"'. Those who find Henry Corbin's dense and allusive style comprehensible might want to look at his 'Sabian Temple and Ismailism'; at least I found the footnotes helpful. All of these stud- ies deal with the historical Sabians. On the role of Sabianism in Maimonides' thought, see Pines, 'Translator's Introduction', pp. cxxiii–cxxiv; J. Stern, *Problems and Parables*; Stroumsa, 'Entre Harran et al-Maghreb'; and id., 'Sabians of Haran'. For an interesting account of the 'afterlife' of Maimonides' account of the Sabians, see Elukin, 'Maimonides on the Rise'. I suspect that in many cases Maimonides attacks the Sabians in places where it would have been impolitic to attack the true objects of his ire directly.

[26] Maimonides cannot avoid this conclusion without compromising freedom of the will and concomitant moral responsibility. Once given, the Torah makes promises, threats, and prophecies; in the eighth of his *Eight Chapters* Maimonides makes an effort to reconcile these phenomena with absolute freedom of the will, something which he is unwilling to sacrifice, and which he emphasizes at length and in detail in that chapter. It ought to be noted that an implication of all this is that Maimonides' God takes a largely 'hands off' approach to history. In this connection, my student Nurit Feinstein pointed out something quite fascinating in her MA thesis, 'Reflections of Jewish and General Philosophy' (p. 67): in his edition of the Passover Haggadah (attached to *MT* 'Laws of *Ḥamets*'), Maimonides' text omits the words 'forced by God's words' which standard Haggadah texts attach to Deut. 26: 5. In his commentary on the Haggadah passage, Isaac Abravanel (1437–1508) takes note of this fact and implies that Maimonides' version of the Haggadah reflects his commitment to free will. To my great surprise, I found a passage in Abravanel in which he explicitly affirms that the com- mandments of the Torah could have been different: had the Jews not sinned with the golden calf, the commandments of the Torah would have dealt only with the sabbath and civil relations. See Abravanel's commentary on Jer. 7 (p. 328) and below, Ch. 4 n. 56. In his Haggadah commentary Abravanel merely explains Maimonides; in the Jeremiah commentary he interprets him as I do here, and adopts that position.

Maimonides' Motivation

As noted in Chapter 1, Maimonides was confronted with a form of Judaism which found perhaps its most sophisticated exponents in Judah Halevi, who preceded Maimonides, and in Nahmanides, who followed him. For Halevi, the commandments of the Torah reflect an antecedent reality. This is a function of what Y. Tzvi Langermann has called Halevi's 'hyperrealism'. Halakhic distinctions for Halevi reflect a reality which is really 'out there', an actual facet of the cosmos, even if it is a reality not accessible to our senses. Holiness, for example, is something which actually inheres in holy places, things, people, and times. Were we able to invent a 'holiness counter' it would click every time its wand came near something holy, just as a Geiger counter clicks in the presence of radioactivity. Radioactivity, of course, is present in the physical universe, while holiness is present only in the metaphysical universe, as it were. Just as radioactivity can have effects, even though it is not apprehended by the senses, so holiness can have effects, even though it cannot be apprehended by the senses—there really is something there, though not on the plane of existence accessible to people who lack Halevi's *inyan elohi*.[27]

Halevi and Nahmanides represent an important aspect of the mainstream in Judaism against which Maimonides felt compelled to swim. As I argued above in Chapter 1, Maimonides was forced to do this, in large measure, because of his consistent nominalism and because of his insistence on the absolute transcendence of God.

It must be emphasized that Maimonides' philosophical nominalism is not conventionalism. He may think that the difference between a holy object and a profane object is to be found, not 'out there' in the world, but 'only' in halakhic institutions, but that does not mean that he holds the difference to be a matter of social convention and nothing more. One can be a nominalist without being a conventionalist. For Maimonides, halakhic institutions are grounded in the Torah, revealed by God to Moses at Sinai.

It must be further emphasized that Maimonides was convinced that the Torah reflects the wisdom of a beneficent God. Thus, to take a simple example, eating kosher food is a halakhic requirement; but it is *also* good

---

[27] Arabic: *al-amr al-ilahi*. Kogan translates this term as 'divine order'. It is an all-purpose term used by Halevi to denote that characteristic present in Jews (and which enables those among them who are capable of it to achieve prophecy) and absent in non-Jews. For discussion and bibliography see Lobel, 'Dwelling Place', 117.

for you. One should keep kosher because of the command, not because of the benefit, but that does not mean that the benefit will not accrue. The Land of Israel is holy *and* it is a pleasant land, flowing with milk and honey.

In the chapters that follow I shall prove that holiness is not a property but an institutional status for Maimonides; that Hebrew, the holy language, is not holy in any essentialist, ontological sense; that the distinction between ritual purity and impurity reflects no extra-halakhic reality; that Jews and non-Jews are distinguished by nothing beyond history, belief, and behaviour; that there is no entity denoted by the term 'Israel' beyond living, breathing Jews; that the terms *kavod* and *shekhinah* do not denote actual aspects of divinity; and that there are no angels in the accepted sense of the term. In the present chapter, I propose to address the nature of halakhah.

Mistakes and Errors in Halakhah/Science/Dogma

A good way of accessing this point is through a distinction drawn by Giora Hon. In a valuable study in which he analyses the concepts of mistake and error, Hon associates 'mistake with avoidable ignorance. A mistake can be avoided since checking procedures are known and available. By contrast, error is associated with unavoidable ignorance.' After analysing the distinction, Hon suggests 'that the distinction between mistake and error can constitute a clear demarcation line between propositions whose truth-values depend on rules and their applications, and those which involve in the assignment of their truth-values elements of reality other than rules, that is, elements whose claim to knowledge is incomplete, for example, sense data'.[28]

Hon's distinction, I think, is useful in helping us to understand Maimonides' attitudes towards science, dogma, and halakhah. In scientific and dogmatic contexts, Maimonides holds that one can fall into error, while in halakhah one can make mistakes. For Maimonides, halakhah is a system of formal rules, independent of 'reality'. The consequences of an 'honest mistake' in the observance of halakhah are relatively modest.[29] Maimonidean science and dogma, on the other hand, relate to 'elements of reality other than rules'. Going astray in these contexts has extremely serious consequences: one loses one's immortality.[30] Another way of putting

---

[28] Hon, 'Going Wrong', 6, 19.

[29] For Maimonides on mistakes in determining halakhah, see Blidstein, *Authority and Dissent.*   [30] More precisely, one thereby fails to gain immortality.

this point, highlighting its importance for understanding the kind of religious thinker Maimonides was, is as follows: for Maimonides, halakhah in a significant sense could have been other than it is, while science could not.

Maimonides discusses the issue of going wrong in three contexts: halakhah, physics and metaphysics, and dogma. With respect to the first he makes a number of distinctions: between mistakes in the context of teaching what the halakhah says on the one hand, and actually instructing people on how to behave on the other; other distinctions relate to the status of the person making the mistake.

It turns out that, with very few exceptions, Maimonides follows well-established precedent, being long-suffering when it comes to mistakes in halakhic contexts but very 'short-suffering' when it comes to errors in what I will call, for the sake of convenience, the 'scientific' context (which, for Maimonides, includes at least some of the dogmas of Judaism).[31] This follows from his view of (at least part of) science as dealing with ultimate reality and his view of halakhah as being a structure or construct which in a real sense is independent of that reality.

Let us begin by examining some core texts concerning mistakes in strictly halakhic contexts.

1. *MT* 'Laws of Sanhedrin', 6: 1

In the event a judge gave a mistaken decision in a non-capital case, if his mistake is one with regard to a matter that is obvious and well known, that is, a mistake in a law that is explicitly stated in the Mishnah or the Gemara, the decision is revoked, the case reconsidered, and decided according to the law. If reversal is impossible . . . he is exempt from making good the loss, for, though he caused the loss, he did it unintentionally.[32]

In other words, if a judge makes a mistake in a matter of law, *even where he should have known better*, he is not made to restore any loss he may have caused. In cases where no restitution is possible (as in a case where the judge's mistake cost a person his or her life, or where the money which the judge's mistake cost the defendant is unrecoverable), the judge is not held formally accountable or punished for judicial malpractice.[33]

[31] This point is explicated in Kellner, *Must a Jew Believe Anything?*, 61–5.

[32] I cite from the translation of Hershman, *Book of Judges*, 21. Following Hon, I have emended Hershman's 'error' to 'mistake'.

[33] For more on judicial error, see *MT* 'Laws of Transgressions through Error', 14: 1–2.

2. *MT* 'Laws of the Rebellious Elder', 3: 4–7

The rebellious elder of whom the Bible speaks is one of the wise men of Israel who is at home in traditional lore, functions as judge, imparts instruction in the Torah as do all the wise men of Israel, but is in disagreement with the Supreme Court with regard to a question of law, refuses to change his view, persists in differing with them, gives a practical ruling which runs counter to that given by them. The Torah condemns him to death, and if he confesses before his execution he has a portion in the world to come. . . .

A rebellious elder is not liable to death unless he is qualified to render decisions, that is, has been ordained by the Sanhedrin, takes issue with the latter . . . [and] communicates his ruling to others who act upon it or acts upon it himself, and dissents from the ruling of the Supreme Court while that tribunal is meeting in the Hall of Hewn Stones. But if a disciple who is not qualified to render decisions gives a practical ruling, he is not liable. . . .

If the elder is the outstanding member of a court and he dissents from a decision by the Supreme Court, persists in communicating his opinion to others, but does not give it in the form of a practical ruling, he is not liable. . . .

If he meets the members of the Supreme Court outside the place assigned for their sessions and defies their ruling, he is not culpable.

In paragraph 8 Maimonides summarizes all of the preceding. In order to be executed as a rebellious elder, a member of the Sanhedrin must persist in teaching his opinion in the face of the opposition of three separate courts (at the entrance to the Temple Mount, at the entrance of the court, and in the Hall of Hewn Stones) of ascending authority, must return to his home city, and there 'give his opinion in the form of a practical ruling to be acted upon by others or acts upon it himself'.[34]

It is clear from this that the rebellious elder is not culpable simply for having made a mistake in a halakhic decision. No attempt is made to stifle his teaching. He is executed only so that the Torah may not become many Torahs in terms of actual practice. On a theoretical level, he may retain his views and even teach them, so long as he acts in accordance with the majority view and instructs others to do so.

The material adduced here may be summarized briefly: mistakes in deciding or teaching halakhah only have consequences in the social sphere. Maimonides gives us no reason to suspect that he holds that such mistakes carry with them any sort of metaphysical consequences whatsoever, as would be the case had he held an 'ontological' view of halakhah. After all, if fulfilling the laws of the Torah properly both effects actual ontological

---

[34] For an exhaustive and penetrating analysis, see Blidstein, *Authority and Dissent*.

change in the universe (as Halevi, for example, appears to believe) and eventually ushers one into the world to come, it makes excellent sense to think that failing to fulfil the laws of the Torah properly will have deleterious effects (and this, as we shall see below, is indeed the view of Nahmanides).

But what if someone makes a mistake, not in the teaching of halakhah, or in judging cases before a rabbinic court (*beit din*), but in his or her own practice? Our next text relates to that issue.

3. *Guide of the Perplexed* iii. 41

Maimonides devotes chapters 25–50 of the third part of the *Guide of the Perplexed* to an examination of the reasons for the commandments. In chapter 35 he divides all the commandments into fourteen classes. Chapter 41 is devoted to the sixth class, those commandments concerned with punishments.

Having discussed the punishments laid down in the Torah, Maimonides notes that punishment presupposes the presence of judges. This leads him to comment on some of the issues gathered together in his *Book of Judges*, the fourteenth book of the *Mishneh torah*; most particularly, he explains some features of the 'rebellious elder' (*zaken mamre*) discussed there. Laws require interpretation, application, adjudication. The authority to do this, and, in extraordinary circumstances, to lay aside legal requirements temporarily, was vested in the Sanhedrin, the 'great court of law'. But, Maimonides cautions, if 'every man of knowledge had been permitted to engage in this speculation concerning particulars, the people would have perished because of the multiplicity of the differences of opinion and the subdivisions of doctrines' (p. 563). It is in this context that Maimonides then writes:

Know that with regard to the perpetration of things forbidden by the Law there are four categories: the first being that of the compelled transgressor [*he'anus*]; the second that of the inadvertent transgressor [*hashogeg*]; the third that of the deliberate transgressor [*hamezid*]; the fourth that of him who transgresses in a high-handed manner [*oseh beyad ramah*].[35]

The compelled transgressor (such as an engaged woman who is the victim of rape) has not sinned and, of course, is not punished. Such a person's behaviour is not in any sense blameworthy.

The inadvertent transgressor, on the other hand, is guilty of sin (i.e. is blameworthy), since had sufficient care been taken, there would have been

---

[35] See Num. 15: 30.

no transgression. Such a person, however, is not punished (the sin, after all, was indeed inadvertent). But, the inadvertent transgressor must still perform an act of atonement, through the bringing of a sacrifice, the *korban shegagah*.[36]

At this point in his discussion Maimonides introduces a distinction 'between a private individual, a king, a high priest', on the one hand, and 'a man qualified to give decisions on points of the law', on the other hand. This distinction relies upon Leviticus 4: 27–8: 'If any person from among the populace unwittingly incurs guilt by doing any of the things which by the Lord's commandments ought not to be done, and he realizes his guilt— or the sin of which he is guilty is brought to his knowledge—he shall bring a female goat without blemish as his offering for the sin of which he is guilty.' Thus far, Maimonides' 'private individual'. We read of the king's inadvertent sin in verse 22: 'In case it is a chieftain who incurs guilt by doing unwittingly any of the things which by the commandment of the Lord his God ought not to be done, and he realizes his guilt—or the sin of which he is guilty is brought to his knowledge—he shall bring as his offering a male goat without blemish.' The priest is discussed in verse 3: 'If it is the anointed priest who has incurred guilt, so that blame falls upon the people, he shall offer for the sin of which he is guilty a bull of the herd without blemish as a sin offering to the Lord.' The Torah thus explicitly recognizes the possibility of inadvertent sinning in the case of the private individual, the king, and the priest.

However, a person who is neither a high priest nor a member of the Sanhedrin, and who incorrectly decides a point of law on his own ('everyone that accomplishes an action or gives a decision on a point of the law in accordance with a doctrine established by his own efforts') is included in the class of deliberate transgressors. By contrast, the Sanhedrin *as a body* 'have the right to establish a doctrine by their own effort. Accordingly if they are mistaken, they are held to have been so *inadvertently*.' This is based upon Leviticus 4: 13–14: 'If it is the whole community of Israel that has erred and the matter escapes the notice of the congregation, so that they do

---

[36] The point here is important for our purposes: one ought not to think that inadvertent sinning adversely affects the soul or nature or essence of the sinner in a way which can only be set right through an act of atonement (as Nahmanides was later to claim, as we shall see below). Were this Maimonides' position, my claim that he regards halakhah is institutional, not ontological, would be refuted. But Maimonides hastens to reassure us: no sin is truly inadvertent and all such sins therefore impose an act of atonement upon the violator.

any of the things which by the Lord's commandments ought not to be done, and they realize their guilt—when the sin through which they incurred guilt becomes known, the congregation shall offer a bull of the herd as a sin offering, and bring it before the Tent of Meeting.' An individual member of the Sanhedrin who rules or acts in opposition to the determinations of that body is considered a 'rebellious elder', and is to be executed. It is only if *the whole community of Israel* (as embodied in the Sanhedrin) makes a mistake in law that the transgression is considered inadvertent. One who opposes the decisions of the Sanhedrin is by definition a deliberate transgressor.

At this point in his discussion Maimonides cites a passage from Mishnah *Avot* (4: 13) which in effect summarizes his entire approach to inadvertence: 'Rabbi Judah said: Be cautious in teaching, for an error in teaching amounts to deliberate transgression.' Maimonides explains this mishnaic text to mean 'that one who, while being deficient in doctrine, gives decisions on points of the Law *and acts in accordance with this deficiency* is regarded as a deliberate transgressor'.[37]

[37] Emphasis added. It behoves us, as Pines' Maimonides would say, to digress for a moment to pay special attention to the way in which Maimonides may have understood the mishnaic text he cites here. The Hebrew text says, *hevei zahir betalmud, sheshegagat talmud olah zadon*. The word *talmud* deserves special attention. Twersky, *Introduction*, 489, has drawn attention to the way in which Maimonides uses the term in *MT* 'Laws of Torah Study', 1: 11: 'The time allotted to study should be divided into three parts. A third should be devoted to the written Law; a third to the Oral Law; and the last third should be spent in reflection, deducing conclusions from premises, developing implications of statements, comparing dicta, studying the hermeneutic principles by which the Torah is interpreted, till one knows the essence of these principles, and how to deduce what is permitted and what is forbidden from what one has learned traditionally. This is termed Talmud.'

Maimonides expands on this in the following paragraph, explaining that 'the words of the prophets are comprised in the Written Law, while their exposition falls within the category of the Oral Law. The subjects styled *pardes* are included in Talmud.' Careful readers of the *Mishneh torah* will at this point recall that in 'Laws of the Foundations of the Torah', 1–4, especially in 4: 13, Maimonides makes clear that *pardes* means the study of physics and metaphysics. Thus, when Mishnah *Avot* 4: 13 says 'Be cautious in teaching [*talmud*], for an error in teaching [*talmud*] amounts to deliberate transgression', Maimonides probably understands the Mishnah to be talking about errors in physics and metaphysics. People may thus be faulted for making errors in matters of doctrine/science, and will be 'punished' for those errors (by not earning a share in the world to come), since these errors could, and therefore should, have been avoided. I shall return to this issue below. For more on Maimonides' use of the term *talmud* here, see H. Kasher, 'Talmud Torah', and Kellner, 'Mishneh Torah: Why?'.

Maimonides goes on to distinguish several cases:

For the status of one who eats a piece of [forbidden] fat from the kidneys thinking that it is [permitted] fat from the rump is not like the status of one who eats fat from the kidneys knowing what it is, but without knowing that it is one of the forbidden fats. For the latter, though he may offer an atoning sacrifice is *close to being a deliberate transgressor*; and he is this by merely acting in this manner.

In the first of these cases one has made a simple mistake of fact, while in the second one has made a mistake in law. Mistakes of fact are in many cases unavoidable; ignorance of the law never is. However, Maimonides continues, there is a case much more serious than either of these: 'one who gives decisions on points of the Law in accordance with his ignorance is indubitably a deliberate transgressor; for the text [of the Law] excuses a mistake in a decision on a point of the Law in the case of the Great Court of Law only.'

For our purposes, the material adduced here may be summarized as follows: mistakes in deciding or teaching halakhah only have consequences in the social sphere. Maimonides gives us no reason to suspect that he holds that such mistakes carry with them any sort of metaphysical consequences whatsoever. I realize that I am making an argument from silence: Maimonides makes no reference to possible damage to the soul of the sinner in any of these cases.

In order to strengthen my argument, I will digress to show how another medieval thinker, Nahmanides, handled the same issue. The contrast between Maimonides and Nahmanides will be most instructive. In *Guide* iii. 41, as we saw above, Maimonides divides halakhic violations into four categories. With respect to the 'compelled transgressor', Maimonides affirms that 'no sin whatever lies upon him'. This is to be contrasted with the inadvertent transgressor, who does sin, 'for if he had made efforts to be firm and cautious there would have been no inadvertence on his part. But he is not to be punished in any way, though he needs atonement and hence must bring a sacrifice' (pp. 563–4). A thinker who saw sin in ontological terms, as leaving some kind of actual trace in the soul of the sinner and thereby diminishing the purity of the individual, could not express herself or himself as did Maimonides here. The inadvertent sinner, in Maimonides' eyes, must make atonement, not as an act of self-purification but because in a certain sense a deliberate transgression transpired: the transgression of negligence. For Maimonides, it is clear that the sinful act itself is essentially neutral, having no consequences in the world outside the psycho-social realm; what is to be deplored is the negligence with which the act was performed. If precisely the same act had been done under compulsion, no sacrifice would have to be brought.[38]

This may be contrasted with the view of a thinker like Nahmanides, for whom sinning diminishes the soul of the sinner, even when done inadvertently. In his comment on Leviticus 4: 2 ('Speak to the Israelite people thus: When a person [*nefesh*] unwittingly incurs guilt in regard to any of the Lord's commandments about things not to be done, and does one of them'), Nahmanides writes:

Since the process of sinning is centred in the soul, and it is the soul which commits the inadvertent transgression, Scripture mentions here *nefesh* [soul, person]. The reason for the offerings of the *nefesh* which inadvertently transgresses is that *all* sins produce a defacement in the soul and constitute a disfigurement thereon, and the soul is only worthy to be received by the countenance of its Creator when it is pure of all sin . . . It is on account of this that Scripture mentions here *nefesh* [soul].[39]

Here we see a clear statement of an ontological understanding of sin. Even an inadvertent sin defaces the soul of the transgressor. This defacement can only be put right by a divinely ordained action which has the power to undo this spiritual (ontological) damage.[40]

Nahmanides agrees with Maimonides that the issue here is one of intention, but then their ways part. Maimonides explains that a sacrifice is necessary because not enough care was taken by the inadvertent sinner. Nahmanides is apparently willing to admit that the inadvertent sinner may have taken all necessary care; but the sinful act itself harms the soul of the

[38] Note also Maimonides' claim in *Guide* iii. 36 (p. 540) to the effect that 'sacrifices in expiation of negligence' teach an important lesson: that sinners can repent. (On the importance of repentance, see *Guide* iii. 41; p. 561.) Here, the point of the sacrifice is didactic. Once again, Maimonides avoids attributing to sacrifices the kind of 'ontological' significance found in the writings of Halevi and Nahmanides (as we shall see immediately below).

[39] Trans. Chavel, 45–6. I have heavily emended the translation in this case, making it much more literal; I also added the emphasis. The material in the ellipsis, not directly relevant to our concerns here, is of interest nonetheless: 'Were it not so, then all the fools of the nations of the world [i.e. the non-Jews] would be deserving to come before Him.'

[40] It is worth noting further that presumably Nahmanides would hold that these behaviours do not deface the soul of a non-Jew. His view of the 'ontological damage' to the soul of an inadvertently sinning Jew is thus based upon a notion of the qualitative difference between the souls of Jews and non-Jews. This is a view which Maimonides certainly rejected. For details, see Kellner, *Maimonides on Judaism and the Jewish People*.

person sinning. The sinful act is not in and of itself neutral, as Maimonides held; it carries with it deleterious consequences for the soul of the sinner, on some actual (if not some physically examinable) plane. The sinful act itself, even if carried out inadvertently, distances one from God.[41]

Just as Judah Halevi maintains that obedience to the commandments actually accomplishes something 'out there' in some actual if physically unexaminable realm,[42] here we see that Nahmanides maintains that sin damages something 'out there' in some actual if physically unexaminable realm. Maimonides, as he must, rejects both positions. Obedience to the commandments is extremely important for one's own personal spiritual health and can contribute to the workings of a just and humane society; violation of the commandments is damaging to one's spiritual health and can contribute to the destruction of society; but in neither case does anything actually occur outside the psychosocial realm.

Maimonides makes the point himself (in the context of a discussion of the 'scapegoat'):

No one has any doubt that sins are not bodies that may be transported from the back of one individual to that of another. But all these actions are parables serving to bring forth a form in the soul so that a passion toward repentance should result: we have freed ourselves from all our previous actions, cast them behind our backs, and removed them to an extreme distance.[43]

Halakhic obedience and disobedience have no consequences in some objectively existent, supersensible, metaphysical realm; they have consequences in the realm of interpersonal relations and in the realm of a person's self-understanding.

Error in 'Science'

We may now turn to texts which relate to errors in scientific contexts. I use the term 'science' here in a Maimonidean way, as translating the Hebrew word *ḥokhmah*,[44] and as referring in the first instance to Aristotelian physics and metaphysics.

---

[41] Compare also Nahmanides on Lev. 18: 29, a passage which reads as if it were written as an anti-Maimonidean polemic.   [42] See e.g. *Kuzari* i. 79.

[43] *Guide* iii. 46 (p. 591). Nahmanides' notorious discussion of the scapegoat (as a sacrifice mandated by God to propitiate the demons of the wilderness) should be recalled here. For a detailed discussion of the text (Nahmanides' comment on Lev. 16: 8) see J. Stern, 'Fall and Rise of Myth', repr. in id., *Problems and Parables*, ch. 6.

[44] For Maimonides on *ḥokhmah* see *Guide* iii. 54; Twersky, *Introduction*, 366–8, 395, 473–6, and 495–7; and Septimus, 'What Did Maimonides Mean by *Madda*?'.

1. *Guide of the Perplexed* iii. 46

In this passage Maimonides takes up the question of why sin-offerings always consist of he-goats. The explanations offered are irrelevant to our discussion here,[45] but what is relevant is that Maimonides distinguishes between different kinds of sins which need atonement: acts of disobedience in connection with property, in connection with corporeal pleasures, in connection with morals, and in connection with opinions.[46] It is with respect to this last category that he writes:

If *the act of disobedience* consists in a speculation—I mean by this that if he believes in any opinion that is not sound because of his incapacity and his slackness in inquiry and in devoting himself to speculation—he must counter this by suppressing his reflection and prevent it from reflecting about anything pertaining to the things in this world, but direct it exclusively to the intelligible and to an exact study of what ought to be believed.[47]

Maimonides teaches here that scientific errors may be construed as acts of disobedience, even if they are the outcome of 'incapacity' as opposed to 'slackness in inquiry'. In the same chapter Maimonides calls wrong opinions 'diseases of the human soul' (p. 582). What he calls 'diseases of the human soul', we call 'immorality'.[48] Such diseases are to be 'cured by their contrary found at the other extreme'.[49]

In what sense can errors concerning philosophical and/or scientific matters be construed as acts of disobedience? Another text in the *Guide* helps us to understand this.

2. *Guide of the Perplexed* i. 5

Exodus 24: 9–11 represents a problem for Maimonides. The text says:

Then Moses and Aaron, Nadab and Abihu, and seventy elders of Israel ascended; and they saw the God of Israel: under His feet there was the likeness of a pavement of sapphire, like the very sky for purity. Yet He did not raise His hand against the leaders of the Israelites; they beheld God, and they ate and drank.

[45] Though they are an excellent example of Maimonides' refusal to accord the sacrifices any intrinsic value. See my discussion below in Ch. 4.

[46] This fourfold distinction is Maimonides' own.

[47] p. 589; emphasis added. In this text, we see philosophy being assimilated into halakhah, through the application of halakhic categories to philosophical issues. This is not directly relevant to our concerns here, but has implications for Maimonides' understanding of the nature of dogma.

[48] See the third and fourth of Maimonides' *Eight Chapters*.

[49] Compare further *Guide* iii. 8 (pp. 434–5).

The anthropomorphism here was terribly troubling to Maimonides. In *Guide* i. 5 (p. 30) he attempts to draw the sting from these verses. He blames the leaders of the Israelites; they 'were overhasty, strained their thoughts, and achieved apprehension [of God], but only an imperfect one'. The Bible's affirmation that the elders saw God and saw God's feet is taken as a criticism of the elders:

For these words are solely intended to present a criticism of their act of seeing, not to describe the manner of their seeing. Thus they were solely blamed for the form that their apprehension took inasmuch as corporeality entered into it to some extent—this being necessitated by their overhasty rushing forward before they had reached perfection.

The elders were blameworthy because they had rushed into metaphysical matters before they were properly prepared to do so. In the words quoted from *Guide* iii. 46 just above, each of them held an 'opinion that is not sound because of his incapacity and his slackness in inquiry and in devoting himself to speculation'. Because of this they deserved punishment: 'They deserved to perish. However [Moses], peace be on him, interceded for them; and they were granted a reprieve until the time they were burnt at Taberah.'[50] If the noble elders of Israel could incur the wrath of God through their attempts to study metaphysics before being properly pre-pared for it, how much more careful must we be! This is the lesson Maimonides derives from this passage:

This having happened to these men, it behooves us, all the more, as being inferior to them, and it behooves those who are inferior to us, to aim at and engage in per-fecting our knowledge in preparatory matters and in achieving those premises that purify apprehension of its taint, which is error. It will then go forward to look upon the divine holy presence.[51]

The irresponsible behaviour of the noble elders of Israel is explained indir-ectly in another passage in the first part of the *Guide*, chapters 32–3. There we learn how dangerous it can be to jump into deep intellectual waters before learning how to navigate them safely.[52]

---

[50] See Num. 11: 1–3: 'The people took to complaining bitterly before the Lord. The Lord heard and was incensed: a fire of the Lord broke out against them, ravaging the outskirts of the camp. The people cried out to Moses. Moses prayed to the Lord, and the fire died down. That place was named Taberah, because a fire of the Lord had broken out against them.'

[51] On this passage in Maimonides, see Regev, 'Vision of the Nobles of Israel', and Levene, 'Maimonides' Philosophical Exegesis'.   [52] Compare also *Guide* i. 60 (p. 153).

3. *Guide of the Perplexed* i. 32–3

In *Guide* i. 32 (pp. 68–9), addressing his reader directly, Maimonides contrasts the individual who studies metaphysics in an appropriate manner (and who thereby may be compared to Rabbi Akiva) with the individual who aspires to

apprehend things beyond your apprehension; or if you hasten to pronounce false, assertions the contradictories of which have not been demonstrated or that are possible, though very remotely so—you will have joined Elisha Aher.[53] That is, you will not only not be perfect, but will be the most deficient among the deficient; and it shall so fall out that you will be overcome by imaginings and by inclination towards things defective, evil, and wicked.

The study of the sciences, Maimonides explains, is a very good thing, and Scripture, he says, compares it 'to the most delicious of foods, namely honey'.[54] But even honey, if eaten improperly, 'upsets the stomach and causes vomiting'. Thus, if scientific investigation is not carried out properly, it 'may be perverted into a defect, just as the eating of honey may be'. Thus Elisha ben Abuyah, tannaitic Judaism's most notorious apostate, is described as a person who made errors in scientific matters.

Beginning one's studies with metaphysics, Maimonides explains in *Guide* i. 33 (p. 71), will result, not in 'a mere confusion . . . but, rather, absolute negation'. This is dangerous in the same way that feeding an infant bread and meat is dangerous.

Another chapter of the *Guide* (i. 50; p. 112) hints that those who erroneously attribute essential attributes to God are wicked sinners. Here is what he writes:

When you shall have cast off desires and habits, shall have been endowed with understanding, and shall reflect on what I shall say in the coming chapters, which shall treat of the negation of attributes, you shall necessarily achieve certain knowledge of it. Then you shall be one of those who represent to themselves *the unity of the Name* and not one of those who merely proclaim it with their mouth without representing to themselves that it has a meaning. With regard to men of this category, it is said: 'You are present in their mouths but far from their thoughts' (Jer. 12: 2). But men ought rather belong to the category of those who represent the truth[55] to themselves and apprehend it, even if they do not utter it, as

---

[53] For a nuanced study of Maimonides on Elisha, see Diamond, 'Failed Theodicy'.

[54] For an important discussion of this passage with special emphasis on Maimonides' use of his talmudic sources, see Stroumsa, 'Elisha ben Abuyah', 175–83.

[55] Pines: 'The word may also mean "God"'.

the virtuous are commanded to do—for they are told: 'ponder it on your bed, and sigh' (Ps. 4: 5).[56]

Of great interest here are the two verses cited by Maimonides. In each case he only cites part of the verse. Supplying the full verses and their immediate contexts is most instructive. Jeremiah 12: 1–3 reads:

You will win, O Lord, if I make claim against You, yet I shall present charges against You: Why does the way of the wicked prosper? Why are the workers of treachery at ease? You have planted them, and they have taken root, they spread, they even bear fruit. You are present in their mouths, but far from their thoughts. Yet You, Lord, have noted and observed me; You have tested my heart, and found it with You. Drive them out like sheep to the slaughter, prepare them for the day of slaying!

Those who merely proclaim God's unity without truly understanding what they proclaim are wicked, even if their ways prosper; they are workers of treachery, who spread and bear fruit. They should be driven like sheep to the slaughter. A similar point arises when we look at the second verse in context (Ps. 4: 1–6):

For the leader; with instrumental music. A psalm of David. Answer me when I call, O God, my vindicator! You freed me from distress; have mercy on me and hear my prayer. You men, how long will my glory be mocked, will you love illusions, have recourse to frauds? Know that the Lord singles out the faithful for Himself; the Lord hears when I call to Him. So tremble, and sin no more; ponder it on your bed, and sigh. Offer sacrifices in righteousness and trust in the Lord.

Here those who merely proclaim God's unity without truly understanding what they proclaim mock God's glory, love illusions, and have recourse to frauds. They are *not* those whom the Lord singles out for Himself, whom the Lord hears when they call. They are sinners who ought to tremble.

4. *Commentary on the Mishnah, Ḥagigah 2: 1*

The Mishnah in *Ḥagigah* 2: 1 states:

One does not expound upon forbidden sexual relations in the presence of three, nor upon *ma'aseh bereshit* in the presence of two, nor upon the *merkavah* in the presence of one, unless that one were wise and understood on his own. All who look upon four things, it were better had they not come into the world: what is above, what is below, what is in front, and what is behind. All who are not protective of the honour of their master, it were better had they not come into the world.

---

[56] The verses here are cited according to the NJPS; Pines translates them slightly differently.

In his comment on this text,[57] Maimonides explains that the term *ma'aseh merkavah* means 'the divine science'.[58] He further explains that the phrase 'It were better had they not come into the world' refers to individuals who attempt to study metaphysics without appropriate preparations. Such an individual, Maimonides informs us, 'is removed from the ranks of humanity, and classifying him in one of the other species of animal would be better for existence[59] than his being a human'. These harsh words are appropriate, Maimonides explains, since these individuals 'are not protective of the honour of their master', i.e. 'are not protective of their intellects, for the intellect is the honour of God [*kevod hashem*]'.[60] Such a person 'does not know the value of this matter which was given him, he is abandoned into the hands of his desires, and becomes like an animal'.[61]

[57] For the full text see Kellner, 'Maimonides' Commentary'.

[58] *Al-ʿilm al-ilahi* in Arabic. This is the standard Arabic term for metaphysics. Compare further Maimonides' early work *Treatise on Logic*, ch. 14.

[59] i.e. for the existing universe.

[60] The intellect is that by virtue of which we can be said to have been created in the image of God. For texts and discussion see Kellner, *Maimonides on Human Perfection*, 1–5. See also p. 214 below.

[61] This can only be understood in the context of Maimonides' Aristotelian definition of human beings as 'rational animals'—humans become such only to the extent that they actualize their intellectual potential to some degree or other. In his earliest work, *Treatise on Logic*, Maimonides wrote: 'Rationality we call man's difference, because it divides and differentiates the human species from others; and this rationality, i.e. the faculty by which ideas are formed, constitutes the essence of man' (*Treatise on Logic*, 10; trans. Efros, 51–2). Herbert A. Davidson has raised questions about whether or not Maimonides actually wrote this text. There can be no doubt, however, that he held the view here attributed to him. The very first chapter of the *Guide* makes no sense unless one understands Maimonides as defining humans as rational animals. For explicit statements, see e.g. *Guide* iii. 8 (pp. 433–4): 'It behooves him who prefers to be a human being in truth, not a beast having the shape and configuration of a human being, to endeavour to diminish all the impulses of matter—such as eating, drinking, copulation, anger, and all the habits consequent upon desire and anger, to be ashamed of them, and to set for them limits in his soul.' See further *Guide* i. 51 ('For being a rational animal is the essence and true reality of man' (p. 113), and see Michael Schwartz's note in his Hebrew translation of the *Guide*), i. 52 (pp. 114, 116), ii. 48 (p. 422 n. 8; p. 410 in Schwartz), iii. 8 (p. 432), iii. 12 (p. 444), and iii. 14 (p. 458). For more discussion, see Kellner, 'Is Maimonides' Ideal Person Austerely Rationalist?'. For Davidson's reservations about the Maimonidean authorship of *Treatise on Logic* see his 'Authenticity of Works' and *Moses Maimonides*, 313–22. Davidson's thesis is criticized in Hasnawi, 'Réflexions', 69–73. Note further M. Z. Cohen, 'Logic to Interpretation', who shows that, in the *Guide*, Maimonides makes use of the Farabian notions put forward in *Treatise on Logic*.

The texts adduced here all share an important element in common: error in scientific contexts can be dangerous. In the *Guide* (i. 34; p. 73) Maimonides uses an interesting allegory to explain the danger:

One of the parables generally known in our community is that likening knowledge to water. Now the Sages, peace be on them, explained several notions by means of this parable; one of them being that he who knows how to swim brings up pearls from the bottom of the sea, whereas he who does not know, drowns. For this reason, no one should expose himself to the risks of swimming except he who has been trained in learning to swim.

Maimonides' view of the danger of scientific error is a reflection of his adoption of the theory of the acquired intellect, according to which the children of human parents are born as human beings only *in potentia*; if they do not actualize their intellects and thus realize the specific difference of human beings (*rational* animals), they remain as they were born, potential but not actual human beings. One actualizes oneself as a human being through the correct apprehension of metaphysical truths. Errors in metaphysics, therefore, keep one from becoming fully human and in addition keep one from one of the consequences of being human, achieving a share in the world to come.[62]

5. *Commentary on the Mishnah, Sanhedrin* 10: 1

We may now turn to a discussion of error in dogmatic contexts. There is one core passage that must be addressed. In commenting on the mishnaic text, 'All Israel have a share in the world to come' (*Sanhedrin* 10: 1) Maimonides lays down thirteen beliefs as 'foundations of the Torah'. After presenting and discussing them in detail, he adds the following peroration:

When all these foundations are perfectly understood and believed in by a person, he is within the community of Israel and one is obligated to love and pity him and to act towards him in all the ways in which the Creator has commanded that one should act towards his brother, with love and fraternity. Even were he to commit every possible transgression, because of lust and because of being overpowered by the evil inclination, he will be punished according to his rebelliousness, but he has a portion [of the world to come]; he is one of the sinners of Israel. But if a man doubts any of these foundations, he leaves the community [of Israel], denies the fundamental, and is called a sectarian, *epikoros*, and one who 'cuts among the

---

[62] For a detailed defence of this interpretation of Maimonides, see the discussion of the theory of the acquired intellect below, in Ch. 7.

plantings'. One is required to hate him and destroy him. About such a person it was said, 'Do I not hate them, O Lord, who hate thee?' (Ps. 139: 21).[63]

Maimonides allows no room here for error or inadvertence: a mistake concerning them *for any reason* costs one her or his share in the world to come. Maimonides actually means what he says, at least so far as the first five principles are concerned.[64]

Maimonides' first five principles (that God exists; that God is one; that God is incorporeal; that God is ontologically prior to the cosmos; that God alone may be worshipped) express metaphysical truths. Not any metaphysical truths, but precisely those which must be held *and understood* if one is to achieve any measure of intellectual perfection and thereby create for oneself a place in the world to come. If one *for any reason* errs concerning these truths, i.e. holds objectively incorrect notions concerning the existence and nature of God, one fails to achieve any measure of intellectual perfection, and thus fails to create for oneself a share in the world to come.

In this section I have presented evidence to the effect that Maimonides distinguishes between mistakes in halakhic contexts, which have relatively modest consequences, and errors in scientific and dogmatic contexts, which have profound consequences. This reflects his perception of halakhah as a system of rules which constitute social reality but do not reflect a prior ontological reality. In subsequent chapters I will try to prove that this is indeed the case by showing that Maimonides holds views of the nature of ritual purity and impurity, of holiness, and of other similar matters which contradict those of many of his predecessors and successors in the Jewish tradition, and which only make sense in the context of a view of halakhah as a system of rules fundamentally independent of reality.

At this point, however, I can strengthen my interpretation of Maimonides as holding an institutional, rather than ontological, view of halakhah by addressing his comments on the instrumental character of halakhah.

Halakhah as Instrumental

One text which expresses the point well is found in *Guide* iii. 27 (pp. 510–11):

The Law as a whole aims at two things: the welfare of the soul and welfare of the body. As for the welfare of the soul, it consists in the multitude's acquiring correct opinions corresponding to their respective capacity . . . As for the welfare of the

---

[63] I have analysed this crucial statement in several contexts. See, most recently, 'Could Maimonides Get into Rambam's Heaven?' and *Must a Jew Believe Anything?*.

[64] See the discussion below on pp. 233–8.

body, it comes about by the improvement of their ways of living one with another. This is achieved through two things. One of them is the abolition of their wronging each other. This is tantamount to every individual among the people not being permitted to act according to his will and up to the limits of his power, but being forced to do that which is useful to the whole. The second thing consists in the acquisition by every human individual of moral qualities that are useful for life in society so that the affairs of the city may be ordered.

The Torah thus has two aims: the welfare of the soul, and the welfare of human society. The second aim is achieved by laws which abolish mutual wrongdoing and which inculcate elevated moral dispositions in the members of the society. Of these two aims, one is more sublime than the other:

Know that as between these two aims, one is indubitably greater in nobility, namely, the welfare of the soul—I mean the procuring of correct opinions—while the second aim—I mean the welfare of the body—is prior in nature and time . . . His ultimate perfection is to become rational *in actu*, I mean to have an intellect *in actu;* this would consist in his knowing everything concerning all beings that it is within the capacity of man to know in accordance with his ultimate perfection.

The Torah emphasizes the second aim more than the first because it applies to all Jews, while the first aim applies only to a relatively small subset of Jews. This is Maimonides' explanation for the fact that, while the first aim is more sublime than the second, and served by the second, the Torah spends much more time and energy on the second aim. Maimonides summarizes all this as follows:

The true Law then . . . has come to bring us both perfections, I mean the welfare of the states of people in their relations with one another through the abolition of reciprocal wrongdoing and through the acquisition of a noble and excellent character. In this way the preservation of the population of the country and their permanent existence in the same order become possible, so that every one of them achieves his first perfection; I mean also the soundness of the beliefs and the giving of correct opinions through which the ultimate perfection is achieved.

The commandments of the Torah are thus a tool, not an end in themselves.[65] They were ordained in the Torah to educate Jews away from violence and oppression, and towards a morally elevated life.

[65] This view of Maimonides was well understood by Shem Tov ben Shem Tov Ibn Shem Tov (15th cent.) in his *Sefer ha'emunot*; he criticizes Maimonides for denying that any of the commandments is intrinsically valuable (*mekhuvenet le'atsmah*); see *Sefer ha'emunot*, Gate 1, ch. 1, p. 7*a*. For a recent exhaustive discussion of Ibn Shem Tov's critique of Maimonides, see Peleg, 'Between Philosophy and Kabbalah'. For other criticisms by Ibn Shem Tov of Maimonides, see H. A. Davidson, *Moses Maimonides*, 415.

The point of all the commandments is summarized in the following passage, from *Guide* iii. 31 (p. 524):

Rather things are indubitably as we have mentioned: every commandment from among these six hundred and thirteen commandments exists either with a view to communicating a correct opinion, or to putting an end to an unhealthy opinion, or to communicating a rule of justice, or to warding off an injustice, or to endowing men with a noble moral quality, or to warning them against an evil moral quality. Thus all [the commandments] are bound up with three things: opinions, moral qualities, and political civic actions.

All the commandments are tools, designed by God to teach truth, institute justice, or inculcate morality. There is no room here for a view of the commandments as effecting change in the world around us, still less in the world above.

The instrumental, educational character of the commandments is made clear in the following passage in *Guide* iii. 51 (p. 622):

Know that all the practices of the worship, such as reading the Torah, prayer, and the performance of the other commandments, have only the end of training you to occupy yourself with His commandments, may He be exalted, rather than with matters pertaining to this world; you should act as if you were occupied with Him, may He be exalted, and not with that which is other than He.[66]

This passage, both when read by itself and all the more when read in light of those cited just above, clearly teaches that fulfilling the commandments of the Torah does not accomplish anything 'pertaining to this world'; the commandments are part of a divinely ordained educational institution, not parts of a recipe for effecting ontological change in the universe.[67]

Our point is made even clearer in *Guide* iii. 54 (pp. 635–6), in the context of Maimonides' discussion of various human perfections:

---

[66] Compare *MT* 'Laws of Substituted Offerings', 4: 13. See the translation of that text and the discussion in Twersky, *Introduction*, 416–17. See also the following sentence in *Guide* iii. 52 (p. 630): 'the end of the actions prescribed by the whole Law is to bring about the passion of which it is correct that it be brought about . . . I refer to the fear of Him . . . and the awe before His command.' The commandments, Maimonides goes on to explain, bring one to awe of God, while the doctrines taught in the Torah bring one to love of God. The commandments are all means to an end external to them. On how the passage adduced here fits into Maimonides' doctrine of the reasons for the commandments (*ta'amei hamitsvot*), see J. Stern, *Problems and Parables*, chs. 4 and 6.

[67] Compare also *Guide* i. 39 (p. 89) and the texts to which Maimonides apparently refers there (*Eight Chapters*, 2, and *MT* 'Foundations of the Torah', 2: 2).

The third species is a perfection that to a greater extent than the second species subsists in the individual's self. This is the perfection of the moral virtues. It consists in the individual's moral habits having attained their ultimate excellence. Most of the commandments serve no other end than the attainment of this species of perfection.[68] But this species of perfection is likewise a preparation for something else and is not an end in itself. For all moral habits are concerned with what occurs between a human individual and someone else. This perfection regarding moral habits is, as it were, only the disposition to be useful to people; consequently it is an instrument for someone else. For if you suppose a human individual is alone, acting on no one, you will find that all his moral virtues are in vain and without employment and unneeded, and that they do not perfect the individual in anything; for he only needs them and they again become useful to him in regard to someone else.[69]

In case the point hasn't been made clearly enough, Maimonides reiterates it a few paragraphs later:

The Sages, may their memory be blessed, apprehended from this verse[70] the very notions that we have mentioned and have explicitly stated that which I have explained to you in this chapter: namely that the term wisdom [*ḥokhmah*], used in an unrestricted sense and regarded as the end, means the apprehension of Him, may He be exalted; that the possession of the treasures acquired, and competed for, by man and thought to be perfection are not a perfection; and that similarly all the actions prescribed by the Law—I refer to the various species of worship and also the moral habits that are useful to all people in their mutual dealings—that all this is not to be compared with this ultimate end and does not equal it, being but preparations made for the sake of this end.

All of the actions commanded by the Torah, Maimonides informs us in this final chapter of his *magnum opus*, are not to be compared to the ultimate

[68] 'Most' but not all; as we saw above in the text cited from *Guide* iii. 27, the commandments that do not inculcate virtuous behaviour teach metaphysical truths. There is thus no comfort here for those who might seek to read Maimonides as a halakhic ontologist.

[69] This passage is truly remarkable. One could, mistakenly in my view, read it as implying that a Jew living alone on a desert island has no need to fulfil most of the commandments (although she would still have to build the proverbial two synagogues). For a bibliography of sources relating to a figure who apparently read Maimonides in that fashion, see Dienstag, 'Nachman Krochmal's Defence'.

[70] Jeremiah 9: 22–3: 'Thus says the Lord: Let not the wise man glory in his wisdom, neither let the mighty man glory in his might, let not the rich man glory in his riches; but let him that glories glory in this, that he understands and knows Me.' For discussions of this verse by Maimonides and other medieval Jewish thinkers, see Melamed, '*Al yithalel*'.

end of the Torah (the teaching of true beliefs concerning metaphysical matters), nor are they its equal; rather, they serve as instruments which prepare people to seek their truly human end, the cognition of intelligibles about God.[71] One must feel sympathy for those many of Maimonides' rabbinic contemporaries who, when faced with a passage such as this, responded, in effect, 'That's Greek to me!'.[72] Indeed, he himself anticipated such a response, writing (in *Guide* iii. 32, in the context of his historical explanation of the sacrifices): 'I know that in thinking about this at first your soul will necessarily have a feeling of repugnance toward this notion and will feel aggrieved because of it; and you will ask me in your heart and say to me: How is it possible that *none* of the commandments, prohibitions, and great actions—which are very precisely set forth and prescribed for fixed seasons—should not be intended for its own sake, but for the sake of something else' (p. 527; emphasis added).

The position found here at the end of the *Guide* is also found, at least indirectly, at the very beginning of the work. Discussing biblical parables in the introduction, Maimonides writes:

Know that the key to the understanding of all that the prophets, peace be on them, have said, and to the knowledge of its truth, is an understanding of the parables, of their import, and of the meaning of the words occurring in them. . . . And it is said in the Midrash: 'To what were the words of the Torah to be compared before the

---

[71] For Maimonides moral perfection is a necessary, but not sufficient, prerequisite for intellectual perfection. For sources, see *Guide* i. 34 (pp. 76–7, where Maimonides writes: 'the moral virtues are a preparation for the rational virtues, it being impossible to achieve true, rational acts—I mean perfect rationality—unless it be by a man thoroughly trained in his morals and endowed with the qualities of tranquillity and quiet'), i. 62 (p. 152), iii. 27 (p. 510), and iii. 54 (p. 635) and *Commentary on the Mishnah, Ḥag.* 2: 1. For discussion, see Kellner, *Maimonides on Human Perfection*, 26–8; id., 'Is Maimonides' Ideal Person Austerely Rationalist?', and Kreisel, *Maimonides' Political Thought*, 160, 238, 317. Charles Manekin suggests the following analogy (in a letter which I paraphrase here): 'To be a physicist one has to know math. Without knowing math, no matter how much physics one has managed to learn, one is not a physicist. And yet, knowing math is not part of being a physicist *per se*; it is not what distinguishes physicists from, say, mathematicians. In Maimonides' (and Gersonides') world, there can be no "Nazi scientists", although there can be Nazis who practice science. For true science entails morality. Morality is not something one can shed; if one does, one loses one's knowledge.' See also below, Ch. 3 n. 40.

[72] Just to put the matter in sharp focus, compare Maimonides' devaluation of prayer here with Judah Halevi's elevation of it. For a wonderful discussion, see Schweid, 'Prayer in the Thought of Yehudah Halevi'.

advent of Solomon? To a well the waters of which are at a great depth and cool, yet no man could drink of them. Now what did one clever man do? He joined cord with cord and rope with rope and drank. Thus did Solomon say one parable after another and speak one word after another, until he understood the meaning of the words of the Torah.'[73] This is literally what they say.[74] I do not think that anyone possessing an unimpaired capacity imagines that *the words of the Torah* referred to here that one contrives to understand through understanding the meaning of the parables are ordinances concerning the building of tabernacles, the *lulab*, and the law of the four trustees. Rather, what this text has in view here is, without any doubt, the understanding of obscure matters (p. 10).[75]

Maimonides makes a clear distinction here between halakhah and the inner meaning of the Torah (which for him means physics and metaphysics, i.e. *ma'aseh bereshit* and *ma'aseh merkavah*). Halakhah has no inner meaning which must be discovered with great difficulty and patience; it is what it is, namely, a social construct ordained by God, not a reflection of some deeper, truer, more inner reality.

Lest it be thought that only in his *Guide* does Maimonides make the point I have been describing here, I would like to cite a passage from one of his halakhic works, the *Commentary on the Mishnah*, a text which every student of Maimonides would admit is addressed to all Jews and not just to the philosophers among them. In the sixth of the *Eight Chapters* with which he prefaces his commentary on Mishnah *Avot*, Maimonides distinguishes between a virtuous person and a self-disciplined person. The philosophers, he says, appear to prefer the former, the Sages of the Talmud, the latter. Against this background he writes:

If the external meaning of the two accounts [i.e. by the philosophers and the Jewish sages] is understood superficially, the two views contradict each other. However, that is not the case; rather, both of them are true, and there is no conflict between them at all. For the bad things to which the philosophers referred when they said that someone who does not desire them is more virtuous than someone who does desire them and restrains himself—these are the things generally accepted by all the people as bad, such as murder, theft, robbery, fraud, harming an innocent man, repaying a benefactor with evil, degrading parents, and things like these. They are the laws about which the sages, peace be upon them, said [BT *Yoma* 67b]: 'If they were not written down, they would deserve to be written

---

[73] *S. of S. Rabbah* 1: 1.

[74] This is not literally what they say in the texts before us today.

[75] For a profound discussion of this passage in the *Guide*, see Diamond, *Maimonides and the Hermeneutics of Concealment*, 13–20.

down'. . . . There is no doubt that the soul which craves and strongly desires any of them is defective and that the virtuous soul neither longs for any of these bad things at all nor suffers pain from the prohibition against them. When the sages said that the continent man is more virtuous and his reward is greater, they had in mind the traditional laws. This is correct because if it were not for the Law, they would not be bad at all. Therefore they said that a man needs to let his soul remain attracted to them and not place any obstacle before them other than the Law.[76]

What are the 'traditional laws' to which Maimonides refers here? He cites the following as examples: 'meat with milk, mixed fabric [*sha'atnez*], and illicit sexual unions'. A virtuous person will not want to kill, steal, or lie (Maimonides' examples), while such an individual may indeed want to eat non-kosher food, wear *sha'atnez*, or engage in illicit sex. Were it not for Torah prohibitions, such things 'would not be bad at all'.[77] Indeed, Maimonides believes that a normal person will be attracted to such activities, and there is clearly nothing wrong with that. It is the institution of Torah which makes such behaviour wrong (for a Jew); there is nothing about the ontological nature of the world which would make engaging in such behaviour damaging to the soul of a Jew. Maimonides clearly teaches here that halakhah does not reflect some antecedent reality, but rather creates a social reality, without making any explicit or implicit claims whatsoever about the extra-social world.

Maimonides' text here coheres perfectly with a passage already cited from *Guide* iii. 51 (p. 622):

Know that all the practices of the worship, such as reading the Torah, prayer, and the performance of the other commandments, have only the end of training you to occupy yourself with His commandments, may He be exalted, rather than with matters pertaining to this world.

The practices of Judaism, I take Maimonides to be teaching here, were ordained *only* for purposes of training. To play on Maimonides' words, the commandments do not relate to matters pertaining to any objectively existent entities and distinctions in this world. Halakhah is therefore an instrument, not an end in itself; theoretically, it could have been different; it does not reflect any antecedent metaphysical reality—rather, it is a divinely ordained response to historical realities and a divinely bestowed gift to be

---

[76] I cite the text as translated in Maimonides, *Ethical Writings*, 79–80.

[77] As we saw above, for Nahmanides, practices outlawed by the ceremonial law of the Torah are bad (at least for Jews) in and of themselves; here Maimonides tells us that in and of themselves, they are not bad at all.

used as a tool for the religious, moral, and intellectual improvement of those bound to obey it.[78]

Halakhah and Theology

Maimonides divorces halakhic observance from theological orthodoxy, elevating the latter at the expense of the former. This is another implication of his instrumental, historicist understanding of halakhah. The clearest statement of his position is found at the end of his Thirteen Principles, cited above. In that text, Maimonides maintains that a person may 'commit every possible transgression'—i.e. fail to fulfil even one of the commandments—and still have a share in the world to come, provided that he or she perfectly understands and accepts the Thirteen Principles. Maimonides

---

[78] Another text in which these ideas find indirect expression is the concluding chapter of the *Book of Knowledge*, namely, 'Laws of Repentance', 10. 'Laws of Ritual Slaughter', 14: 11, is also relevant. 'Laws of Trespass [*Me'ilah*]', 8: 8 (following the textual discussion and analysis of Henshke, 'On the Question of Unity') also supports our interpretation. I cite and discuss that text below in Ch. 3. Maimonides' understanding of the nature of the commandments is thrown into greater relief if we compare his view to that of Gersonides, as my student Oded Horetzky pointed out to me. Gersonides, ordinarily painted as an extreme Aristotelian (which he surely was), is actually much more conservative than Maimonides when it comes to the nature of the commandments. As he makes clear in his introduction to his Torah commentary and in many places in the commentary itself (see e.g. his explanation of why the Tabernacle in the wilderness had to have been built precisely as it was, at the end of his commentary on the Torah portion 'Terumah'), Gersonides believed that the specific details of even the most 'ritualistic' of the commandments hinted at important lessons concerning the structure of the physical universe. This being the case, the commandments could not easily be other than as they are. Given his attempt to connect the commandments to history as opposed to physics, that possibility makes more sense for Maimonides than it can for Gersonides. Further, as Mr Horetzky noted, for Maimonides, the point of many, if not most, of the commandments is educational and moral: to bring about better individuals and a better society. For Gersonides, in addition to these ends, the commandments are also meant to lead those capable of understanding their hidden message to a deeper understanding of the nature of the physical world. Once again, Gersonides sees the commandments in a much less changeable light than does Maimonides. Another example of this difference between the two thinkers is the issue of *sha'atnez* (Lev. 19: 19). Maimonides explains it historically (which means that the commandment has no intrinsic significance; *Guide* iii. 37; p. 544), while Gersonides sees it as embodying a lesson in physics (Gersonides' commentary on Leviticus, pp. 302–3). We have here more examples of what Charles Manekin has called 'conservative tendencies in Gersonides' religious philosophy'. See his article by that name.

there demands strict and unwavering orthodoxy; if a person even doubts any single one of the Thirteen Principles they exclude themselves from the community of Israel, are reviled, and must be hated (bearing in mind that hating a fellow-Jew is forbidden by Leviticus 19: 17). At the same time he is remarkably latitudinarian when it comes to halakhic violations in consequence of human weakness. This is the case, I submit, because in his eyes halakhah is an instrument, not an end; it reflects historical experience but not prior ontological reality; it is institutional but not essentialist.

1. Objection: Commandments and the World to Come

The following objection to all that I have written in this chapter is bound to be raised: halakhah must have some extra-social effect since its observance is the key to enjoying a share in the world to come. It will also be objected that my description of the commandments in social, historicist, institutional terms cannot be true since the Torah pre-exists the universe.

I have written in great detail about the first objection elsewhere,[79] and there is no point in repeating those discussions here. Let me just say briefly that Maimonides seeks to provide a philosophically acceptable explanation of the rabbinic doctrine of the survival of the soul after the death of the body. The explanation he offers is that to the extent that anything survives the death of the body, it is only the knowledge that one has acquired of abstract metaphysical truth. Historians of medieval philosophy generally call this doctrine the theory of the acquired intellect. One of the consequences of his adoption of this theory is that Maimonides has no way of including in the world to come individuals who have fulfilled the commandments of the Torah but who have not achieved at least some minimal level of intellectual perfection. He simply has no mechanism, acceptable to him philosophically, which would make this possible. This is not to say that obedience to halakhah is irrelevant to earning a share in the world to come, since, for Maimonides, a high level of morality is a necessary prerequisite for achieving anything more than a minimal level of intellectual perfection (would that were so!), and the world certainly knows no moral regimen superior to the divinely authored Torah.[80]

[79] *Must a Jew Believe Anything?* (2nd edn.), 149–63 and the sources cited there, and n. 80 below.

[80] According to Maimonides, obedience to halakhah is certainly not a sufficient condition for achieving a share in the world to come, and it is not even a necessary condition. For details, see below in Ch. 7, where I provide a fuller discussion of the theory of the acquired intellect.

2. Objection: Ante-Mundane or Primordial Torah

A second objection relates to the notion that the Torah existed before the creation of the universe. There is a small number of rabbinic texts that teach that the Torah pre-exists the cosmos.[81] Thus, for example, Mishnah *Avot* 3: 14 states that the Torah is a 'desirable instrument' (*keli ḥemdah*) through which the world was created. In some early midrashim, God is depicted as using the Torah as a template or blueprint for creation.[82] According to the eighth-century midrash, *Chapters of Rabbi Eliezer* (*Pirkei derabi eli'ezer*, chapter 3), seven things were created before the world: 'The Torah, Gehenna, the Garden of Eden, the Throne of Glory, the Temple, repentance, and the name of the Messiah.'[83] We shall return to this particular text below. Another expression of this idea is found in BT *Shabat* 88*b*:

R. Joshua ben Levi also said: When Moses ascended on high, the ministering angels spake before the Holy One, blessed be He:
'Sovereign of the Universe! What business has one born of woman amongst us?'
'He has come to receive the Torah,' answered He to them.
Said they to Him: 'That secret treasure, which has been hidden by Thee for nine hundred and seventy-four generations before the world was created, Thou desirest to give to flesh and blood! "What is man, that thou art mindful of him, And the son of man, that thou visitest him?" (Ps. 8: 5). "O Lord our God, How excellent is thy name in all the earth! Who hast set thy splendour[84] upon the Heavens!"' (Ps. 8: 2).[85]

The Torah, God's 'secret treasure', is presented here as pre-existing the world by 974 generations.

---

[81] There are biblical antecedents for this. In Prov. 3: 19 and 8: 22–36 wisdom is described as ante-mundane. On this, see N. G. Cohen, 'Context and Connotation', 46.

[82] *Gen. Rabbah* 1: 1, 4, and 8: 2. For references to other relevant texts, see E. Urbach, 'Fragments', 20.

[83] In this, *Chapters of Rabbi Eliezer* apparently reflects BT *Pes.* 54*a*, which presents the list in the following order: 'The Torah, repentance, the Garden of Eden, Gehenna, the Throne of Glory, the Temple, and the name of the Messiah'. Compare *Midrash tehilim*, 90: 12; in 93: 3 God is represented as having *thought* of the Torah (and other things) before creation, not that the Torah was already in existence before creation. Passages from *Chapters of Rabbi Eliezer* will be cited from the translation of Gerald Friedlander, with emendations (to bring it line with Pines' translation of the *Guide*). *Chapters of Rabbi Eliezer*, it is interesting (and, given Maimonides' problems with it, not surprising) to note, is one of the principal 'rabbinic' sources of the Zohar. See Giller, *Reading the Zohar*, 11. For an interesting sidelight on the text from BT *Pes.* cited here see the discussion of Abravanel's use of it in Borodowski, *Isaac Abravanel on Miracles*, 114–16.

[84] Here understood as signifying the Torah.   [85] I cite the Soncino translation.

There are perhaps a dozen places in rabbinic literature in which this idea finds clear expression.[86] It has had quite an impressive afterlife, however.[87] One example is found in Rashi's comment on Genesis 1: 1, in which it is implied that the cosmos was created so that the Torah could be given to the Jews.[88] The idea was also to become very important in kabbalistic texts.[89]

That most enigmatic of ancient Jewish texts, *Sefer yetsirah*, has a role to play in this discussion. If the book is as ancient as some scholars think, and if it indeed teaches that the cosmos was created out of the letters of the Hebrew alphabet, then it may at the very least hint at the notion of the ante-mundane Torah, which is, after all, the quintessential Hebrew document.[90]

[86] For discussion, see E. Urbach, *Sages*, 180–2. See also *Gen. Rabbah* 49: 2, in which God is presented as giving a new interpretation of the Torah every day, and the description of the 'academy on high' in BT *BM* 86*a*. Both stories reflect a view of Torah as in some sense existing independently of God.

[87] It was a popular motif in *piyutim*, ancient synagogue poetry. See Weinberger, *Jewish Hymnography*, 54 and 69, and Swartz, 'Ritual about Myth about Ritual'. Compare also Baer, 'Towards a Clarification', 111–12.

[88] See Pearl, *Rashi*, 49. Rashi's comment, of course, could be interpreted as teaching that God *planned* to create the Torah and give it to the Jews *after* the creation of the cosmos, but that, to my mind, is a useless quibble since, even according to this interpretation, the idea of the Torah pre-exists creation.

[89] See most recently, and in great detail, Moshe Idel's absorbing book, *Absorbing Perfections*. The entire book is relevant, but see esp. pp. 31–53 and 358–89. For an earlier study, which connects the idea of the ante-mundane Torah to magic, see Scholem, *On the Kabbalah and its Symbolism*, 38–40. See also Idel, 'Midrashic versus Other Forms of Jewish Hermeneutics'. Other sources are listed and discussed in Lamm, *Torah Lishmah*, 103 and 121 (n. 14).

[90] See references to literature on *Sefer yetsirah* above, in Chapter 1. On the specific issue raised here, see Gruenwald, '*Haketav, Hamikhtav*, and the Articulated Name', and Rubin, 'Language of Creation'. Gershom Scholem summarizes the attitude of many generations of Jewish mystics concerning the notion of an ante-mundane Torah in the following passage: 'All Jewish mystics, from the Therapeutae, whose doctrine was described by Philo of Alexandria, to the latest Hasid, are at one in giving a mystical interpretation to the Torah; the Torah is to them a living organism animated by a secret life which streams and pulsates below the crust of its literal meaning: every one of the innumerable strata of this hidden region corresponds to a new and profound meaning of the Torah. The Torah, in other words, does not consist merely of chapters, phrases and words; rather it is to be regarded as the living incarnation of the divine wisdom which eternally sends out new rays of light. It is not merely the historical law of the Chosen People, although it is that too; it is rather, the cosmic law of the Universe, as

Was Maimonides familiar with this notion of a pre-existent Torah? Undoubtedly[91]—he certainly knew the texts just cited and quotes one of them himself, as we shall see immediately. Did he accept it as literally true? There is very little reason to think so. Harry A. Wolfson analysed the notion of what he calls a 'primordial' Torah in post-rabbinic texts and showed that a long line of thinkers was familiar with the idea, but refused to take it literally.[92] In particular, Sa'adiah did not feel bound by the literal meaning of the idea.[93] Even Judah Halevi, in *Kuzari* iii. 73, refuses to take the idea literally, understanding it as an expression of God's ante-mundane intention to give the Torah to Israel.[94] Maimonides, I want to show here, was aware of the idea and consciously rejected it. This rejection is important, not just for what it teaches concerning the issue at hand, but for what it indicates about Maimonides' notion of Torah generally.

Let us first quote and analyse the relevant passage from *Chapters of Rabbi Eliezer*:

R. Eliezer ben Hyrcanos opened and said: . . . seven things were created before the creation of the world: the Torah, Gehenna, the Garden of Eden, the Throne of Glory, the Temple, repentance, and the name of the Messiah. . . . Forthwith the Holy One, blessed be He, took council with the Torah, whose name is *tushiyah*,[95] with reference to creation of the world. . . . Wherefrom were the heavens created? From the light of His garment.[96] He took some of it, stretched it like a cloth, and thus they were extending continually, as it is said: 'Who coverest Thyself with

God's wisdom conceived it. Each configuration of letters in it, whether it makes sense in human speech or not, symbolizes some aspect of God's creative power which is active in the universe' (see Scholem, *Major Trends*, 13–14).

[91] Not every doctrine taken as 'orthodox' today was even known to Maimonides, let alone accepted by him. For an important example of this, see Kellner, *Maimonides on the 'Decline of the Generations'*.

[92] H. A. Wolfson, *Repercussions*, 85–113. Wolfson's discussion also focuses on the Islamic idea of a pre-existent Koran; it may be that part of Maimonides' motivation in denying the pre-existence of the Torah is to polemicize against this Islamic doctrine. Similarly, the connection between Torah and *logos* (as implied in John 1: 1 and many other places) may have played a role in bringing Maimonides quietly to take issue with the notion of a pre-existent Torah.

[93] See H. A. Wolfson, *Repercussions*, 92–3, and Altmann, 'Saadya's Theory of Revelation'.   [94] See Baron, 'Yehudah Halevi', 141.   [95] i.e. 'resourcefulness'.

[96] For the use of similar expressions in Heikhalot literature see Scholem, *Jewish Gnosticism*, 58–64; id., *On the Mystical Shape of the Godhead*, 29; and R. Loewe, 'Divine Garment'. Might Maimonides' discussion of this text, analysed below, be, among other things, a silent polemic against the use of this expression in Heikhalot texts?

light as with a garment; who stretchest out the heavens like a curtain' (Ps. 104: 2). Wherefrom was the earth created? From the snow under the throne of His glory. He took some of it and threw it, as it is said: 'For he saith to the snow, Be thou earth' (Job 37: 6).

This text may be understood as teaching that reward and punishment (Gehenna and the Garden of Eden) precede creation; in other words, right and wrong are not socially determined,[97] but part of the very fabric of the universe. In this context, the inclusion of the Temple, the site at which Jews brought the sacrifices which atoned for their sins, makes excellent sense: God knows that people will sin, and graciously created the tools for overcoming sin (sacrificial cult and repentance) even before creating the world. By including the messiah in this list, the authors of this text make clear that in their eyes the destruction of the Temple is part of a much larger historical plan, and that exile will ultimately end in redemption. To teach that God 'consulted' the Torah in order to create the cosmos implies that nature is not value-neutral. But it can be taken to imply much more; it can be and was taken to imply that the cosmos reflects the Torah and that the Torah, in a real sense, is therefore linked to the nature of the universe at the deepest possible levels. A thinker who takes this view seriously will be led to believe that the ceremonial laws of the Torah are not simply historically conditioned institutions, many or perhaps all of which could be other than they are. No; such ceremonials reflect an antecedent reality, itself conditioned by the ante-mundane Torah. A person who takes this view is likely to arrive (as did Nahmanides) at the view that Torah and nature are one and the same thing; there is no objective nature which follows its own immanent and essential character[98]—it is all Torah.[99] Such a person would have to be convinced (as were Halevi and Nahmanides) that obedience to these laws was directly beneficial to the Jew who obeyed them, and that disobedience to them was directly harmful to the Jew who disobeyed them.[100]

[97] Maimonides *appears* to have held that right and wrong are socially determined (*Guide* i. 2); the literature on this question is vast, and has involved heated polemics. For references see Dienstag, 'Natural Law' and, more recently, Rynhold, 'Good and Evil'.

[98] In our terms: which follows its own immanent laws.

[99] I owe the ideas in this paragraph to discussions with Jolene S. Kellner.

[100] This helps us to understand the particularism of Halevi and Nahmanides: the Torah reflects reality; the Jews have the Torah; all other people thus live at a lower level of reality (and, I dare add, of goodness) than do the Jews; what they do, what becomes of them, are matters are much less important than what Jews do and what becomes of them.

Maimonides' treatment of the idea of an ante-mundane Torah is thus more important than the question of how he understood a particular midrashic motif—it goes to the very heart of his view of Torah and cosmos. Maimonides discusses our passage from the *Chapters of Rabbi Eliezer* in several places in the *Guide of the Perplexed*. Let us look at two of them.

Discussing God's names in *Guide* i. 61 (pp. 148–9) Maimonides writes:

Hence Scripture promises that an apprehension that will put an end to this delusion [that God has many attributes] will come to men. Thus it says: 'In that day shall the Lord be one, and His name one' (Zech. 14: 9); which means that in the same way as He is one, He will be invoked at that time by one name only, by that which is indicative only of His essence and which is not derivative. In the *Chapters of Rabbi Eliezer* they have said: 'Before the world was created there were only the Holy One, blessed be He, and His name.' Consider how this dictum states clearly that all the derivative names have come into being after the world has come into being.

What is at stake here is God's unity (which, for Maimonides, also means God's uniqueness). Had anything existed with God before creation, God's uniqueness would be put in doubt. Maimonides uses a text from *Chapters of Rabbi Eliezer* to prove that such was not the case: before creation *nothing* whatsoever existed but God and God's name.[101] Maimonides' use of this text in our context is particularly suggestive, since the passage quoted by Maimonides is followed almost immediately by the text cited above, concerning the seven things which were created (and thus already existed) before the creation of the cosmos. In itself, then, Maimonides' source does not really teach what Maimonides wants it to teach, that nothing existed with God (even 'temporarily') before creation. His use of selective quotation here may very well be meant to hint to his reader that the sequel in *Chapters of Rabbi Eliezer* should be read in light of the message of the earlier text, that nothing coexisted with God before creation.[102] This

---

[101] In his introduction to his commentary on the Torah, Nahmanides famously maintained that the Torah was indeed the name of God. I doubt that he made this claim in order to avoid the conclusion that I think ought to be derived from Maimonides' comment here (that the Torah did not pre-exist the cosmos); rather, this is one more reflection, if one were needed, of the vast gulf between Maimonides and Nahmanides.

[102] Another relevant text, Mishnah *Avot* 5: 5, teaches that ten things were created at twilight (of the sixth day of creation); among these are the *ketav* and the *mikhtav*. In his comment on this text Maimonides explains that the former refers to the written Torah and the latter to the tablets of the Decalogue. That being so, not only did the Torah not pre-exist the world, it was one of the last things created. My thanks to James Diamond for pointing these texts out to me.

interpretation is supported by an earlier passage (which may be construed as hinting at our text in *Chapters of Rabbi Eliezer*).

Guide of the Perplexed i. 9 (pp. 34–5) is devoted to the term 'throne' (*kise*). Maimonides explains that the term indicates grandeur, high rank, and dignity. Thus, the heavens are called 'throne' since they bear witness (to those who study them properly) to God's greatness, grandeur, and power. He goes on to explain:

> The matter is just as we have pointed out: namely, every place such as the Sanctuary or the heaven, distinguished by God to receive His light and splendour, is called a throne. The term is given a wider meaning in the Hebrew language when it says: 'For my hand upon the throne of the Lord' (Exod. 17: 16). What is meant is the attribute of His greatness and sublimity; this ought not to be imagined as a thing outside His essence or as a created being from among the beings created by Him, so that He, may He be exalted, should appear to exist both without a throne and with a throne. That would be infidelity beyond any doubt. For it states explicitly: 'Thou, O Lord, sittest for all eternity, Thy throne is from generation to generation' (Lam. 5: 19); whereby it indicates that the throne is a thing inseparable from Him. Hence the term throne signifies, in this passage and in all those similar to it, His sublimity and greatness and does not constitute a thing existing outside His essence, as will be explained in some of the chapters of this treatise. (p. 35)

To say that something exists alongside God before creation is 'infidelity [i.e. heresy] beyond any doubt'.[103] Maimonides talks of the throne here, but there is no doubt that the same reservation applies to any other entity thought to exist, along with God, before creation. It is likely that his strong language reflects his abhorrence of the idea that anything might be co-eternal with God. As he notes elsewhere: 'For the purpose of every follower of the Law of Moses and Abraham our Father or of those who go the way of these two is to believe that there is nothing eternal in any way at all existing simultaneously with God' (*Guide* ii. 13; p. 285). In *Guide* i. 68 he calls this belief a 'foundation of the Torah', writing: 'We have mentioned this likewise in our great compilation, since this, as we have made clear there, is one of the foundations of our Law; I mean the fact that He is one only and that no other thing can be added to Him, I mean to say that there is no eternal thing other than He' (p. 163). But could one not say that God

---

[103] Indeed, in *MT* 'Laws of Repentance', 3: 7 Maimonides states the same point in a halakhic context, calling a person who holds that anything exists along with God before creation a sectarian (*min*) and excluding that person from the world to come. One wonders how he squared this with his claim in *Guide* ii. 25 to the effect that Plato's doctrine of creation was Jewishly acceptable.

created the Torah, throne, etc., and then created the 'rest' of the cosmos? I think that Maimonides would respond as follows: there was no 'before' before creation (time, as I will note below, being one of the created things). Anything which exists with God 'before' creation is by definition eternal and God is no longer one. It is for this reason that denial of any antemundane entities but God is a foundation of Judaism, and affirming such existents is 'infidelity beyond any doubt'.[104]

Maimonides' second explicit citation from the *Chapters of Rabbi Eliezer* is found in *Guide* ii. 26 (pp. 330–2). This is a long passage, but worth quoting at length:

I have seen a statement of Rabbi Eliezer the Great, figuring in the celebrated *Chapters* known as *Chapters of Rabbi Eliezer*, which is the strangest statement I have seen by one who follows the Law of Moses our Master. Here is the text of the statement he made. He says: 'Wherefrom were the heavens created? From the light of His garment. He took some of it, stretched it like a cloth, and thus they were extending continually, as it said: "Who coverest Thyself with light as with a garment, Who stretchest out the heavens like a curtain" (Ps. 104: 2). Wherefrom was the earth created? From the snow under the throne of His glory. He took some of it and threw it, as it is said: "For he saith to the snow, Be thou earth." (Job 37: 6)'. This is the text of the statement he made there. Would that I knew what that Sage believed. Did he believe that it is impossible that something should come into being out of nothing and that there must necessarily be matter out of which that which is generated is produced? Did he for this reason seek to find wherefrom were created the heavens and the earth? However, whatever results from this answer, he ought to be asked: Wherefrom was the light of His garment created? Wherefrom was the snow under the throne of glory itself created? If, however, he wished to signify by the light of His garment an uncreated thing and similarly by the throne of glory something uncreated, this would be a great incongruity. For he would have admitted thereby the eternity of the world, if only as it is conceived according to Plato's opinion. As for the throne of glory belonging to the created things, the Sages state this expressly, but in a strange manner. For they say that it was created before the creation of the world. But the scriptural texts, in

[104] Idel, *Absorbing Perfections*, 45, expresses the point made here as follows: 'Ancient Jewish monotheism was generally uncomfortable with the idea of the preexistence of any entity to the creation of the world, a premise that would imperil the uniqueness of God as the single creator. The coexistence of an additional entity would produce a theological dynamics that would question the most singular religious achievement of ancient Judaism. Implicitly, allowing any role to such a founding and formative entity would reintroduce a type of myth that could recall the pagan mythology, where once again the relationship between the preexistent deities as a crucial condition for the cosmogonic process would be thrown into relief.'

connection with it, do not refer in any way to creation, with the exception of David's statement: 'The Lord hath established His throne in the heavens' (Ps. 103: 19), which statement admits very well of figurative interpretation. . . . Now, if Rabbi Eliezer believed in the eternity a *parte ante* of the throne, the latter must have been an attribute of God, and not a created body. But how is it possible for a thing to be generated from an attribute?[105]

Implying that 'the light of God's garment' or 'the throne of glory' were uncreated entities, existing alongside God before the creation of the Universe 'would be a great incongruity'.[106] Maimonides goes on to describe the incongruities, pointing out that the scriptural basis for believing in ante-mundane existence is nearly non-existent; the one verse which might be taken to teach this idea is easily interpreted metaphorically.

The throne of glory is one of the seven things which *Chapters of Rabbi Eliezer* teaches existed before creation; it beggars imagination to think that Maimonides would be any happier with any of the other six.[107] Believing that the Torah existed before creation, I submit, is 'infidelity beyond any doubt' in Maimonides' eyes and leads to great incongruities.[108] It is also, to put it mildly, incongruous with the many Maimonidean texts analysed above in this chapter.

Typically, Maimonides made this point indirectly, by implication. This is a further reflection of his overall strategy of fighting his wars without

[105] *Chapters of Rabbi Eliezer* 3 is also cited in *Guide* ii. 30 (p. 349), but the issue discussed there (temporal creation) is not directly related to our question.

[106] For an interesting discussion of this passage, see Langermann, 'Cosmology and Cosmogony', 212–13.

[107] One might further note that, given his understandings of Gehenna and the Garden of Eden, Maimonides could not possibly take the idea that they are ante-mundane in any literal sense. For Gehenna and the Garden of Eden, see his 'Introduction to *Perek ḥelek*'. A translation may conveniently be found in Twersky, *Maimonides Reader*, 402–23, esp. 413–14. It may be that Maimonides discusses the throne explicitly because of its centrality in ancient Jewish mysticism. For details, see Scholem, *Major Trends*, 43–6, Bar-Ilan, 'Throne of God', and most recently, Deutsch, *Gnostic Imagination*, 68–79.

[108] Possibly relevant is the following from *Guide* i. 65 (p. 158): 'I do not consider that . . . you require that the denial of the attribute of speech with reference to Him be explained to you. This is the case particularly in view of the general consensus of our community on the Torah being created. This is meant to signify that His speech that is ascribed to Him is created.' Implied here is the claim that the Torah does not pre-exist the cosmos, but that is not definite since it could be argued that God created the cosmos and then immediately created the Torah.

declaring them. In an important sense, however, this whole discussion is 'academic': for Maimonides it makes no sense whatsoever to speak of anything pre-existing the world, since time itself was created along with the cosmos. To speak of an ante-mundane Torah in any but the most allegorical sense is not only to commit a religious error, but also to make a logical blunder.[109]

3. Objection: The Patriarchs and Obedience to the Commandments

A staple of rabbinic literature is the idea that the patriarchs observed all the 613 commandments of the Torah. This idea is expressed in several places.[110] If I am correct in my interpretation of Maimonides as rejecting the notion of a primordial Torah and holding that the details of the Torah were determined by contingent historical factors, then it is obvious that he could not accept this doctrine.

This view has become very popular in traditionalist Judaism today, and was held by some important early authorities (e.g. Nahmanides on Genesis 26: 5). But, so far as I (and many kind friends) have been able to discover, Maimonides makes no explicit reference to this idea anywhere in his writings. There are plenty of good reasons for him to have rejected the notion (over and above the fact that it is incompatible with the thesis advanced in this chapter). It is incompatible with *MT* 'Laws of Idolatry', 1, according to which Abraham taught philosophical monotheism, which, it turns out, could not hold its own against the pressure of idolatry, and had to be supplemented with the 613 commandments of the Torah. *MT* 'Laws of Kings', 9: 1 also militates against the possibility that Maimonides accepted the notion under discussion. In that text Maimonides lists the single commandment given to each of the patriarchs (circumcision, in the case of Abraham; tithes, in the case of Isaac; and the sinew of the thigh, in the case of Jacob). I have also found a passage in the *Guide* (iii. 49; pp. 603–4) relevant to the issue:

From the story of Judah a noble moral habit and equity in conduct may be learnt; this appears from [Judah's] words: 'Let her take it, lest we be put to shame;

---

[109] On time as created, see *Guide* ii. 13. Kenneth Seeskin has recently subjected Maimonides' discussion of creation to careful analysis. See his *Searching for a Distant God*, 66–90, and 'Maimonides, Spinoza, and the Problem of Creation'.

[110] Mishnah *Kid.* 4: 14. The relevant part of the mishnaic text is missing from Maimonides' edition; not only did he not comment on it, he did not count it as part of the Mishnah. On the textual issues, see Epstein, *Introduction*, ii. 976–7, and Lieberman, *Tosefta kifshuta*, vol. viii (*Seder nashim*), 986. My thanks to Hillel Newman for sending me to these sources. See also BT *Yoma* 28b and *Ned.* 32a, and JT *Ber.* 2: 3/4c.

behold, I sent this kid' (Gen. 38: 23). Before the giving of the Torah sexual intercourse with a harlot was regarded in the same way as sexual intercourse with one's wife is regarded after the giving of the Torah. I mean to say that it was a permitted act that did not by any means arouse repugnance.

Judah's behaviour is here explained by the fact, that before the Torah was given, sex with a prostitute was not forbidden. Maimonides' point is not that the patriarch Judah flouted the prohibition against having sexual intercourse with a prostitute; rather, he explicitly says that for the patriarch Judah (and by implication the other patriarchs) sex with a prostitute in his day was permitted in the same way as sexual intercourse with one's wife was permitted after the giving of the Torah. Just as sexual intercourse within marriage after the giving of the Torah arouses no repugnance, so sexual intercourse with a prostitute before the giving of the Torah aroused no repugnance. I do not know if Maimonides was consciously trying to signal his rejection of the idea that the patriarchs observed the commandments, but that certainly appears to be the upshot of this passage.

God and Abraham: Who Chose Whom?

I claimed above that, according to Maimonides, God's choice of the Jews as the chosen people was actually a consequence of Abraham's discovery of God and not a historically necessary event. Before closing this chapter, I need to prove that point.

The founder of the Jewish people is the patriarch Abraham. It is worth paying close attention to Maimonides' description of Abraham's career, as presented in the first chapter of *MT* 'Laws Concerning Idolatry'.[111] In this chapter Maimonides presents what might be called a natural history of religion. The Bible presents its readers with an implicit problem: given that Noah and his immediate descendants knew God, how did the world become entirely idolatrous by the time of Abraham, ten generations after Noah? Here is Maimonides' explanation:[112]

In the days of Enosh [Gen. 4: 26, 5: 7–11] mankind fell into grave error; the wise of that generation turned brutish in counsel; and Enosh himself was among the

---

[111] For a helpful discussion of this text, which supports the reading I am about to give it, see L. Kaplan, 'Maimonides on the Singularity'.

[112] I cite Bernard Septimus's translation from his forthcoming translation of the *Book of Knowledge* for the Yale Judaica series. I have eliminated almost all of Professor Septimus's extremely learned notes. It is my pleasant duty to thank him here for his kindness in furnishing me with an advance copy of his translation.

errant. Their fallacy was to say as follows: 'Since God created the stars and spheres to govern the world, set them on high, and granted them honor, and [since] they are ministers who serve Him, they deserve to be praised, extolled and honored. Indeed, it is the will of God (blessed be He) that [we] magnify and honor those whom He has magnified and honored, just as a king wants his servants and attendants to be honored—for this redounds to the honor of the king.' Once this notion got into their heads, they began to build temples to the stars, offer them sacrifices, praise and extol them verbally, and bow down toward them, in order to win divine favor, by their corrupt lights. That was the root of alien worship.

Having explained the origin of idolatry,[113] Maimonides describes Abraham's rebellion against it:

After much time had passed, false prophets arose among the human race, claiming that God had commanded them: 'Worship such and such a star (or all the stars): offer it these sacrifices and libations; build it a temple; and fashion its image' . . . Thus it was that they began to make images in temples, under trees, atop mountains and on hills. They would come together, bow down to them, and tell the whole populace: 'This image can help or harm, and ought to be worshiped and feared.' The priests would then tell them: 'Through this worship you will multiply and prosper: do such and such; don't do such and such.' . . . It thus became the universal practice to worship the [various] images with distinct rites, and to sacrifice and bow down to them. With the passage of time, the Honored and Revered Name sank [into oblivion, fading] from the mouths and minds of all beings: they recognized it not. So all the commoners, women, and children, knew nothing but the wood or stone image and fabricated temple that they were brought up from childhood to bow down to, worship, and swear by. The wise among them—priests and the like—imagined there was no deity save the stars and spheres, for which those images had been made as [symbolic] representations. But as to the Eternal Source, none recognized or knew Him save singular individuals like Enoch, Methuselah, Noah, Shem, and Eber. Thus was the world declining by degrees, till the World's Pillar, our Father Abraham, was born. No sooner was this hero weaned than he began to ponder, though but a child, and to meditate day and night, wondering: 'How can the Sphere forever follow its course with none to conduct it? Who causes it to rotate? For it cannot possibly cause *itself* to rotate?' He had no one to teach or instruct him in anything, but was immersed in [the culture of] Ur of the Chaldees among the foolish adherents of alien worship. His father, mother and the entire populace worshiped alien deities, and he worshiped along with them, while his mind was searching and seeking to understand—till he grasped the true way and understood the right course of his own sound reason: He realized that: there is a single God, He conducts the Sphere, He created the universe, and, in all that exists, there is no god but He. And he realized that all

---

[113] *Avodah zarah*; Septimus translates this more literally as 'alien worship'.

the people were in error, and [that] what had caused them to err was worshiping the stars and images for so long that the truth [of God's existence] was lost to their minds. It was at age forty[114] that Abraham recognized his Creator.

Maimonides goes on to describe how Abraham then refuted the inhabitants of Ur, argued with them, broke their images, and began instructing them in the truth. After convincing his fellow-countrymen (and thus apparently upsetting the traditional order), the king sought to kill him. He was miraculously saved, whereupon he emigrated and 'began to call out loudly to all the people, teaching them that the world has [but] one God, who [alone] ought to be worshiped'. He travelled from city to city and from kingdom to kingdom, teaching this truth which he had discovered. Arriving in the land of Canaan, he proclaimed his message, instructed the inhabitants, implanted truth in their hearts, composed books on it, and taught it to his son Isaac.[115]

   Prominent in these texts is the noteworthy emphasis on the activity of Abraham. God is entirely absent from this account as anything but the object of philosophical speculation. According to this account, God does not even issue the command which opens the Abraham story in the Torah (Gen. 12: 1), 'Get thee hence . . .'. Even the (midrashically based) miracle by which Abraham was saved from the king of Ur is presented without

---

[114] When he had reached intellectual maturity, and not at the age of 3, as *Gen. Rabbah* 95 has it. See Abraham ben David's gloss here.

[115] Compare Maimonides' account in *Guide* iii. 29: 'However, when the Pillar of the World grew up and it became clear to him that there is a separate deity that is neither a body nor a force in a body and that all the stars and the spheres were made by Him, and he understood that the fables upon which he was brought up were absurd, he began to refute their doctrine and show up their opinions as false; he publicly manifested his disagreement with them and called "in the name of the Lord, God of the world" (Gen. 21: 33)—both the existence of the deity and the creation of the world in time by that deity being comprised in that call' (p. 516). For other parallels in the *Guide*, see ii. 39 (p. 379) and iii. 24 (p. 502). See also *Book of Commandments*, positive commandment 3. The issue also comes up in Maimonides' famous responsum to Obadiah the Proselyte. The slight variations in the text as cited by Blau (*Responsa*, no. 293, p. 549) and by Sheilat (*Letters*, 232–3) are of great interest. Sheilat, true to his vision of Maimonides, chooses readings which subtly but clearly diminish the universalist impact of the passage; Blau chooses readings which subtly but clearly augment the universalist impact of the passage (the former seems more likely an explanation than the latter, given what I know of R. Sheilat's other writings). I examine this matter in Kellner, ' "Farteitsht un Farbessert" '.

directly and clearly involving God—the text literally says: 'a miracle was performed for him' (*na'asah lo nes*).[116] Throughout these passages it is Abraham, and not God, who is the subject of active verbs: Abraham meditated, pondered, wondered, searched, grasped, understood, realized, recognized, refuted, argued, broke images, convinced, emigrated, proclaimed, travelled, taught, instructed, implanted, and composed.[117] God is cognized, according to this account, but does not act.[118]

---

[116] BT *Pes.* 118a. The Talmud here has God insisting on saving Abraham Himself (the angel Gabriel had sought the assignment); Maimonides clearly presents the story in an entirely different light. See also *Gen. Rabbah* 39: 3.

[117] My thanks to Zev Harvey for drawing my attention to this point.

[118] The God described here is the 'God of the philosophers'. Compare Kreisel, *Maimonides' Political Thought*, 43: 'What is crucial to stress in this context is that Abraham is depicted by Maimonides as an Aristotelian philosopher. His deduction that God "created" everything as depicted in "Laws of Idolatry", I. 3, is in reality the Aristotelian view that God is the first Cause of all existence.' Agreeing as I do with Kreisel's interpretation, I think it apposite to quote Judah Halevi's parallel account of Abraham in *Kuzari* iv. 17: 'The Sage said: Well, then, by that standard, it was right for Abraham to have undergone all that he did in Ur of the Chaldees, and then in departing from his homeland, and also in accepting circumcision, and again in expelling Ishmael, and even further in his anxiety about slaughtering Isaac, since all that he experienced with respect to the divine order [*al-amr al-ilahi*], he experienced by savouring [*dhawq*], not by reasoning.' This passage is found in the context of Halevi's distinction between the philosophic God of Aristotle (and of Abraham, according to Maimonides!), known in the tradition as *elohim*, and the experienced God of the patriarchs, known in the tradition by the Tetragrammaton. Halevi's Abraham goes beyond the God of the philosophers to the God of experience. Halevi makes this clear in the sequel: 'God ordered him to abstain from his scientific studies based on reasoning . . . and to take upon himself the duty of obeying the One he had experienced by savouring, just as it says: "Savour and see how good the Lord is" (Ps. 34: 9).' On this passage, see the discussion in Lobel, *Between Mysticism and Philosophy*, 89–93. Compare also Hasdai Crescas's comment (*Or hashem*, i. iii. 6, p. 122) to the effect that while it was Abraham's philosophical reasoning which *prepared* him for prophecy, this reasoning did not bring him to certain knowledge of God, which is the province of prophets, not philosophers: 'even though he desired the truth, he did not escape all doubt until God caused His light to emanate upon him, it [i.e. God's light] being prophecy'. This passage is discussed by W. Z. Harvey in *Physics and Metaphysics*, 47–8 and 60–5. Note Harvey's comment (p. 48) about the Maimonides whom Crescas criticized: 'His Abraham is an Aristotelian philosopher, or, if you prefer, his Aristotle was an Abrahamic philosopher.' It is noteworthy also that a rabbinic text (BT *Shab.* 156a, *Ned.* 32a), 'abandon your astrology [= philosophical—scientific research]', used by both Halevi and Crescas in the present context, is nowhere cited by Maimonides.

The upshot of all this is that Abraham discovered God on his own, so to speak.[119] God did not choose Abraham, God did not seek him out, God did not make Himself known to Abraham. God waited till someone discovered the truth about Him; that someone happened to be Abraham, progenitor of the Jews. It did not have to be Abraham. Had the first human being to discover the truth about God been, say, a Navajo, and had that Navajo philosopher possessed the courage and effectiveness of Abraham, then the Navajos would be the chosen people, the Torah would have been composed in the Navajo language, its narratives would reflect their history, and many of its commandments would reflect that history and the nature of Navajo society at the time of the giving of the Torah to them. The inner meaning of the Torah, its philosophical content, and spiritual message would all be equivalent to the inner meaning, philosophical content, and spiritual message of the Torah as it was indeed revealed to Moses at Sinai, but its outer garment would be dramatically different.

Here in its starkest fashion is the profound gulf which separates Maimonides from Halevi and thinkers like him.[120] For Halevi, God chose the Jews because of their antecedent special character, the only people on earth in whom the *inyan elohi* was permanently lodged. For Maimonides, it is Abraham's choice of God which makes his descendants special, so long as they remain loyal to that choice.[121]

---

[119] In other words, Abraham discovered God through *hekhre'a hada'at*, reasoned conviction. He also brought his contemporaries (Noahides in the most literal sense of the term) to acceptance of monotheism through *hekhre'a hada'at*. It is a safe assumption that, according to Maimonides' view, Abraham himself and those whom he brought near to God achieved shares in the world to come; that being the case, the standard reading of *MT* 'Laws of Kings', 8: 11 cannot be correct. See below, Ch. 7. My thinking here was stimulated by a comment I found in an unpublished paper by Mark A. Kaplowitz, though he wanted to take this issue in another direction.

[120] Compare also below, in my account of the holiness of the Jewish people, Ch. 3, for more on the comparison of Maimonides and Halevi vis-à-vis Abraham. See Ravitzky, 'Image of the Leader', and id., 'Introduction', esp. pp. 15–19.

[121] I was once discussing conversion to Judaism in a class in the United States. Two of my students, both daughters of Baptist ministers, asked me, in amazement: 'The Jews are God's chosen people; how can one choose to be chosen?'. This question goes to the heart of the debate between the Judaism of Judah Halevi, the Zohar, Nahmanides, etc. and the Judaism of Maimonides. In a very real sense, for the former, one cannot choose to be chosen. For Halevi, converts remain unequal to born Jews; for the Zohar there really is no such thing as conversion—true proselytes are persons born to gentile parents into whose bodies Jewish souls have fallen. For Maimonides, on the other hand, in

Our point finds further expression in the continuation of Maimonides' account:

Our Father Jacob taught all his children; but he singled out Levi, appointing him 'head' and installing him in an academy to teach 'the way of the Lord' (Gen. 18: 19) and keep Abraham's charge. He directed his children that there be an uninterrupted succession of Levite appointees, so that the teaching not be forgotten. This enterprise was gathering strength among Jacob's children and those who joined them, a God-knowing nation was coming into being—till Israel's stay in Egypt became prolonged and they retrogressed, learning [the Egyptians'] deeds and worshiping alien deities like them (the sole exception being the tribe of Levi, which remained steadfast to the patriarchal charge: never did the tribe of Levi worship alien deities). The root planted by Abraham was on the verge of being uprooted and Jacob's descendants were on the verge of reverting to the error and aberrance of the nations.[122] But because God loved us and stood by [his] oath to our Father, Abraham, he elected Moses—our Master and the Master of all the Prophets—and charged him with his [prophetic] mission. When Moses our Master attained to prophecy and God chose Israel as His own, He crowned them with commandments, and taught them: how to worship Him and what rules should govern alien worship and all who stray after it.

a very real sense, true Jews are not chosen by God, but, rather, are individuals (whoever their parents might be) who choose God. For Maimonides, as I argued in *Maimonides on Judaism and the Jewish People* (see the next note), *all* Jews are converts to Judaism.

[122] This last point deserves expansion, since it is important for the thesis being developed here. Following midrashic tradition (*Mekhilta*, 'Bo', 5; ed. Lauterbach, vol. ii, p. 36; *Exod. Rabbah*, 19: 5), Maimonides maintains that the Jews in Egypt (with the exception of the tribe of Levi) had assimilated to the idolatrous norms of the Egyptian culture around them (compare the opposed picture drawn by Halevi in *Kuzari* i. 95). Maimonides repeats this claim in a number of places. See e.g. his response to Obadiah the Proselyte in *Letters* (ed. Sheilat), 235, and his *Essay on Resurrection* (see *Letters*, ed. Sheilat, pp. 335–6 for the Arabic text and p. 369 for a Hebrew translation; for an English translation, see Halkin and Hartman, *Epistles of Maimonides*, 230). Those of Abraham's descendants who stood at Sinai quite literally converted to Judaism (the new religion expressed in the Torah of Moses). This may be seen from the way in which Maimonides opens his discussion of the laws of conversion in *MT* 'Laws of Forbidden Intercourse', 13: 'With three things did Israel enter the covenant: circumcision, immersion, and sacrifice.' Just so, Maimonides continues, must converts today undergo circumcision and immersion (sacrifice being no longer possible). See the fuller development of this point in Kellner, *Maimonides on Judaism and the Jewish People*, 85–7.

Israel thus becomes God's chosen people because of Abraham's antecedent choice of God.[123] I shall revisit this issue in Chapter 7, where I discuss Maimonides' account of 'Israel' and the chosen people.

❦

For Halevi and thinkers like him, the commandments of the Torah reflect an antecedent ontological reality; indeed, for the authors of the Zohar, having the Jews fulfil these commandments is a divine need.[124] Thus the commandments could not be other than they are. For Maimonides, on the other hand, the commandments of the Torah reflect historical events and

---

[123] Compare *Guide* iii. 51 (p. 623): 'This was also the rank of the Patriarchs, the result of whose nearness to Him, may He be exalted, was that His name became known to the world through them: "The God of Abraham, the God of Isaac, and the God of Jacob . . . this is my name forever" (Exod. 3: 15). Because of the union of their intellects through apprehension of Him, it came about that He made a lasting covenant with each of them . . . Also the providence of God watching over them and over their posterity was great.' This idea even finds expression in Maimonides' *Epistle to Yemen*, a text in which he must have been greatly tempted to use a stronger notion of the choice of Israel than the one expressed here. Towards the beginning of the *Epistle*, he emphasizes the importance of the following teaching: 'Ours is the true and divine religion, revealed to us through Moses, chief of the former as well as of the later prophets. *By means of it God has distinguished us from the rest of mankind*, as He declares: "Yet it was to your fathers that the Lord was drawn in His love for them, so that He chose you, their lineal descendants, from among all the peoples" (Deut. 10: 15). This choice was not made thanks to our merits, but was rather an act of grace, on account of our ancestors who were cognizant of God and obedient to Him, as He states: "It is not because you are the most numerous of peoples, that the Lord set His heart on you and chose you—indeed, you are the smallest of peoples [but it was because the Lord loved you and kept the oath He made to your fathers]" (Deut. 7: 7[–8])' (emphasis added). I cite from the translation in Halkin and Hartman, *Epistles of Maimonides*, 96–7. This text reads as if it were written in direct opposition to the views of Judah Halevi on the election of Israel (as expressed, for example, in *Kuzari* i. 27, 48, 95, and 103; several of these texts are quoted below in Ch. 7).

[124] See Faierstein, '"God's Need for the Commandments"'; for context and background, see Idel, *Kabbalah: New Perspectives*, ch. 7. Other relevant studies include Matt, 'The Mystic and the *Mizwot*', and Schwartz, 'From Theurgy to Magic'. The notion that in some sense the fulfilment of the commandments on the part of Israel is crucial for God's own 'well-being', as it were, is a reflection of the ancient idea of theurgy. See Dodds, *The Greeks and the Irrational*, 283–311, and Luck, 'Theurgy and Forms of Worship'.

constitute a social or institutional reality; they could certainly be other than they are.[125]

[125] But they are not; I do not for a moment believe that Maimonides entertained the idea that his historical explanation of (a huge number of) the commandments in any way diminished the obligation of each Jew to obey them all. He sharply distinguished explanations of why commandments were given from explanations of why they ought to be obeyed. For valuable studies of this issue, see J. Stern, *Problems and Parables*, and Seeskin, *No Other Gods*. See also Ch. 4 n. 57 and Ch. 7 n. 63 below.

THREE

Holiness

❧

Introduction

WHAT IS HOLINESS? Is it something actual which inheres in holy persons, places, times, and objects or is it a matter of institutional status? This question has very rarely been asked of Jewish texts, perhaps because the notion of holiness is so pervasive in Judaism that asking Jewish texts about the nature of holiness is like asking fish about the nature of water.[1] By focusing here on the way in which Maimonides understood the nature of holiness, I hope to show that the question is worth asking.

In one of his many illuminating studies the late Isadore Twersky wrote that for Maimonides holiness 'is a transcendent separate essence. It is not a *segulah* [= special characteristic, property] embodied in a physical object, which transfers by itself or which can be transferred from a sacred object to those who use it or respect it.'[2] If I understand Twersky correctly, he is maintaining that, for Maimonides, there is actually something in the universe called holiness, over and above holy persons, places, times, and objects.

Well, of course! Why should it be surprising that a medieval Jew would think that persons, places, times, and objects can be holy in some actual, intrinsic, objectively real sense? It may not be surprising for other Jews, but, and this is what I wish to prove in this chapter, it would be surprising were Maimonides to hold this view. So much so, that in another context Twersky himself writes that 'the holiness ascribed [by Maimonides] to various objects (such as Torah scrolls, *mezuzot*, phylacteries, the holy language) is teleological',[3] i.e. not intrinsic, and certainly not real in the sense of being 'a transcendent separate essence'.

---

[1] Compare Jacobs, 'Holy Places', who points to 'the absence of anything like a systematic treatment of the topic [of holiness in Judaism]' (p. 4). My claim here is well illustrated in a fascinating study by Peters, *Jerusalem and Mecca*. The question of how Judaism and Islam understand the nature of holiness is nowhere addressed in this book.

[2] Twersky, 'Martyrdom and Sanctity of Life', 172–3.

[3] Id., 'Maimonides on Eretz Yisrael', 285–6.

What, then, is Maimonides' position? In order to answer that question, it will be useful to distinguish three different views of sanctity.[4] According to one view, holiness is an essential feature of certain places, people, objects, or times; on this view, holiness is 'hard-wired' into parts of the universe. Judah Halevi apparently held this view, at least with respect to the holiness of the Land of Israel,[5] the holiness of the commandments, and probably with respect to the special character of the Jewish people, the 'holy nation'. Fairly clear evidence that Halevi held the view that I am attributing to him may be seen in *Kuzari* iii. 53. Explaining how two distinct domains can be joined, Halevi cites examples of other changes in status brought about by halakhic procedures (such as marriage and divorce, and many matters connected to the priestly ritual and to ritual purity and impurity). He then explains:

> The divine order [*al-amr al-ilahi*] used to indwell with every single one of these acts because the practices [prescribed by] the religious Law are like beings that are generated naturally, all of which are determined by God, inasmuch as their determination is [obviously] not within the power of a human being, just as you see [that] beings generated naturally are determined, given proper balance and appropriately related to one another in terms of their physical constitutions [which ultimately derive] from the four natures. Thus, they are rendered complete and prepared [for their various tasks] by [even] the slightest thing; and the form that they are worthy of [having] . . . comes to dwell within them.

Changes in nature, Halevi explains here, are brought about by the indwelling of forms in properly prepared material substrates. This makes perfect sense in the physics of his day, and the Khazar king has no trouble accepting it. That being so, Halevi then asks rhetorically, 'Who, then, but God alone is able to determine works [in this way] so that the divine order [*al-amr al-ilahi*] dwells within them?'

The analogy drawn here is very important for our purposes. Given the proper circumstances, a hen's egg can develop into a chicken. A chicken is not an egg; chickens are ontologically distinct from eggs. Similarly, a married woman is in some real sense distinct from her former unmarried self; a house declared ritually impure by a priest (Lev. 13: 47–59, 14: 33–53) is, in a real sense, not the same house it was before the priestly declaration. Before the declaration, the house was ritually pure, after the declaration, it

---

[4] I am deeply grateful to Professor Joshua Golding for helping me to think through this issue; he is no way responsible for the use to which I put his insights here. I use the terms 'holiness' and 'sanctity' interchangeably.

[5] On which see below, nn. 68 and 69.

is ritually impure, and more has changed here than 'just' the halakhic status of the house.

'Actions [prescribed] by the religious Law', Halevi continues, when properly performed, have actual, not 'only' statutory or institutional consequences:[6]

when it has been completed in the proper way, and you see the heavenly fire, or discover another spirit within yourself, which you did not know [beforehand], or [you witness] veridical dreams and miracles, you know that they are the result of all you did before and of the mighty order with which you have come into contact and which you have [now actually] attained.

It appears that Halevi holds that proper fulfilment of the commandments of the Torah thus brings about real change in the universe. On his view, holiness can inhere in certain things, not in others; just as non-Jews cannot prophesy, so not everything can be or become holy. The substrate makes a difference.

According to a second view, the universe, as it were, starts out all of a piece, at least with respect to sanctity. At various times God renders certain times, places, or objects holy. This is certainly one way of reading verses such as 'And God blessed the seventh day and declared it holy, because on it God ceased from all the work of creation that He had done' (Gen. 2: 3). A reasonable way of understanding this and similar verses is that God took a day like every other day (the seventh) and rendered it sacred, changing its nature from that time on.

An example of this second view, it appears to me, may be found in the commentary of Hayim ben Moses Attar (1696–1743) on the Torah, *Or haḥayim* (on Numbers 19: 2). According to Rabbi Hayim, before receiving the Torah the Jews were like any other people; upon accepting the Torah the people of Israel became ontologically distinct (my language, not his) from all other nations. Rabbi Hayim writes: 'The distinction by virtue of which the Jewish people were elevated above the other nations is the acceptance of the Torah, for without it, the House of Israel would be like all the other nations.'[7] In the sentences which follow Rabbi Hayim makes it

---

[6] I put the word 'only' in quotation marks to emphasize that, according to the view I find in Maimonides, holiness is, indeed, 'only' institutional, but still extremely important; but as Halevi would understand him, Maimonides' view makes holiness *only* institutional, i.e. relatively unimportant.

[7] I assume that R. Hayim has in mind passages such as BT *Shab*. 145*b*–146*a*. Maimonides treats this passage as metaphorical in *Guide* ii. 30 (pp. 356–7); see below, Ch. 7 n. 137.

very clear that the Jews are distinguished from non-Jews on a very basic, spiritually fundamental level. After Sinai, the Jews are ontologically distinct from non-Jews, even if before Sinai they were not.

Both these views share the idea that, however it becomes holy, a holy place, person, time, or object is, once holy, objectively different from profane places, persons, times, and objects. According to both these views, sanctity is real, it inheres in sacred places, etc., it is intrinsic to them; it is, one might say, part of their metaphysical make-up. I will characterize both these approaches, therefore, as 'ontological' or 'essentialist' views of the nature of holiness. Holy places, persons, times, and objects are ontologically distinct from (and religiously superior to) profane places, persons, times, and objects. This distinction is part of the universe.

In Chapter 1 I used an analogy with radioactivity to make this point. Just as radioactivity was a feature of the universe before it was known to science, so, according to these two views, holiness is a feature of certain persons, places, times, and objects, even though there is no way to measure it. It is a feature of the objectively real world, even if not part of the world susceptible to laboratory examination.

Maimonides, I will show, held a different view of holiness. Holy places, persons, times, and objects are in no objective way distinct from profane places, persons, times, and objects. Holiness is the *name* given to a certain class of people, objects, times, and places which the Torah marks off. According to this view holiness is a status, not a quality of existence. It is a challenge, not a given; normative, not descriptive. It is institutional (in the sense of being part of a system of laws) and hence contingent. This sort of holiness does not reflect objective reality; it helps constitute social reality. Holy places, persons, times, and objects are indubitably holy, and must be treated with all due respect, but they are, in and of themselves, like all other places, persons, times, and objects. What is different about them is the way in which the Torah commands that they be treated. Their sanctity derives from the uses to which they are put; in that sense it is teleological, using Twersky's language.

For the purposes of this study, the distinction between the first and second views of holiness is unimportant. If I can prove that Maimonides held the third, institutional/teleological view, it will follow that he rejected both types of ontological view.[8]

---

[8] Support for the distinction drawn here, and for my interpretation of Maimonides, is found in the three essays by Yochanan Silman—'Halakhic Determinations', 'Commandments and Transgressions', and 'Introduction'. See p. xii in the last of these for brief comments on holiness.

The two views I will be contrasting here were ably summed up by Joyce Carol Oates in a parenthetical aside to an essay on Auden: 'a profane sort of art, perhaps, in Auden's vocabulary. (The value of a profane thing lies in what it usefully does, the value of a sacred thing lies in what it *is* . . .).'[9] In partial contradiction to Oates, I will prove here that, for Maimonides, the sacred character of persons, places, times, and objects lies precisely in what they *do* (or the *use* to which they are put), not in what they *are*. In other words, I will argue that, for Maimonides, holiness is institutional, not essentialist; teleological, not ontological.

Given Maimonides' nominalism and his insistence upon the absolute transcendence of God, he could not attribute extra-mental existence to a general term like 'sanctity', and he could not have held that there is any property shared by God and humans. If God is holy (and so the Torah affirms), then humans can be called holy only if the terms are used in an absolutely equivocal sense. The upshot of the textual discussion upon which we are about to embark is precisely that: people, places, times, objects are sacred 'only' in an institutional sense.

It is also crucial to emphasize that holiness may exist 'only' at the level of halakhic institutions, but this does not mean that a person who holds this view must be insensitive to the emotional consequences of encountering a place or thing or person which she or he holds sacred. There is no reason to think that Maimonides did not prize such experiences. In short, a nominalist can also have religious experiences![10]

A Glance at the Biblical Evidence

What is called holy in the Torah? First and foremost, obviously, God. In a text which was to have profound influence on Jewish liturgy, the prophet Isaiah wrote:

In the year that King Uzziah died, I beheld my Lord seated on a high and lofty throne; and the skirts of His robe filled the Temple. Seraphs stood in attendance on Him. Each of them had six wings: with two he covered his face, with two he covered his legs, and with two he would fly. And one would call to the other, 'Holy, holy, holy! The Lord of Hosts! His glory fills all the earth!' (Isa. 6: 1–3)

[9] Oates, 'Depth-Sightings'.

[10] I would like to avoid being drawn into a discussion of the extent to which Maimonides' intellectualism shades off into intellectualist mysticism. For that position, see Blumenthal, 'Maimonides: Prayer'. S. Harvey, 'Meaning of Terms', 188–96, shows that Maimonides was read in this fashion in Egypt, while Langermann, 'Saving the Soul', puts this way of reading Maimonides into its Yemenite context.

God is also called 'the Holy One of Israel' some fifteen times in the Bible (most of these occurrences being in Isaiah). God's being the Holy One *of* Israel has direct consequences:

For I the Lord am your God: you shall sanctify yourselves and be holy, for I am holy. You shall not make yourselves unclean through any swarming thing that moves upon the earth. For I the Lord am He who brought you up from the land of Egypt to be your God: you shall be holy, for I am holy. (Lev. 11: 44–5)

Verses such as this, and others, for example 'Speak to the whole Israelite community and say to them: You shall be holy, for I, the Lord your God, am holy' (Lev. 19: 2), admit, it seems to me, of very different interpretations. One way of looking at them is to see them as teaching that God is holy and through the process of election Israel also becomes holy.[11] Just as God's holiness is essentialist, so also is Israel's. But all these verses admit of a different interpretation, one which I will try to show was held by Maimonides. According to this interpretation, Israel is holy when it behaves in certain ways. Holiness on this view is a challenge and not a gift.[12] I do not want to make any claims about the way in which the biblical books understood holiness, only that their words are ambiguous and can be, and have been, interpreted in very different ways.[13]

The same ambiguity, I submit, may be found in the language of the opening formula of blessings ordinarily recited before the fulfilment of any positive commandment: 'Blessed are You, Lord our God, Who has sanctified us with His commandments and commanded us to . . .'. Following Hayim ben Moses Attar, one can understand this language as affirming that the imposition of the commandments has made Israel intrinsically holy, or, on the other hand, as affirming that holiness is a consequence of fulfilling the commandments and that it means nothing more than that. Again, I am

[11] Judah Halevi attributes intrinsic holiness to the people of Israel even before Sinai. See the extended discussion in Ch. 7 below.

[12] Even 2 Sam. 6 and 1 Chron. 13, often thought of as teaching that the ark of the covenant had some sort of inherent and dangerous holiness, do not teach that. Uzziah's death was not an automatic consequence of his having touched the holy ark; it was a *punishment* by God for having done so. Similarly with the account in 1 Sam 5: the sufferings of the Philistines were *inflicted* by God as punishment and warning. There is nothing of Indiana Jones in the biblical text itself.

[13] My friend Hayim Shahal pointed out to me that the Hebrew *kedoshim tihiyu* ('You shall be holy') can be read in the future tense (as a promise) or in the imperative (as a commandment or challenge). Maimonides, I will show here, must have read it in the latter sense.

making no claims about what the talmudic Sages intended when they instituted this formula (assuming they all intended the same thing by it, which I consider unlikely); rather, I want to show how Maimonides must have understood it.

Maimonides on the Nature of Holiness in General

What does Maimonides himself actually say on our topic? There are a small number of texts in which he explicitly addresses the definition of holiness. The most important of these, I think, is found in *Guide* iii. 47:

As for His dictum, may He be exalted, 'Sanctify yourselves therefore and be ye holy, for I am holy' (Lev. 11: 44), it does not apply at all to ritual impurity and purity. *Sifra* states literally: This concerns sanctification by the commandments. For this reason, transgression of the commandments is also called ritual impurity. . . . The term ritual impurity is used equivocally in three different senses: it is used of disobedience and of transgression of commandments concerning action or opinion; it is used of dirt and filth . . . and it is used according to these fancied notions,[14] I refer to touching or carrying certain things or being under the same roof with certain things.[15] With reference to this last sense, we say: 'The words of the Torah are not subject to becoming impure.'[16] Similarly, the term holiness [*al-kedushah*] is used equivocally in three senses opposed to those three senses.[17]

'Holiness', therefore, can mean one of three things:

1. obedience to the commandments concerning action or opinion;

2. physical cleanliness;

3. ritual purity.

With respect to the first and second, it is readily apparent that there is nothing 'essentialist' or 'ontological' at stake here. When one obeys the Torah, when one holds true views, one has achieved a state of holiness. When one is physically clean, one may be called holy. With respect to the third meaning, Maimonides explicitly teaches that matters of ritual purity and impurity are institutional, not ontological:

[14] Arabic: *wa-ala hadha al-ma'ani al-mutawahima*; ibn Tibbon: *medumim*; Kafih: *mahshavti'im*; Schwartz: *hamedumim*. Friedlaender: 'imaginary defilement'. On *wahm*, the term in question here, see Jospe, *Torah and Sophia*, 226–31, and Friedman, 'Tamar', 50 n. 68.

[15] i.e. matters of ritual purity and impurity are 'fancied notions', having no objective correlates in the 'real' world.   [16] BT *Ber.* 22a.

[17] The passage here is on pp. 595–6. We shall consider it again in Ch. 4 in the context of ritual purity and impurity.

It is plain and manifest that the laws about ritual impurity and purity are decrees laid down by Scripture[18] and not matters about which human understanding is capable of forming a judgment; for behold, they are included among the divine statutes [*ḥukim*].[19] So, too, immersion as a means of freeing oneself from ritual impurity is included among the divine statutes. *Now 'ritual impurity' is not mud or filth which water can remove, but is a matter of scriptural decree and dependent upon intention of the heart.* Therefore the Sages have said, If a man immerses himself, but without special intention, it is as though he has not immersed himself at all. Nevertheless we may find some indication of all this: just as one who sets his heart on becoming ritually pure becomes so as soon as he has immersed himself, *although nothing new has befallen his body*, so, too, one who sets his heart on purifying himself from the impurity that besets men's souls—namely, evil thoughts and wicked moral qualities[20]—becomes pure as soon as he consents in his heart to shun those counsels and brings his soul into the waters of pure reason. Behold, Scripture says, 'I will sprinkle pure water upon you, and you shall be pure: I will purify you from all your ritual impurity and from all your fetishes' (Ezek. 36: 25). May God, in His great mercy, purify us from every sin, iniquity, and guilt. Amen.[21]

Could we ask for a clearer statement? Matters of ritual purity and impurity are decrees of the Torah, having no objective correlation in the 'real' world. These laws reflect no objective reality, on any level or in any dimension; rather, they create social/halakhic reality.

Thus, if we take Maimonides at his word in *Guide* iii. 47, 'holiness' is the term used by the Torah to characterize obedience, cleanliness, or ritual purity. It refers to nothing which can actually and objectively inhere in entities, persons, places, or times. This point is emphasized in an earlier chapter of the *Guide* as well. In iii. 33 (p. 533), Maimonides writes:

Similarly, one of the intentions of the Law is purity and sanctification; I mean by this renouncing and avoiding sexual intercourse and causing it to be as infrequent

[18] *Gezerat hakatuv*. On this expression see the discussion in J. Stern, *Problems and Parables*, 49–66.

[19] This statement is interesting in light of the claim made by Maimonides in the *Guide* that the divine statutes (*ḥukim*) can be understood. On the whole issue see J. Stern, *Problems and Parables*.

[20] *De'ot raot*. For many reasons I would prefer to follow Herbert Danby and translate this as 'false convictions', but I fear that would be incorrect. On the expression *de'ah* as 'moral quality' in Maimonides, see *Guide* iii. 35 (p. 535). For discussion, see Septimus, 'What Did Maimonides Mean by *Madda*?'.

[21] *MT* 'Laws of Immersion Pools', 11: 12. I cite from the translation of Danby, *Book of Cleanness*, 535, with emendations and emphases added. For an extended discussion of this passage see below, Ch. 4 on ritual purity and impurity.

as possible, as I shall make clear. Thus, when He, may He be exalted, commanded the religious community to be sanctified with a view to receiving the Torah, and he said: 'And sanctify them today and tomorrow' (Exod. 19: 10), He said: 'Come not near a woman' (Exod. 19: 15). Consequently He states clearly that sanctity consists in renouncing sexual intercourse, just as He states explicitly that giving-up of the drinking of wine constitutes sanctity, in what He says about the Nazirite: 'He shall be sacred'[22] (Num. 6: 5). A text of *Sifra* reads: '"Sanctify yourselves therefore, and be ye holy" (Lev. 11: 44)—This concerns sanctification by the commandments.' And just as the Law designates obedience to these commandments as sanctity and purity, it also designates transgressions of these commandments and the perpetration of evil actions as impurity, as I shall make clear. Cleaning garments, washing the body, and removal of dirt, also constitute one of the purposes of this Law. But this comes after the purification of actions and purification of the heart[23] from polluting opinions and polluting moral qualities.[24]

The clear implication of this passage is that sanctity consists of modes of behaviour, among which are the renunciation of sexual intercourse, the renunciation of wine, obedience to the commandments, and the attainment of pure actions and ideas. This is certainly very far from any ontological conception of holiness.

Holy Persons

The term 'holiness' may have no actual referent in any dimension of the real world, but Jewish tradition is hardly hesitant about applying the term to people, to places, to times, and to objects, and Maimonides is certainly part of that tradition. It will be useful to focus our attention first on the way in which Maimonides describes the holiness attainable by people.

The fifth of the fourteen volumes of the *Mishneh torah* is *Sefer kedushah*, the *Book of Holiness*. This volume contains three sections: 'Laws of Forbidden Intercourse', 'Laws of Forbidden Foods', and 'Laws of [Kosher] Slaughtering'. What do these three issues have in common? Maimonides explains in *Guide* iii. 35. The purpose of the laws concerning forbidden foods, he tells us there, 'as we have explained in the Commentary on the Mishnah in the Introduction to *Aboth*,[25] is to put an end to the lusts and licentiousness manifested in seeking what is most pleasurable and to taking the desire for food and drink as an end' (p. 537). The laws concerning

---

[22] Pines translates: 'He shall be saintly.' [23] The seat of the intellect.

[24] My thanks to Mr Yisrael Ben-Simon for drawing my attention to this passage.

[25] See the fourth of Maimonides' *Eight Chapters*.

forbidden intercourse, he also explains, are designed 'to bring about a decrease of sexual intercourse and to diminish the desire for mating as far as possible, so that it should not be taken as an end, as is done by the ignorant, according to what we have explained in the Commentary on Tractate *Aboth*.' Maimonides does not explicitly explain the purpose of the laws concerning ritual slaughter here (indeed, he does not mention them at all in this passage in the *Guide*), but it is not hard to see how they would fit into the rubric of forbidden foods.

Indeed, Maimonides makes this tolerably clear in his introduction to the *Mishneh torah*, where he describes the *Book of Holiness* as follows:

Fifth Book. It includes in it precepts having reference to illicit sexual unions, and those that relate to forbidden foods; because in these two regards, the Omnipresent sanctified us and separated us from the nations, and of both classes of precepts it is said, 'And I have set you apart from the peoples' (Lev. 20: 26), 'Who have set you apart from the peoples' (Lev. 20: 24). I have called this book: The Book of Holiness.[26]

One achieves holiness by refraining from forbidden food and from forbidden sexual activity.[27] That is why the laws concerning forbidden foods and the laws concerning ritual slaughtering (which turn certain classes of edibles from forbidden to permitted) are classed together in the *Book of Holiness*.

Maimonides derives this connection between holiness and refraining from forbidden activies from a midrashic passage cited in the fourth introductory principle to his *Book of Commandments*:

We are not to include charges which cover the whole body of the commandments of the Torah. There are injunctions and prohibitions in the Torah which do not pertain to any specific duty, but include all commandments . . . With respect to this principle other scholars have erred, counting 'You shall be holy' (Lev. 19: 2) as one of the positive commandments—not knowing that the verses, 'You shall be holy' (Lev. 19: 2) [and] 'Sanctify yourselves, and be you holy' (Lev. 11: 44) are charges to fulfill the whole Torah, as if He were saying: 'Be holy by doing all that I have commanded you to do, and guard against all things I have enjoined you from doing.' The *Sifra* says: '"You shall be holy": keep apart'; that is to say, hold aloof from all the abominations against which I have admonished you. In the *Mekhilta* the Sages say: 'And you shall be holy men unto Me' (Exod.

---

[26] *Book of Knowledge*, trans. Hyamson, 18*b*.

[27] For more on this connection, see *MT* 'Laws of Moral Qualities', 5: 4, and *Guide* iii. 33 (p. 533), cited above. Also relevant is *MT* 'Laws of Forbidden Intercourse', 22: 20.

22: 30)—Issi the son of Yehudah says: With every new commandment the Holy One, blessed be He, issues to Israel He adds holiness to them.' That is to say, this charge is not an independent one, but is connected with the commandments wherein they have been enjoined there, since whoever fulfills that charge is called holy. Now this being so, there is then no difference between His saying, 'You shall be holy', and 'Obey My commandments' . . . The *Sifrei* says: ' "And you be holy" (Num. 15: 40), this refers to the holiness of the commandments.'[28]

Maimonides explains here that the biblical statement, 'You shall be holy', is not to be counted as one of the 613 commandments of the Torah, since it encompasses the whole Torah. While doing so, Maimonides lets slip, as it were, a point crucial to our purposes: Jews are not made holy by having been given the commandments; rather, they become holy when they fulfil them. That does not mean that as one fulfils commandments one's onto-logical status changes from profane to holy; rather, it means that 'holiness' is the way in which the Torah characterizes obedience to the command-ments. As Maimonides says at the end of the passage, holiness refers to the holiness of [fulfilling] the commandments.

Returning to the exposition of this passage, Maimonides cites the expla-nation of *Sifra* on 'You shall be holy': keep yourself apart or separate your-self from illicit enjoyments (*perishut*). From what in particular must one refrain in order to achieve holiness? In the *Mishneh torah* Maimonides explains: forbidden foods and forbidden sexual activity.

Maimonides connects the *perishut* spoken of here with the *perushim*, or Pharisees, in *MT* 'Laws of Ritual Impurity of Foodstuffs', 16: 12:

Although it is permissible to eat ritually impure foodstuffs and to drink ritually impure liquids, the pious of former times used to eat their common food in condi-tions of ritual purity, and all their days they were wary of every ritual impurity. And it is they who were called Pharisees, 'separated ones', and this is a higher holi-ness. It is the way of piety that a man keep himself separate and go apart from the rest of the people and neither touch them nor eat and drink with them. For separa-tion leads to the purification of the body from evil deeds, and the purification of the body leads to the hallowing of the soul from evil thoughts, and the hallowing of the soul leads to striving for imitation of the Shekhinah; for it is said, 'Sanctify yourselves therefore and be ye holy' (Lev. 11: 44), 'for I the Lord Who sanctify you am holy' (Lev. 21: 8).[29]

[28] See Chavel translation, ii. 380–1 (emended).

[29] *Book of Cleanness*, trans. Danby, 393. Compare *Guide* iii. 33 (p. 533) and, on the con-nection between holiness and *perishut*, *MT* 'Laws of the Foundations of the Torah', 7: 1 and 7. See further Maimonides' *Commentary on the Mishnah*, Sotah 3: 3.

Acting like the Pharisees is a form of 'higher holiness'. It involves separating oneself from all forms of ritual impurity and from all people who are in
a state of ritual impurity. This is not because there is anything intrinsically
wrong with being ritually impure.[30] It is because such separation 'leads to
the purification of the body from evil deeds', which, in turn, 'leads to the
hallowing of the soul from evil thoughts', which itself 'leads to striving for
imitation of the Shekhinah'.

I understand Maimonides to be saying here that the aim of holiness, of
perishut, is moral behaviour (separation from evil deeds),[31] which in turn
makes possible intellectual perfection (separation from evil thoughts); that,
in turn, brings one to strive for *imitatio Dei*.[32] This is to translate Maimonides' rabbinic vocabulary into the language of medieval Aristotelianism.[33]
But one need not agree with this translation to see that, on the evidence of
the text presented here, for Maimonides holiness means the outcome of a
kind of behaviour. It is nothing which can be said to exist in and of itself,
it is not some sort of superadded essence, it is nothing ontological. It is
simply a name given to certain types of (extremely important, highly

[30] Maimonides writes in para. 9: 'Just as it is permissible to eat and drink common
food that is ritually impure, so it is permissible to allow ritual impurity to befall common food in the Land of Israel; and ritual impurity may be imparted to common food
that is at the outset in fit and proper condition. Similarly, it is permissible to touch any
things that are ritually impure, and to incur ritual impurity from them, for Scripture
warns none but the sons of Aaron and the Nazirite against incurring ritual impurity
from a corpse, thereby implying that for all other people it is permissible, and that it is
permissible even for priests and Nazirites to incur ritual impurity from other ritually
impure things, except only the ritual impurity of corpses.'

[31] On which see pp. 148–51 below.

[32] The point made here is well stated in Kreisel, *Maimonides' Political Thought*, 156:
'The dominant motif characterizing Maimonides' discussions of God is the negation of
corporeality. His view of holiness as lying in the ethical virtues in general, and restraint
of corporeal desires in particular, connects this notion with the negation of one's own
corporeality. One must particularly negate that which is associated with the most corporeal of our senses.' The literature on Maimonides' conception of human perfection is
vast. Much of it is summarized and analysed in Kellner, *Maimonides on Human
Perfection*. More recent studies include: Benor, *Worship of the Heart*; Bruckstein, 'How
Can Ethics be Taught'; W. Z. Harvey, 'Political Philosophy and Halakhah'; H. Kasher,
'Three Punishments'; Kreisel, *Maimonides' Political Thought*; Rosenberg, 'You Shall
Walk in His Ways'; Seeskin, *Searching for a Distant God*, 97–106; Shatz, 'Worship,
Corporeality and Human Perfection'; and Lorberbaum, 'Maimonides on *Imago Dei*'.

[33] For a defence of this approach, see Kellner, *Must a Jew Believe Anything?*(2nd
edn.), Appendix 1, 149–63.

valued) behaviour, and, by extension, to persons, places, times, and objects. It is, and this is a point which must be emphasized, something which is not given, but must be earned. Holiness is not an inheritable status.[34]

Before carrying on with the line of interpretation being developed here, it is important to note that for Maimonides holiness in this sense is not restricted to Jews. While I am not a devotee of the sort of Maimonidean numerology indulged in by Leo Strauss, sometimes it is simply too striking to be ignored. The *Mishneh torah* comprises fourteen volumes. The precise mid-point, then, is the end of volume vii. This (and only this) volume is itself divided into precisely seven sections. Devoted to laws relating to agricultural matters, volume vii ends with a section called 'Laws of the Sabbatical Year and Jubilee'.[35] This seventh section of the seventh volume is divided into thirteen chapters. The thirteenth chapter is divided into twelve paragraphs in standard editions.[36] The last of these paragraphs reads:

Not only the Tribe of Levi, but each and every individual human being,[37] whose spirit moves him and whose knowledge gives him understanding to set himself apart[38] in order to stand before the Lord, to serve Him, to worship Him, and to know Him, who walks upright as God created him to do, and releases himself from the yoke of the many foolish considerations which trouble people—such an

[34] In general, I agree with Abraham Nuriel's criticism of Yeshayahu Leibowitz's interpretation of Maimonides, to the effect that there is relatively little actually of Maimonides in Leibowitz's exposition of his thought; but on at least one important issue, I believe that Leibowitz was absolutely correct. As Leibowitz used to like to say in his many public lectures on Maimonides, the latter insisted that humans are given nothing on a silver platter; everything must be earned. It can be shown that for Maimonides this 'everything' includes one's humanity, one's status as a Jew, providence, prophecy, a share in the world to come, and, as I am arguing here, holiness. See Nuriel, 'Are There Really Maimonidean Elements?'.

[35] For Maimonides, the reinstitution of the Jubilee is intimately connected to the messianic era. See *MT* 'Laws of Kings', 11: 1.

[36] The significance of the number thirteen in Judaism and for Maimonides (the author, it must be recalled of 'Thirteen Principles' of Judaism) is addressed in Abravanel, *Rosh amanah*, ch. 10, p. 79 of my Hebrew edition and p. 98 in my English translation. Abravanel missed an important source: *MT* 'Laws of Circumcision', 3: 9.

[37] *Kol ish va'ish mikol ba'ei olam*. On the significance of the term *ba'ei olam* in rabbinic Hebrew, see the remarkable study by Hirshman, *Torah for the Entire World*. That Maimonides understands the term to mean all human beings is made clear in *MT* 'Laws of Sanhedrin', 12: 3, and 'Laws of Kings', 8: 10.

[38] *Lehibadel*. It would have been helpful for the argument being made here had Maimonides used some variant of the root *p-r-sh* in this passage, but one must deal with texts as written, not as one would like them to have been written.

individual is as sanctified as the Holy of Holies, and his portion and inheritance shall be in the Lord forever and ever. The Lord grant him adequate sustenance in this world, the same as He had granted to the priests and to the Levites. Thus indeed did David, peace upon him, say, 'O Lord, the portion of mine inheritance and of my cup, Thou maintainest my lot' (Ps. 16: 5).[39]

Any human being (Jew or non-Jew) who sets herself apart from the foolishness of ordinary pursuits, behaves properly, worships God, and comes to know God,[40] is as sanctified as the Holy of Holies in the Temple in Jerusalem. Again, we see that holiness is a function of a kind of behaviour; it is not any sort of essentialist quality having any sort of ontological status. It is a name, not something really 'out there' in the universe.

The universal character of holiness emerges in a second passage in the *Mishneh torah*:

It is among the foundations of religion to know that God causes human beings to prophesy, and that prophecy does not rest upon anyone but a sage great in wisdom, powerful with respect to his [moral] qualities—[i.e.] one whose passions do not overpower him with respect to anything in the world, but, rather, through his intellect he always subdues his passions—and who has a very broad and well-established intellect. A person filled with all these qualities, sound of body, upon entering 'pardes' [i.e. Aristotelian physics and metaphysics, as Maimonides explained in *MT* 'Laws of the Foundations of the Torah', 4: 13] and continuously dwelling upon those great and remote matters, and having an intellect prepared to understand and conceive them, and who continues to *sanctify* himself, by separating himself from the ways of most people who walk in the darkness of the times, and who zealously trains himself and teaches his mind not to have any thoughts concerning vain things, the nonsense of the time and its snares, but his mind is always directed above, bound under the throne in order to understand those sacred and pure forms, and who examines the entire wisdom of God from the first form till the navel of the world, learning from this God's greatness; the holy spirit immediately rests upon him, and at the time the spirit rests upon him, his soul mingles with the degree of the angels known as Ishim and he becomes another man, and understands through his intellect that he is not as he was, but has risen above the degree of other wise humans, as it says of Saul: 'You will prophesy and become another man' (1 Sam 10: 6).[41]

---

[39] I quote (with emendations) from *Book of Agriculture*, trans. Klein, 403.

[40] By which I take Maimonides to mean that one can achieve intellectual perfection only after having achieved moral perfection (through performance of the commandments, at least where Jews are concerned); see above, Ch. 2 n. 71. I need not insist on this interpretation, however, in order to advance the argument being made here.

[41] 'Laws of the Foundations of the Torah', 7: 1, emphasis added, quoted from *Book of*

The sanctification spoken of here relates to the process of becoming a prophet. As is well known, Maimonides teaches that prophecy is a natural, human quality.[42] All humans (Jew and non-Jew) can, in principle, aspire to prophecy. One sanctifies oneself by separating oneself 'from the ways of most people who walk in the darkness of the times'. Becoming holy is a status open to all, and is achieved through certain kinds of elevated behaviour. If anyone can aspire to holiness, and if achieving it is consequent upon behaviour, holiness can hardly be ontological in any of the senses discussed above.

We may now return to our argument. In the *Mishneh torah* Maimonides makes holiness mean refraining from forbidden foods and forbidden sex. In his *Book of Commandments* he in effect explains this by connecting holiness to *perishut*. After explaining (again in the *Mishneh torah*) that the Pharisees were so called because they strove for a higher level of holiness through separation from improper behaviour and thoughts, Maimonides connects two distinct verses to make a single argument: 'Sanctify yourselves therefore and be ye holy' (Lev. 11: 44), 'for I the Lord Who sanctify you am holy' (Lev. 21: 8). Holiness, as defined here, leads to *imitatio Dei*.

The notion of *imitatio Dei*, in turn, is connected by Maimonides to holiness in a variety of interesting ways. In order to see this, we must look at the first text in which Maimonides discusses the imitation of God, *Book of Commandments*, positive commandment 8:

Walking in God's ways. By this injunction we are commanded to be like God (praised be He) as far as it is in our power. This injunction is contained in His words, 'And you shall walk in His ways' (Deut. 28: 9), and also in an earlier verse in His words, ['What does the Lord require of you, but to fear the Lord your God,] to walk in all His ways?' (Deut. 10: 12). On this latter verse the Sages comment as follows: 'Just as the Holy One, blessed be He, is called merciful [*raḥum*], so should you be merciful; just as He is called gracious [*ḥanun*], so should you be gracious; just as he is called righteous [*tsadik*], so should you be righteous; just as He is called saintly [*ḥasid*], so should you be saintly.'[43] This injunction has already appeared in another form in His words, 'After the Lord Your God shall you walk' (Deut. 13: 5), which the Sages explain as meaning that we are to imi-

Knowledge, trans. Hyamson, 42*a*. On this passage, see Kellner, 'Literary Character of the *Mishneh Torah*', 36–42.

[42] *Guide* ii. 32. See below, Ch. 7 nn. 7 and 123.

[43] Maimonides quotes here (in the original Hebrew, even though the *Book of Commandments* was written in Arabic) from *Sifrei Deut.*, 49, without the prooftexts found there.

tate the good deeds and lofty attributes by which the Lord (exalted be He) is described in a figurative way—He being immeasurably exalted above all such description.[44]

One imitates God through merciful, gracious, righteous, and saintly behaviour. The point is reiterated in the second text in which Maimonides deals with the imitation of God, in *MT* 'Laws of Moral Qualities', 1: 5–6:

The ancient saints trained their dispositions away from the exact mean towards the extremes; in regard to one disposition in one direction, in regard to another in the opposite direction. This was supererogation. We are bidden to walk in the middle paths which are the right and proper ways, as it is said, 'and you shall walk in His ways' (Deut. 28: 9). In explanation of the text just quoted, the sages taught, 'Even as He is called gracious, so be you gracious; even as He is called merciful, so be you merciful; even as He is called holy, so be you holy.' Thus too the prophets described God by all the various attributes, 'long-suffering and abounding in kindness, righteous and upright, perfect, mighty, and powerful', and so forth, to teach us that these qualities are good and right and that a human being should cultivate them, and thus imitate God, as far as he can.[45]

Maimonides changes his source here in interesting ways. *Sifrei*, followed by Maimonides in the *Book of Commandments*, spoke of mercy, graciousness, righteousness, and saintliness. The text here speaks of graciousness, mercy, and holiness. I will discuss the possible significance of this below, but let it be noted here that there is no known source for Maimonides' formulation. I have not examined all the known manuscripts of the *Sifrei*, but in printed texts the first time that 'holiness' is introduced into this discussion is here in 'Laws of Moral Qualities'.[46]

In the third text in which Maimonides discusses *imitatio Dei*, *Guide* i. 54 (p. 128), he reverts to the original formulation of *Sifrei*, or at least quotes part of it without the addition of holiness:

For the utmost virtue of man is to become like unto Him, may He be exalted, as far as he is able; which means that we should make our actions like unto His, as the

[44] Quoted, with emendations, from the Chavel translation, i. 12–13.

[45] Quoted, with emendations, from *Book of Knowledge*, trans. Hyamson, 47b–48a.

[46] The *Sifrei* passage is found, in various forms, in half a dozen places in rabbinic literature. Thanks to the help of my colleague Hillel Newman and of two computerized databases of rabbinic texts, I have found variants in *Midrash tana'im*, Deut. 11: 22; *Mekhilta derabi yishma'el*, 'Masekhet shirah', 'Beshalah', 3; *Mekhilta derabi shimon bar yohai*, 15; JT *Pe'ah*, 1: 1 (15b); BT *Shab.* 133b; Tractate *Soferim* 3: 17; and Tractate *Sefer torah* 3: 10. While some of the traditional commentaries on the *Mishneh torah* take note of the textual discrepancy, none seem to think it worthy of particular attention.

Sages made clear when interpreting the verse, 'Ye shall be holy' (Lev. 19: 2). They said: 'He is gracious, so be you also gracious; He is merciful, so be you also merciful' (*Sifrei* on Deut. 10: 12). The purpose of all this is to show that the attributes ascribed to Him are attributes of His actions and that they do not mean that He possesses qualities.[47]

Becoming God-like, Maimonides makes very clear here, means behaving in a particular fashion. To achieve holiness, and thus to imitate God, one must act graciously and mercifully. Maimonides is not even willing to attribute holiness to God in any sort of essential or ontological fashion. 'Holy, holy, holy! The Lord of Hosts! His glory fills all the earth!', said the prophet Isaiah, and what the prophet must have meant, according to Maimonides, is that God's actions are gracious and merciful. If Maimonides is so unwilling to attribute holiness to God in any sort of essential or ontological fashion, how reluctant must he be to attribute it to any other entities, persons, places, and times.

It is very difficult to know what the addition of holiness to the passage from *Sifrei* in 'Laws of Moral Qualities' signifies. It is possible that Maimonides had a different text in front of him, but I consider that highly unlikely, for a number of reasons. He quotes the received text in the *Book of Commandments* and repeats at least part of it in the *Guide of the Perplexed*. Second, it seems odd that only Maimonides should have had access to a version including holiness, one which is quoted in no other source. It seems more likely to me (as has been suggested by most of Maimonides' commentators) that he purposefully introduced into the passage from *Sifrei* a portion of another midrashic text, *Sifra* on Lev. 19: 2. That verse reads, 'You shall be holy, for I, the Lord your God, am holy', and on it *Sifra* says: 'As I am holy, so you be holy'.[48]

Is there any significance to this? In the context of our present discussion the following suggestion makes sense to me, but I must offer it tentatively, since there is no way of knowing whether it is true. By introducing 'holiness' into a passage talking of mercy and graciousness, Maimonides emphasizes the non-ontological character of holiness. Just as mercy and graciousness are matters of action and character, so also is holiness. It is just possible, in other words, that Maimonides alters the text of the *Sifrei* in a

[47] For a discussion of some of the textual issues here, see Michael Schwartz's note on this passage in his Hebrew translation of the *Guide* (p. 135 n. 35).

[48] This passage from *Sifra* is quoted by Maimonides in the text from *Guide* iii. 47, cited above, p. 91. For more on the textual issues here, see Schwartz's n. 18 on his translation of *Guide* iii. 33.

way not likely to arouse comment in order to hint at his non-ontological understanding of the holiness of persons.[49]

Up to this point I have focused on how a person achieves holiness. I have argued that, for Maimonides, holiness is not some sort of superadded property; it is the way in which Judaism characterizes what we might call (in a very non-Maimonidean idiom), 'God-liked' behaviour. One achieves holiness, not by becoming like God (hardly a possibility for any creature), but by imitating God's attributes of action; by acting, as it were, like God and, thus, in a way, being 'liked' by God. This being so, it should not surprise us to discover that it is behaviour too which brings about the opposite of holiness, profanation:

There are other things that are a profanation of the Name of God. When a man, great in the knowledge of Torah and reputed for his piety, does things which cause people to talk about him, even if the acts are not express violations, he profanes the Name of God. As, for example, if such a person makes a purchase and does not pay promptly, provided that he has means and the creditors ask for payment and he puts them off; or if he indulges immoderately in jesting, eating, or drinking, when he is staying with ignorant people or living among them; or if his mode of addressing people is not gentle, or he does not receive people affably, but is quarrelsome and irascible. The greater a man is the more scrupulous he should be in all such things, and do more than the strict letter of the law requires. And if a man has been scrupulous in his conduct, gentle in his conversation, pleasant towards his fellow-creatures, affable in manner when receiving them, not retorting, even when affronted, but showing courtesy to all, even to those who treat him with disdain, conducting his commercial affairs with integrity, not readily accepting the hospitality of the ignorant nor frequenting their company, not seen at all times, but devoting himself to the study of Torah, wrapped in Talith and crowned with phylacteries, and doing more than his duty in all things, avoiding, however, extremes and exaggerations—such a man has sanctified God, and concerning him, Scripture saith, 'And He said unto me, "Thou art My servant Israel, in whom I will be glorified"' (Isa. 49: 3).[50]

God's name can be sanctified or profaned: it depends entirely on how one behaves.[51]

---

[49] Note the discussion of this text in L. Kaplan, 'Maimonides and Soloveitchik', 504.

[50] *MT* 'Laws of the Foundation of the Torah', 5: 11, quoted from *Book of Knowledge*, trans. Hyamson,. 41a–b.

[51] Maimonides' view should be contrasted with that of Nahmanides, who glosses Lev. 19: 2 as commanding that Jews avoid ritual impurity. For discussion, see Silman, 'Introduction', p. xii, and Faur, *In the Shadow of History*, 12–13.

The People of Israel

Are the people of Israel holy? I will defend the view that, according to Maimonides, Jews as such are in no way distinct from non-Jews. By this I mean that Maimonides rejected any understanding of the election of Israel which presented Jews as ontologically distinct from non-Jews and superior to them. In whatever sense Israel may be called holy, it cannot be in ontological or essentialist terms.

Maimonides held Jews to be distinct from non-Jews only to the extent that the former adhered to the Torah. In that he never doubted the divinity of the Torah, Maimonides also never doubted that true adherents of the Torah were, with very few exceptions, better people than those who did not adhere to it. I am not trying to say that Maimonides denied the idea of the election of Israel; that would be ridiculous. He held the idea, but in an unusual fashion.

Maimonides' conception of the election of Israel reflects other ideas of his. One of these is his adoption of the Aristotelian notions that human beings are rational animals[52] and that, when born, humans are only potentially rational. Adopting a useful analogy suggested by Daniel J. Lasker, all humans are born with the same hardware. What we do with that hardware (i.e. the software we run) determines the kind of people we become.[53] Torah on this account is a challenge, not a gift; a demand, not an endowment.

Connected to all this is Maimonides' uncompromising and unprecedented insistence on strict doctrinal orthodoxy. In effect, for Maimonides, in the final analysis, it is what we affirm (after we have learned to behave properly) that makes us what we are.

All this being so, it should come as no surprise that Maimonides does not count belief in the election of Israel as one of the dogmas of Judaism; indeed, to the best of my knowledge, he only mentions the doctrine explicitly once in all of his writings.[54] In fact, Maimonides' nominalism makes it

---

[52] Discussed above, Ch. 2 n. 61.　　　　　　[53] Lasker, 'Proselyte Judaism'.

[54] *MT* 'Laws of Idolatry', 1: 3: 'After Moses had begun prophesying and God chose Israel as an inheritance, He crowned them with commandments and taught them how to worship Him.' God sent Moses to save the Jews in Egypt from a total relapse into idolatry. This, Maimonides says, God did 'out of His love for us and in order to keep His oath to Abraham'. God loves the Jews, not because they are ontologically unlike other nations, but because of the love Abraham showed God and the oath God in consequence made to him. My thanks to Professor Zev Harvey for drawing this text to my attention.

impossible for him to attach any special qualities to the people of Israel as such (as opposed to individual Jews). 'Israel' as a Platonic idea, so to speak, cannot exist. The term can be no more than a name, a convenient short-hand expression.[55]

Indeed, I think a case can be made that Maimonides distinguishes Jews, constituted by the descendants of Abraham through Isaac and Jacob, from Israel, constituted by a narrower circle of these descendants (and selected non-Jews[56]) who understand properly what the Torah demands of them and who satisfy those demands to some degree (see also the discussion in Chapter 7 below).

What, then, can we make of the holiness of the Jewish people? After all, the Torah itself teaches that the nation of Israel is holy:

'Now then, if you will obey Me faithfully and keep My covenant, you shall be My treasured possession among all the peoples. Indeed, all the earth is Mine, but you shall be to Me a kingdom of priests and a holy nation.' These are the words that you shall speak to the children of Israel (Exod. 19: 5–6).

and

For you are a people consecrated to the Lord your God: of all the peoples on earth the Lord your God chose you to be His treasured people. (Deut. 7: 6).

It seems clear to me that Maimonides must interpret passages such as these as normative and not descriptive. Indeed, this is precisely what he does with the first of them (he nowhere mentions the second[57]) in his *Book of Commandments*, as we saw above.[58]

In a passage from the introduction to the *Mishneh torah* cited above we find Maimonides explaining that Israel is sanctified through observance of the commandments. A fair way of reading this text[59] is that Israel is in no ontological sense holy; holiness is not what distinguishes Jew from non-Jew 'up front', so to speak. It is sanctificatory behaviour that sets Israel apart from all other peoples.

[55] It is relevant in this context to note that, while Maimonides devotes much attention to the question of how humans are to love God, with the sole exception of the text cited in the previous note he appears to avoid any mention of God's love for humans generally and for the people of Israel in particular.

[56] See *MT* 'Laws of the Sabbatical Year and the Jubilee', 13: 13.

[57] I rely here on Kafih, *Maimonides on the Bible*.

[58] In *Guide* ii. 35 (p. 368) Maimonides cites Exod. 19: 6 to emphasize the greatness of Moses; he cites the verse in a clearly normative and prescriptive fashion in iii. 8 (p. 435) and also in iii. 32 (p. 526).   [59] See above, p. 94 n. 27.

A number of other passages support the interpretation advanced here. In his famous responsum on music, Maimonides says as follows:

The truth has been clearly proven that the intent of our being a holy nation is that there be no action nor speech among us which does not concern itself with perfection or with that which leads to perfection; it is not in the release of forces which interfere with all that is good, nor that we abandon ourselves to debauchery and lightheadedness.[60]

Israel is a holy nation because of its behaviour; there is nothing intrinsic about it which makes it holy.

The same point, it appears to me, may be seen in a passage in *Guide* ii. 29 (p. 342) where Maimonides writes (apparently following Sa'adiah Gaon[61]):

For it sometimes happens that the seed remains while the name does not. Thus you can find many peoples that are indubitably the seed of Persia or Greece, but are not known by a special name, being absorbed in another religious community. This, to my mind, is likewise an indication of the eternity of the Law because of which we have a special name.

A reasonable reading of this passage is that Israel is Israel not because of any ontological characteristic, or special holiness, but because of its loyalty to the Torah.

I have found two places in his writings, however, in which Maimonides might be thought to be attributing holiness to the people of Israel in a descriptive, as opposed to a prescriptive, fashion. The first of these is *MT* 'Laws of Forbidden Intercourse', 19: 17:

All families are presumed to be of valid descent and it is permitted to intermarry with them in the first instance. Nevertheless, should you see two families continually striving with one another, or a family which is constantly engaged in quarrels and altercations, or an individual who is exceedingly contentious with everyone, and is excessively impudent, apprehension should be felt concerning them, and it is advisable to keep one's distance from them, for these traits are indicative of invalid descent . . . Similarly, if a person exhibits impudence, cruelty, or misanthropy, and never performs an act of kindness, one should strongly suspect that he is of Gibeonite descent, since the distinctive traits of Israel, the holy nation

---

[60] Maimonides, *Letters*, ed. Sheilat, 429. This is responsum no. 244 (p. 398) in Maimonides, *Responsa*, ed. Blau. For an English translation of the responsum, see Rosner, 'Moses Maimonides on Music Therapy', 8–10. For an easily accessible study of the responsum and its background, see B. Cohen, 'Responsum of Maimonides'. For an extensive bibliography of studies concerning the responsum, see Dienstag, 'Art, Science, and Technology', 165–8.   [61] Sa'adiah Gaon, *Book of Beliefs and Opinions*, iii. 7.

[*ha'umah hakedoshah*], are modesty, mercy, and lovingkindness, while of the Gibeonites it is said, 'Now the Gibeonites were not of the children of Israel' (2 Sam. 21: 2), because they hardened their faces and refused to relent, showing no mercy to the sons of Saul, nor would they do a kindness unto the children of Israel, by forgiving the sons of their king, notwithstanding that Israel showed them grace at the beginning and spared their lives.[62]

I think that it is fair to read Maimonides in this passage as writing persuasively. He wants to convince Jews to act with 'modesty, mercy, and lovingkindness' *so as to be* a holy nation.[63] This is certainly consistent with the way in which Maimonides reads texts attributing holiness to (or, actually, demanding it of) individuals, as we saw above.

The second passage is from *MT* 'Laws of the Sanhedrin', 25: 1–2:

It is forbidden to lead the community in a domineering and arrogant manner. One should exercise one's authority in a spirit of humility and reverence. The man at the head of the congregation who arouses excessive fear in the hearts of the members thereof for any but a religious purpose will be punished. It will not be given to him have a son who is a scholar, as it is written: 'Men do therefore fear him; he will not see any [sons] that are wise of heart' (Job 37: 24). He is also forbidden to treat the people with disrespect, even if they are ignorant. He should not force his way through the holy nation [*am hakodesh*][64] [to get to his seat].[65] For even if they be simple and lowly, they are the children of Abraham, Isaac, and Jacob, the hosts of God, brought forth out of Egypt with great power and with a mighty hand.[66]

In this passage Maimonides calls the Jewish people *am hakodesh*. The source of this expression is instructive: the prophet promises that the Jews will be called by a new name after the future redemption, 'the holy people, the redeemed of the Lord'.[67] The prophet is not characterizing the Jews as a

---

[62] *Book of Holiness*, trans. Rabinowitz and Grossman, 125.

[63] In Ch. 7 below I analyse this passage and show that it makes little sense to read it as if Maimonides is actually attributing particular moral qualities to Jews and to Gibeonites.

[64] See Isaiah 62: 12: 'And they shall be called the holy people, the redeemed of the Lord'.

[65] Literally: 'march over the heads of the holy nation'. As Herbert Davidson pointed out to me in a personal communication, Maimonides is simply using the language of his talmudic source here (BT *San.* 7*b*). This certainly weakens the position of any who might want to use this passage to support the claim that Maimonides attributes ontological holiness to the Jewish people.

[66] Cited, with emendations, from *Book of Judges*, trans. Hershman, 75.

holy people in the present, he is prophesying that they will be so called after the redemption. The appellation is predictive, not descriptive. Further, given the point Maimonides is driving home in this passage, that leaders should be meek in their demeanour (like Moses, as he explains in the continuation), it makes excellent sense for him to emphasize the special character of those led. Isaiah's expression works well for him in that fashion. It would be a mistake, it appears clear to me, to read out of this isolated expression a retreat from Maimonides' repeated position that holiness in people is a matter of their behaviour, not of their essence.

The Sanctity of the Land of Israel and of Jerusalem

A large number of scholars have written about Maimonides' understanding of the sanctity of the Land of Israel.[68] It is no doubt unfair to summarize a large number of fine studies in one sentence, but they all make much the same claim: for Maimonides, the Land of Israel is special because of what has taken place there and because of the commandments which can only be fulfilled there. Unlike Halevi, who held the sanctity of the Land of Israel to be something built into the universe from the instant of creation,[69] Maimonides understands its sanctity as historically contingent.[70] We see this in the following passage from the *Mishneh torah*:

All territories held by the Jews who came up from Egypt, and consecrated with the first consecration, subsequently lost their sanctity when the people were exiled therefrom, inasmuch as the first consecration was due solely to conquest and therefore was effective only during its duration and not for all future time. When

---

[67] Malbim's comment on this verse is exquisitely Maimonidean: the Jews will be *called* a holy nation thanks to the sanctity of their actions and their righteousness.

[68] In addition to Twersky, 'Maimonides on Eretz Yisrael', see Henshke, 'Legal Source'; Idel, 'Some Conceptions'; Kreisel, 'Land of Israel'; Levinger, *Maimonides as Philosopher and Codifier*, 88–99; Nehorai, 'Land of Israel'; Ravitzky, 'Awe and Fear', esp. pp. 18–22; Rosenberg, 'Link to the Land of Israel'; and Schweid, *The Land of Israel*.

[69] Most of the studies listed in the previous note also contain references to Halevi. In addition, see Alloni, *'Kuzari'*; Altmann, 'Climatological Factor'; Baer, 'Land of Israel'; and Melamed, 'Land of Israel and Climatology'.

[70] In a recent study, Ya'akov Blidstein summarizes the scholarly consensus (to which I subscribe) as follows: 'Halevi is presented as holding a "mythic" position, which attributes inherent meaning to the Land, while Maimonides is described as holding an "halakhic" view which attributes to it primarily an instrumental meaning' ('Living in the Land of Israel', 171). It is worth emphasizing that, for Halevi, prophecy is a phenomenon intimately connected with the Land of Israel, while for Maimonides prophecy is a perfection of the prophet, wherever she or he may reside.

the exiles returned and held part of the Land, they consecrated it a second time with a consecration that is to endure forever, both for its duration and for all future time. [The Sages, however,] left the places held by those who came up from Egypt, but not held by those who came up from Babylonia, in their former status and did not exempt them from the heave offerings and tithes, in order that poor people might derive sustenance from them during the Sabbatical year. Our saintly Rabbi [Judah the Prince], however, granted a dispensation to Beth-Shean, out of the places not held by those who came up from Babylonia, and it is counted with Ashkelon and is exempt from tithes.[71]

It is evident from Maimonides' discussion here and in many other places that the sanctity of the Land of Israel is a consequence of the commandments which obtain only in the land, and is so far from essentialist that in the past this holiness came and went, so to speak.[72] Maimonides is so clear in his position that even traditionalist non-academics among his students occasionally acknowledge this to be the case.[73] In most other cases this community of scholars seeks to read Maimonides as if he diverged very little from what they take to be the consensus of the Jewish tradition.

There is, however, one text in the *Mishneh torah* which seems to attribute to at least one place in the Land of Israel a holiness which goes beyond history and commandments. In 'Laws of the Temple', 6: 16, Maimonides writes:

Now why is it my contention that as far as the Sanctuary and Jerusalem were concerned the first sanctification hallowed them for all time to come, whereas the sanctification of the rest of the Land of Israel, which involved the laws of the Sabbatical year and tithes and like matters, did not hallow the land for all time to come?[74] Because the sanctity of the Sanctuary and of Jerusalem derives from the Divine Presence, which could not be banished.[75] Does it not say 'and I will bring

[71] 'Laws of Heave Offerings', 1: 5; quoted from *Book of Agriculture*, trans. Klein, 99.

[72] It is not my purpose here to argue whether or not Maimonides' understanding of holiness (as elucidated in this study) accurately captures normative Jewish teaching on the subject. I would like to note, however, that his approach seems accurately to reflect a reasonable way of reading the *locus classicus* for halakhic discussions of the holiness of the Land of Israel, Mishnah *Kel.* 1: 6–9. The Mishnah discusses rising levels of sanctity, all in terms of what may or may not be done in these places. Holiness in this text appears to be nothing more than a function of halakhah (and not the other way round).

[73] I have never seen this in print, but have heard it in public lectures.

[74] In his gloss on this sentence, Maimonides' critic, Abraham ben David of Posquières (*c.* 1125–98), rejects the distinction drawn here between Jerusalem and the rest of the Land of Israel, saying that Maimonides had no source for it.

your sanctuaries unto desolation' (Lev. 26: 31), wherefore the Sages have averred: even though they are desolate, the sanctuaries retain their pristine holiness. By contrast, the obligations arising out of the Land as far as the Sabbatical year and the tithes are concerned had derived from the conquest of the Land by the people (of Israel), and as soon as the Land was wrested from them the conquest was nullified. Consequently, the Land was exempted by the Law from tithes and from (the restrictions) of the Sabbatical year, for it was no longer deemed the Land of Israel. When Ezra, however, came up and hallowed the Land, he hallowed it not by conquest but merely by the act of taking possession. Therefore, every place that was possessed by those who had come up from Babylonia and hallowed by the second sanctification of Ezra is holy today, even though the land was later wrested from them; and the laws of the Sabbatical year and the tithes appertain thereto in the matter we have described in 'Laws of Heave Offerings'.[76]

This passage is important for our purposes for two reasons. On the one hand it confirms the widely accepted reading of Maimonides according to which the sanctity of the Land of Israel is historically conditioned, a *consequence* of Jewish possession of the land, not a precondition of it. As we see, this holiness 'comes and goes'.[77] All this seems to reflect the fact that for Maimonides, in principle, some other territory could have become the Holy Land had history worked out differently.[78] This passage is equally important, however, for appearing to affirm that, while all this is true of the Land of Israel in general, it is not true of Jerusalem, 'because the sanctity of the Sanctuary and of Jerusalem derives from the Divine Presence, which could not be banished'.[79]

A number of scholars have seen this passage as possibly expressing a

[75] Compare Maimonides' *Commentary on the Mishnah, Zev.* 14: 8, translated in Twersky, 'Maimonides on Eretz Yisrael', 286.

[76] I quote (with emendations) from *Book of Temple Service*, trans. Lewittes, 28–9.

[77] Which is most emphatically *not* to say that this holiness is unimportant in Maimonides' eyes, or that he did not have great affection for the Land. With respect to the former, see the analogy drawn above in Ch. 2 n. 11. That the holiness of the Land of Israel is strictly institutional, historical, and sentimental in no way diminishes its sanctity in the eyes of Maimonides—it is as sacred as any piece of territory can be. Continuing the analogy to which I just referred, we might say that, for Maimonides, God brought about a 'marriage' between the Jewish people and the Land of Israel. Seth Kadish originally suggested this line of thought to me. Maimonides' affection for the Land of Israel finds clear expression in *MT* 'Laws of Kings', 5: 9–12, on which see the important analysis by Blidstein, 'Living in the Land of Israel'.

[78] This, in turn, reflects the fact that, for Maimonides (as I understand him), Abraham chose God, not the other way round. See pp. 77–83 above.

[79] On the special sanctity of Jerusalem in Maimonides' thought, see Freudenthal, 'Jerusalem ville sainte?'.

'retreat' from Maimonides' generally teleological, historical, and institutional account of the holiness of the Land of Israel.[80] Eliezer Schweid has argued effectively against this, with specific reference to *MT* 'Laws of the Temple', 2: 1–2, where Maimonides writes:

The site of the altar was defined very specifically and it was never to be changed . . . It was on the site of the Temple that the patriarch Isaac was bound. . . Now there is a tradition known to all that the place where David and Solomon built the altar . . . was the same place where Abraham built the altar upon which he bound Isaac.[81] This, too, was the place where Noah built an altar when he came out of the ark. It was also the place of the altar upon which Cain and Abel offered sacrifice. There it was that Adam offered a sacrifice after he was created. Indeed Adam was created from that very ground; as the Sages have taught: Adam was created from the place where he made atonement.[82]

In connection with this passage, Schweid claims that Maimonides attributes to the Temple Mount no intrinsic (what I have been calling 'ontological') holiness; rather, he 'describes a history of sanctificatory acts which have marked it for the service of God and the atonement of sin. It is history, then, that has given this place peculiar significance.' Schweid sees the 'uniquely and eternally holy' character of the site of the altar as symbolizing 'on the one hand the fundamental relationship between God and His people, which He has undertaken to sanctify His name in the world, and on the other the status of this people's role in the history of the nations, from the very beginning of the human race'.[83]

I think that Schweid has made a valuable point, but it needs to be

---

[80] See e.g. Twersky, 'Maimonides on Eretz Yisrael', 285–6, and Ravitzky, 'Awe and Fear', 21 n. 86.

[81] Of course, if the entire event took place only in a prophetic vision, then Maimonides' words here take on a meaning very different from their plain sense, though certainly remaining amenable to the thrust of my discussion. This interpretation of Maimonides (quite reasonable in light of his claim in *Guide* ii. 42 that every time a prophet talks with an angel the conversation takes place in a vision of prophecy) was held by some of his medieval interpreters, as is demonstrated by Abravanel's impassioned response to them in his comment on *Guide* i. 8. Abravanel there faults Joseph ibn Kaspi (1279–1340) for holding this position. On Kaspi's position, see H. Kasher, ' "How Could God Command Us?" ', and Goetschel, 'Le Sacrifice d'Isaac'. Abraham Nuriel suggests that this interpretation, so disdainfully rejected by Abravanel, may very well have been Maimonides' actual position: see 'Are There Really Maimonidean Elements?', 154–7. For a discussion of medieval scholars who interpreted Maimonides in this fashion, see Schwartz, *Amulets*, 71–4.   [82] *Book of Temple Service*, trans. Lewittes, 10.

[83] Schweid, *Land of Israel*, 67. To my ears Schweid's last sentence sounds more Halevian than Maimonidean.

refined. In the passage cited here Maimonides emphasizes the significance of the site of the altar, while not talking of its holiness at all. Indeed, holiness is not at issue. Maimonides is explaining why the site of the altar must never be moved; he emphasizes the importance of its location by connecting it to a series of events of crucial importance for humanity in general (Adam, Cain and Abel, Noah) and to the Jewish people in particular (Abraham and Isaac, David and Solomon). In fact, if one wanted to read this passage as teaching something about the holiness of the site of the Temple, the message would have to be just as universal as Jewish (which calls to mind the passage from 'Laws of the Sabbatical Year and the Jubilee', 13: 13 cited above).

However, if one accepts the reading of 'Laws of the Temple', 2: 1–2, offered here, what of 'Laws of the Temple', 6: 16, according to which the sanctity of Jerusalem appears to be of a different quality than the sanctity of the rest of the Land of Israel? A complete answer to this challenge must involve a discussion of what Maimonides means by *shekhinah* ('divine presence'). He writes in 6: 16: 'Because the sanctity of the Sanctuary and of Jerusalem derives from the Divine Presence, which could not be banished'— a passage which I discuss in Chapter 6 below. Here let me just say that since, like Sa'adiah and others before him,[84] Maimonides takes *shekhinah* as synonymous with *kavod* ('divine glory'), the term cannot refer to any actual entity and must be read in some allegorical fashion. Whatever the *shekhinah* turns out to be for Maimonides, however, it is the presence of the *shekhinah* in the sanctuaries which makes them sacred for all future time.[85] The issue at stake here is not the nature of that sanctity but when it applies. Maimonides is very clear: the site of the Temple was chosen for its historical significance; the sanctity of the site is not a function of that historical significance. It is the sanctuary and not the place in which it stands which creates holiness.[86] The holiness in question is like every other holiness: institutional, instrumental, teleological, historical, but not ontological or essentialist.[87]

Another point must be made here. According to Maimonides' own

[84] See Altmann, 'Saadya's Theory of Revelation'.

[85] This is important: the ground on which the Temple is built is of great historical significance for Jews and for all humanity; but it *becomes* (and remains forever) sacred when the Temple is consecrated; it was not sacred before.

[86] Were that not the case, one would have to hold that the myriad places in the Wilderness of Sinai and in the Land of Israel at which the Tabernacle was 'parked' had permanent sanctity, like Jerusalem.

[87] In a private communication to me, Professor Zev Harvey offered an alternative

account, the Temple in Jerusalem and the Tabernacle in the wilderness before it were concessions to the primitive character of ancient Israel. In the best of all worlds, as it were, God would not have had to command their construction.[88] That makes the presence of the *shekhinah* in the Temple in Jerusalem an outcome of historical events which could have been different. Once again, the historical, contingent nature of the sanctity of the Temple is demonstrated.

This teleological-historical approach to the Temple site finds further expression in *Guide* iii. 45 (p. 575). In the context of explaining the commandments relating to the Temple, he writes:

It is known that idolaters sought to build their temples and to set up their idols in the highest places they could find there . . . Therefore Abraham our Father singled out Mount Moriah, because of its being the highest mountain there, proclaimed upon it the unity [of God], and determined and defined the direction toward which one would turn in prayer, fixing it exactly in the West. For the Holy of Holies is in the West.

According to this passage, Mount Moriah was chosen by Abraham, not because of its historical significance, not because of any essential holiness inhering in it, but simply because it was the highest mountain in the area.[89] Abraham needed a high mountain for the prosaic reason that idols were worshipped in high places. In establishing the worship of the one true God, Abraham chose a mountain which overshadowed those devoted to the service of false gods.

Maimonides also tells us here that it was Abraham's decision that anyone worshipping God on the Temple Mount would face west. For this reason, when the Temple was eventually built, the Holy of Holies was placed in its westernmost part. What is the reason for this? Again, the need to refute idolatry takes centre stage:

In my opinion, the reason for this is as follows: Inasmuch as at that time the opinion

explanation for Maimonides' comments on the special sanctity of Jerusalem: 'The root of Maimonides' special attitude toward Jerusalem is the halakhic directive that the Great Court sits in Jerusalem. The Shekhinah speaks through the decisions of the Great Court in Jerusalem, which constitutes the Oral Torah. The Great Court does not sit in Jerusalem because Jerusalem is holy, but Jerusalem is holy because the halakhah has determined that the Great Court sits there.' For more on the connection between *shekhinah* and Jerusalem, see my discussion in Ch. 6 below.

[88] For details see Ch. 4 below.
[89] This claim will surely surprise anyone who has had the privilege of looking *down* at the Temple Mount from Mount Scopus or from the Mount of Olives.

generally accepted in the world was to the effect that the sun should be worshipped and that it is the deity, there is no doubt that all men turned when praying toward the East. Therefore, Abraham our Father turned, when praying on Mount Moriah—I mean in the Sanctuary[90]—toward the West, so as to turn his back upon the sun.

The Holy of Holies is placed in the west for the simple reason that this opposes idolatrous belief—not because there is anything significant about this placement in and of itself.

Maimonides then goes on to claim that Abraham singled out the Temple Mount not just because of the accidental feature of its height, but by means of prophetic inspiration. The identity of the site was later known by Moses and others:

In my opinion there is also no doubt that the place singled out by Abraham in virtue of prophetic inspiration was known to Moses our Master and to many others. For Abraham had recommended to them that that place should be a house of worship, just as the translator sets forth when he says [in the Targum to Gen. 22: 14]: 'Abraham worshipped and prayed in that place and said before the Lord: Here will worship the generations', and so on.

What is the role of prophetic inspiration here? Maimonides may mean that through prophetic insight he knew of the other great events that had transpired at this site, or it may simply mean what the text says: that he knew prophetically that Israel would one day worship God on this site in a temple devoted to that purpose. In no way does it involve a retreat from Maimonides' non-essentialist understanding of the sanctity of the spot.[91]

A little further on in the chapter Maimonides refers to Mount Moriah as the 'place [which] is the final purpose of the Law on earth'. That may sound as if he is according the site much more than purely historical or teleological significance; he very quickly gives us reason to understand that such is not his intent. A few lines on, he writes:

It is known that these people built temples for the stars and that in that temple an

[90] It is not clear to me what Maimonides means by this. Kafih, in his comment on this passage, indicates that Maimonides held that Abraham, who is traditionally thought to have instituted the morning prayer, may have established a permanent place on the site in which he prayed every morning.

[91] It may even only mean that Abraham in this case had functioned with the first degree of prophecy (*Guide* ii. 45). Such an individual 'receives a divine help that moves and activates him to a great, righteous, and important action' (p. 396) but does not really prophesy. If this is the correct interpretation, then all that Maimonides is saying here is that Abraham was inspired (in the most general sense of the term) in his battle against idolatry.

idol whose worship was agreed upon was set up, I mean an idol assigned to a certain star, or to a portion of a Sphere. Consequently we were commanded to build a Temple for Him, may He be exalted, and place within it the ark within which were the two Tablets containing the words 'I [am the Lord]' and '*You shall not have*'.[92]

The 'final purpose of the Law on earth' is the utter destruction of idolatry and the establishment of the worship of the one true God.[93] It is *because* (and only because) idolatrous temples existed (and the Jews could not understand divine worship without sacrifices) that Israel was commanded to build a Temple to God, and to place within it the ark of the covenant, containing the tablets of the Decalogue, which teach the essence of Judaism: the existence of God and the non-existence of all other deities.

In sum, Maimonides' discussion in *Guide* iii. 45 of the connection between Abraham and the Temple Mount strengthens the claim that he saw the sanctity of the site in terms that were historical (the events of world-historical significance which occurred there) and teleological (the need to eradicate idolatry), and not in any sort of ontological fashion.

This interpretation is further confirmed in an unlikely place in the *Mishneh torah*. Maimonides devotes a whole chapter of 'Laws of the Temple' to a summary of the restrictions governing what may or may not be done on the Temple Mount. Because of the site's great holiness, the behaviour of visitors to the site is strictly regulated. Hardly an auspicious text in which to look for support for the non-ontological interpretation of holiness! However, in what appears to be an attempt to indicate to at least some of his readers that he should indeed be interpreted as I am doing here, he opens his discussion in 'Laws of the Temple', 7 with the following statement: 'It is a positive commandment to reverence the Sanctuary, for it is said: "You shall . . . reverence My Sanctuary" (Lev. 19: 30). This does not bid you revere the Sanctuary itself, but Him who commanded that we reverence it.'[94] The Torah commands one to behave with awe (*yirah*) towards the Tabernacle in the wilderness and later the Temple; not because of the

---

[92] *Guide* iii. 45 (p. 576). Emphasis added.

[93] For more on idolatry as the opposite of the whole Torah, see *MT* 'Laws of Idolatry', 2: 7–8, and the following passages from the *Guide*: iii. 29 (p. 521), iii. 30 (p. 523), iii. 37 (pp. 542, 545). See also *MT* 'Laws of Sabbath', 30: 15, cited at the end of this chapter.

[94] *Book of Temple Service*, trans. Lewittes, 29 (emended). Compare *MT* 'Laws of Ritual Slaughtering', 14: 11 (the very last paragraph in the *Book of Holiness*): 'When one performs the commandment of covering up the blood, he should do it, not with his

buildings or their sites themselves, but out of reverence to God who commanded their construction. The Temple is a tool in the process of purifying humanity from immorality and ignorance, and as such is very sacred. But this sanctity is a function of the Temple's glorious purpose, not a function of any essential characteristic which sets it apart from other buildings.[95]

Before ending this discussion, it is important to emphasize that Maimonides expresses great love for the Land of Israel. *MT* 'Laws of Kings', 5: 9–12, is a moving panegyric to the land and the love expressed for it by the talmudic Sages.[96] One can be deeply attached to a place because of its signficance without thinking that the place is in any way ontologically distinct from and superior to other places.[97]

Holiness, in people, is a function of what they do, not of what they are. To say that a person (or nation) is holy is to say nothing 'ontological' about them; it is to say much about how that person or nation acts. Similarly, to say that a place is holy is to say nothing 'ontological' about it; it is to say much about the history of the place and about how that place must be treated in a halakhic framework.[98]

---

foot, but with his hand, or with a knife or utensil, so as not to conduct the performance of the commandment in a contemptuous manner, thus treating God's commandments with scorn. For reverence is due not to the commandments themselves, but to Him who had issued them, blessed be He, and had delivered us from groping in the darkness by making the commandments a light to straighten out the crooked places and a light to teach us the paths of uprightness. And so indeed Scripture says, "Thy word is a lamp unto my feet, and a light unto my path"' (Ps. 119: 105). I cite the translation by Rabinowitz and Grossman, p. 322.

[95] Maimonides includes his discussion of the synagogue in the *Book of Love* and not in the *Book of Temple Service*. He apparently chooses to discuss the synagogue in its capacity as a venue for worship for all Jews, and not in its capacity as a replacement for the Temple. I wonder if this might be a subtle devaluation of the Temple: it is defined fundamentally as a place for sacrifices, not as a place for prayer, a higher form of worship for Maimonides.

[96] On this passage, see the discussion in Blidstein, 'Living in the Land of Israel'.

[97] One could, of course, examine the sanctity of the Temple implements (*kelei mikdash*), but since their sanctity is surely not qualitatively greater than that of the Temple, I do not see how such a discussion would add anything of significance to our understanding of Maimonides' conception of the nature of holiness. The same obtains with respect to tithes, etc.

[98] An interesting sidelight to our discussion of holy places is provided by *MT* 'Laws of Mourning', 4: 4. Maimonides writes there (about burial): 'A cave is dug in the earth. On the side thereof, a niche is opened, where the body is buried face upward; then the

Holy Things: Torah, *Tefilin*, *Mezuzot*

Maimonides devotes chapter 10 of *MT* 'Laws of *Tefilin*, *Mezuzah*, and the Torah Scroll' to a discussion of the sanctity of Torah scrolls. The chapter opens with a list of twenty defects, 'each of which renders a Torah scroll unfit; if one of them is found, the scroll becomes like the Pentateuchs from which children are taught. It does not have the sanctity of a Torah scroll and it is not read from publicly.'[99] But a Torah scroll written in the proper manner, with the proper implements, on the proper parchment, by a qualified scribe, is an object of great holiness.

Let us ask ourselves how and when the Torah scroll becomes holy. Apparently, this is at the moment when the scribe writes the last letter of the last word. Until this point, the scroll is like 'the Pentateuchs from which children are taught. It does not have the sanctity of a Torah scroll and it is not read from publicly.' What happens when the last letter is written? Were Maimonides an adherent of the ontological view of holiness, he would have to hold that, with the completion of the last letter, some superadded property becomes attached to what has up to that moment been a collec-

---

grave is covered with dust and stones. The dead may be buried in a wooden casket. The escorts say to the deceased: "Go in peace", as it is said, "But you shall go to your fathers in peace" (Gen. 15: 15). All the graves in the cemetery are marked, and a monument is erected over each. For the righteous, however, no monument need be reared; their words [*divreihem*] are their memorial; one ought not visit graves.' I cite *Book of Judges*, trans. Hershman, 174, liberally emended and corrected. The last phrase, 'one ought not visit graves', is found in no known source earlier than this text of Maimonides; see Kanyevsky, *Kiryat melekh*, ad loc. It appears to be his own addition. (In searching for a source, I checked the Bar Ilan University Responsa Project CD-ROM and discovered there that the passage in question came from the Higger edition of *Baraitot lemasekhet soferim*. But Higger, it turns out, cites Maimonides as his source! See Higger, *Masekhet semahot*, 246.) This phrase troubled some of Maimonides' commentators—medieval (Radbaz = David ben Solomon ibn Abi Zimra, 1479–1573) and modern (Kafih)—who went to great lengths not to take it literally. Assuming that Maimonides meant what he said (and I can see no reason not to take him literally here, and many reasons why one should), we find Maimonides teaching that one ought not to visit a whole class of sites—graves of the righteous—treated as holy by many Jews. For further discussion of this Maimonides text, see Horowitz, 'Speaking to the Dead', 313; Lichtenstein, 'Rambam's Approach Regarding Prayer', 28 ff.; and Bar-Levav, 'We Are What We Are Not', 19*–20*.

[99] 'Laws of *Tefilin*, *Mezuzah*, and the Torah Scroll', 10: 1. I cite my translation of the *Book of Love*, 107.

tion of skins and ink, rendering it holy. While I cannot prove textually that Maimonides did not hold this position, anyone familiar with the whole body of his writings is sure to find it unlikely. So what does happen when the last letter is properly written? With the writing of that letter, I submit, our collection of skins and ink achieves the *status* of a kosher Torah scroll. Because of that status, Jews are commanded to treat the scroll 'with extreme sanctity and great respect'. So much so, Maimonides continues, that 'it is forbidden to sell a Torah scroll, even if one has nothing to eat, and even if one owned many scrolls, and even in order to replace an old one with a new one'. In general, he goes on, 'It is never permissible to sell a Torah scroll except for two things: to study Torah with the money or to wed a woman with it. This on condition that one has nothing else to sell.'[100]

There is nothing in this passage that is not found in Maimonides' sources, and there is nothing in it which proves conclusively whether or not he held the sanctity of a Torah scroll to be ontological or institutional. Given the analysis of his attitude towards the holiness of persons, of nations, and of places presented here, however, it seems that the burden of proof is on one who wishes to attribute to Maimonides the view that the holiness of the Torah scroll is in some sense essentialist and ontological, not teleological and institutional.

Indirect support for the thesis that Maimonides did not attribute ontological holiness to Torah scrolls may be found if we take note of a distinction made by Boaz Huss in a study of the Zohar. Huss distinguishes between (*a*) an emphasis on the authoritative character of canonical texts; (*b*) an emphasis on the sanctity of the information contained in those texts (such that 'the text is believed to be a textual conduit between the community and the divine world . . . the study and exegesis of [such] sacred texts has a ritualistic character and may become part of the community's established rites'); and (*c*) an emphasis on the holy character of the non-semantic aspects of the book (such 'as the sound of its words, the form of its letters, as well as in the physical volume itself'). The recitation of such texts, 'even without understanding its content, is perceived as religiously potent'.[101] I have demonstrated elsewhere that, for Maimonides, the sanctity of the Torah is a function of its origin and its meaning;[102] its non-semantic aspects are important because of that origin and meaning, and as such are carefully defined by halakhah, but have no discernible significance

---

[100] *MT* 'Laws of *Tefilin*, *Mezuzah*, and the Torah Scroll', 10: 2.
[101] Huss, 'Sefer ha-Zohar': see pp. 262, 263, 295.
[102] See Kellner, 'Revelation and Messianism', and Ch. 5 below.

in and of themselves.[103] Maimonides' emphasis throughout is on the *authority* of the Torah and the role it plays in Jewish life.[104] He is interested in the message contained in the Torah scroll, and only secondarily in the scroll itself.

This interpretation of Maimonides is strengthened by a much-debated responsum of his. *MT* 'Laws of *Tefilin*, *Mezuzah*, and the Torah Scroll', 10: 1, reads:

> We thus find twenty matters, each of which renders a Torah scroll unfit; if one of them is found, the scroll becomes like the Pentateuchs from which children are taught. It does not have the sanctity of a Torah scroll and it is not read from publicly.

Despite this straightforward position, there is a responsum of Maimonides written in the margin of his own copy of 'Laws of *Tefilin*, *Mezuzah*, and the Torah Scroll', 7: 14, which complicates the picture. The text itself here reads:

> A Torah may be written book by individual book; these do not have the sanctity of a complete Torah scroll. One does not write a partial Torah,[105] containing various passages. Nor is a partial Torah to be written for children to study from; this is permissible if the scribe plans to finish at least one volume of the Pentateuch. It is permissible to write a partial Torah if one writes only three words on each line.

Maimonides was asked how a community which only had an invalid Torah scroll, or was without a Torah scroll altogether, should act:[106] should the public reading be done at all, and, if so, with or without the blessings over the reading of the Torah? In the responsum that appears in the margin Maimonides is quite emphatic: one ought to read, and one may make the blessing. The commandment over which the blessing is made, he insists, is studying Torah, not reading from a kosher Torah scroll: 'It is the study of the Torah [*hehagiyah batorah*] which is the commandment over which we make the blessing.' Making the blessings over readings from an invalid Torah scroll, he says, was the practice of the scholars of the West (i.e. Spain

---

[103] Thus it is not likely that Maimonides would attach much importance to the recitation of Torah texts without understanding them, and, so far as I know, there is not a single example of *gematriyah* or *notarikon* in all his writings. (Even in places where his sources use *gematriyah*, Maimonides does not; compare *Guide* i.15 with *Gen. Rabbah* 68: 12.) Compare also *MT* 'Laws of the Recitation of the Shema', 2: 8–10, with the glosses of R. Abraham ben David and my discussion of this text below in Ch. 5.

[104] This has interesting parallels to his views concerning the authority of the Sages (which is institutional, and not 'ontological'); see Kellner, *Maimonides on 'The Decline of the Generations'*.   [105] Here, and in the rest of the paragraph, *megilah*.

[106] *Responsa* (ed. Blau), no. 294.

and North Africa), such as Rabbi Joseph Halevi (ibn Megash) and Rabbi Isaac of Fez (Alfasi).[107] Most of the scholars of the East (presumably a reference to geonic Babylonia), on the other hand, did not understand the distinction between the act of reading and the act of studying and insisted that blessings be made only when a kosher Torah scroll was used.

This responsum has been the subject of considerable discussion and debate.[108] Solomon ben Abraham Adret (Rashba, *c*.1235–*c*.1310, cited in Joseph Karo, *Kesef mishneh* on 'Laws of *Tefilin*', 10: 1) asserted that this was a juvenile responsum by Maimonides, and that 'Laws of *Tefilin*', 10: 1, reflects his mature position. In his commentary, Karo opines that 'Laws of *Tefilin*' relates to behaviour in the first instance (*lekhathilah*,[109] while the responsum deals with a case where no kosher Torah scroll is to be had (*bede'avad*, *post factum*). Among our contemporaries, while Rabbi Rabinovitch cites the responsum without comment, Rabbi Kafih cites Rashba's position, to the effect that the responsum was written by a younger Maimonides, while the text in 'Laws of *Tefilin*', 10: 1, reflects his settled position. Karo's *Shulḥan arukh*, by the way ('Oraḥ ḥayim' 143: 2–3), rules that one may not make a blessing over an invalid Torah scroll.[110]

For our purposes, the distinction drawn by Maimonides in his responsum is most suggestive. That blessings are made over the reading of the Torah means that there is a commandment to so read. What is the nature of that commandment? Apparently, for Rashba, *Kesef mishneh*, *Shulḥan arukh*, and Rabbi Kafih (and many others), Jews are commanded to read from a kosher Torah scroll and it is only that reading which fulfils the commandment. For Maimonides, on the other hand, the commandment is to study what the Torah teaches, and for that an invalid Torah scroll, or even a Pentateuch, suffices. It seems to me that this much-debated responsum indicates that what primarily interested him was the Torah as an educational vehicle, not as a holy object.

These considerations, I admit, do not prove that Maimonides understood the nature of the sanctity of Torah scrolls in 'non-ontological' terms,

---

[107] On the scholars of the West, see Twersky, *Introduction*, 54 n. 85.

[108] See the notes in Blau's edition of the *Responsa*, and in Yosef's edition, pp. 29–33.

[109] In Jewish religious law, there are acts which are forbidden, yet, having been performed, bear no culpability. The term *lekhathilah* (roughly: 'before the act') relates to the question as to whether or not a certain act is permissible *ab initio*. *Bede'avad* (roughly: 'after the act') responds to the retrospective question of whether or not one has satisfied a requirement if it has been fulfilled incorrectly or in a less than optimal way.

[110] See also Levy, *Fixing God's Torah*, 188, 220.

but they surely add weight to that claim. So, too, does the following passage in 'Laws of *Tefilin*', 1: 19: '*Tefilin* and *mezuzot* may only be written in Assyrian script. It was permitted to write Torah scrolls in Greek as well, but in no other script. But Greek has sunk into oblivion, become corrupted, and lost. Today, therefore, all three are only written in Assyrian script.' In principle, a valid Torah scroll could be written in Greek (were the Greek language sufficiently well known), a point which strengthens the claim that it is the content of the scroll, and not the scroll itself as a physical object, which is the primary locus of its sanctity.[111]

Maimonides may not be unambiguous about the nature of the sanctity of Torah scrolls. Such, however, is not the case when we examine what he says about *tefilin* and *mezuzot*. In *MT* 'Laws of *Tefilin, Mezuzah*, and the Torah Scroll', 4: 25, we read:

The sanctity of *tefilin* is great since all the while *tefilin* are on a man's head and arm he is humble and filled with awe, is not attracted to laughter and wasted talk, and does not think bad thoughts; rather, he directs his heart to matters of truth and righteousness.[112] One should therefore strive to have them on him all day long, for that constitutes the commandment concerning them. It was said about Rav, the student of our Holy Rabbi [Judah Hanasi], that in his whole life he was never seen walking more than four cubits without Torah,[113] fringes, or *tefilin*.

This passage clearly presents what Twersky has called an 'instrumental' understanding of the sanctity of *tefilin*.[114] Their holiness consists in their impact upon the wearer.

It should be emphasized that *tefilin* are very holy indeed. Following the Talmud (*Men.* 36*b*, *Shab.* 12*a*), Maimonides writes:

One must touch one's *tefilin* continuously while wearing them, so that his attention not be diverted from them even for a moment, their sanctity being greater even than that of the High Priest's frontlet,[115] since on the frontlet God's name is written only once, while the Tetragrammaton occurs twenty-one times in the

---

[111] The interpretation of Maimonides urged here is hardly routine. Note the following comment by William Scott Green: 'These regulations suggest that rabbis regarded Torah-writing itself as a sacred object. The idea that a missing or added letter in the Torah's transcription could "destroy the world" (BT *Eruv.* 13*a*) and the notion that one grieves for damaged writing as one does for a deceased human being implied that rabbis construed the very letters of the Torah-writing not as mere signs of an immaterial discourse but as sacred in themselves' ('Writing with Scripture', 13).

[112] There are no clear rabbinic sources for Maimonides' assertions in this sentence.

[113] i.e. without studying the words of Torah (following Rashi on BT *Meg.* 28*a*).

[114] Twersky, 'Martyrdom and Sanctity of Life', 173.   [115] See Exod. 28: 36.

tefilin of the head, and similarly in the *tefilin* of the hand. ('Laws of *Tefilin*, *Mezuzah*, and the Torah Scroll', 4: 14)

This great holiness, however, is instrumental, teleological, and institutional, not essentialist or ontological.

Mezuzot are less sacred than *tefilin* ('Laws of *Tefilin*, *Mezuzah*, and the Torah Scroll', 5: 1), but hardly profane items. The *mezuzah*, like *tefilin*, is given a teleological or instrumental explanation:

One must take great care to fulfil the commandment of *mezuzah*, since it obliges everyone always. Every time one enters or leaves [his home] he will encounter the unity of God's name, remember His love,[116] awaken from his sleep and from his concentration on temporal vanities, and realize that nothing exists forever and ever but knowledge of the Rock of the Universe; one is immediately restored to one's senses[117] and follows the paths of the upright. The Sages said:[118] one who has *tefilin* on his head and his arm, and fringes [*tsitsit*] on his clothing,[119] and a *mezuzah* on his doorway is assured of not sinning, since he has many reminders; these are the angels which save him from sinning, as it says, 'The angel of the Lord camps around those who fear Him and rescues them' (Ps. 34: 8).[120]

One is commanded to wear *tefilin* and *tsitsit*, and to affix a *mezuzah* to one's doorpost in order to be reminded of what is truly important: God and the Torah. The *mezuzah* itself is not an amulet and does nothing; rather, it reminds us of things we ought to know. The instrumental character of this explanation is clear. Typically, Maimonides kills two birds with one stone here: he demystifies the *mezuzah* and at the same time takes advantage of an opportunity to explain that when the Sages (not only Maimonides) speak of angels in this context, they are speaking figuratively, and mean

---

[116] Although the Hebrew is ambiguous, it is clear that Maimonides means human love of God, as opposed to God's love of humans, since the text in the *mezuzah* includes the words (Deut. 6: 5), 'You shall love the Lord your God'; my thanks to Eliezer Zitronenbaum for pointing this out to me.

[117] i.e. focuses on what is truly important.

[118] BT *Men.* 43*b*. [119] See Num. 15: 37–41.

[120] *MT* 'Laws of *Tefilin*, *Mezuzah*, and the Torah Scroll', 6: 13. Anyone familiar with Maimonides' treatment of angels in the *Mishneh torah* and in the *Guide* will immediately realize that his use of the term here is figurative; see the discussion below in Ch. 8. Not everyone reads the passage in this fashion. See the translation by Touger, *Book of Love*, 130, who comments, '"these are the angels"—who are brought into being by his fulfillment of the mitzvot [of *tefilin*, *tsitsit*, and *mezuzah*].' This certainly proves the truth of Maimonides' observation in *Guide* ii. 25 (p. 327) to the effect that the gates of interpretation are never closed.

reminders. He thus furthers his project of reading the Sages as purveyors of the kind of Judaism that he himself taught.

Fringes (*tsitsit*) do not fit into our discussion here, since Maimonides codifies as law that they have no particular sanctity. Thus he writes:

> One may enter a privy or a bathhouse while wearing fringes. Torn white or azure threads may be thrown in the garbage, since the commandment bestows no sanctity on the object. One may not sell a *tallit* with fringes on it to a Gentile unless one unties the fringes first; not because the object has any sanctity, but lest the Gentile wrap himself in it, and accompany a Jew who will think that he is Jewish also, and thus the Gentile will be enabled to kill the Jew. ('Laws of Fringes', 3: 9)

Ignoring the sad comment on gentile–Jewish relations embodied in the last sentence of this extract, we see that fringes, unlike *tefilin* and *mezuzah*, have no sanctity, whether institutional or ontological.

It will be useful, I believe, to summarize this discussion of the nature of the sanctity of holy objects according to Maimonides with the following text from *MT* 'Laws Concerning Trespass in Regard to Sacred Objects [*me'ilah*]',[121] 8: 8:

> It is fitting for man to meditate upon the laws of the holy Torah and to comprehend their full meaning to the extent of his ability. Nevertheless, a law for which he finds no reason and understands no cause should not be trivial in his eyes. Let him not 'break through to come up against the Lord, lest the Lord break forth upon him' (Exod. 19: 24); nor should his thoughts concerning these things be like his thoughts concerning profane matters. Come and consider how strict the Torah was in the law of trespass! Now if sticks and stones and earth and ashes become hallowed by words alone, as soon as the name of the Master of the Universe was invoked upon them, and anyone who comported with them as with a profane thing committed trespass and required atonement even if he had acted unwittingly, how much more should man be on guard not to rebel against a commandment decreed for us by the Holy One, blessed be He, only because he does not understand its reason; or to heap words that are not right against the Lord; or to regard the commandments in the manner in which he regards ordinary affairs . . .[122] All of the sacrifices are included among the statutes (*hukim*); therefore the Sages said that the world depends even upon[123] the sacrificial cult,

---

[121] i.e. making profane use of hallowed things.

[122] Up to this point I cite the translation in Twersky, *Introduction*, 409. What follows from this point is my own translation, based upon the text as established in Henshke, 'On the Question of Unity', 38. See both Twersky (pp. 407–15) and Henshke (*passim*) for extremely valuable discussions of this passage.

[123] And not 'for' or 'thanks to' (*bishvil*) as many of the edd. have, as Henshke points out.

since it is through the performance of the statutes and ordinances (*mishpatim*) that the upright merit life in the world to come. The Torah commanded the statutes first, as it says, 'You shall keep My statutes and My ordinances, by the pursuit of which man shall live; I am the Lord' (Lev. 18: 5).

This is, of course, an important text for understanding Maimonides' explanation of the reasons for the commandments. Here, however, I want to focus on another aspect of this passage: 'sticks and stones and earth and ashes become hallowed by words alone', Maimonides tell us here, 'as soon as the name of the Master of the Universe was invoked upon them.' Items pledged to the Temple become sanctified, but 'all' that changes in them is their status, nothing else. That, at least, is how I think this passage must be read. There is another important point which this passage helps us to understand: holiness may reflect nothing ontological, nothing really 'out there' in the world, but that does not make it unimportant: 'Come and consider how strict the Torah was in the law of trespass!' Items pledged to the Temple are in no essential way different from identical items not so pledged; but the Torah is very strict concerning improper treatment of these pledged items. Holiness may be 'only' institutional in Maimonides' eyes, but that does not make it trivial.

Holy Times

The holiest of all Jewish holy days is the sabbath. Classic Jewish texts may not explicitly distinguish the sanctity of the sabbath from that of other holy times, but they certainly treat profanations of the sabbath as more severe violations than profanations of other holy times.[124] In one important sense the sanctity of the sabbath differs from that of all the other festivals: it occurs every seventh day; its occurrence is a direct function, so to speak, of God's creation. But the occurrence of other holy days (including even the Day of Atonement) depended originally upon the recognition of a new moon by the Sanhedrin in Jerusalem and depends today upon a humanly instituted calendar. God makes the sabbath; Israel makes the festivals.

If we can show that for Maimonides the holiness of the sabbath is not ontological, then we do not have to make a similar argument for other holy

---

[124] This point is made succinctly by Maimonides himself in *MT* 'Laws of the Sabbath', 1: 1–4, 'Laws of Repose on the Tenth of Tishrei', 1: 1–2, and 'Laws of Repose on a Festival', 1: 1–4. Violations of the sabbath are punished more severely than violations of the Day of Atonement, and violations of the Day of Atonement are punished more severely than violations of the three pilgrim festivals.

times; it will follow *a fortiori*.[125] Maimonides devotes a whole chapter of the *Guide* to the sabbath; it closes his discussion of creation. *Guide* ii. 31 (p. 359) opens with:

Perhaps it has already become clear to you what is the cause of the Law's establishing the Sabbath so firmly . . . It comes third after the existence of the deity and the denial of dualism.[126] For the prohibition of the worship of anything except Him only aims at the affirmation of the belief in His unity. You know from what I have said that opinions do not last unless they are accompanied by actions that strengthen them, make them generally known, and perpetuate them among the multitude. For this reason we are ordered by the Law to exalt this day, in order that the principle of the creation of the world in time be established and universally known in the world through the fact that all people refrain from working on one and the same day.

Maimonides explains here that there is a hierarchy of importance in Jewish beliefs: first in importance is God's existence; second is God's unity and

[125] The idea that the sabbath is in some ontological fashion distinct from the other days of the week (more correctly: that the sabbath is distinct from the days of the week, since it is not itself one of the days of the week) became a staple of kabbalistic thought. On this, see Idel, 'Sabbath'. On p. 82, for example, Idel states that Moses Cordovero 'conceives Sabbath not just as a moment in time propitious for the revelation of the holy, but as an entity, consisting of holiness and light, which descends in a certain moment upon the material world and is experienced by those who prepare themselves and their belongings so as to contain the presence of Sabbath.' As he explains (p. 88): 'It is their [i.e. the kabbalists'] belief in an ontology that relates special moments of time to divine hypostases that underlies the possibility of [the] experience [of the sabbath].' See also Idel's discussion of the theurgic character of the sabbath in kabbalistic thought in the same article (p. 76). According to Idel, the ontological and theurgic character of the sabbath reflects 'the creation of a strong metaphysics, of a supernatural realm that governs the lower world continuously, and in accordance to some recognizable laws, [which] affected dramatically the forms of experience that populate Kabbalistic literature' (p. 89).

[126] The first of Maimonides' Thirteen Principles teaches the existence of God, the second God's unity, the third God's incorporeality, and the fourth, creation. Creation is thus the third after 'the existence of the deity'. For discussion, see Kellner, *Dogma*, 54–61. Alternatively, as suggested to me by Seth Kadish, the first statement in the Decalogue teaches God's existence, the second forbids idolatry, the third forbids taking God's name in vain, and the fourth teaches about the sabbath, which makes 'it come third after the existence of the deity and the denial of dualism'. R. Kadish's interpretation involves taking 'the existence of the deity and the denial of dualism' to be the message of the first statement in the Decalogue, which is certainly an acceptable interpretation of Maimonides.

incorporeality;[127] and third is the creation of the world.[128] He then points out that even if one learns true opinions, such opinions will be forgotten or corrupted unless they are 'accompanied by actions that strengthen them, make them generally known, and perpetuate them among the multitude'. That is the purpose of the sabbath: to strengthen, make generally known, and perpetuate among the multitude the recognition that the world was created by God.[129]

The didactic character of the sabbath is made clear in an earlier text of Maimonides, his concluding peroration to *MT* 'Laws of the Sabbath', 30: 15:

Observance of the Sabbath and abstention from idolatry are each equivalent to the sum total of all other commandments of the Torah.[130] Furthermore, the Sabbath is an eternal sign between the Holy One, blessed be He, and ourselves. Consequently, if one transgresses any of the other commandments he is a wicked Jew, but if he publicly desecrates the Sabbath he is the same as an idolater; both are considered as Gentiles in every respect.

Jews are commanded to exalt the sabbath day, not because of anything intrinsic about it, not because in and of itself it is ontologically distinct from other days of the week, but so that they will not forget important philosophical and religious truths.[131] One could hardly ask for a clearer statement of the non-ontological character of sabbath holiness.[132]

---

[127] Views which, according to Maimonides, imply each other: if God is one, God cannot be corporeal, and if God is incorporeal, God must be one. See *MT* 'Laws of the Foundations of the Torah', 1: 7.

[128] On the importance of creation in Maimonides, see *Guide* ii. 25. In the sequel to the passage cited here, he writes: 'the belief in a true opinion—namely the creation of the world in time, which, at the first go and with the slightest of speculations, shows that the deity exists' (*Guide* ii. 31; p. 360).

[129] This point is repeated at the end of *Guide* iii. 32.   [130] See above, n. 93.

[131] The sabbath also serves to remind Jews of the Exodus from Egypt and to provide them with weekly rest, issues which Maimonides discusses in the remainder of *Guide* ii. 31.

[132] The startling nature of Maimonides' claims becomes clear if we examine a comment made by Joseph Dan, in the context of a discussion of certain kabbalistic views of holy times: 'If the universe is eternal, the concept of a "holy day" loses its meaning. Sabbath cannot be the seventh day after the creation, and Rosh Hashanah cannot be the day creation began. The division of the year into weeks and months becomes arbitrary, as there is no meaningful starting point. As so much of the *halachah* is based on specific

Maimonides' statements on the nature of holiness should be understood in the light of his position that, according to the Torah, nothing is handed to one on a silver platter. Yeshayahu Leibowitz used to proclaim that Judaism is not an 'endowing' religion but a 'demanding' religion. In this, at least, he appears to reflect a Maimonidean perspective faithfully. In place of what I have been calling the 'ontological' view of holiness, according to which holiness is a 'gift' granted by God, Maimonides proposed a view of holiness which granted little, but demanded much. He did so in a finely nuanced and subtle fashion, without calling attention to the unusual character of his views. Jews found it comforting to read Leviticus 11: 45, 'You shall be holy', as a statement of the special character of their God-given nature. Maimonides read that verse as an imperative—as a challenge to Jews to act in a way befitting the nation that had received the Torah. The job of the Torah is not to make Israel comfortable with the real, but to challenge it to draw ever closer to the ideal.

sacred times, the adoption of the concept of a noncreated world is intrinsically anarchic and antinomianistic? The upshot of Maimonides' view of sacred times is not that the cosmos is uncreated, but, rather, that it is not truly important that the sabbath is actually the seventh day after creation or that Rosh Hashanah actually marks the day creation began. Anyone brought to Jewish maturity believing that sabbath and Rosh Hashanah actually mark the weekly and annual anniversary of creation will have a hard time not seeing Maimonides' view as 'intrinsically anarchic and antinomianistic' (even though he or she would be clearly wrong). See Dan, 'Nachmanides', 413. For further background on the sabbath in kabbalah, see Ginsburg, 'Sabbath' and, more recently, Hallamish, 'Sabbath'. For a discussion which emphasizes the radical differences between Maimonidean and kabbalistic views on the sabbath (and, in the eyes of its author, the radical differences between Maimonidean and rabbinic thought on the sabbath), see Tishby, *Wisdom of the Zohar*, iii. 1216–18 and 1261.

FOUR

Ritual Purity and Impurity

֍

Introduction: Two Ancient Views on Ritual Purity and Impurity

IN ONE OF ITS SENSES, as we have just seen, the term 'holiness' stands in opposition to ritual impurity. Biblical and rabbinic texts, when taken together, seem to allow for a wide variety of approaches to the meaning of ritual purity and impurity (*toharah* and *tumah*).[1] Here I want to focus on two such approaches, arguing that Maimonides was familiar with them both and that he adopted one and consciously rejected the other.[2] His

[1] Translating these terms into English is problematic. The translation used here is rejected in Neusner, *Idea of Purity*, 1, on the grounds that the terms 'ritual purity and impurity' imply that we are dealing with something which is not real, substantive, or actual, and because it appears to be the antonym of 'moral' purity and impurity. Since my argument here is meant to show that Maimonides denies that *toharah* and *tumah* have any real, substantive, or actual existence, using the translation 'ritual purity and impurity' seems perfectly apt (although by using these terms I do not mean to beg the question at issue here). Moreover, my ears do not pick up the opposition to moral purity that Neusner hears in the term 'ritual purity'. Maimonides' understanding of the moral character of *toharah* and *tumah* will be discussed below. For the sake of consistency, I have emended all the translations used below so that *toharah* is always translated 'ritual purity' and *tumah* as 'ritual impurity'.

[2] Scholars are deeply divided over how the authors of the Bible and of rabbinic texts understood the nature of ritual purity and impurity. Neusner contrasts the views of W. Robertson Smith and Yehezkel Kaufmann, on the one hand, with the view of Baruch Levine on the other. The former, as cited by Neusner, see purity 'as a status, and not as expressive of the presence of demonic forces operating independently of the will of one, omnipotent God. Baruch Levine has most recently formulated the second view. It holds that impurity results from the working of destructive or demonic forces which may operate independently of the will of God and may threaten the deity in the same way as man. Impurity is not merely a status and is not limited to the cult, though it is most dangerous there, because in the cult the domicile of the deity is affected' (p. 8). According to Smith, as presented by Neusner, 'Taboos about purity are reduced to an aspect of the will of the divinity'; while according to Levine, 'priestly literature takes for granted the independent, active existence of demonic forces. Impurity is not a state of being, but an

position on this matter is another expression of the sort of religious sensibility he sought to inculcate in his readers, and in addition teaches us about the sort of religious sensibility against which he sought to inoculate them.[3]

Maimonides made a conscious choice between two competing views of the nature of ritual purity and impurity, accepting one and rejecting the other. What are these two views? They are well captured by a pair of texts. *Heikhalot rabati* reports that the students of Rabbi Nehuniah ben Hakanah wished to recall him from what appears to have been a mystical experience without endangering him. The text reports as follows:

Immediately I took a very fine woollen cloth[4] and gave it to Rabbi Akiba, and Rabbi Akiba gave it to a servant of ours, saying: 'Go and lay this cloth beside a

active force. Impurity is demonic, and demonic forces of impurity endanger men and deities, just as in other ancient Near Eastern religions' (pp. 9–10). For Smith and Kaufmann, monotheism 'effects so complete a revolution in the antecedent Israelite cult that all traces of polytheist conception of impurity as a source of independent demonic power are wiped out. For Levine the Israelite cult is perceived in the context of the other cults of the same time and place' (p. 11). Neusner agrees with Levine with regard to the biblical materials. Rabbinic texts, he holds, teach an entirely different theory of purity and impurity. 'In talmudic law purity is indeed made relative. The talmudic purity laws comprise and create a wholly abstract set of relationships, a kind of non-Euclidean geometry of the cultic realm' (p. 16). For a view similar to Levine's, see Milgrom, *JPS Torah Commentary, Numbers*, 161, who holds that the original biblical notion of impurity was of 'a dynamic, physical substance exuded by the contaminated body'. He sees it as a 'physical miasma'. Neusner's claims that the Bible sees ritual purity and impurity in what I would call ontological terms, and that there is a radical break between biblical and rabbinic perspectives, were criticized in Maccoby, *Ritual and Morality*. Maccoby argues that the biblical system of ritual purity and impurity serves a consciously moral end. The issue of who is right in these debates is not really important to me here. What is important is that the scholars mentioned all agree that biblical texts and rabbinic texts teach *either* that laws of ritual purity and impurity reflect what might be called ontologically significant distinctions or that they do not. For a recent and extremely lucid study, see Klawans, *Impurity and Sin*. Some of Klawans's distinctions seem to have been anticipated by Maimonides. Klawans is also the author of a detailed critique of some of Milgrom's views; see Klawans, 'Ritual Purity'.

[3] Of course, I am not the first student to take note of the unusual character of Maimonides' views on the subject of ritual purity and impurity (see, for example, the very important comments of Henshke, 'On Judicial Reality'), but I am not aware of other attempts to see in these views a reflection of a much broader religious orientation on Maimonides' part, as I do here.

[4] A soft, white cloth, appropriate for intimate examinations of menstrual purity.

woman who immersed herself a second time.[5] For if that woman will come and declare the circumstances of her menstrual flow[6] before the company, there will be one who forbids her to her husband and the majority will permit. Say to that woman: "Touch this cloth with the end of the middle finger of your hand, and do not press[7] the end of your finger upon it, but rather as a man who takes a hair which had fallen therein from his eyeball, pushing it very gently". They went and did so, and laid the cloth before Rabbi Ishmael. He inserted it into a bough of myrtle full of oil [of foliatum] that had been soaked in pure balsam[8] and they placed it upon the knees of Rabbi Nehuniah ben Hakanah; and immediately they dismissed him from before the throne of glory where he had been sitting and beholding:

> Wonderful loftiness and strange dominion,
> Loftiness of exaltation and dominion of majesty,
> Which come to pass before the throne of glory,
> Three times each day, in the height,
> From the time the world was created and until now, for praise.[9]

As Lawrence Schiffman points out, the principle operating here seems to be that of the least possible impurity.[10] The real, objective power of menstrual impurity is such that if a woman who is ritually pure halakhically, but about whom a minority of authorities would hold that she might still be ritually impure, were to touch glancingly a clean cloth, and that cloth was wrapped around a myrtle bough full of oil which had been soaked in an extremely valuable spice (balsam), and the bough then placed upon the knees of a person engaged in a heavenly ascent, this would be enough to shatter the connection between the person making the heavenly ascent and his or her heavenly partners. Ritual impurity, according to the evidence of

---

[5] BT *Nid*. 67a.   [6] i.e. a minor question concerning her ritual purity persists.

[7] From the root *d-r-s*, which indicates a form of contact which imparts ritual impurity.

[8] i.e. the myrtle bough had been soaked in pure balsam and was itself full of oil of foliatum; the fine white cloth was wrapped around this bough.

[9] I cite the translation by Morton Smith published in Scholem, *Jewish Gnosticism*, 10.

[10] See Schiffman, 'Recall', 274. Seth Kadish pointed out to me that one of the matters at issue here is that, according to this text, an entity held to be ritually impure only by minority opinion (which means that in technical halakhic terms it is ritually pure) can still have an extremely minor but actual ritual impurity. In other words, according to this view the power of ritual impurity is greater than or at least independent of established halakhah.

this text, is a powerful force in the universe.[11] This force exists independently of halakhah, or, perhaps better, prior to halakhah. It can effect real changes in the world of objective reality.[12] According to the view found in this text, ritual impurity is hypostasized—it is seen as a force or substance having objective reality, a force or substance which can harm and which must be resisted, subdued, overcome. In line with my discussions above, I call this the 'ontological' view of ritual impurity.

Another view of ritual purity and impurity is also found in ancient Jewish literature:

An idolater asked Rabban Johanan ben Zakai: 'These rites that you perform look like a kind of witchcraft. You bring a heifer, burn it, pound it, and take its ashes. If one of you is defiled by a dead body you sprinkle upon him two or three drops and you say to him: "Thou art ritually pure!"' Rabban Johanan asked him: 'Has the demon of madness ever possessed you?' 'No,' he replied. 'Have you ever seen a man possessed by this demon of madness?' 'Yes,' said he. 'And what do you do in such a case?' 'We bring roots,' he replied, 'and make them smoke under him, then we sprinkle water upon the demon and it flees.' Said Rabban Johanan to him: 'Let your ears hear what you utter with your mouth! Precisely so is this spirit a spirit of ritual impurity; as it is written, "And also I will cause the prophets and the ritually impure spirit to pass out of the land" (Zech. 13: 2). Water of purification is sprinkled upon the ritually impure and the spirit flees.' When the idolater had gone Rabban Johanan's disciples said to their master: 'Master! This man you have put off with a mere makeshift, but what explanation will you give to us?' Said he to them: 'By your life! It is not the dead that defiles nor the water that purifies! The Holy One, blessed be He, merely says: "I have laid down a statute, I have issued a decree. You are not allowed to transgress My decree"; as it is written, "This is the statute of the law" (Num. 19: 2)'.[13]

---

[11] For a clear expression of ritual purity thus understood, see the following comment in Douglas, *Purity and Danger*, 114: 'It follows from this that pollution is a type of danger which is not likely to occur except where the lines of structure, cosmic or social, are clearly defined. A polluting person is always in the wrong. He has developed some wrong condition or simply crossed some line that should not have been crossed and this displacement unleashes danger for someone. Bringing pollution, unlike sorcery and witchcraft, is a capacity which men share with animals, for pollution is not always set off by humans. Pollution can be committed intentionally, but intention is irrelevant to its effect—it is more likely to happen inadvertently.'

[12] For more on this text, see Lieberman, 'Knowledge of the Halakhah', and Swartz, *Scholastic Magic*, 170–2.

[13] The text is found in *Num. Rabbah* 19: 8. I cite the Soncino translation with minor changes. For parallels, see *Tanḥuma*, 'Ḥukat' 8, *Pesikta rabati* 14: 14, and *Pesikta derav kahana*, 4: 7. For discussion of the text, see Neusner, *Idea of Purity*, 105; E. Urbach, *Sages*, i. 99; Goldin, 'Magic of Magic', 342–3, and Silman, 'Introduction', pp. viii–x.

It is reasonable, I think, to read this passage as does Urbach: 'this ritual of the sprinkling of the water of purification, which was prepared with the ashes of the heifer, has only a ceremonial significance. A corpse defiles, for this is the halakhic rule, but this ritual impurity is not an independent power, nor has the water any magical force; however, it is a precept, and by virtue of the precept, the corpse defiles and the water purifies.'

If the text from *Heikhalot rabati* sees the laws of ritual purity and impurity as reflecting an objective reality, I take the story here as teaching that the laws of ritual purity and impurity do not reflect any objective reality, though they certainly create a halakhic reality.

I should like to try to explain this point further with the example of an allergy: I am deeply allergic to cats, and if exposed to them usually get an attack of asthma. Similarly, there is a long tradition in Judaism which holds that Jews are 'allergic' to ritual impurity and that exposure to ritually impure objects actually affects Jews in a way parallel to that in which exposure to cats actually affects me. The effects of ritual impurity on Jews may not be measurable by any known sensing device, but they are none the less real and important. This seems to be the view of *Heikhalot rabati* and a long tradition of subsequent Jewish texts.[14] The same tradition seems to hold that eating unkosher food, for example, does not harm non-Jews, but in some real (but not physical) way harms Jews.[15]

Judah Halevi on Ritual Purity and Impurity

The debate I find between the text from *Heikhalot rabati* and the story about Rabban Johanan ben Zakai is reflected in medieval Jewish thought. Judah Halevi seems close to the position reflected by the *Heikhalot rabati* text, while Maimonides adopts that expressed in the story of Rabban Johanan.

---

[14] The most emphatic of which appears to be an unusual and controversial composition called *Baraita demasekhet nidah*, the text of which was edited by Evyatar Marienberg in his doctoral dissertation, 'Niddah'. Several scholars have examined aspects of this tradition, with special reference to menstrual impurity. See S. J. D. Cohen, 'Purity and Piety'; Dinari, 'Customs'; id., 'Profanation of the Holy'; Woolf, 'Medieval Models'; Kanarfogel, '*Peering through the Lattices*', 127–30; and Swartz, *Scholastic Magic*, 164, 214–15. On *Baraita demasekhet nidah* in particular see the comments by Lieberman, 'Knowledge of the Halakhah'. For more on this, see the very helpful dissertation by Koren, ' "The Woman from whom God Wanders" '.

[15] For an example of how these ideas developed in Judaism after Maimonides, see Idel, ' "Reasons for Unkosher Birds" '.

While Judah Halevi never addresses the point directly (not that there is any reason for him to have done so), there are a number of passages in the *Kuzari* from which it seems fairly apparent that he attributed some sort of reality to matters of ritual purity and impurity, i.e. that he attributed to them what I have been calling ontological as opposed to purely institutional standing.

One such indication is found in *Kuzari* ii. 14. Just as a fruit tree growing poorly in the desert will flourish if moved to a more appropriate place, so the Jewish people flourish when in the Land of Israel. The Jews 'grew numerous during their stay in the Holy Land in conjunction with those concomitants that are helpful [in this regard], such as rites of purification [*al-taharat*], acts of worship, and sacrifices, especially when these were carried out in the presence of the Divine Presence.' Even a fruit tree moved to a fertile place needs water and other care if it is to flourish, and so, too, the Jews in the Land of Israel need to 'water themselves spiritually' if they are to flourish. A Jew wishing to flourish Jewishly in the Land of Israel must, among other things, perform the rites of purification.

This passage seems to indicate that, for Halevi, being ritually impure is a state to be avoided and that purifying oneself from states of impurity is a condition for Jewish flourishing. In contrast, as we shall see below, Maimonides holds that if one has no technical need for ritual purity (such as entering the Temple precincts), one may remain ritually impure without being harmed in any way.

Another passage relevant to our theme is found in *Kuzari* ii. 60. It is there that Halevi makes his well-known and influential claim that most forms of ritual impurity are connected in one way or another to death. Leprosy (i.e. the biblical *tsora'at*, not the illness today known as Hansen's disease) and seminal emissions, he explains, are 'contrary to the specific character of life and spirit'. They reflect a corruption which is objectively real. 'Because of its fineness, corruption like this may not be perceived except by those who are endowed with refined spirits and noble souls'; but that does not make it any less real. Gamma rays, for example, objectively existed before their effects were noticed and a way was invented to detect them; similarly, the effects of ritual impurity objectively exist and are evident to those 'endowed with refined spirits and noble souls'.

This, Halevi asserts, is a matter of empirical truth:

Of course, some people have found a certain heaviness within their souls whenever they are not purified of their major ritual impurities. It is already well attested by experience that they [the major forms of ritual impurity] corrupt fine things like flowers and wines by their touch, and most of us also undergo some change on coming close to corpses and graves. Their souls are also disturbed for a while when they are in a house in which there was a dead body, whereas someone whose heart is insensitive undergoes no change on that account.

As I understand him, Halevi is not here describing emotional reactions to death, but reactions on another plane altogether, which have emotional consequences. Dead bodies are corrupting, both psychologically and onto-logically, as it were.

In *Kuzari* iii. 21 Halevi indicates that one should be mindful of ritual impurity when mentioning God—that is, one should strive to be ritually pure when saying God's name. Since God is mentioned in all the prayers, and since the truly worshipful human being should have God in mind at all times, it would appear that ritual impurity is not simply a technical prob-lem but a serious impediment to the religious life.

Kuzari iii. 53 discusses the power of the Torah to effect change in the world in which we live. It is through pronouncements made in accordance with specific intentions, sometimes coupled with specific behaviours, that objects become sanctified, for example, or women betrothed. The thrust of Halevi's discussion here is that these changes are not just matters of con-vention but, rather, that some real change takes place in some super-social realm. This becomes clear when he says:

The divine order [*al-amr al-ilahi*] used to indwell with every single one of these acts because the practices prescribed by the religious Law are like beings that are generated naturally, all of which are determined by God, exalted be He, inasmuch as their determination is obviously not within the power of a human being, just as you see that beings generated naturally are determined, given proper balance, and appropriately related to one another in terms of their physical constitutions.

Halevi concludes this discussion by asking rhetorically, 'Who, then, but God alone is able to determine works in this way so that the divine order dwells within them?' Properly incubated eggs become chickens, Halevi explains, thanks to the way in which God ordered the natural universe. Similarly, it seems fair to say in Halevi's name that Jews who touch a corpse become ritually impure in the first degree, thanks to the way in which God has ordered the supernatural universe.

My interpretation is supported by the sequel. 'Actions prescribed by the religious Law', Halevi argues, 'when completed in the proper way', have concrete results in the world:

You see the heavenly fire or discover another spirit within yourself, which you did not know beforehand, or you witness veridical dreams and miracles, you know that they are the result of all that you did before and of the mighty order with which you have come into contact and which you have now actually attained.

So, if I understand Halevi correctly, rites of purification remove something in the person that was really there; they do not simply change the person's status in the eyes of the law. In this, as in so many matters, Maimonides wrote as if one of his main objectives was to replace the Judaism of Judah Halevi with a very different version of the faith.[16]

Maimonides on Ritual Purity and Impurity

Maimonides consciously adopted the position I find expressed in the Rabban Johanan story and consciously rejected the position apparently expressed by *Heikhalot rabati*.[17] It is important to note that in making this

[16] Not surprisingly, Nahmanides seems to follow Halevi, not Maimonides, in his view of the nature of ritual impurity. For an indication of this, see his comment on Lev. 16: 4 (near the end). More evidence of this may be found in his comment on Lev. 19: 2, especially as analysed in Faur, *In the Shadow of History*, 12–13. See also the comment of Yuter, 'Positivist Rhetoric', 156: 'A third critique of Maimonides stems from Nahmanides, who does not believe that Jewish normativity can be defined solely on the basis of the absolute, hard, cold statute.'

[17] I do not mean to imply that Maimonides knew the text from *Heikhalot rabati* cited above (I have no idea whether he did or not), only that he knew and rejected the view of ritual impurity assumed by the text. Nor do I mean to imply that his views are unprecedented. Maimonides' view on the nature of ritual purity and impurity seems to reflect at least one strain of rabbinic thought. A large number of midrashim (among which may be cited *S. of S. Rabbah* 2: 15, *Lev. Rabbah* 8: 3 and 26: 2, and *Midrash Ps.* 12) state that 'children in David's days, before they had yet experienced the taste of sin, knew how to expound the Torah by adducing forty-nine reasons for declaring a thing unclean and forty-nine reasons for declaring it clean'. Similarly, the Talmud (BT *San.* 17*a*) quotes R. Judah in the name of Rav: 'None is to be given a seat on the Sanhedrin unless he is able to prove the ritual purity of a [ritually impure] reptile from biblical texts.' (I might add that Tosafot ad loc. were clearly troubled by this statement; it is more than likely that the authors of the Tosafot, by and large, held to an ontological view of the nature of ritual purity and impurity and would therefore find this statement puzzling in the extreme.) The upshot of these two passages is that ritual purity/impurity is a matter of law, not nature. My thanks to Dr Avram Montag for drawing my attention to the significance of these passages in this context. Maimonides is, furthermore, preceded by Sa'adiah Gaon, who, in *Beliefs and Opinions* vi. 4, wrote: 'the body of man contains no ritual impurity at all. It is, on the contrary, entirely ritually pure, for ritual impurity is neither a thing that is subject to sense perception nor a requirement of logic. It is purely a decree of the law of the Torah. This law has declared ritually impure certain secretions of human beings after they discharge from the body, although they do

claim I am not stating the obvious. For a clear expression of this, see the *Or hahayim* of Hayim ben Moses Attar on Numbers 19: 2. The *Or hahayim* is a widely influential commentary on the Pentateuch and in the passage in question the author attributes a profoundly ontological understanding of the nature of ritual impurity to Maimonides, and does so without the least awareness that this attribution is at all questionable.[18] That it is questionable is apparent from Maimonides' discussion of the reasons for the commandments of ritual purity and impurity in *Guide* iii. 47:

As for His dictum, may He be exalted, 'Sanctify yourselves therefore and be ye holy, for I am holy' (Lev. 11: 44), it does not apply at all to ritual impurity and purity. *Sifra* states literally: This concerns sanctification by the commandments. For this reason, transgression of the commandments is also called ritual impurity . . . The term ritual impurity is used equivocally in three different senses: It is used of disobedience and of transgression of commandments concerning action or opinion; it is used of dirt and filth . . . and it is used according to these fancied notions,[19] I refer to touching or carrying certain things or being under the same roof with certain things.[20] With reference to this last sense, we say: 'The words of the Torah are not subject to becoming impure'.[21] Similarly, the term holiness is used equivocally in three senses opposed to those three senses.[22]

not render ritually impure while in the body.' I cite the passage as translated by Samuel Rosenblatt, p. 249, corrected according to Kafih's Arabic text and Hebrew translation, p. 206. See further *Beliefs and Opinions* iii. 2 (trans. Rosenblatt, 144; trans. Kafih, 122).

[18] It is likely that R. Hayim took it as a given that the ontological understanding of Judaism was normative. Compare the following comment of Moshe Idel: 'Unlike the rabbinic treatment of the mitzvot as basically non-constelled, namely as ungoverned by metaphysical structures, most of the kabbalists subordinated them to supernal entities and processes, thus creating more comprehensive frameworks' ('On Some Forms of Order in Kabbalah', p. xxxviii).   [19] On the terminology here, see above, Ch. 3 n. 14.

[20] i.e. matters of ritual purity and impurity are 'fancied notions', having no objective correlates in the 'real' world. As R. Kafih says in a note on this text, 'He [Maimonides] called ritual impure things "matters of thought" [*mahshavti'im*], since they are not anything real [*mamashi*], but matters of thought.' I might note that in my estimation, the late R. Kafih is one of the few rabbinic (as opposed to academic) interpreters of Maimonides consistently to read what Maimonides actually wrote, as opposed to what 'he must have meant'.   [21] BT *Ber.* 22*a*.

[22] The passage here is on pp. 595–6. One wonders if Maimonides wrote this paragraph partially in reaction to *Kuzari* iii. 49: 'The Sage said: Ritual impurity and sanctity are correlative notions, neither one of which exists without the other. Thus, where there is no sanctity there is no ritual impurity either, because the meaning of ritual impurity is simply: something that restricts the one who has it from coming into close contact

Ritual impurity in the sense under discussion here is a matter of 'fancied notions'. It refers to the halakhic status of certain implements, places, or people and to nothing beyond that halakhic status.

Maimonides makes this point explicitly, not only here in the *Guide* but also in at least two places in the *Mishneh torah*. He ends his formal discussion of ritual purity and impurity in that book with the following peroration:

It is plain and manifest that the laws about ritual impurity and purity are decrees laid down by Scripture[23] and not matters about which human understanding is capable of forming a judgment; for behold, they are included among the divine statutes [*ḥukim*].[24] So, too, immersion as a means of freeing oneself from ritual impurity is included among the divine statutes. *Now 'ritual impurity' is not mud or filth which water can remove, but is a matter of scriptural decree and dependent upon intention of the heart.* Therefore the Sages have said, 'If a man immerses himself, but without special intention, it is as though he has not immersed himself at all'.[25] Nevertheless we may find some indication of all this: just as one who sets his heart on becoming ritually pure becomes so as soon as he has immersed himself, *although nothing new has befallen his body,* so, too, one who sets his heart on purifying himself from the impurity that besets men's souls—namely, evil thoughts and wicked moral qualities[26]—becomes pure as soon as he consents in his heart to shun

with some other thing characterized by sanctity, which belongs to the dominion of what is consecrated to God, like the priests, their various foods, their garments, their *terumot*, the sacrifices, the Sanctuary, and much else besides. In the same way, the meaning of sanctity is: something that restricts the one who has it from coming into close contact with many commonly recognized things. Most of that which is characterized by sanctity is associated with the presence of the Divine Presence. However, we have been deprived of it. Moreover, the prohibition in force among us against sexual intercourse with a menstruating woman (Lev. 18: 19), and also with a woman who has just given birth (Lev. 12: 2) is not something derived from her impurity. Rather, it is simply a commandment of God.' Far from seeing sanctity and ritual purity as distinct issues, Halevi here seeks to make them one.

[23] *Gezerat hakatuv*. On this expression, see the discussion in J. Stern, *Problems and Parables*, 49–66.

[24] This statement is interesting in light of the claim made by Maimonides in the *Guide* that the divine statutes (*ḥukim*) can be understood. On the whole issue see J. Stern, *Problems and Parables*.

[25] Mishnah *Ḥag.* 2: 6. In his comment ad loc. Maimonides generalizes from the specific discussion in this passage to all cases: immersion for the purposes of removing ritual impurity always requires specific intention (since, for Maimonides, I urge, the important change is in our self-understanding, and not in the physical or metaphysical realms).

[26] See above, Ch. 3 nn. 16–18.

those counsels and brings his soul into the waters of pure reason. Behold, Scripture says, 'I will sprinkle pure water upon you, and you shall be pure: I will purify you from all your ritual impurity and from all your fetishes' (Ezek. 36: 25). May God, in His great mercy, purify us from every sin, iniquity, and guilt. Amen.[27]

Maimonides often takes advantage of the end of a section of the *Mishneh torah* to deliver a sermonette on the broader moral and spiritual consequences of the technical halakhic issues under discussion. His point here seems to be that the laws of ritual purity and impurity, important as they are in their own right, must be understood as symbolizing something deeper: the need to purify oneself of bad moral qualities in order to bring one's 'soul into the waters of pure reason'.[28] This must be the explanation of why Maimonides finds it necessary to polemicize against a view which sees ritual impurity as something actual (on the spiritual, if not necessarily physical level), similar to 'mud or filth which water can remove'. Seeing ritual impurity as an ontological issue might lead one to miss its ethical significance.

A similar point is made at the end of *MT* 'Laws of the Ritual Impurity of Foodstuffs'. Maimonides ends this section of his code by pointing out that, even though 'it is permissible to eat ritually impure foodstuffs and to drink ritually impure liquids',[29] the Pharisees[30] sought for a higher level of holiness

---

[27] 'Laws of Immersion Pools', 11: 12. I cite from the *Book of Cleanness*, trans. Danby, 535, with emendations and emphases added. For valuable discussion of this passage, see J. Stern, *Problems and Parables*, 34, 60–3. On pp. 34 and 61 Stern draws our attention to the important point that Maimonides' decision to characterize the laws of ritual purity and impurity as *ḥukim* is, apparently, unprecedented.

[28] Maimonides repeatedly emphasizes the necessity of achieving moral perfection as a prerequisite for intellectual (= truly human) perfection. See above, Ch. 2 n. 71 and Ch. 3 n. 40.

[29] A point worthy of emphasis in and of itself, especially in light of some of the texts adduced from Halevi above: if one does not need to be ritually pure for some specific reason, there is nothing wrong with remaining ritually impure. Had Maimonides thought that ritual impurity had some sort of objective existence he could not have viewed remaining in a state of ritual impurity with such equanimity. On this matter, see Maimonides' *Commentary on the Mishnah*, introd. to *Toharot*, trans. Kafih, 22, col. b, top, and, emphatically, *Book of Commandments*, positive commandments 96 and 109. Feintuch, in *Pikudei yesharim*, his commentary on the *Book of Commandments* (i. 313–14), points out that, according to Maimonides, the Torah instituted the laws of ritual purity and impurity so that a person's normal state would be that of ritual impurity (so as to limit contact with the Sanctuary, and the familiarity that follows from such contact).

[30] For a Maimonidean characterization of the Pharisees, see his comment on Mishnah *Sot.* 3: 3.

and avoided ritually impure implements, foods, and even people. Did they do this because they found some objective (spiritual) defect in being ritually impure? Maimonides hastens to assure us that this is not the case:

Separation leads to the purifying of the body from evil deeds, and the purifying of the body leads to the sanctification of the soul from evil moral qualities,[31] and the sanctification of the soul leads to the imitation of the Divine Presence; for it is said, 'Sanctify yourselves therefore and be ye holy' (Lev. 11: 44), 'for I the Lord who sanctify you am holy' (Lev. 21: 8).[32]

The Pharisees avoided ritual impurity, not because there was anything objectively wrong with it, but because they understood its importance in teaching us to avoid immorality and thus better imitate God.[33] As he does with the notion of holiness,[34] Maimonides presents the issue of ritual purity and impurity as a moral category, not an ontological one.[35]

It seems clear that in these two passages Maimonides is polemicizing against a view which he evidently rejects, one which attributes some sort of ontological status to ritual impurity. It is against the background of these two passages that we should reread a text cited above in a different context in Chapter 3, from *MT* 'Laws Concerning Trespass in Regard to Sacred Objects [*Me'ilah*]', 8: 8:[36]

It is fitting for man to meditate upon the laws of the holy Torah and to comprehend their full meaning to the extent of his ability. Nevertheless, a law for which

---

[31] *De'ot*; Danby: 'thoughts'.

[32] 'Laws of the Ritual Impurity of Foodstuffs', 14: 12. See discussion at pp. 95–6 above.

[33] The entire section at the end of 'Laws of the Ritual Impurity of Foodstuffs' (paras. 8–12) is important in this context. Maimonides repeatedly emphasizes in these paragraphs that the laws of ritual purity and impurity relate only to the Temple (on which, see below, p. 146) and that, in and of itself, there is nothing wrong with being ritually impure, eating ritually impure food, and allowing ritually pure food to become ritually impure. It is against that background that he must explain, in para. 12, why it is that 'although it is permissible to eat ritually impure foodstuffs and to drink ritually impure liquids, the pious of former times used to eat their common food in conditions of ritual purity and all their days they were wary of every ritual impurity?' I should note that Maimonides' halakhic position here is in no way unusual; what is unusual is the repeated emphasis he places on the idea that there is nothing wrong with being ritually impure in and of itself. For an opposing view, see Nahmanides on Lev. 19: 2.

[34] See Silman, 'Halakhic Determinations', 'Commandments and Transgressions', and 'Introduction', and Seeskin, 'Holiness as an Ethical Ideal', and W. Z. Harvey, 'Holiness'.

[35] See further *Guide* iii. 33 (p. 533)

[36] This is the last section of the *Book of Temple Service* in the *Mishneh torah* and thus serves as a transition to the next section of the work, the *Book of Sacrifices*.

he finds no reason and understands no cause should not be trivial in his eyes. Let him not 'break through to come up against the Lord, lest the Lord break forth upon him' (Exod. 19: 24); nor should his thoughts concerning these things be like his thoughts concerning profane matters. Come and consider how strict the Torah was in the law of trespass! Now if sticks and stones and earth and ashes become hallowed by words alone, as soon as the name of the Master of the Universe was invoked upon them, and anyone who comported with them as with a profane thing committed trespass and required atonement even if he had acted unwittingly, how much more should man be on guard not to rebel against a commandment decreed for us by the Holy One, blessed be He, only because he does not understand its reason; or to heap words that are not right against the Lord; or to regard the commandments in the manner in which he regards ordinary affairs. All of the sacrifices are included among the statutes [*ḥukim*]; therefore the Sages said that the world depends even upon the sacrificial cult, since it is through the performance of the statutes and ordinances [*mishpatim*] that the upright merit life in the world to come.[37] The Torah commanded the statutes first, as it says, 'You shall keep My statutes and My ordinances, by the pursuit of which man shall live; I am the Lord' (Lev. 18: 5).[38]

As already noted in Chapter 3, this is an important text for understanding Maimonides' account of *ta'amei hamitsvot*, the reasons for the commandments. But, for our purposes here, the passage is crucial for teaching the following: items pledged to the Temple become sanctified, but 'all' that changes in them is their status, nothing else. It may not be accidental that Maimonides introduces this idea in a paragraph serving as a transition to his discussion of sacrifices. He may be indicating something to the perceptive reader about the status of sacrifices. Be that as it may, it serves my purposes well, since I want to move to a discussion of one aspect of Maimonides' explanation of why sacrifices were ordained in the Torah.

[37] Maimonides' statement here makes sense in light of his comment on Mishnah *Avot* 1: 2. The text there reads: 'Simeon the Righteous was of the survivors of the Great Assembly. He used to say: "By three things is the world sustained—by the Torah, the Temple Service [*avodah*], and deeds of lovingkindness".' On this, Maimonides comments: 'He said that by means of wisdom, represented by the Torah, and by means of the moral virtues, represented by deeds of lovingkindness, and by means of observing the precepts of the Torah, represented by the offerings, shall the perpetual improvement of the world and the order of its existence be in the perfect path' (I cite the translation of David, p. 2). The world is no longer sustained by the sacrificial service, as the text of *Avot* would appear to teach, but by the observance of *all* the commandments, *represented* by the sacrificial service! For useful background to this, see Goldstein, 'Sacrifice and Worship'. I discuss this text again at the end of this chapter.

[38] On the textual issues in this passage, see Ch. 3 nn. 121–2.

Maimonides on the Sacrificial Cult and the Laws of Ritual Purity and Impurity

Maimonides, as is well known, holds that the sacrificial cult was not part of God's primary intention, as it were, but represents an accommodation on God's part to the (historically contingent) spiritual weakness of the Jews leaving Egypt. The sacrifices, that is, serve no purpose of their own, but were instituted against God's will, so to speak. But, as we shall see, the Tabernacle in the wilderness and the Temple after it were ordained by God only in order to serve as a venue for sacrifices. The laws of ritual purity and impurity, in turn, were ordained in order to emphasize to the Jews the special character of the Tabernacle and Temple. In other words the laws of ritual purity and impurity exist, in effect, in order to make the Temple special, and the Temple exists only to serve as a place in which to bring sacrifices; sacrifices, in turn, were ordained, not because the Torah as ideally constituted must include them, but because the Jews who received it could not manage without them. This being the case, the laws of ritual purity and impurity are themselves a product of contingent historical circumstance and obviously cannot reflect real distinctions in the cosmos.

Guide iii. 47 is devoted to a discussion of the laws of ritual purity and impurity. Maimonides explains that the laws of the Torah, when compared to those of the idolaters who existed when the Torah was given, 'come to facilitate the actions of worship and to lighten the burden' (p. 593). Thus, for example, he says, one ought 'to compare a rite in which for reasons of divine worship a man burns his child with one in which he burns a young pigeon'. 'This', he goes on to say, 'is a premise of great importance that must not be lost from your mind.' At the very beginning of his discussion of the laws of ritual purity and impurity, Maimonides thus indicates that the context of this discussion is the sacrificial cult.

Maimonides explains this 'premise of great importance' by saying, 'We have already explained[39] that the whole intention with regard to the Sanctuary [*mikdash*] was to affect those that came to it with a feeling of awe and fear. Now if one is continually in contact with a venerable object, the impression received from it in the soul diminishes and the feeling it provokes becomes slight.' This being the case, Maimonides explains, God 'forbade the ritually impure to enter the Sanctuary in spite of there being many species of ritual impurity, so that one could—but for a few exceptions—

---

[39] In ch. 45, p. 577.

scarcely find a ritually pure individual.' After specifying many of the myriad ways by which one can become ritually impure, Maimonides asserts: 'Thus all of this was a reason for keeping away from the Sanctuary and for not entering it at every moment' (p. 594).[40] 'In consequence of such actions', Maimonides elucidates, 'fear [*al-yirah*] will continue and an impression leading to the humility that was aimed at will be produced.'[41]

But the laws of ritual purity and impurity have many purposes:

One of them is to keep men away from disgusting things. The second is to safeguard the Sanctuary. The third is to protect what is generally accepted and customary, for, as you will hear presently, unpleasant things were imposed on the Sabians in cases of ritual impurity. The fourth is to ease unpleasant restrictions and to order things in such a manner that questions of ritual impurity and ritual purity should not prevent a man from engaging in any of his occupations; for this matter of ritual impurity and ritual purity concerns only the Holy Place and holy things, nothing else: 'She shall touch no holy thing, nor come into the Sanctuary' (Lev. 12: 4). As for the rest, there is no sin if one remains ritually impure as long as one wishes and eats, as one wishes, ordinary food that has become ritually impure.

---

[40] Here and below I have changed Pines' 'clean' to 'ritually pure' and his 'unclean' to 'ritually impure'.

[41] See also the introduction to his commentary on the Order Toharot in the Mishnah, trans. Kafih, 22, col. 2. There he says that 'most of the need for these matters [the laws of ritual purity and impurity] is only for the Sanctuary and its sancta'. Maimonides makes the point even more clearly and emphatically in *MT* 'Laws of Ritual Impurity of Foodstuffs', 12: 8 (*Book of Cleanness*, trans. Danby, 392, with emendations): 'Whatever [*kol*] is written in Scripture and in traditional teaching about the laws relating to things ritually impure and ritually pure is relevant only to the Temple and to its hallowed things and to heave offerings and second tithe, for it warns those who are ritually impure against entering the Temple or eating in ritual impurity anything that is hallowed or heave offering or tithe.' The same point comes up in the *Book of Commandments*, positive commandment 109: 'This points to the principle which I have explained, namely that the law of immersion applies only to one who wants to become ritually pure, and [for such a one] this law is a commandment; but there is no absolute obligation to immerse oneself, and anybody who wishes to remain ritually impure, and is prepared to forgo entering the camp of the Divine Presence for a time, is at liberty to do so' (trans. Chavel, i. 110). Feintuch, *Pikudei yesharim*, i. 313, points out that in the *Book of Commandments* the laws relating to ritual purity and impurity follow immediately upon the laws concerning the Sanctuary and the sacrifices since 'the purpose of all of them is in general to make people avoid entering the Sanctuary, so that it should be considered as great by the soul and feared and venerated' (*Guide* iii. 35; p. 537).

Two issues must be emphasized here. First, Maimonides informs us that there is nothing wrong with being ritually impure,[42] and that if one has no need to deal with sacred matters, there is no need to undertake rites of purification. One could, in theory, spend one's whole life in a state of ritual impurity without that in any way diminishing one's religious purity, saintliness, closeness to God, etc. This contrasts sharply with Halevi's view, as seen above. Second, Maimonides lists four purposes of the laws of ritual purity and impurity. Of them, only the second could possibly be interpreted in what I have been calling ontological terms, and that is clearly not the way in which Maimonides interprets it, as should be evident by now.

At this point Maimonides explains that the biblical laws of ritual purity and impurity are much less onerous than those of the ancient Sabians and their contemporary remnant, the Zoroastrians. He places special emphasis on the burdensome restrictions on menstruating women in those societies:

the menstruating woman remains isolated in her house; the places upon which she treads are burnt; whoever speaks with her becomes ritually impure; and if a wind that blows passes over a menstruating woman and a ritually pure individual, the latter becomes ritually impure. (p. 595)

The difference between this and Jewish law is 'great':

All the various kinds of work that a wife does for her husband, are also done by a menstruating woman for her husband, except for washing his face, and so on.[43] It is only forbidden to have intercourse with her in the days in which she is ritually impure and defiled.

After describing other Sabian usages, Maimonides summarizes the point: 'They have many burdensome usages of this kind, whereas as for us we only claim that something is ritually impure or ritually pure with regard to holy things and to the Sanctuary.'

One can think of many reasons why Maimonides saw fit to emphasize the distinction between the biblical laws of ritual purity and impurity and those of the Sabians,[44] but for our purposes we need only focus on one: he

---

[42] As opposed to being simply dirty. Compare the following suggestive decision in *MT* 'Laws of *Tefilin*', 10: 8: 'Those ritually impure, even menstruants and Gentiles, may hold a Torah scroll and read from it, since words of Torah cannot become ritually impure. This, on condition that their hands are not soiled or muddy. If they are, they must wash their hands and then they may touch it.' Maimonides' sources (BT *Ber.* 22*a*, *Meg.* 9*a*) do not compare ritual impurity and filth in this context as he does.

[43] BT *Ket.* 4*b*, 61*a*.

[44] One reason may have been his interest in distinguishing Rabbanite from Karaite Judaism. On this, see the studies by Cohen, Dinari, and Woolf, cited above in n. 14, and

clearly plays down, and indeed actually denies, the objective reality of ritual impurity here (and, I might add, subtly associates those who affirm it with Sabian idolaters).

Maimonides goes on, in a text worth quoting a second time:

As for His dictum, may He be exalted, 'Sanctify yourselves therefore and be ye holy, for I am holy' (Lev. 11: 44), it does not apply at all to ritual impurity and purity. *Sifra* states literally: This concerns sanctification by the commandments. For this reason, transgression of the commandments is also called ritual impurity . . . The term ritual impurity is used equivocally in three different senses: it is used of disobedience and of transgression of commandments concerning action or opinion; it is used of dirt and filth . . . and it is used according to these fancied notions, I refer to touching or carrying certain things or being under the same roof with certain things. With reference to this last sense, we say: 'The words of the Torah are not subject to becoming impure.' Similarly, the term holiness is used equivocally in three senses opposed to those three senses. (pp. 595–6)

It would be hard to be more explicit than this. The laws of ritual purity and impurity refer to matters that exist only in the mind (which does not make them unimportant!); they are halakhic institutions, with no objective referent in the super-social universe.[45] Although this is not his concern here, Maimonides also takes this opportunity to make sure we realize that holiness is like ritual purity: an idea, an institution, a halakhic and hence social reality, but not something having intrinsic, objective existence.

Maimonides reiterates that there is nothing wrong with being ritually impure. Even priests avoid ritual impurity only because they 'were always in need of entering the Sanctuary for the purpose of sacrificing' (p. 596). But, Maimonides makes clear, this restriction relates only to priests, and only for the practical reason just cited. It does not relate to their wives and daughters: 'Do you not see that this prohibition does not extend to women? It is said: "the sons of Aaron" (Lev. 21: 1), and not "the daughters of Aaron", women not being needed in sacrifice.' A priest having no need to enter the Sanctuary (one living, say, in Brooklyn), would have no reason to avoid ritual impurity.

The rest of chapter 47 deals with other matters relating to the laws of ritual purity and impurity, but they do not impinge directly on the issue under study, so I shall pass them over in silence.

Friedman, 'Social Realities in Egypt'. Another possible reason is to counter the trends which later found expression in the influential *Baraita demasekhet nidah*.

[45] I must clarify: something can be deemed ritually impure because it is disgusting; calling it ritually impure adds nothing to its nature but—and this is a big 'but' in the eyes of Maimonides—determines how halakhah commands one to relate to it.

For our purposes, the lessons of *Guide* iii. 47 are two: (*a*) the laws of ritual purity and impurity relate to matters of halakhic import, but to no realities over and above or outside humans and their social relations, and (*b*) they were instituted first and foremost in order to inculcate a sense of reverence towards the Tabernacle in the wilderness and, later, the Temple in Jerusalem.

But why does the Torah command the erection of such sanctuaries? Maimonides answers this question in *Guide* iii. 32, where he describes God's 'wily graciousness and wisdom'[46] (p. 525) in accomplishing ends indirectly. God created the world in such a way that individuals have to move through many stages of growth before they attain their full maturity. 'Many things in our Torah', he then points out, 'are due to something similar to this very governance on the part of Him who governs, may He be glorified and exalted. For a sudden transition from one opposite to another is impossible. And therefore man, according to his nature, is not capable of abandoning suddenly all to which he was accustomed.'

Jews in the time of the Exodus had become accustomed to religious worship which revolved around animal sacrifice.[47] This being so, God's wisdom and 'gracious ruse, which is manifest in regard to all His creatures, did not require that He give us a Torah prescribing the rejection, abandonment, and abolition of all these kinds of worship'. Had God done so, the Israelites coming out of Egypt would not have been able to accept the Torah. In explaining this, Maimonides offers an analogy. Just as the Israelites coming out of Egypt could not relate to worship without sacrifices, so also, Jews of Maimonides' own day could not relate to worship without ritual and prayer.[48] Demanding of the ancient Israelites that they worship without sacrifices was as impossible as sending a prophet today (in Maimonides' time, although I doubt that things have changed much since) who, 'calling upon the people to worship God, would say: "God has given you a Torah forbidding you to pray to Him, to fast, to call upon Him for help in misfortune. Your worship should consist solely in meditation without any works at all."'

---

[46] On this expression and its background, see Pines, 'Translator's Introduction', pp. lxxii–lxxv, and Stroumsa, 'Sabians of Haran', 283.

[47] Maimonides holds that most of the Jews in Egypt were idolaters. See above, Ch. 2 n. 122.

[48] On this, see W. Z. Harvey, 'Les Sacrifices'. It might not be too extreme to suggest that, in his own mind, Maimonides regarded *piyut*, ritual poetry, as a parallel to animal sacrifice. See above, Ch. 1 n. 98.

This being the case, Maimonides continues, God 'suffered the above-mentioned kinds of worship [i.e. animal sacrifices] to remain, but transferred them from created or imaginary or unreal things [i.e. the objects of idolatrous worship] to His own name, may He be exalted, commanding us to practise them with regard to Him, may He be exalted.'

The sacrificial cult is an example of divine accommodation: God accommodates the Torah to the primitive needs of the Jewish people at an early stage of their development (just as a wise parent feeds a newborn milk or soft food).[49] As Maimonides says a few paragraphs further on, responding to a possible objection to this proposal, the sacrificial cult, in all its myriad impressive and colourful detail, was not intended by God 'for its own sake, but for the sake of something else, as if this were a ruse invented for our benefit by God in order to achieve His first intention [the correct apprehension of God and rejection of idolatry]' (p. 527).[50]

Returning to the order in which Maimonides himself develops his ideas, a cult needs a place in which to be performed. Having commanded the sacrifices, God 'commanded us to build a temple for Him . . . to have an altar for His name . . . to have the sacrifice offered up to Him . . . to bow down in worship before Him; and to burn incense before Him' (p. 526).[51]

All this (including everything to do with the priests) Maimonides calls a successful 'divine ruse' which brought it about that 'the memory of idolatry was effaced and that the grandest and true foundation of our belief—namely the existence and oneness of the deity—was firmly established' (p. 527). God's wily and gracious ruse worked so well that 'the souls had no feeling of repugnance and were not repelled because of the abolition of the modes of worship to which they were accustomed and [other] than which no other mode of worship was known at that time'.

[49] On the notion of divine accommodation here, see Benin, *Footprints of God*; Funkenstein, *Theology and the Scientific Imagination*, 231–49; and Socher, 'Of Divine Cunning'.

[50] A text at the end of *MT* 'Laws Concerning Trespass with Respect to Sacred Objects' has been taken as an indication that in the *Mishneh torah*, at least, Maimonides held a less extreme positition on the nature of sacrifices. However, this interpretation is based upon a faulty text. See above, Ch. 3 nn. 121, 122, 123.

[51] Maimonides is quite explicit about this point; compare the following from *Guide* iii. 32 (p. 530): 'Those laws concerning sacrifices and repairing to the Temple were given only for the sake of the realization of this fundamental principle [that God alone be worshipped]. It is for the sake of that principle that I transferred these modes of worship to My name, so that the trace of idolatry be effaced and the fundamental principle of My unity be established.'

After dealing with a number of objections to his explanation for the sacrificial cult and the establishment of the priesthood, Maimonides points out that the biblical sacrificial cult was in many ways more refined than the idolatrous practices that it replaced. One important difference was that sacrifices could no longer 'be offered in every place and at every time. Nor could a temple be set up in any fortuitous place, nor could any fortuitous man offer the sacrifice . . . On the contrary, He forbade all this and established one single house [as the Temple] . . . so that sacrifices should not be offered elsewhere. Also only the offspring of one particular family can be priest[s]' (p. 529). All of these restrictions were designed by God to limit and restrict sacrificial worship as much as possible: 'All this was intended to restrict this kind of worship, so that only the portion of it should subsist whose abolition is not required by His wisdom.' Maimonides contrasts this with other forms of worship, including prayer, fringes,[52] *mezuzot*,[53] and *tefilin*,[54] which may be observed 'in every place and by all people'.

The point of interest to us in all this is the connection made by Maimonides between the sacrificial cult and the commandments concerning the sanctuary. He makes the point yet again: 'Those laws concerning sacrifices and repairing to the Temple were given only for the sake of the realization of this fundamental principle [the apprehension of God and rejection of idolatry]' (p. 530).[55]

Connecting chapters 47 and 32 of part iii, as Maimonides instructs his readers to do in the 'Instruction with Respect To This Treatise' found near the end of his introduction to the *Guide* (p. 15), we are led to the following chain of reasoning:

1. Sacrifices are not part of what might be called God's ideal plan for the Torah but rather represent an accommodation to the unfortunately primitive character of the ancient Israelites.[56]

---

[52] See *MT* 'Laws of Fringes', 3: 13, cited above in Ch. 3.

[53] See *MT* 'Laws of *Tefilin*', 6: 13, cited above in Ch. 3.

[54] See ibid. 4: 25, cited above in Ch. 3.

[55] Compare Halevi's view of the sacrifices as expressed in *Kuzari* iii. 51 (which follows from his general account of the commandments in *Kuzari* iii. 23).

[56] Abravanel interprets Maimonides as teaching that God's original intention had been to command only the sabbath and civil laws (see Maimonides' gloss on Exod. 15: 25–6, Jer. 7: 9–10 and BT *Shab.* 87*b*, in *Guide* iii. 32; p. 531); after the sin of the golden calf God 'realized' that the Jews were too primitive to manage without a full panoply of sacrifices and hence commanded them. See Abravanel's comment on Jer. 7 (p. 328) and above, Ch. 2 n. 26.

2. Once sacrifices had been ordained, an attempt was made to limit their extent.

3. No matter how restricted, a sanctuary (but only one) still had to be ordained, and a priesthood established.

4. Laws of ritual purity and impurity were issued concerning the sanctuary to make sure that it was treated with awe and respect.

5. The laws of ritual purity and impurity cannot, therefore, be seen as reflecting some objective quality in the world since they were ordained only as a consequence of the sacrifices, which themselves were only God's 'second intention'.[57]

While this conclusion is surprising in light of what were apparently the standard orthodoxies of Maimonides' day (and ours), it should not actually be surprising in the context of his thought. He was, after all, the person who wrote explicitly: 'Know that all the practices of the worship, such as reading the Torah, prayer, and the performance of the other commandments, have only the end of training you to occupy yourself with His commandments, may He be exalted, rather than with matters pertaining to this world.'[58]

The practices of Judaism, I take Maimonides to be teaching here, were ordained only for purposes of training. To play on Maimonides' words, the

[57] Given Maimonides' historicization of so many of the commandments, readers unfamiliar with the long history of discussion on this topic might wonder how Maimonides expected Jews familiar with his account to be motivated to obey the commandments. This is hardly the place to go into this issue. An important discussion of it is found in Twersky, *Introduction*, 374–484. It ought to be noted that, once commanded, the sacrifices are entirely obligatory, and Maimonides nowhere intimates the contrary. On this, see the discussion in Blidstein, *Prayer in Maimonidean Halakhah*, 73–4, and the sources cited there. For further discussion of this issue, see Ch. 2 nn. 21, 125 and Ch. 7 n. 63.

[58] *Guide* iii. 51 (p. 622). Compare *MT* 'Laws of Substituted Offerings [*Temurah*]', 4: 13. See the translation of this text and discussion in Twersky, *Introduction*, 416–17. See also the following sentence in *Guide* iii. 52 (p. 630): 'the end of the actions prescribed by the whole Law is bring about the passion of which it is correct that it be brought about . . . I refer to the fear of Him . . . and the awe before His command.' The commandments, Maimonides goes on to explain, bring one to awe of God, while the doctrines taught in the Torah bring one to love of God. The commandments are all means to an end external to them. My concern here is with the question of ritual purity and impurity; on how the passage adduced here fits into Maimonides' doctrine of the reasons for the commandments (*ta'amei hamitsvot*), see above, Ch. 2 n. 65, and J. Stern, *Problems and Parables*, chs. 4 and 6.

commandments do not relate to matters pertaining to any objectively existent entities and distinctions in this world.

Maimonides on the Moral Significance of the Laws of Ritual Purity and Impurity

I do not want the reader to leave this chapter with the impression that, in the absence of the Temple in Jerusalem, the laws of ritual purity and impurity have lost all significance for Maimonides. On the contrary, he was convinced of their permanent significance as metaphors having moral import. I made this claim briefly above, and would like to conclude the discussion in this chapter by revisiting the issue in greater detail.

As already noted, Maimonides concludes 'Laws Concerning Immersion Pools' (ii: 12) in particular, and the *Book of Purity* as a whole, with what appears to be an impassioned peroration. 'It is plain and manifest', he teaches there, that the laws concerning ritual purity and impurity in the Torah are scriptural decrees, included in the category of divine statutes. Concerning these statutes, Maimonides writes:

> They are not believed by the multitude of the Sages to be things for which there is no cause at all and for which one must not seek an end. For this would lead, according to what we have explained, to their being considered as frivolous actions. On the contrary, the multitude of the Sages believe that there indubitably is a cause for them—I mean to say a useful end—but that it is hidden from us either because of the incapacity of our intellects or the deficiency of our knowledge. (*Guide* iii. 26; p. 507)

One ought to note in passing a point immediately relevant to our discussion in this chapter: Maimonides could argue on the basis of the passage just cited that were there an objective, ontological basis for the laws of ritual purity and impurity, they should not have been included among the *ḥukim*, those statutes for which no reason is immediately available. Were it in some way dangerous—physically, mentally, or spiritually—to touch a ritually impure object, then the laws governing such contact should not have been included among the *ḥukim*. But it is not my point in this book to argue that Maimonides understood his sources correctly, so let us return to the issue at hand.

The laws concerning ritual purity and impurity are not just *ḥukim*; Maimonides calls them 'scriptural decrees'. What are such decrees? In *Guide* iii. 38 (p. 550) he writes: 'Know that certain commandments also contain prescriptions that are intended to lead to a useful moral quality, even if they prescribe certain actions that are deemed to be merely decreed by Scripture and not to have a purpose.' Scriptural decrees are *deemed* not to have a purpose (and some of these lead to a useful moral quality, a point to which I shall return presently). In his letter on astrology to the rabbis of Montpellier Maimonides further clarifies the nature of these decrees:[59]

I have . . . read in all matters concerning all of idolatry, so that it seems to me that there does not remain in the world a compilation on this subject, having been translated into Arabic from other languages, but that I have read it and have understood its subject matter and have plumbed the depth of its thought. From those books it became clear to me what the reason is for all those commandments that everyone comes to think of as having no reason at all other than the decree of Scripture. I already have a great compilation on this subject in the Arabic language with lucid proof for every single commandment, but this is not required of us now.[60]

Scriptural decrees, then, are commandments and prohibitions which can only be understood against the background of ancient (Sabian) idolatry. Scriptural decrees are thus to be understood as historically conditioned commandments, commanded in order to uproot specific (and historically contingent) idolatrous practices.

Having determined what *ḥukim* and scriptural decrees are, we can return to the second and third sentences in the passage quoted above from *MT* 'Laws Concerning Immersion Pools', 11: 12: 'So, too, immersion as a means of freeing oneself from ritual impurity is included among the divine statutes. Now "ritual impurity" is not mud or filth which water can remove, but is a matter of scriptural decree and dependent upon intention of the heart.' Since ritual impurity is not an objective status, like being dirty but, rather, a matter of halakhic status, it follows that the process which frees one from such impurity is entirely a matter of halakhic status as well, and, Maimonides adds crucially, depends upon 'intention of the heart'.

In support of this claim, Maimonides cites the following mishnaic text:

If one ritually immersed himself for unconsecrated food, and intended to be rendered fit solely for unconsecrated food, one is prohibited from partaking of second tithe. If one ritually immersed himself for second tithe, and intended to be

---

[59] 'But this reason is exactly the type of historical explanation of the commandments Maimonides would also want to conceal from a general audience—and elsewhere does. Calling it a *gezerat hakatuv* [scriptural decree] serves exactly this function'; J. Stern, *Problems and Parables*, 59.

[60] I cite the translation of Lerner, *Maimonides' Empire of Light*, 180.

rendered fit solely for second tithe, one is prohibited from partaking of *terumah*. If one ritually immersed himself for *terumah*, and intended to be rendered fit solely for *terumah*, one is prohibited from partaking of hallowed things. If one ritually immersed himself for hallowed things, and intended to be rendered fit solely for hallowed things, one is prohibited from touching the waters of purification. If one ritually immersed himself for something possessing a stricter degree of sanctity, one is permitted to have contact with something possessing a lighter degree of sanctity. If one ritually immersed himself but without special intention, it is as though one had not bathed.[61]

This text deals with Jews who came to Jerusalem to celebrate one of the pilgrim festivals. In his *Commentary on the Mishnah*, Maimonides explains:

If one had ritually immersed himself with the intention of eating unconsecrated food and remained in that state, he is not permitted to eat [second] tithe until he immerses himself a second time with the intention of becoming ritually purified for [second] tithe. Everyone [who immerses himself] must do so with the intention of becoming ritually purified for that for which he ritually purifies himself. One who simply immersed himself with no special intention, neither for [second] tithes nor for anything else, it is as if he did not immerse himself and with that immersion he can only eat unconsecrated foods.

The Mishnah in *Ḥagigah* as adumbrated by Maimonides deals with a specific case; in our passage from the *Mishneh torah* Maimonides generalizes from this specfic case and maintains that all matters of ritual purity and impurity depend upon one's intention.

'Nevertheless', Maimonides says, 'we may find some indication of all this.' To what does the word 'nevertheless' refer? I submit that it refers to the claim that ritual purity and impurity deal 'only' with halakhic status; they have no correlate in the world of extra-social reality. What is the indication or hint (the Hebrew here is *remez*)? Maimonides hastens to tell us, in *MT* 'Laws Concerning Immersion Pools', 11: 12:

Just as one who sets his heart on becoming ritually pure becomes so as soon as he has immersed himself, although nothing new has befallen his body, so, too, one who sets his heart on purifying himself from the impurity that besets men's souls—namely, evil thoughts and wicked moral qualities—becomes pure as soon as he consents in his heart to shun those counsels and brings his soul into the waters of pure reason.

Parallel to ritual impurity Maimonidean Judaism recognizes a category of moral impurity. Just as one can free onself from ritual impurity, so one can

---

[61] *Ḥagigah* 2: 6; I cite the Soncino translation with slight emendations.

free oneself from moral impurity. To accomplish the former, one must immerse oneself in a ritual bath with the proper intention.[62] So, too, to accomplish the latter: one must immerse onself in 'the waters of pure reason'[63] with the proper intention. Moral purity thus involves some measure of intellectual perfection.[64] That, however, is a big issue, and not relevant to our concerns here. The laws of ritual purity and impurity may be scriptural decrees meant to combat ancient idolatry, long gone from the world, but they remain ever relevant as metaphorical expressions of the obligation to strive for moral purity.[65]

[62] In *Guide* iii. 33 (p. 533) Maimonides makes even ritual purification depend upon 'the purification of actions and purification of the heart from polluting opinions and polluting moral qualities'. My thanks to Mr Yisrael Ben-Simon for drawing my attention to this passage.

[63] The Hebrew word translated as 'reason' here is *da'at*. On this term in Maimonides, see Baneth, 'Maimonides' Philosophical Terminology', 16, and Septimus, 'What Did Maimonides Mean by *Madda*?', 90.

[64] See *Guide* i. 5 (p. 30), where Maimonides writes that 'it behooves us, all the more, as being inferior to them, and it behooves those who are inferior to us, to aim at and engage in perfecting our knowledge in preparatory matters and in achieving those premises that purify apprehension of its taint, which is error. It will then go forward to look upon the divine holy Presence.' As much as moral perfection is a prerequisite for intellectual perfection (above, Ch. 2 n. 71), some knowledge is a prerequisite for moral perfection.

[65] For another expression of the moral message of the laws of ritual purity and impurity, see the following passage from the end of *MT* 'Laws Concerning the Ritual Impurity of Leprosy' (16: 19):' "Leprosy" is a comprehensive term covering sundry incompatible matters . . . Now this change in garments and in houses which Scripture includes under the general term leprosy was no normal happening, but was a portent and a wonder among the Israelites to warn them against slanderous speaking. For if a man uttered slander the walls of his house would suffer a change: if he repented the house would again become clean . . . [if he persisted in his slander after several intermediate stages of 'leprosy'] his skin would suffer a change and he would become leprous and set apart and exposed all alone until he should no more engage in the conversation of the wicked, which is raillery and slander . . . Such is the conversation of the wicked, occasioned by their idling at street corners, in the gatherings of the ignorant, and in the feastings of drunkards. But the conversation of the worthy ones of Israel is none other than the words of Torah and wisdom; therefore the Holy One, blessed is He, aids them and bestows wisdom upon them.' I cite *Book of Cleanness*, trans. Danby, 203–4. This text is subjected to detailed analysis in Diamond, 'Maimonides on Leprosy'.

Critiques of Maimonides' Account of the Sacrifices

Maimonides' historicizing explanation of the sacrificial cult has scandalized generations of readers—including, emphatically, Nahmanides.[66] It was not only kabbalistically inclined thinkers like Nahmanides who rejected this account of the sacrifices; even a 'radical rationalist' such as the fourteenth-century Nissim of Marseilles was taken aback by Maimonides' position that sacrifices in and of themselves effect nothing. Citing with approval Halevi's position (*Kuzari* iii. 51) that bringing sacrifices is a necessary preparation for achieving prophecy, Nissim says of Maimonides: 'But the opinion of Rabbi Moses, his memory for a blessing, that the only purpose of the sacrifices is to transfer them from being offered to demons, *ba'alim*, and *ashtarot* is insufficient.'[67]

Abravanel may have been the first person to point to *Leviticus Rabbah* 22: 8 as a possible source for Maimonides' doctrine of sacrifices. He does this in his introduction to Leviticus, where he defends Maimonides' explanation of the sacrifices from the strictures of Nahmanides.[68] The passage in *Leviticus Rabbah* reads:

Rabbi Phinehas in the name of Rabbi Levi said: The matter may be compared to the case of a king's son who thought he could do what he liked and habitually ate the flesh of dead and torn animals. Said the king: 'I will have him always at my own table and he will automatically be hedged round.' Similarly, because Israel were passionate followers after idolatry in Egypt and used to bring their sacrifices to the satyrs, as it is written, 'And they shall no more sacrifice their sacrifices unto the satyrs' (Lev. 17: 7)—and these satyrs are nought but demons, as is borne out by the text which says, 'They sacrificed unto demons, no-gods' (Deut. 23: 17), these

[66] See Nahmanides' comment on Lev. 1: 9, with its mystical approach to sacrifices and the affirmation of their permanent psychological validity, and, for a very perceptive analysis, Pinchot, 'Deeper Conflict'. On Nahmanides and other kabbalists on sacrifices, see Idel, 'On the Significances'. For a recent and valuable discussion of Maimonides' rationale for sacrifices, see J. Stern, *Problems and Parables*, 23–35, 140–50.

[67] I cite from *Ma'aseh nisim*, 361. I borrow the characterization of Nissim as a 'radical rationalist' from Kreisel, 'Torah Commentary', 32.

[68] See also Abravanel's comment on Jer. 7 (p. 328), where he adopts Maimonides' position (*Guide* iii. 32; pp. 530–1) that God's original plan had been to limit the commandments of the Torah to the sabbath and civil laws. See above, n. 56. James Diamond pointed out to me that the division between sabbath and civil laws corresponds to Maimonides' distinction (*Guide* iii. 27; p. 510) between laws which aim at the welfare of the soul (sabbath) and those which aim at the welfare of the body (civil laws). This text is quoted on p. 59 above.

demons being nought but satyrs, as it says, 'And satyrs shall dance there' (Isa. 13: 21)—and they used to offer their sacrifices in the forbidden high places, on account of which punishments used to come upon them, the Holy One, blessed be He, said: 'Let them offer their sacrifices to Me at all times in the Tent of Meeting, and thus they will be separated from idolatry and be saved from punishment.' Hence it is written, 'what man soever there be of the house of Israel that killeth an ox . . . and hath not brought it unto the door of the tent of meeting' (Lev. 17: 8–9).[69]

The whole issue has been taken up recently and exhaustively by Jonathan Klawans in a discussion of Jacob Milgrom's *Leviticus*.[70] Klawans discusses Milgrom's use of this midrashic text (in which Milgrom follows Abravanel) and then comments perceptively:

Interestingly enough, Maimonides himself did not quote the Lev. R. passage in his own historicist interpretation of sacrifice. Scholars have continued to debate whether the passage really means what Abarbanel (and now, Milgrom) says it means . . . The upshot is this: Lev. R 22: 8 doesn't 'clearly' imply anything. Milgrom's reading of the Lev. R passage is clearly shaped by those exegetes who took Maimonides' side in the debate about the future of sacrifice. Yet one can certainly wonder whether the fourth- or fifth-century rabbis responsible for Lev. R 22: 8 really meant what the Maimonidean medievals and reforming moderns make them say.

Klawans's point is convincing: had Maimonides seen in this text a source for his own ideas, he would surely have quoted it. There are over two dozen other citations from *Leviticus Rabbah* in the *Guide*,[71] so there is no reason to suspect that Maimonides was not familiar with the text.

I should like to note in passing here that Maimonides' account of the sacrifices makes excellent sense in the context of what I see as his overall approach to Judaism, which seeks to place maximum responsibility on the shoulders of each individual. One of the problems with a sacrificial cult is

---

[69] I cite the Soncino translation, based on standard printed editions of the text. A critically edited text of *Lev. Rabbah* appears in *Midrash vayikra rabah*, ed. Margulies; our passage is on p. 517. In his notes to the text Margulies cites it as a possible source for Maimonides. In this he is followed by E. Urbach, *Sages*, i. 368. The issue had been taken up earlier in Hoffmann, *Leviticus*, 60. Hoffman noted that Abravanel's version of the text was faulty. Abravanel and Hoffmann are both discussed in N. Leibowitz, *Studies in Vayikra*, 16–17. Funkenstein, *Perceptions*, 95, discusses the text from *Lev. Rabbah* as an example of divine accommodation.   [70] Klawans, 'Ritual Purity', 23–4.

[71] According to Michael Swartz's index of rabbinic citations in his translation of the *Guide*.

the human propensity to see it as a technique for the absolution of sin through the manipulation of things (in this case, animals) as opposed to the manipulation, so to speak, of the self. The sacrificial cult lends itself (and this appears to be Maimonides' point in the last paragraphs of *Guide* iii. 32) to the sort of attitude which led, in its extreme form, to the scandal of the sale of indulgences in the medieval church. It is important to take note of the fact that Maimonides' views on the sacrificial cult are, to put it mildly, unusual in the context of Judaism as it developed before and after him. It must be recalled that a substantial percentage of the 613 commandments of the Torah deals with sacrifices, priesthood, the Temple, and matters of ritual purity and impurity (according to Rabbi Kafih, twenty-one of the 248 positive commandments and eleven of the 365 negative commandments deal with ritual purity and impurity).[72] It should be further noted that roughly one-third of the Mishnah is devoted to these topics.[73] In terms of what may be called pre-Maimonidean popular Judaism, Michael D. Swartz notes in connection with the *piyutim* of the Day of Atonement liturgy: 'A major theme in these poems is that creation itself took place for the sake of cult. This notion complements the rabbinic idea that the world was created by the pre-existent Torah and humankind was created for its sake.'[74] A separate study of *piyutim* as a source of ideas distinctly uncongenial to Maimonides is a scholarly desideratum.

---

[72] Kafih, *Writings*, i. 94.   [73] As noted in Swartz, *Place and Person*, 3.
[74] Swartz, 'Ritual about Myth about Ritual', 142.

FIVE

The Hebrew Language

꤯

Introduction

YOM TOV BEN ABRAHAM OF SEVILLE (Ritva, *c*.1250–1330) was a
student of Solomon ben Abraham Adret and a great admirer of
Nahmanides. He is remembered primarily as the author of influential
novellae on the Talmud. Despite these rabbinic, as opposed to philosophical, credentials, Rabbi Yom Tov wrote a little work called *Sefer hazikaron*,
dedicated to defending Maimonides from the criticisms levelled at him by
Nahmanides in the latter's commentary on the Bible. In this work, there is
only one issue on which Rabbi Yom Tov sides with Nahmanides against
Maimonides: the status of the Hebrew language.

Rabbi Yom Tov wrote: 'Heaven forfend that I offer my soul as a pledge
in defence of the essence of what Maimonides wrote, and may the Lord
forgive him for it, since he made such a great and terrible matter depend
upon something this insignificant.'[1]

What great and terrible matter was it that Maimonides had slighted in
this fashion and for which he needed God's forgiveness? He had denied
that there is anything intrinsically unique about Hebrew. He maintained,
in effect, that the sanctity of Hebrew has nothing to do with the facts that
the Bible was written in it, that God said 'Let there be light' in it and in so
doing created the universe, that it is the language of prophecy, that it was
the 'ur-language' of humankind, or that it is the most exalted language,
spiritually and poetically, on earth. No, Maimonides maintained that
Hebrew is called holy simply because it is a language without words for
foul and disgusting matters, especially concerning sex and defecation. He
thus claims that Hebrew is holy because of one of its characteristics, a

---

[1] *Sefer hazikaron*, 72. For further criticisms of Maimonides by R. Yom Tov (on the
former's explanation of the sacrificial cult), see Idel, 'Maimonides and Kabbalah', 46,
and Schwartz, 'From Theurgy to Magic', 182. On R. Yom Tov's general intellectual
stance, see Schwartz, 'Rationalism and Conservatism'.

characteristic which could, in principle, be shared by other languages. Hebrew is a language like other languages, only more refined.[2]

Rabbi Yom Tov—and not only he[3]—found this intolerable. I will try to show that he was right, according to his lights, to refuse to defend only this of all the many Maimonidean positions attacked by Nahmanides. Maimonides' claims about the 'normality' of Hebrew reflect a much deeper agenda, one which could not have failed to arouse the ire of thinkers like Rabbi Yom Tov. This agenda is the subject of our study in this book.

Judah Halevi on the Hebrew Language

A brief glance at the stream against which Maimonides swam is in order, particularly as regards the special nature of language in general and of Hebrew in particular. Helpful here is the insight of Brian Vickers, who, as I discussed in Chapter 1, points out that the relationship between language and reality is a useful way of distinguishing between the occult and the scientific. The scientific tradition distinguishes between words and things, while the occult tradition fudges the distinction. This leads to the idea that one can manipulate objects in the world by performing manipulations upon their names, which in turn leads to the idea that knowledge of God's true name gives the knower power over the cosmos God created.[4]

---

[2] See Septimus, 'Maimonides on Language', 48: 'Maimonides was opposed to the conception of language as fundamentally related to the ultimate order of things and possessed of power. This conception of language or more precisely Hebrew is an old one. It can be traced back to classical rabbinic literature and assumes great importance throughout the history of Jewish mysticism. Linguistic conventionalism cuts the ground out from under this conception.' In this, as I will show in this chapter, Maimonides is the polar opposite of Judah Halevi.

[3] Moshe Idel has explored the great weight many kabbalists place upon the inherent sanctity of Hebrew and its utility in theurgic contexts in many valuable studies: see Idel, *Language, Torah, and Hermenutics*; id., 'Reification of Language'; id., 'Midrashic versus Other Forms of Jewish Hermeneutics'. See also Altmann, 'Maimonides' Attitude'.

[4] See pp. 20–1 above. Compare Septimus, 'Maimonides on Language', 50: 'For many, it was crucial that the sacred be seen as embedded in the cosmic order. This applies to the sacred language, its words and letters, and especially to the text of the Torah and the names of God. It applies to prayer, as it does to the other sacred commandments[;] they have an inherent relationship to the world order, and an ability to set in motion powerful cosmic forces. Maimonides, on the other hand, rejected the religious outlook that sees language and law built into the basic order of things. For once religious

Maimonides' approach to the nature of Hebrew is but a reflection of his deeper adherence to the scientific culture of his day, and of his rejection of the occult.

Before turning to an examination of Maimonides' views on the nature of the Hebrew language,[5] it will be useful to glance at what Halevi has to say on the subject. In what sense is Hebrew special? For Halevi, Hebrew is superior to all other languages '[both] with regard to the essence of language and with regard to all that it embraces by way of meanings'.[6] Hebrew is essentially nobler than all other languages, as demonstrated by the fact that it was used by the prophets (*Kuzari* ii. 68).[7] Hebrew is holy because it is the only language directly created by God. God taught the language to Adam and it is thus the only truly perfect language; as such, only its nouns convey true information about the essential characteristics of the entities they name:

However, the [various] languages and forms of writing differ in excellence with respect to one another. Some of their names correspond very closely to the things named by them, while some of them [correspond only] remotely. The divine[ly] created language which God taught Adam and placed [both] on his tongue and within his mind, is undoubtedly the most perfect language and also the one that corresponds most closely to the things named by it. [Thus, it is] just as [Scripture] said: 'And whatever the man would call each living creature, that would be its name' (Gen. 2: 19), meaning that [the creature] deserves [just] that name, while [the name] corresponds to it, and tells about its nature. Thus, the superior status of the holy language [relative to other languages] and [the fact] that the angels are more strongly affected by it than [by] any other[8] was entirely necessary.

With respect to this relation [of correspondence between word and object in Hebrew], one may also say of [Hebrew] writing that the forms of its letters are not haphazard and accidental, but rather [are designed] for a purpose corresponding to what is intended by each and every letter.[9] In this theory, therefore, it is not

words and performances are accorded a role in the operation of the world-order, the idea of "nature" is radically altered and one can seem perilously close to the world of magic. Maimonides' doctrine of the conventionality of language was an expression of his rationalistic conception of both Judaism and the natural order.'

[5] For important discussions of Maimonides' views on the nature of language, see J. Stern, 'Language', and, in much greater detail, id., 'Maimonides on Language'.

[6] *Kuzari* ii. 66.

[7] One gets the impression that Halevi held that not only is it the case that in actual fact prophecy has only occurred in Hebrew, but that it can only occur in Hebrew, and that this was too obvious to mention. My thanks to Professor Diana Lobel for discussing these points with me.   [8] BT *Shab.* 12*b*. See also BT *Ḥag.* 16*a* and *Sot.* 33*a*.

farfetched for names[10] and whatever resembles them in [both oral] expression and in writing to have an efficacy [of their own], and, prior to both of them, a determinate measure, [by which] I mean, the thinking of [a] soul that is pure, [and] similar to the angels.[11]

Hebrew, the most perfect of all languages, is the only language created by God. It was not learned by Adam, but placed directly in his mind. Given this origin, it is no surprise that its letters are not random or historically conditioned marks, but have special purposes. Its words, too, are not the consequence of happenstance, convention, or history, but actually teach something important about the things they name or describe.[12] This close correspondence between names and the things named is unique to Hebrew. As a divinely originated language it affects angelic beings more than any other. Hebrew words (or names), when used appropriately, have powerful effects in the world.

For Halevi, Hebrew's holiness is thus a consequence of some essential characteristic of the language, one which it in principle cannot share with other, conventional, languages.[13]

---

[9]   BT *Shab.* 104a.

[10]   Original: *al-shemot*; Halevi uses a combination of Arabic (*al-*) and Hebrew (*shemot*) here. The reference is almost certainly to the use of God's names in order to accomplish the user's ends. On this, see Swartz, 'Magical Piety', 171, and Ch. 1 n. 64 above.

[11]   *Kuzari* iv. 25. Studies on Halevi on the Hebrew language include: Bacher, 'Views of Jehudah Halevi'; Friedlaender, 'Jehudah ha-Levi'; Septimus, 'Maimonides on Language', 48–9; H. A. Wolfson, 'Veracity of Scripture', 224–34; and Zwiep, *Mother of Reason*, 137 (for a parallel between Halevi and Menahem ibn Saruk, see p. 151).

[12]   Compare Nahmanides' comment on Gen. 2: 20: 'The Holy One, blessed be He, brought before Adam all the beasts of the field and all the fowl of the heavens, and he, recognizing their nature, called them names, that is, names appropriate to them. By the names it was made clear who is fit to be the help for another, meaning, fit to procreate with one another' (trans. Chavel, 78).

[13]   Halevi's attitude to Hebrew may be explained, in part, as a reaction to contemporary claims concerning the superiority of Arabic over all other languages; Alloni, '*Kuzari*', 133–5. A consequence of Halevi's view, pointed out to me by Mr Adam Smith of Boston, is that to the extent that classical Hebrew is what we would today call a male chauvinist language, that chauvinism reflects the true nature of the universe. Maimonides' views on Hebrew allow him to adopt a much less 'chauvinist' view of the nature of women. See Kellner, 'Philosophical Misogyny', and Melamed, 'Maimonides on Women'.

Maimonides on the Hebrew Language

1. *The Guide of the Perplexed*

Turning back to Maimonides,[14] we find him asserting that 'language is one of the [specific] properties of a human being and a benefit that is granted him by which he is distinguished'.[15] It is thus no surprise that humans were given language 'with a view to perfection in order that we learn and teach'. The gift of speech should be used appropriately, and must not be 'used with a view to the greatest deficiency and utter disgrace, so that one says what the ignorant and sinful Gentiles say in their songs and stories'. Against this background, Maimonides writes:

I can also give the reason why this our language is called the Holy Language. It should not be thought that this is, on our part, an empty appellation or a mistake; in fact it is indicative of true reality.[16] For in this holy language no word at all has been laid down in order to designate either the male or female organ of copulation, nor are there words designating the act itself that brings about generation, the sperm, the urine, or the excrements. No word at all designating, according to its first meaning, any of these things has been laid down in the Hebrew language, they being signified by terms used in a figurative sense and by allusions. It was intended thereby to indicate that these things ought not to be mentioned and consequently that no terms designating them should be coined. For these are things about which one ought to be silent; however, when necessity impels mentioning them, a device should be found to do it by means of expressions deriving from other words, just as the most diligent endeavor should be made to be hidden when necessity impels doing these things.[17]

[14] After writing this chapter I discovered Ravitzky, 'Maimonides and his Students'. Ravitzky supports the thrust of my discussion here.

[15] *Guide* iii. 8 (p. 435). In that Maimonides defines humans as rational animals (i.e. humans belong to the genus 'animal', and to the species 'rational'), if language is a property by which humans are distinguished from all other animals, it must be intimately connected to rationality. Thus, it is no surprise that in Tibbonian Hebrew, the term 'rational animal' is translated *ḥai medaber* (= speaking animal); see e.g. Samuel ibn Tibbon's translation of the *Guide* i. 51, i. 52, iii. 48, and iii. 12. Ibn Tibbon makes this explicit in his *Perush hamilot hazarot*, *alef* (s.v. *ma'amorot–gader*), *heh* (s.v. *higayon*), and *kaf* (s.v. *ko'aḥ medaber*). See also in *Treatise on Logic* (whether or not this text was indeed written by Maimonides is irrelevant here, since our interest is medieval Hebrew usage in general), chs. 10 and 13.

[16] It is suggestive in the extreme that Maimonides assumed that readers of the *Guide* might think that calling Hebrew the holy language is 'an empty appellation or a mistake'.   [17] *Guide* iii. 8 (pp. 435–6).

Hebrew is called holy, not because of any intrinsic characteristic, not because it, unlike other languages, was directly implanted by God in the heart of the first human and is thus divine, not conventional. No, Hebrew is called holy because of a moral consideration:[18] it is a language which inculcates the values of sexual modesty and personal delicacy. In this sense, it is indeed holy. But in this sense, one supposes, Victorian English might also be called holy, although it is likely that Maimonides would say that Hebrew is still superior to Victorian English, in that the latter had words for earthy matters but simply chose not to use them.[19] The special characteristic of Hebrew is that it had no such words: euphemisms were all it had.[20]

This view of Hebrew follows from the views of sanctity and of ritual purity and impurity discussed above in Chapters 3 and 4. We saw that the term 'holiness' can stand in opposition to 'ritual impurity'. One of the senses of ritual impurity is 'dirt and filth'. Hebrew, as a language free of native expressions denoting aspects of dirt and filth, may be truly called holy.

In another passage in the *Guide of the Perplexed* Maimonides makes his opposition to the Halevi–Nahmanides line concerning the nature of Hebrew explicit:[21]

[18] Maimonides notes at the end of the chapter, 'In the greater part of this chapter we have turned aside from the purpose of the treatise to deal with moral and also religious matters. However, though these matters do not wholly belong to the purpose of the treatise, the order of the discourse has led to that' (p. 436).

[19] Isadore Twersky notes that Joseph Ibn Kaspi (1279–1340) 'asserts in a very positivistic manner that Hebrew is a holy tongue because it is grammatically correct': *Introduction*, 324 n. 1. Ibn Kaspi's comment is found in *Asarah kelei kesef* ii. 17. Twersky's note contains a wealth of other references relevant to Maimonides' view of Hebrew as conventional.

[20] In a personal communication, Josef Stern suggests that, for Maimonides, 'Hebrew expresses a sense of shame with respect to topics such as matter, material impulses, and material organs by not containing any explicit words for these things. This "personification" of Hebrew as a language with a sense of shame is what makes it a Holy Language.'

[21] My attention was drawn to this passage by Faur, *Golden Doves with Silver Dots*, 71. Faur cites Gen. 2: 19, 'and whatever the man called it, that was its name' and asserts that Maimonides interprets the verse to mean that 'it was Adam, and not God, who instituted language' (including, I might emphasize, Hebrew), and as indicating 'the arbitrariness of the [Hebrew] word itself', since '*whatever* the man called it, that was its name'. Faur's insights help to highlight the radical difference between Maimonides' view of the nature of Hebrew and those of Halevi and of Nahmanides. See also Levinger, *Maimonides as Philosopher and Codifier*, 97. Levinger discusses kabbalistic and halakhic opposition to Maimonides' views on the nature of the Hebrew language.

Among the things you ought to know and have your attention aroused to is the dictum: 'And the man gave names [to all the cattle and to the birds of the sky and to all the wild beasts; but for Adam no fitting helper was found]' (Gen. 2: 20). It informs us that languages are conventional and not natural, as has sometimes been thought.[22]

Here Maimonides informs us that the pure Hebrew language spoken by Adam is conventional, like all other languages. Halevi and Maimonides cite the very same verse, the former to prove the uniqueness of Hebrew, the latter to prove the reverse! This is the clearest possible rejection of the idea that Hebrew is in some significant way intrinsically distinct from all other languages, holy in and of itself.

Harry Wolfson read this passage differently.[23] He understands Maimonides here as affirming that 'languages are "conventional" in the sense that they are founded by somebody, that is, Adam, who was taught by God, and are "not natural" in the sense that they have not grown up spontaneously without a founder'. In this he rejects the interpretations of Narboni and Shem Tov on this passage,[24] according to which names of things 'are only arbitrary terms without telling us anything of the nature of the things of which they are names, thus siding with Aristotle's view against the view which is generally identified with Plato and the Stoics'.[25] Wolfson, in other words, is trying to make Maimonides more of a Halevian than he actually was on the question of whether Hebrew is natural or conventional.[26] He was misled on this score, I believe (and that he was

---

[22] *Guide* ii. 30 (pp. 357–8). See Uriel Simon's interesting exposition of Abraham ibn Ezra on this issue: 'common nouns are not arbitrary, but essential: "You see that he [Adam] gave names to all of the animals and birds according to the nature of each and every one of them, and he was a very wise man" (comm. on Gen. 2: 17). But whereas for Yehudah Halevy this supported his view that Hebrew is "the language created by God, which he taught Adam and placed on his tongue and in his heart" (*Kuzari* iv. 25), Ibn Ezra saw Adam as the creator of the Hebrew language . . . therefore he accorded the Hebrew language no more than the status of "the first language" . . . and of a "lucid language", unique in that it is the holy tongue, since "only it contains the great divine name"' (Simon, *Four Approaches*, 267–8 n. 53). For more on Ibn Ezra on this issue, see Zwiep, *Mother of Reason*, 156.   [23] See H. A. Wolfson, 'Veracity of Scripture', 235.

[24] As well as that of José Faur. See above, n. 21.

[25] Commentators on Plato are actually divided on the question of whether he held language to be natural as opposed to conventional. On this issue, see White, *Plato on Knowledge and Reality*, 131–56. White argues that Plato holds language to be neither conventional nor natural.

[26] For a discussion of this issue in Sa'adiah Gaon, see Dotan, *Dawn of Hebrew*

actually misled will be become clearer as we progress), because he did not see that Maimonides' stance on Hebrew was simply an aspect of a much broader rejection of the 'proto-kabbalistic' vision of Judaism adopted by Halevi and Nahmanides (and many others).[27]

In the *Guide* Maimonides consistently treats Hebrew as an example of language in general and not as something *sui generis*. It will be useful to glance at a few examples of this. Like all 'normal' languages, Hebrew grows and changes, even within the Bible itself. This claim comes up several times in the 'lexicographical' chapters of the *Guide*. Here is an example from i. 8 (p. 33):

Place [*makom*]. Originally this term was given the meaning of particular and general place. Subsequently, language extended its meaning and made it a term denoting an individual's rank and situation . . . It is in this figurative manner that it is said: 'Blessed be the glory of the Lord from His place' (Ezek. 3: 12), meaning, according to His rank and the greatness of His portion in existence.

Here we have a term, which in Ezekiel is intimately associated with God (and which, in rabbinic Hebrew, even came to denote God), but which originally had no such meaning. Its meaning was extended in a fashion apparently common to all languages.[28]

Similarly, in *Guide* i. 67 (p. 162):

The doing away with the notion in question, which gives rise to vain imagining, should not be negated because of the rules of conjugation obtaining in the [Hebrew] language, for we know that today we have no complete understanding of the science of our language and that in all languages rules merely conform to the majority of cases.

In Hebrew, as in all languages, 'rules merely conform to the majority of cases'. This comment in and of itself does not prove that Maimonides held

---

Linguistics, i. 96–104. Sa'adiah's view of all language (including Hebrew) as conventional is also discussed in Brody, *Geonim of Babylonia*, 322.

[27] For the philosophical background to many of the issues discussed here, see Goodman, 'Jewish and Islamic Philosophy of Language'.

[28] See *Guide* i. 9 (p. 34) for a similar example. Note also Maimonides' comment in *Guide* i. 57 (pp. 132–3), concerning the question of divine attributes (surely an issue that one would expect Hebrew to handle very well): 'For the bounds of expression in all languages are very narrow indeed, so that we cannot represent this notion to ourselves except through a certain looseness of expression.' Hebrew is in no way excepted from this stricture but is treated even on this crucially important religious issue as one language among others.

Hebrew to be a language like all other languages, but it surely renders more difficult the case of those who would deny that claim.[29]

In the context of the Judaism which he inherited from his forebears and teachers, Maimonides' views on Hebrew are surely unusual.[30] The very first verses of the Bible teach that the cosmos was created through a Hebrew utterance.[31] Hebrew is the language in which God addresses humankind and in which the Torah was couched. It is hardly surprising, therefore, that many Jewish thinkers attached special significance to the Hebrew language and saw in it a tool which not only reflects reality at its deepest level but creates realities as well.[32]

Just as Halevi affirmed the special character of Hebrew before Maimonides, so did Nahmanides after him, and in direct opposition to

[29] For more on the natural way in which Hebrew evolves, see the sources cited in Twersky, *Introduction*, 330.

[30] So much so that even so radical a Maimonidean as Joseph ibn Kaspi held that Hebrew terms express the essence of the objects they name. See Herring, *Joseph ibn Kaspi's Gevia Kesef*, 52–60. See above, n. 19.

[31] See e.g. BT *Ber. 55a*: 'Rab Judah said in the name of Rab: Bezalel knew how to combine the letters by which the heavens and earth were created. It is written here, "And He hath filled him with the spirit of God, in wisdom [*ḥokhmah*] and in understanding [*tevunah*], and in knowledge [*da'at*]" (Exod. 35: 31) and it is written elsewhere, "The Lord by wisdom [*ḥokhmah*] founded the earth; by understanding [*tevunah*] He established the heavens" (Prov. 3: 19) and it is also written, "By His knowledge [*da'at*] the depths were broken up" (Prov. 3: 20).' See further BT *Men. 29b*, BT *AZ 3a*, *Gen. Rabbah* 18, and E. Urbach, *Sages*, i. 197–213. For another interesting text, from Merkavah literature, see Scholem, *Jewish Gnosticism*, 79. For Maimonides on this, see *Guide* i. 65 (p. 158) on the equivocality of the term 'speech': to say that God spoke is simply to say that God acted. This certainly deflates the notion that Hebrew was actually used in the creation of the world. My thanks to Josef Stern for pointing this out to me.

[32] This is certainly the view of *Sefer yetsirah*. Idel, 'Reification of Language', 47, comments: *Sefer yetsirah* 'contributed the theory that the letters of the Hebrew alphabet entered the process of creation not only as creative forces but as the elements of its material structure'. *Sefer yetsirah* was seen as a legitimate expression of talmudic Judaism by most of Maimonides' philosophic predecessors and successors. On the 'ontological' status of Hebrew in *Sefer yetsirah*, see further Altmann, 'Saadya's Theory of Revelation'; Dan, 'Religious Meaning'; Idel, 'Midrashic versus Other Forms of Jewish Hermeneutics'; Jospe, 'Early Philosophical Commentaries'; Pines, 'Quotations from Saadya's Commentary'; Sirat, *History of Jewish Philosophy*, 10; and Zwiep, *Mother of Reason*, 54. It is surely worthy of note that, while Halevi included a commentary on *Sefer yetsirah* in the *Kuzari* (iv. 25) Maimonides, so far as is known to us, never mentioned the work. It is hardly credible that he had never heard of it. See Ch. 1 n. 48.

him. But before examining Nahmanides' criticisms of Maimonides we need to look at other instances in which the latter's view of the nature of Hebrew finds apparent expression.

In general, it might be thought that Hebrew, the language of divine communication with human beings, is uniquely qualified to express divine matters. But this is not the case. In this respect, all languages are limited. Maimonides gives us no reason to think that Hebrew is superior to other languages in this regard:

> These subtle notions [concerning God's existence] that very clearly elude the minds cannot be considered through the instrumentality of the customary words, which are the greatest among the causes leading unto error. For the bounds of expression in all languages are very narrow indeed, so that we cannot represent this notion to ourselves except through a certain looseness of expression.[33]

Language under the best of circumstances is heuristic,[34] pointing us in the right direction, never metaphysical, in the sense of adequately expressing true reality.[35]

2. Other Writings

There are a number of places in his letters, commentaries, and halakhic writings in which Maimonides makes direct or indirect references to the Hebrew language which are relevant to the present inquiry. In these passages Maimonides makes an important distinction between content and language.[36] Wherever Maimonides' hands are not tied, so to speak, by

---

[33] *Guide* i. 57 (pp. 132–3).

[34] Kenneth Seeskin notes that Maimonides shares with Plato and Plotinus a view of language as heuristic, not referential: 'its function is not to depict the structure of an underlying reality but to prepare the mind for a particular kind of reflection' ('Sanctity and Silence', 9).

[35] For more on Maimonides' views on the conventional nature of the Hebrew language, see Rosenberg, 'Bible Exegesis in the *Guide*', 98–103. Compare also Botwinick, *Skepticism, Belief, and the Modern*, 36, where the author discusses what he calls Maimonides' nominalist philosophy of language. I ought to note that not all students of Maimonides accept at face value what he says about Hebrew (or, more correctly, are unwilling or unable to read his words without forcing upon them a more traditionalist interpretation). For a particularly egregious example see Amitai, 'Maimonides on Hebrew'.

[36] In the texts that follow I will be discussing the distinction between content and language in the context of Hebrew vis-à-vis other languages. But Maimonides makes the distinction in a broader context as well in *Guide* i. 50 (p. 111): 'Know, thou who studiest this my treatise, that belief is not the notion that is uttered, but the notion that is represented in the soul when it has been averred of it that it is in fact just as it has been represented.'

settled halakhic precedent, he insists that the language in which something is said is less important than what is being said.

Maimonides makes this distinction clearly in one of his earliest references to the question of language. In Mishnah *Avot* 1: 17 we read:

Simeon, his son, used to say: all my days I grew up among the sages, and I have found nothing better for a person than silence. Study is not the most important thing, but deed; whoever indulges in too many words brings about sin.

In his long comment on this passage, Maimonides takes critical note of the behaviour of some of his rabbinic contemporaries. He tells of having seen great and righteous people who, if they happened to be at a drinking party or a wedding, stopped people from reciting Arabic poetry, even if the subject of the poem was praise of courage or seriousness, while they had no objection to the recitation of poems in Hebrew, even if these contained deprecated or forbidden speech. This is the height of folly, Maimonides insists, since speech is to be prized or deprecated on the basis of its content, not the language in which it is expressed. However, he goes on to admit, foolishness expressed in Hebrew is worse than if it were expressed in other languages, because of Hebrew's sanctity. Maimonides here affirms that Hebrew is the holy language (and we have seen just above why it is called holy) and ought not to be abused, but still, what makes speech noble or ignoble is not the language in which it is couched, but the ideas it expresses.[37]

Maimonides refers back to this passage in a responsum addressed to a correspondent in Aleppo, Syria, concerning the permissibility of listening to Arabic music: 'We have already explained in our commentary on *Avot* that there is no difference between things said in Hebrew and things said in Arabic, since things are forbidden or permitted according to the meaning of what is said.'[38] The point is quite clear: meaning, not language, is what is fundamental. Our issue comes up in another letter, this one written by Maimonides to a simple Jew in Baghdad named Joseph ibn Jabar. Ibn Jabar had been mocked for his inability to read Hebrew, and Maimonides, seeking to encourage him, wrote that he considered him his beloved student, as was

anyone who wishes to cleave to the study of Torah, even if he understood [only] one verse or one law—and it makes no difference if he understood the matter in

---

[37] This passage is discussed in Kozodoy, 'Reading Medieval Hebrew Love Poetry', and Brann, *The Compunctious Poet*, 77.

[38] *Letters*, ed. Sheilat, 429, and Maimonides, *Responsa*, ed. Blau, 398 (responsum no. 244). On this responsum see above, Ch. 3 n. 60.

Hebrew[39] or Arabic or Aramaic, [since] the point is to understand the matter in any language. [Since] the Shema may be recited in any language, how much more so the commentaries and compositions![40]

Even though Maimonides goes on in this letter to encourage ibn Jabar to learn enough Hebrew to understand the *Mishneh torah*, and rejects the idea of translating that work into Arabic (because its beauty will thereby be lost),[41] his overall point is clear: Torah study is central to Judaism, and there is no necessity to do it in Hebrew as opposed to other languages.

Maimonides alludes to our subject in a passage in his *Medical Aphorisms* (*Pirkei mosheh*), in connection with a discussion of the climatological theory, according to which human beings reflect the special characteristics of the climes from which they hail. In chapter 25, paragraphs 57–8 he writes:

Moses states: These are Galen's words in regard to the Greek language which he claims is superior to all other tongues of the world. Razi and others questioned this statement of Galen and the question consists of the fact that he places Greek above other languages of man and degrades every other tongue. It is known that every tongue is conventional and every language with which one is not familiar and with which one is not raised is disagreeable and difficult and burdensome. This is the viewpoint of those who question this.[42] It seems to me that the [following] words of Galen in this assertion are correct: that the differences in the pronunciation of the elements of speech and the differences of the organs of speech are in accordance with the nature of the different climates, meaning the differences in body constitution and the difference in the form of their organs and the internal and external measurements, as Abu Nasser Alfarabi mentioned in the *Book of Letters*.[43] People living in temperate climes are more perfect in intelligence

[39] Lit. 'the holy language'.

[40] *Letters*, ed. Sheilat, 408; English trans. Stitskin, 87–94. Our passage appears on p. 87.

[41] It is important to note that nothing I write here should be taken as meaning that Maimonides did not love Hebrew or did not take pride in it. Indeed, in his comment on Mishnah *Avot* 2: 1, Maimonides cites learning Hebrew as an example of a commandment of which people make light, but which should be taken seriously. There does not seem to be any place where Maimonides actually counts learning Hebrew as a commandment, however.

[42] i.e. who question Galen's claims about the superiority of Greek.

[43] On this source, see S. Harvey, 'A New Islamic Source', 39; I follow Harvey in the translation here. Kafih, in his notes on this text, detects a (temporary, since it pre-dates the *Guide*) retreat from the view that languages are conventional; this may or may not be the case, but is unimportant for our purposes, since here too Hebrew is treated in no way as unlike other languages, be they all natural or be they all conventional. See further Langermann, 'Maimonides and Miracles', 171 n. 31.

and, in general, better in form, that is, their shape is more orderly, the composition of their organs is better and their constitution is better proportioned than people living in the far northern or southern climes.[44] So too the pronunciation of letters by people from temperate climes, and the movement of their organs of articulation during speech is more even. They are closer to the human language and the enunciation of letters, and the articulation of their speech organs is clearer than that of the people of the distant climates and their language, just as Galen asserted it. Galen did not mean the Greek language alone,[45] but it and similar ones, such as the Greek language, the Hebrew, the Arabic, the Persian and the Aramaic. These are the languages of [people in] temperate climates, and they are natural to them, according to the different places and their proximity [or distance from one another]. Regarding the Hebrew and Arabic languages, it is accepted by everyone who knows these two languages that they undoubtedly are a single language, and the Aramaic is very closely related to them. Greek is close to Aramaic, and the source of the letters of these four languages is the same, and only few letters are different, perhaps three or four letters. However, Persian is far removed from these [four languages], and the enunciation of its letters is quite different.[46]

In this passage Maimonides discusses Hebrew in the same breath, so to speak, as other languages spoken by peoples who were born and reared in temperate climes. Such people are better suited by nature than individuals from more extreme climes to use that properly human tool, speech. From this perspective there is no difference between Hebrew, Arabic, Aramaic, and Greek, which are related languages; nor is there is any difference of rank between these four and Persian.[47] Offered a golden opportunity, so to

[44] For studies on the doctrine of 'climatology', here attributed to Alfarabi, see Altmann, 'Climatological Factor'; Baer, 'Land of Israel'; Melamed, 'Land of Israel and Climatology'; S. Harvey, 'A New Islamic Source'; and Kreisel, 'Land of Israel'. For a discussion of climatology and language, see Zwiep, *Mother of Reason*, 192–200. Other relevant and useful studies include Alloni, *'Kuzari'*; R. Fontaine, 'Between Scorching Heat and Freezing Cold'; id., 'Inhabited Parts of the Earth'; Goldenberg, 'Development of the Idea of Race'; and Regev, 'Land of Israel in Sixteenth-Century Jewish Thought'.

[45] Maimonides here maintains that Galen did not mean to assert that only Greek is a truly perfected language. There can be little doubt that Maimonides misinterprets Galen's actual intention here.

[46] I cite the translation of Rosner and Muntner (Maimonides, *Medical Aphorisms*, i. 202–3), corrected according to the text and (Hebrew) translation of Maimonides, *Letters*, ed. Kafih, 149–50. For discussion of this passage, see Septimus, 'Maimonides on Language', 48–9, and Silman, *Philosopher and Prophet*, 90–1 n., 241 n.

[47] Zwiep, *Mother of Reason*, 202, points to parallels to some of these ideas in Abraham Ibn Ezra. Y. Tzvi Langermann maintains that in this passage Maimonides sees

speak, to emphasize the special character of Hebrew, Maimonides resolutely refuses to do so. Indeed, outside the *Guide* he seems to write as if he
were unaware of the extravagant claims made for the special character of
Hebrew by many of its enthusiasts.

There is a passage in the *Commentary on the Mishnah* in which our issues
find interesting and clear expression. In connection with the Mishnah's use
of the word *taram* ('gave the heave offering'), Maimonides notes:

The modern grammarians[48] object to [the Sages'] use throughout the Mishnah of
taram . . . saying that the correct form is *herim*. But in truth this is no objection.
For correct form in any language depends upon what the people of that language
speak and [what] is heard from them. Now [these teachers of the Mishnah] were
without a doubt Hebrews in their [native] place, namely the Land of Israel. And
they have been heard to use *taram* and its conjugations. This is proof that it is permitted in the [Hebrew] language and that it is one of the expressions of the
Hebrews. And after this fashion should your response be to any one of the moderns who claims that the speech of the Mishnah is not pure . . . And this principle,
which I have mentioned to you, is considered quite sound by the perfect scholars
who discuss the universal matters which are common to all languages.[49]

Septimus here contrasts Maimonides' 'linguistic empiricism' with the 'clas-
sicism' of thinkers like Abraham Ibn Ezra. For our purposes, however, the
interesting element in this passage is the way in which Maimonides treats
Hebrew as he would any other language. Languages grow and develop
according to apparently universal rules. This growth and development is
entirely acceptable and in this Hebrew is like every other language. Mishnaic
sages, as native speakers in their native land, determine what Hebrew is, as
opposed to some frozen classical (i.e. biblical) model of the language.[50] This

Hebrew as natural as opposed to conventional. But, as such, it is no different from other
natural languages. In the *Guide* Maimonides adopts a much more radical claim: language (including Hebrew) is conventional, not natural. See Langermann, 'Maimonides
and Miracles'. In this, Langermann follows Kafih ad loc.

[48] Kafih cites Menaham ibn Saruk.

[49] *Commentary on the Mishnah*, *Terumot* 1: 1. Cited from Septimus, 'Maimonides on
Language', 43–4, slightly emended according to Maimonides, *Letters*, ed. Kafih, i. 167.
For similar language, compare *Treatise on Logic*, p. xiv. Josef Stern suggests that these
texts echo battles between 'logicians' and 'grammarians' in the contemporary Muslim
world. For details, see his 'Maimonides on Language'.

[50] Indeed, as Maimonides notes in another context, we know only a 'scant portion'
of the original Hebrew language and barely know how to pronounce it. See *Guide* i. 61
(p. 148). I might note that this would seen to render the theurgic use of Hebrew problematic, or at least of limited efficacy.

approach seems hard to reconcile with the view that Hebrew, the language used by God to create the cosmos, and implanted in the minds of Adam and Eve (or taught to them by God), is in some essential way wholly unlike all other languages. After all, the Hebrew which God used to create the cosmos was biblical, not mishnaic!

There are a number of passages in the *Mishneh torah* which are relevant to our theme. In 'Laws of the Recitation of the Shema', 2: 10, we learn:

One may recite the Shema in any language he knows. One who recites in any language [other than Hebrew] must also diligently avoid mistakes in that language, and must take care to pronounce the words properly in that language just as he must take care when reciting it in the holy language [Hebrew].

The first sentence of this paragraph is based on an explicit mishnaic text (*Sotah* 7: 1) and presents no problems. The second sentence refers back to issues discussed by Maimonides in the two paragraphs which precede this one. At the end of paragraph 8 Maimonides had written: 'One must take care to pronounce the letters clearly; if he did not, he still fulfilled his obligation.' In paragraph 9 he explains what he means by this:

How does one take care to pronounce the letters clearly? He should exercise care not to pronounce a stop as a spirant, nor a spirant as a stop, nor a quiescent *sheva* as a mobile *sheva*, nor a mobile *sheva* as a quiescent *sheva*. Therefore, he must pause between two similar letters, when one ends a word and the other begins the following word, as in 'with all your heart'.[51] He must recite *bekhol*, pause and then continue and recite *levavkha*. So also with *ve'avadetem meherah* (Deut. 11: 17) and *hakanaf petil* (Num. 15: 38). One must clearly pronounce the *zayin* of *tizkeru* (Num. 15: 40). One must extend the *dalet* of *eḥad* ('one', Deut. 6: 4) sufficiently to proclaim God's sovereignty over the heavens, the earth, and the four corners of the world.[52] One must not cut the *ḥet* in the word *eḥad* short such that it sound like *eiḥad*.[53]

What does Maimonides teach us? Let us say that someone does not know Hebrew, and chooses to recite the Shema in English translation. It is not sufficient that the translation should be precise (i.e. that one 'diligently avoid mistakes in that language', paragraph 8); one 'must take care to pronounce the words properly in that language just as he must take care

[51] *Bekhol levavekha*; the first word ends with the letter *lamed* and the second begins with it.

[52] Lit. 'the four directions'. The point here (based on a discussion in BT *Ber.* 13*b*) is that one ought to extend the word 'one' (or its last letter) long enough self-consciously to (re-)accept God's sovereignty over the universe.

[53] Which could be construed as meaning 'is not one'.

when reciting it in Hebrew'. Take, for example, the first paragraph of the Shema:

Hear, O Israel! The Lord is our God, the Lord alone. You shall love the Lord your God with all your heart and with all your soul and with all your *might. Take* to heart these instructions with which I charge you this day. Impress them upon your children. Recite them when you stay at home and when you are away, when you lie down and when you get up. Bind them as a sign on your hand and let them serve as a symbol on your forehead; inscribe them on the doorposts of your house and on your gates.

The word 'might' ends with the letter 't' and the following word, 'take', begins with it. One must be careful to pronounce these two words so that they are clearly distinct: one 'must recite "might", pause and then continue and recite "take"'.

This, at least, is what Maimonides' irascible glossator, Abraham ben David, takes him to mean—and faults him mightily for it. He says that Maimonides' ruling is rationally unacceptable (*ein zeh mekubal al hada'at*) since all other languages are commentaries (*perush*) on Hebrew, 'and who would diligently avoid mistakes in a commentary?'. I assume that Rabbi Abraham here refers to the idea that Hebrew is the original language of humankind; he even seems to claim that it is the only true language, all others being mere commentaries upon it. But perhaps I am reading too much into his comment. Another issue more clearly arouses his ire: Maimonides' ruling here is without any apparent talmudic source.[54] It is also probably safe to assume that Rabbi Abraham did not like the way in which Maimonides here implicitly equates Hebrew and all other languages.

Joseph Karo (in his commentary *Kesef mishneh*), apparently aware of these issues, seeks to draw the sting of Maimonides' ruling by making the sentence, 'One who recites in any language [other than Hebrew] must also diligently avoid mistakes in that language, and must take care to pronounce the words properly in that language just as he must take care when reciting it in Hebrew' refer entirely to the issue of translation, denying that Maimonides rules that one should read the translation as carefully as one reads the original Hebrew.

I think that any fair-minded reader must agree that Rabbi Abraham presents a less tortured reading of Maimonides' text than does Karo. This is not to say that Karo was not a fair-minded reader of Maimonides. But it is more than a safe assumption that he accepted the views about the special

---

[54] As noted in Levinger, *Maimonides' Techniques of Codification*, 142–3.

nature of the Hebrew language which were widely accepted in kabbalah,[55] and could not believe that Maimonides meant to imply that there is no substantial difference between Hebrew and other languages.

The Shema may be recited in any language; that is settled law. Since the Shema, when read in Hebrew, must be pronounced very carefully, it follows, Maimonides apparently held, that when recited in any language other than Hebrew it must also be pronounced very carefully in that language. Here I think we see an example of the distinction between content and language drawn by Maimonides in his commentary on Mishnah *Avot*, as discussed above.

There is another passage in *MT* 'Laws of the Recitation of the Shema' in which the point comes through even more clearly, in 3: 4–5:

No other sacred matter may be uttered in the bathhouse and the privy, even if not in Hebrew,[56] and not only the recitation of the Shema. Not only is it forbidden to utter Torah matters there, it is even forbidden to think about them in the privy, bath-house, or any other polluted place, i.e. a place with excrement or urine.

Everyday matters may be spoken about in Hebrew in the privy, and so also epithets of God, such as 'Merciful' and 'Faithful', etc. But the specific names of God—i.e. the names which may not be erased[57]—may not be mentioned in a privy or a bathhouse that has been used. But if the opportunity to restrain one from doing something forbidden arose in a bath-house or in privy, it should be done, even in Hebrew, and even if it concerns sacred matters.

In these two paragraphs Maimonides weaves together four distinct talmudic sources (BT *AZ* 44*b*, *Ber.* 24*b*, *Shab.* 10*b* and 40*b*) in order to teach a unified lesson: with the exception of specific names of God, Hebrew may be used in a privy or bath-house to discuss everyday matters, and matters of Torah may not be uttered in a bath-house, even if not in Hebrew. Clearly, it is not the language which is crucial, but what is spoken about.

A third passage relevant to our enquiry is in *MT* 'Laws of the Sanhedrin', 26: 3:

He who curses himself is liable to flogging—the penalty incurred when one curses his neighbour—for it is said: 'Only take heed to thyself and guard well thy life' (Deut. 4: 9). Whether he curses himself or another Israelite or the nasi or a judge, he is not subject to flogging unless he curses by one of the special names of God, such as YH, Elohim, Shaddai, or the like, or by any of the appellations of God, such as the Merciful, the Jealous, or the like. Since cursing by any of the

---

[55] On which see above, n. 32.   [56] Lit. 'in a secular language'.
[57] See *MT* 'Laws of the Foundations of the Torah', 6: 2.

appellations entails the penalty of flogging, it follows[58] that if one curses by the name of God in any language, he is subject to flogging, for the names by which Gentiles refer to God belong to the category of attributes.[59]

The last sentence in this paragraph is apparently Maimonides' own deduction.[60] Just as the Hebrew word *ḥanun*, 'the Merciful', is an appellation (*kinui*) of God, so are words like 'God' in English or 'Allah' in Arabic. So we see again, whenever Maimonides' hands are not tied, so to speak, by halakhic precedent, he makes meaning primary, not the language in which it is expressed.[61]

In apparent contrast to what I have written so far, there is a passage in *MT* 'Laws of Prayer', 1: 4, which might be thought to imply that Maimonides singled out Hebrew as special and superior to other languages:

After the Jews were exiled by the evil Nebuchadnezzar, they mingled with the Persians, Greeks, and other nations and had children in these foreign lands. These children spoke confused languages, composed of many languages, and could not speak well in any single language, as it says, 'their children spoke the language of Ashdod and the language of those various peoples and did not know how to speak Judean' (Neh. 13: 24). Because of this, when one of them prayed, he was unable to ask for what he needed or praise the Holy One, blessed be He, in Hebrew, without mixing in other languages. Seeing this, Ezra and his court ordained eighteen blessings in the following order: the first three consist of praises of God, the last three consist of thanksgiving, while those between consist of requests for the principal desires of individuals and the principal needs of the community. The prayers were thus well ordered and learned quickly, by everyone. In this way, the prayers of the inarticulate could be as perfect as those of the eloquent. For this reason were ordained all the blessings and prayers as regularly recited by all Jews, so that the full meaning of the blessings be well expressed, even by the inarticulate.

This passage, however, does not state that Hebrew is any way superior to other languages, even with respect to prayer. It explains why Judaism has fixed prayers. Originally, prayer was meant to be recited extemporaneously, 'as the spirit moved one', so to speak. When the Jews lived independently

---

[58] This appears to be Maimonides' own conclusion.

[59] I have used the translation in *Book of Judges*, trans. Hershman, 79, with slight alterations.

[60] See Levinger, *Maimonides' Techniques of Codification*, 187.

[61] Other passages in the *Mishneh torah* which may be relevant to our theme include 'Laws of Oaths', 11: 14, 'Laws of Prayer', 14: 11, 'Laws of Blessings', 1: 6, and 'Laws of Tefilin', 1: 19. In each of these passages, Maimonides refuses to grant priority of any sort to Hebrew, but since each is based on clear halakhic precedent, their support for the position being urged here is secondary at best.

in their land, these prayers were, naturally, expressed in Hebrew. The dispersal of the Jews[62] brought it about that they became inarticulate in Hebrew and could no longer frame prayers in that, or indeed, in *any* particular language. It was this deficiency which brought about the establishment of set prayers which, according to Jewish law, may be recited in any language.[63]

Why Did Maimonides Adopt his Position?

We have adduced a wide variety of texts, all of which together lead to the conclusion, not only that Maimonides held Hebrew to be a language like any other (sacred, of course, because it had no foul words and thanks to the uses to which it had been put, but in no intrinsic, inherent, ontological way different from other languages), but that it was also important for him to get that message across, even if he did not wish to draw explicit attention to what he was doing. Why was this so important? A passage in the *Guide of the Perplexed* provides us with one key to understanding this.

In *Guide* i. 61–2 Maimonides discusses God's names. He opens the discussion by stating: 'All the names of God, may He be exalted, that are to be found in any of the books derive from actions. There is nothing secret in this matter' (p. 147). In other words, God's names denote nothing about God's essence, but only describe ways in which God behaves. It follows from this that there is no difference between calling God *ḥanun* in Hebrew, for example, or 'Merciful' in English. This matter is entirely normal and there is nothing unusual or secret about this.

Maimonides goes on to note an exception to this generalization, 'namely, *yod*, *heh*, *vav*, *heh*. This is the name of God, may He be exalted, that has been originated without any derivation, and for this reason it is called the *articulated name*.' This name of God is exceptional and is called articulated (*meforash*) because 'it gives a clear unequivocal indication of His essence, may He be exalted'. But all the other biblical and rabbinic names of God tell us nothing about God, but much about how normal speakers of Hebrew characterize the Deity.

After elaborating these points, Maimonides emphasizes:

Do not think anything other than this and do not let occur to your mind the vain imaginings of the writers of amulets[64] or what names you may hear from them or

---

[62] And not the decline of the generations! See Kellner, *Maimonides on the 'Decline of the Generations'*, 51–2.

[63] Mishnah *Sot.* 7: 1.   [64] Arabic: *al-kame'ot*; Pines translates 'charms'.

may find in their stupid books,[65] names that they have invented, which are not indicative of any notion whatsoever but which they call the names and of which they think that they necessitate holiness and purity and work miracles. All these are stories that it is not seemly for a perfect man to listen to, much less to believe. (p. 149)

The writing of amulets containing holy names and the manipulation of divine names (*shemot* in Hebrew, *al-shemot* in Maimonides' Judaeo-Arabic) were common forms of magical praxis in antiquity, widely accepted among the Jews.[66] Maimonides gives short shrift to these practices.

Maimonides continues his discussion of God's names in *Guide* i. 62, there exhorting his readers in the following fashion:

When wicked and ignorant people found these texts, they had great scope for lying statements in that they would put together any letters they liked and would say: this is a name that has efficacy and the power to operate if it is written down or uttered in a particular way. Thereupon these lies invented by the first wicked and ignorant man were written down, and these writings transmitted to good, pious,

---

[65] Possibly a reference to *Sefer harazim* and books like it. See below.

[66] For background on this, see Groezinger, 'Names of God'. Note well Groezinger's comments on p. 57: 'The distinction and autonomy of the onomatological conception becomes particularly apparent where the names themselves appear in the texts as living, powerful, magnificent and venerable beings, who are granted veneration and praise like a personal god, particularly through the well-known formula: *barukh shem kevod malkhuto*.' Groezinger writes that each divine name in Heikhalot texts is 'a venerable bearer of power, indeed, it is a hypostasis of inherent power and function . . . From the aforesaid it becomes clear why even the slightest change of a name, or an enumeration of too many or too few names, can have dangerous consequences, since through the change of the series of letters a new name comes into being and a new center of power is activated, which eventually can become dangerous to the one who handles the name' (p. 58). On the expression *barukh shem kevod malkhuto le'olam va'ed* see my comments below in Ch. 6 n. 16. For more on these names, see Elior, 'Mysticism, Magic, and Angelology', 11: 'This literature perceives the divine creative force as embodied within the Hebrew letters. Thus reality is no more than the extension and manifestation of the divine word. The divine language by which the world was created becomes *names* possessing creative power and letters which bind heaven and earth. The name embodies the divine essence which is susceptible of being attained, the secret creative powers hidden in the letters and the enigmatic element which links between the world of man and the celestial world. The essence of God is identical to His name, and therefore knowledge of the names and the manner of articulating them is tantamount to a certain comprehension of the divine essence. The name is considered as the embodiment of the creative power and as a means of creation, as a mystical–magical means of ascent and as the secret essence of the celestial world.'

and foolish men who lack the scales by means of which they could know the true from the false. These people accordingly made a secret of these writings, and the latter were found in the belongings left behind them, so that they were thought to be correct. To sum up: 'A fool believes everything' (Prov. 14: 15). We have gone beyond our noble subject and our subtle speculation, turning to speculation designed to invalidate vain imaginings the lack of validity of which is manifest to every beginner in speculation. However, the necessity that made us mention the names and their meaning and the opinion concerning them that is generally accepted by the vulgar has led us to do so. (p. 152)[67]

Maimonides' language here is very strong, even though he tries to exculpate the many people among whom he lived who gave credence to the magical efficacy of amulets and the manipulation of divine 'names'. People who believed these things in his day, he tells us, are 'good, pious, and foolish men', unlike the 'wicked and ignorant' individuals originally responsible for all this nonsense.[68]

An example of the sort of writing Maimonides attacks here is the *Sefer harazim* (Book of Mysteries), discussed above in Chapter 1. *Sefer harazim* and works like it[69] explain, perhaps, the fervour of Maimonides' comments here, and surely explain why he found it of such pressing importance to undermine the theory of Hebrew which makes these works possible.[70]

Nahmanides' Critique

Maimonides' claims about Hebrew are difficult to defend, a point made emphatically by Nahmanides in his critique of *Guide* iii. 8.[71] In his comment on Exodus 30: 13, Nahmanides explains that the perfect silver shekel, weighing precisely what it should, with no imperfections, and no admixture of baser metals, is called the holy shekel. He then explains:

[67] For valuable background to this passage, see J. Stern, *Problems and Parables*, 122–3.

[68] One can hardly help wondering where Halevi would fit in here: 'wicked and ignorant' or 'good, pious, and foolish'?

[69] There is another relevant book now easily accessible which well illustrates the tendencies in Judaism that I think Maimonides was seeking to undermine. This is the *Ḥarva demosheh*, or *Sword of Moses*. See above, Ch. 1 n. 72.

[70] For further background on the magical and theurgic uses of Hebrew in rabbinic texts and culture, see Gruenwald, 'Haketav, Hamikhtav, and the Articulated Name'. For evidence that the magical and theurgic uses of divine names were widespread in the generations immediately after Maimonides, see the text of Abraham Abulafia cited in Idel, 'Judaism, Jewish Mysticism, and Magic', 35–6.

[71] The commentators Narboni and Shem Tov were no more convinced by Maimonides' claims than was Nahmanides.

I hold that this is the same reason why our Rabbis call the language of the Torah 'the sacred language', because the words of the Torah, and the prophecies, and all words of holiness were all expressed in that language. It is thus the language in which the Holy One, blessed be He, spoke with His prophets and with His congregation . . . In that tongue He is called by His sacred names . . . In that tongue He created His world . . . The names of Michael and Gabriel are in this sacred language. In that language He called the names of 'the holy ones that are in the earth' (Ps. 16: 3), Abraham, Isaac, Jacob, Solomon, and others. Now the Rabbi has written in the *Guide of the Perplexed* . . .[72] Now there is no need for this reason, for it is clear that the Hebrew language is most holy, as I have explained. And [Maimonides'] reason is in my opinion not correct . . .[73] And if the reason were indeed as the Rabbi has said, they should have called it the modest language.[74]

In another context Nahmanides argues explicitly against the claim that Hebrew is conventional, without mentioning Maimonides by name.[75] For Nahmanides, the holiness of Hebrew is intrinsic, not, as Maimonides would have it, extrinsic.[76] It is the language used for the actual creation of the cosmos, it is the language in which the Torah is written, it is the language which God uses to communicate with prophets and Jews, it is the language in which God is actually named. It, unlike all other languages, 'is most holy'.

---

[72] Nahmanides here cites *Guide* iii. 8, where Maimonides says that Hebrew is holy because it has no words for indelicate objects and actions, as we saw above.

[73] Nahmanides here adduces examples of Hebrew words for indelicate objects and actions.

[74] Nahmanides, *Commentary*, trans. Chavel, 519–20.

[75] 'Ma'amar al penimiut hatorah' in Nahmanides, *Writings*, 467.

[76] In a personal communication Professor Josef Stern disagrees with my reading of Nahmanides here: 'According to Nahmanides, the Torah calls the sheqel "sheqel haqodesh" [holy shekel], not because it has any special or privileged qualities of its own, a natural perfection or supernatural or divine status. Instead the sheqel is qodesh [holy] only because it is used for various functions that are qodesh, such as redemption of the first-born or the valuation of gifts to the Temple . . . Hence, the sense in which things like the sheqel are qodesh is entirely derivative. No intrinsic property of the sheqel renders it qadosh. Had the US dollar been used instead to fulfill the various Temple functions that in fact happened to be fulfilled by the sheqel, it, the dollar, would instead be qadosh. This functional explanation of the sanctity of the sheqel is, then, by and large deflationary.' Since I am more interested in Maimonides here than in Nahmanides, I leave it to the reader to judge between our different interpretations.

Maimonides' position on Hebrew, as the language of modesty and hence and only hence of holiness, is not only hard to defend, as Nahmanides argued, it is also unprecedented.[77] This is not the only case in which Nahmanides 'caught' Maimonides taking a stand difficult to defend,[78] but in this case in particular, Nahmanides' refutation seems especially strong. It is hard not to ask why Maimonides put himself so far out on such a weak limb.

While Maimonides certainly found no joy in writers of amulets and manipulators of divine names, I think it makes sense to see his consistent and repeated attempts to reduce the level of religious tension, so to speak, around the Hebrew language as a reflection of his much broader agenda, the removal of halakhic issues from the realm of ontology to the realm of morality.

On the basis of the foregoing it seems clear that a proper understanding of Maimonides' thought and that of the school which he in effect founded demands an understanding of the world of Jewish magic and the occult which Maimonides sought (by and large unsuccessfully) to dethrone. Taking note of that world enables us to see that his distinction between ontology and sociology, so to speak, is both pervasive throughout his thought and a conscious (if purposefully muted) reaction to a kind of religious consciousness which he dismissed as little more than paganism. In this chapter I have used his understanding of the nature of the Hebrew language to illustrate this wider claim.

[77] Unprecedented, but not without influence. See Zwiep, *Mother of Reason*.

[78] Maimonides had claimed that the Aramaic translation (Targum) of the Torah attributed to Onkelos was characterized by a consistent attempt to avoid anthropomorphism. Nahmanides takes Maimonides to task for this in his comment on Gen. 46: 1. Their debate is reflected in modern scholarship. See Bacher, *Maimonides as Biblical Commentator*, 39–45 (on which, see Dienstag, 'Binyamin Ze'ev Bacher', 67–8 n. 13) and Halperin, *Faces of the Chariot*, 120, 251, and 406–7, for the 'Maimonidean' perspective. But Klein, 'Translation of Anthropomorphisms', 162–77, argues that had the authors of the Targumim 'truly been concerned about the theological and philosophical implications of anthropomorphisms, they would have avoided them with much greater care and consistency' (p. 168). He faults Maimonides for retrojecting 'his own sensitivity on the issue to the early Aramaic translators' and for incorrectly seeking 'to systematize the obvious inconsistencies in the targum, on the assumption that a system does exist'. Klein notes that both assumptions are also made in modern scholarship. My thanks to Seth Kadish for drawing my attention to Klein's works. For more on Maimonides and Onkelos, see Weiss, 'See No Evil'; Posen, 'Targum Onkelos in Maimonides' Writings'; and id., *Translation Consistency*, 39, 75–6, 131 n. 28, 133–4.

Before closing this discussion I would like to take note of a broader issue. The debate between Maimonides and Halevi over the nature of the Hebrew language is but a reflection of a deeper debate between them. Halevi's views on Hebrew are an expression of his hard-line particularism. If Hebrew is uniquely suited to communication with and from God, if Hebrew has theurgic properties not found in other languages, then non-Jews (and even non-Hebrew-speaking Jews?) are by definition kept further from God than are Jews. In other words, if Hebrew has special and important religious properties, it follows that anyone seeking to approach God using any other language is condemned to remain at a distance. This is hardly a view congenial to Maimonides, and his characterizations of Hebrew should be understood, in turn, as an expression of his hard-line universalism.

SIX

Kavod, Shekhinah, and Created Light

☙

Introduction

THE TERM *KAVOD* OCCURS about a dozen times in the Torah in some sense or other of perceptible divine presence.[1] Rabbinic literature tends to prefer the term *shekhinah* (from the root, *sh-kh-n*, to dwell) for what is apparently the same phenomenon.[2] Heikhalot literature seems to place greater emphasis on *kavod* than on *shekhinah*, while later kabbalah does just the opposite, making *shekhinah* one of the *sefirot* (the ten hypostasized attributes or emanations by means of which the Infinite enters into relationship with the finite). Medieval Jewish philosophers such as Sa'adiah and Judah Halevi added a third term, 'created light', and took all three as synonyms. All of these literatures seem to agree on one thing: the terms *kavod*, *shekhinah*, and 'created light' all denote something in the 'real world'. The terms are not simply metaphors or descriptions of the internal state of an individual undergoing a religious experience. But it is precisely in such a fashion, I will show here, that Maimonides understood the terms. Maimonides' 'non-ontological' view of the terms *kavod*, *shekhinah*, and 'created light' is part and parcel of his campaign against proto-kabbalistic elements in Judaism.

In making this argument, I will be developing and expanding upon brief comments made by my late teacher, Steven S. Schwarzschild, who had

---

[1] The term, deriving from the Hebrew word for 'heavy' and usually meaning 'honour' or 'gravitas' has, when connected to God, often been translated as 'glory', although the NJPS usually prefers 'Presence'.

[2] The identity of *kavod* and *shekhinah* was apparently first pointed out explicitly by Sa'adiah Gaon, as will be seen below. Howard Kreisel notes: 'The identification of the "glory" (*kavod*) and the *shekhinah* occurs in rabbinic literature. Many of the same motifs found in the Bible in conjunction with the *kavod* are employed by the rabbinic Sages in describing the *shekhinah*' (*Prophecy*, 77). In post-Maimonidean kabbalistic texts the identity of *shekhinah* and *kavod* with the *sefirah* Malkhut becomes commonplace. See e.g. Septimus, *Hispano-Jewish Culture*, 106.

argued that the term *shekhinah* should 'be understood as a somewhat poetic, metaphoric name that classical Judaism has given to the idea of the functioning relationship between the transcendent God, on the one hand, and, on the other hand, humanity in general and the people of Israel in particular'. Schwarzschild contrasted this view with attempts at hypostasization, in which '*shekhinah* as a term of art for God's love, care, and nearness becomes a metaphysical (meta-*physical*) ontic entity that, if not actually a part, or aspect, of God, insinuates itself as an intermediary between God and humanity'. In a few brief sentences in his essay, he argued that Maimonides understood the term *shekhinah* as being figurative and metaphorical.[3] Schwarzschild's interest was in making a normative claim about Judaism, and in showing, once again in his view, that the German philosopher Hermann Cohen had got things right and that matters often understood in metaphysical terms ought to be understood in regulative or moral terms. My interest here is historical; I seek to delineate Maimonides' precise views, and to show that his understanding of *kavod*, *shekhinah*, and 'created light' reflects his metaphorical reading of terms which other Jewish thinkers understand as naming real entities in the cosmos. In this we see yet another reflection of Maimonides' opposition to 'hyper-realism', his opposition to the multiplication of entities beyond necessity, his opposition to attempts to 'repopulate' the heavens, and his opposition to seeing what Steven Schwarzschild would call (echoing Hermann Cohen) regulative ideals as reified entities.

Let us look briefly at the way in which the term *kavod* is used in the Torah. Its first occurrence is in Exodus 16, which describes one of the episodes of Israelite grumbling in the wilderness. Moses tells the Jews: 'and in the morning you shall see the *kavod* of the Lord, because He has heard your grumblings against the Lord. For who are we that you should grumble against us?' (Exod. 16: 7). Moses keeps his word: 'Then Moses said to Aaron, "Say to the whole Israelite community: Advance toward the Lord, for He has heard your grumbling." And as Aaron spoke to the whole Israelite community, they turned toward the wilderness, and there, in a cloud, appeared the *kavod* of the Lord' (Exod. 16: 9–10). The ancient Israelites certainly seemed to have beheld something actually visible here, and in a later chapter (Exod. 24: 17) they see the *kavod* as a burning fire on top of Mount Sinai.[4]

---

[3] See Schwarzschild, '*Shekhinah* and Eschatology', 235, 238, and 244.

[4] Compare also Lev. 9: 5–7, 22–4; Num. 14: 10, 20–3 and 16: 6–7; Isa. 40: 3–5 and 60: 1–3; Ezek. 1: 26–8, 3: 22–7, and 8: 1–4.

A further passage on the same theme, in chapter 33, was destined to have great resonance for Maimonides. Moses is shown asking God: 'Oh, let me see Your *kavod*!' God answers:

'I will make all My goodness pass before you, and I will proclaim before you the name Lord, and the grace that I grant and the compassion that I show. But', He said, 'you cannot see My face, for man may not see Me and live.' And the Lord said, 'See, there is a place near Me. Station yourself on the rock and, as My *kavod* passes by, I will put you in a cleft of the rock and shield you with My hand until I have passed by. Then I will take My hand away and you will see My back; but My face must not be seen.' (Exod. 33: 18–23)

The rank anthropomorphism of this passage was problematic for Maimonides, and he turned to it again and again in his writings.[5] Be that as it may, the text itself seems to present the *kavod* as something which may be seen.

Not only visible, but also, apparently, impenetrable: 'When Moses had finished the work, the cloud covered the Tent of Meeting, and the *kavod* of the Lord filled the Tabernacle. Moses could not enter the Tent of Meeting, because the cloud had settled upon it and the *kavod* of the Lord filled the Tabernacle' (Exod. 40: 33–5). This sense of the *kavod* as filling space finds expression several times in the prophetic writings. At the dedication of Solomon's Temple we find:

When the priests came out of the sanctuary—for the cloud had filled the House of the Lord and the priests were not able to remain and perform the service because of the cloud, for the *kavod* of the Lord filled the House of the Lord—then Solomon declared: 'The Lord has chosen to abide in a thick cloud: I have now built for You a stately house, a place where You may dwell forever.' (1 Kgs. 8: 10–13)[6]

Similarly:

In the year that King Uzziah died, I beheld my Lord seated on a high and lofty throne; and the skirts of His robe filled the Temple. Seraphs stood in attendance on Him. Each of them had six wings: with two he covered his face, with two he covered his legs, and with two he would fly. And one would call to the other, 'Holy, holy, holy! The Lord of Hosts! His *kavod* fills all the earth!' The doorposts would shake at the sound of the one who called, and the house kept filling with smoke. I cried, 'Woe is me; I am lost! For I am a man of unclean lips and I live

---

[5] For details, see Hannah Kasher's exhaustive and perceptive study, 'Maimonides' Interpretation'. See also Klein-Braslavi, *King Solomon*, 203–11.

[6] Compare the parallel passage, 2 Chron. 7: 1–3.

among a people of unclean lips; yet my own eyes have beheld the king Lord of Hosts.' (Isa. 6: 1–5)[7]

Another verse that was destined to have profound impact upon Jewish liturgy is Ezekiel 3: 12: 'Then a spirit carried me away, and behind me I heard a great roaring sound: "Blessed is the *kavod* of the Lord, in its[8] place."' Taken at face value, these verses certainly appear to teach a doctrine according to which God's *kavod* is an entity that actually exists in the sensible world.

Shekhinah, Kavod, and Created Light in Rabbinic Texts

The term *shekhinah* is used widely in rabbinic texts, and even the briefest study would take us far afield. Ephraim Urbach writes: 'We may sum up as follows: In Tannaitic literature the term *shekhinah* is used when the manifestation of the Lord and His nearness to man are spoken of.'[9] About rabbinic literature as a whole, he writes: 'A survey of all the passages referring to the *shekhinah* leaves no doubt that the *shekhinah* is no "hypostasis" and has no separate existence alongside the Deity' and 'The concept of the *shekhinah* does not aim to solve the question of God's quiddity, but to give expression to His presence in the world and His nearness to man, without, at the same time, destroying the sense of distance.'[10]

As used in rabbinic literature *shekhinah* may not be a hypostasis in the Neoplatonic sense of the term, but there is no reason to doubt that many rabbinic sources attest to an understanding of *shekhinah* as a phenomenon which can be located in specific places at specific times.[11]

---

[7] Compare also Ezek. 43: 1–9.

[8] NJPS translates 'His'; I follow the Targum and most of the classical commentators in understanding the reference here to be to the *kavod*, and not to God.

[9] E. Urbach, *Sages*, i. 43. For more on *kavod* and *shekhinah* in rabbinic literature, see Abelson, *The Immanence of God* (strongly criticized by Urbach); Fishbane, 'The "Measures" of God's Glory'; E. R. Wolfson, *Through a Speculum that Shines*, 43–9; and Schwarzschild, '*Shekhinah* and Eschatology'. Schwarzschild provides a very useful summary (and critique) of much earlier literature on the subject.

[10] *Sages*, 63, 65. Gershom Scholem, however, sees the notion of *shekhinah* as 'verging on hypostatization'. See Scholem, *On the Mystical Shape of the Godhead*, 147–8. For a critique of Scholem's attempt to draw a sharp distinction between rabbinic views of *shekhinah* and later kabbalistic views, see Idel, 'Rabbinism versus Kabbalism'.

[11] See e.g. *Gen. Rabbah* 19: 7. Indeed, Alan Unterman opens his *Encylopaedia Judaica* article '*Shekhinah*' with the following definition of the term as used in rabbinic literature: 'God viewed in spatio-temporal terms as a presence'.

While the term *kavod*, as opposed to *shekhinah*, does not figure prominently in rabbinic halakhah and aggadah, it is found in crucial passages in another kind of literature created by the rabbis, namely prayer. This should hardly surprise us—after all, so many of the prayers are drawn from biblical texts. But even so, the use of *kavod* (in the sense under discussion in this chapter, and not simply in the sense of 'honour') in so many places that were designed to be or became central to the liturgy indicates the importance of the concept in the world-view of rabbinic Judaism.[12]

The passages from Isaiah and from Ezekiel cited above come together in one of the central texts of the Jewish liturgy, the Kedushah.[13] Here follows my woefully wooden and inadequate translation of part of the Kedushah as found in Maimonides' order of prayer:[14]

We sanctify and revere and multiply Your holiness three times over, as in the word spoken by Your prophet: 'And one would call to the other, "Holy, holy, holy! The Lord of Hosts! His *kavod* fills all the earth!"' (Isa. 6: 3). His *kavod* and greatness fill all the earth, and His ministers ask, 'Where is the place of His *kavod*?' in order to revere Him. They praisefully say one to the other, 'Blessed is the *kavod* of the Lord, in its place.' (Ezek. 3: 12)

Here we have a prayer, versions of which are recited three times in every morning service, a prayer which served as the springboard for scores if not

---

[12] I realize that there is no such thing as 'the worldview of rabbinic Judaism'. But it is a safe bet that Maimonides thought that there was such a thing, and since this sketchy study of rabbinic texts is meant to serve as background to Maimonides, and not as a study of rabbinic Judaism, I shall let the term stand.

[13] The origins of the Kedushah ('doxology') prayer, the focus of the public recitation of the Amidah, are lost in antiquity. It was certainly well established by geonic times, and is included without comment in Maimonides' order of prayer at the end of the second volume of the *Mishneh torah*. For a recent overview, see Raymond Scheindlin's edition and translation of Elbogin, *Jewish Liturgy*, 54–62. For detailed studies of the history and crystallization of the prayer, see Bar-Ilan, 'Major Trends', and Fleischer, 'Kedushah of the Amidah'. Fleischer concludes that the inclusion of the Kedushah in the liturgy was an accommodation by the rabbis to the demands of the masses, who pressed for its inclusion. On the history and significance of the '*keter*' version of Kedushah (ignored, I might note, by Maimonides) see Bar-Ilan, 'Idea of Crowning God'. For a study of one of the two biblical verses which forms the core of the Kedushah (Isa. 6: 3), and its subsequent liturgical importance, see Weinfeld, '"We Will Sanctify Your Name"'. Weinfeld concludes that 'The *kedushah* liturgy is thus based upon the conception that the members of the earthly congregation can join the angels in songs of praise, and sing "together" in one chorus the praises of God' (p. 76).

[14] According to MS Oxford Huntington 80, and not the printed versions.

hundreds of synagogue hymns (*piyutim*),[15] and a prayer given special prominence in the way in which it is recited during the repetition of the Amidah. The prayer is emphatic in its focus on *kavod*.

The Kedushah may or may not have been composed by talmudic rabbis; it was certainly prized by the authors of Heikhalot texts, and found its prominent place in the liturgy by the geonic period. Maimonides had no reason not to attribute its authorship to the rabbis of the Talmud (much as he perhaps would have preferred not to).[16]

It is, of course, possible to read each rabbinic reference to *shekhinah* in metaphorical terms. That is much harder to do with the use of the term *kavod* in Heikhalot texts. Rachel Elior summarizes the matter as follows:

> The term *kavod* has various meanings in *hekhalot* literature; with regard to the characteristics of the Divine, *kavod* is the general name for the celestial worlds unparalleled in the terrestrial realm, for the fixed relationship of God and the celestial retinue, of the enthroned to the throne. As in its biblical sense, *kavod* in *hekhalot* mysticism is an aspect of God with a visual dimension, the figurative hierarchy of the heavens accessible to observation by *hekhalot* mystics.[17]

[15] On the *kedushta* and *yotser* types of *piyutim*, see Weinberger, *Jewish Hymnography*, 50–8.

[16] There is another well-known sentence from the liturgy which ought to be mentioned here. It is the statement *barukh shem kevod malkhuto le'olam va'ed* ('blessed be the name of His glorious sovereignty forever and ever'), inserted into the recitation of the Shema after the first verse (Deut. 6: 4). The word *kavod* here, however, is in the construct state and clearly modifies the following word; thus the translation here. This prosaic linguistic fact did not stop the many Jews who insisted on reading this passage in creative (and fanciful) ways. Useful studies on this sentence include Fleischer, 'Towards a Clarification'; M. Kasher, 'Meaning of the Phrase'; Y. Urbach, 'Concerning the Secret'—an idiosyncratic study but one which cites many useful sources; Elbogin, *Jewish Liturgy*, 21–4, 80, 376–7; and Kimelman, 'Shema' Liturgy', 97–103. Our sentence played an extremely non-Maimonidean role in certain Heikhalot texts; see Groezinger, 'Names of God', 57: 'The distinction and autonomy of the onomatological conception becomes particularly apparent where the names themselves appear in the texts as living, powerful, magnificent and venerable beings, who are granted veneration and praise like a personal god, particularly through the well-known formula: *Barukh shem kevod malkhuto?* According to this view, the sentence means, 'Blessed be the name *Kavod*'—it is no longer God who is blessed after the recitation of the first verse of the Shema (Deut. 6: 4), but God's name. Attributing independent status to God's name violates any number of Maimonidean strictures; see the discussion of the throne of God on p. 73 above.

[17] Elior, 'Concept of God', 110. Other studies relevant to the use of *kavod* in Heikhalot texts include Abrams, '"Secret of Secrets"'; Altmann, 'Saadya's Theory of Revelation'; id., 'Moses Narboni's "Epistle on *Shi'ur Qoma*"'; Dan, *Esoteric Theology*;

Kavod is thus something seen; as such, the term must relate to something locatable in space and time, something that can be apprehended by the human senses.

Sa'adiah Gaon

Consistent with traditional usage, both Sa'adiah Gaon and Judah Halevi understand *kavod* as denoting something corporeal and accessible to the senses.[18] Sa'adiah sought to protect God's absolute incorporeality in the face of biblical passages such as those quoted above. Thus he writes:

Our answer to this objection is that this form was something [specially created]. Similarly the throne and the firmament,[19] as well as its bearers, were all of them produced for the first time by the Creator out of fire for the purpose of assuring His prophet that it was He that had revealed His word to him . . . It is a form nobler even than [that of] the angels, magnificent in character, resplendent with light which is called the *kavod* of the Lord. It is this form . . . that the Sages characterized as *shekhinah*. Sometimes, however, this specially created being consists of light without the form of a person.[20]

We learn a number of important things from this passage. Sa'adiah teaches that what the Torah calls *kavod*, rabbinic literature calls *shekhinah*. It is created out of fire, it is greater than the angels, and it is that which prophets (actually) see when they describe visions of the divine realm. Seeing the *kavod* assures the prophet that his vision is real and not the result of his (fevered) imagination.[21] When one sees the *kavod*, it is not God one sees (God forbid!), but, rather, a special divine creation.

Fishbane, 'The "Measures" of God's Glory'; Freudenthal, 'Stoic Physics'; Jospe, 'Early Philosophical Commentaries'; Kiener, 'Hebrew Paraphrase'; Liebes, *Ars Poetica*, 56; Petuchowski, *Theology and Poetry*, 38; Pines, 'God, the Divine Glory, and the Angels'; id., 'On the Term *Ruḥaniyut*'; Scholem, *Jewish Gnosticism*, 37, 55, 68; E. R. Wolfson, 'Merkavah Traditions'; and id., 'Theosophy of Shabbetai Donnolo'. On the use of *kavod* in the *piyut* literature, see E. Urbach (ed.), *Sefer arugat habosem*, i. 197–203.

[18] For a history of discussions of *kavod*, see Dan, *Esoteric Theology*, 104–68.

[19] The question had been asked with respect to Ezek. 1: 26 ('Above the expanse over their heads was the semblance of a throne, in appearance like sapphire; and on top, upon this semblance of a throne, there was the semblance of a human form') and 1 Kgs. 22: 19 ('But [Micaiah] said, "I call upon you to hear the word of the Lord! I saw the Lord seated upon His throne, with all the host of heaven standing in attendance to the right and to the left of Him"').

[20] Sa'adiah, *Book of Beliefs and Opinions*, ii. 10; p. 121 in the Rosenblatt translation.

[21] Discussing this passage, Diana Lobel writes that the *kavod* 'is an objective light, more sublime than the light of the angels, which God molds into various spiritual forms

Judah Halevi

Judah Halevi's views on the nature of *kavod* are similar to those of Sa'adiah. In *Kuzari* ii. 4 he writes of 'spiritual forms, which are called the *kavod* of the Lord, [which] take shape out of the delicate spiritual stuff that is called the Holy Spirit. It is called the Lord metaphorically [inasmuch] as it descended on Mount Sinai',[22] and in ii. 8: 'the *kavod* [of the Lord] is a ray of divine light, which is beneficial when His people are in His land'. The phenomena to which Halevi refers here are clearly perceptible in the inter-subjective world of human experience.

One of Halevi's more important statements of his position is found in *Kuzari* iv. 3:

Now according to the first opinion[23] the *kavod* of the Lord (Exod. 15: 7) is that delicate body which is subject to the will of God, which takes shape in accordance with whatever He wishes to show to a particular prophet. According to the second opinion, the *kavod* of the Lord is the entire ensemble of angels and spiritual instrumentalities [by means of which God acts, like] the Throne, the Chariot, the firmament, the Wheels, the Spheres, as well as other things that are stable and everlasting . . . Perhaps this was what Moses, peace upon him, was seeking when he said, 'Oh, let me see Your *kavod*!' (Exod. 33: 18). God responded positively to him in that regard on condition that he protect himself against seeing the front [of what would be shown to him], which a human being cannot withstand . . . Now within that *kavod* [there is] something that prophetic sight can withstand. Yes, and among its concomitant effects [there is also] something that [even] our own glances can withstand, like the cloud (Exod. 24: 15) and the consuming fire (Exod. 24: 17), for example, which belong to the class of things familiar to us. . . . when the sun itself is at its brightest, [our] eyesight cannot look at it [directly]; and if someone were to force himself to do that, he would go blind. This is [also the case

when God wants to assure the prophet of the Divine Presence. At certain extraordinary times, such as the revelation at Mount Sinai, the *kavod* also becomes visible to all the people of Israel' (*Between Mysticism and Philosophy*, 112–13). For more on Sa'adiah on *kavod*, see (in addition to the studies by Abrams, Altmann, Freudenthal, Jospe, and Kiener, cited above in n. 17): Kreisel, 'Judah Halevi's Influence on Maimonides', 110–12; Lobel, *Between Mysticism and Philosophy*, 118–19, 164–5; A. Green, *Keter*, 96–8; E. R. Wolfson, *Through a Speculum that Shines*, 126–7; and, in great and illuminating detail, Kreisel, *Prophecy*, 56–67, 76–7.

[22] This passage is discussed in E. R. Wolfson, *Through a Speculum that Shines*, 173. He points out that in this passage Halevi merges 'ancient Jewish theosophy [= notions taken from the Heikhalot literature] and contemporary philosophic terminology'.

[23] Halevi here refers to the opinion of Sa'adiah.

with] the *kavod* of the Lord, the *malkhut*[24] of the Lord, and the *shekhinah* of the Lord as far as terms derived from the religious Law are concerned.

With respect to this passage, Howard Kreisel draws the following distinctions between Sa'adiah and Halevi:

Saadiah clearly has actual physical sight in mind, while Halevi is ambiguous on this point. If the 'inner eye' is the power of imagination under the sway of the intellect, and the angels are the Separate Intellects—notions which Halevi is at least prepared to entertain—then he could not have thought it absolutely necessary to interpret the 'face' as a corporeal entity at all, no matter how subtle its composition.[25]

Diana Lobel agrees:

The Haver [Halevi's spokesperson in the book] is agnostic about the precise ontological status of the *kavod*: whether it is a created light which God molds into the forms he shows the prophet (iv. 3; ii. 4, 7) or represents the permanent forms of the celestial world, such as the throne and the chariot (iv. 3). Ha-Levi emphasizes the affective, experiential dimension, the effect of the vision on the person who holds it.[26]

But whatever Halevi's actual opinion about the experience of the prophet in relation to *kavod* etc., I want to show that he holds that these phenomena have clear manifestations—cloud and fire—in the world in which we (non-prophets) live.

Halevi connects the phenomena under discussion to the Land of Israel. Towards the end of *Kuzari* ii. 14, one of the key texts on the special nature of the Land of Israel, he notes that the Jewish people 'grew numerous during their stay in the Holy Land in conjunction with those concomitants that are helpful [in this regard], such as rites of purification, acts of worship,

[24] 'Kingship'; in kabbalah the *sefirah* identified as *kavod* and as *shekhinah*. See above, n. 2.

[25] Kreisel, 'Halevi's Influence on Maimonides', III. Other studies on Halevi on *kavod*, *shekhinah*, etc. (in addition to Lobel, *Between Mysticism and Philosophy*, 101, 118–19, and Kreisel, *Prophecy*, 111–17) include Lasker, 'Judah Halevi and Karaism'; E. R. Wolfson, *Through a Speculum that Shines*, 163–87; id., 'Merkavah Traditions', 194–203; and Silman, *Philosopher and Prophet*, 203–8.

[26] Lobel, *Between Mysticism and Prophecy*, 119. Interestingly, Lobel also compares Sa'adiah and Halevi: 'In Sa'adya's doctrine, the Glory, or angel, or cloud functions merely to assure the prophet and the people that it is actually God who is addressing them. Ha-Levi develops this idea in the direction of a symbolic language; the image not only tells the prophet from whence the communication comes, but actually instructs him more effectively than could language alone' (p. 113).

and sacrifices, especially [when these were carried out] in the presence of the *shekhinah*'. He goes on here to imply that *shekhinah* and *al-amr al-ilahi* are identical, at least in this context. Be that as it may, *shekhinah* in this passage is clearly more than a metaphor for some notion of God's care for creatures.

In *Kuzari* ii. 16, Halevi asks the Khazar king to describe what he thinks happens when the people of Israel, dwelling in the Land of Israel, properly worship the Lord during the festivals appointed by God for that purpose. The king replies: 'The *kavod* of the Lord should [certainly] appear.' There is no doubt that the king here serves as a spokesman for the views of Halevi, who was convinced that the *kavod* is perceptible and can be made to appear if the proper combination of acts is carried out by the right people in the right place in the right way at the right time.

Statements he makes at the very end of the *Kuzari* strengthen this interpretation of Halevi. In v. 22 the Khazar king seeks to dissuade his friend, the sage who had taught him about Judaism, from leaving for the Land of Israel, and asks: 'What would one seek in the Holy Land today, when the *shekhinah*[27] is no longer there and drawing close to God is something one can attain in any place by means of pure intention and fervent desire?'. The worried king receives the following reply:

It is the *shekhinah* that is visible to the eye that has disappeared, since it reveals itself only to a prophet or to a multitude that is pleasing [to God] in that special place. . . . But the hidden [and] spiritual *shekhinah* is with [every] native-born Israelite [who is] blameless [in his] actions, pure of heart, [and] sincere in his intention towards the Lord of Israel. (v. 23)

God is with good Jews[28] at all times. That presence was actually made visible in the Land of Israel under certain circumstances.

This passage of Halevi's takes on added meaning when read in connection with a recently discovered text, about which Joseph Yahalom writes:

From what Halevi says in the most recent fragment of a letter to have been discovered in the St Petersburg library collection of manuscripts, it would appear that he sought to realize in his pilgrimage to Jerusalem the precise conditions that he had already stated would bring about the revelation of the *Shekhinah* in the Land. As he puts in this letter, his intentions are to gather about him a group of priests (*kohanim*) who, under his charge, would perform the cultic rites on the Mount of Olives: 'And my soul longed / for the mountain of holiness / to bow down in the

---

[27] Halevi uses the Arabic here, *sakinah*.

[28] At least the native-born among them; for an important discussion of Halevi's views on proselytes, see Lasker, 'Proselyte Judaism'.

presence of the sons of Aaron / and the holy ark which has been hidden / and to say before the Lord, Rise and have compassion for Zion.'[29]

Not only was *shekhinah* actually visible in the past, it is entirely possible that Halevi journeyed to the Land of Israel in the hopes of seeing it![30]

Maimonides on *Kavod* in the *Guide of the Perplexed*

Turning now to Maimonides, I propose to examine the ways in which he analyses the terms *kavod*, *shekhinah*, and created light in the *Guide of the Perplexed*, before taking note of some of the places in which these terms are used in his earlier writings.[31] I propose to study his texts in this non-chronological order since, while he uses the terms in his earlier writings, he analyses them only in the *Guide*. I am also operating on the assumption that there are no major discontinuities between Maimonides of the *Guide* and Maimonides of the earlier writings, at least with respect to the issue under discussion. It will turn out that Maimonides most emphatically does not follow Onkelos, Sa'adiah, and Halevi in seeing *shekhinah* as some sort of divine creation which, like all created entities, enjoys some sort of existence of its own.[32]

Not surprisingly, most of the places in which Maimonides treats of these terms are in the first fifty chapters of the *Guide*, those chapters in which he teaches the reader how to read passages in the Torah which might be thought to describe God in corporeal, anthropomorphic, and anthropopathic terms. I propose to examine first passages dealing with *kavod*, then

[29] Yahalom, 'The Journey Inward', 147.

[30] *Shekhinah* comes up in another context which further illustrates the differences between Halevi and Maimonides. For Halevi the authority of the Sanhedrin in Jerusalem is connected to the court's sitting in the Temple, in the presence of the *shekhinah*. Maimonides explicitly denies this connection. This issue reflects Halevi's attempt to intertwine halakhah with prophecy and Maimonides' attempt to distinguish the two. On the issue of the Sanhedrin and the *shekhinah*, see Blidstein, *Authority and Dissent*, 18–19, 155, 268 n. 4. On the issue of halakhah and prophecy see E. Urbach, 'Halakhah and Prophecy', and Arieli, 'Rabbi Judah Halevi and the Halakhah'. For discussion and further references see Kellner, 'Rabbis in Politics'.

[31] On a fourth term, 'created voice', which plays a much smaller role in Maimonides than do the three terms under discussion, see Kreisel, '"The Voice of God"', and Eisenmann, 'The Term "Created Light"', which cites other relevant studies. For background, see H. A. Wolfson, *Repercussions*, 85–92.

[32] In this interpretation, I take issue with Scholem, *On the Mystical Shape of the Godhead*, 154, and, following him, E. Urbach, *Sages*, i. 40.

those dealing with *shekhinah*, and finally those dealing with created light. This will necessitate a certain amount of repetition, since, as it turns out, Maimonides does not hold these terms to be distinct from one another in any important way and thus often treats them together, but approaching the matter in this fashion will make my analysis easier to follow.

In *Guide* i. 4 (pp. 27–8) Maimonides discusses the three terms 'to see' (*ra'oh*), 'to look at' (*habit*), and 'to envision' (*hazoh*), and writes that they are

applied to the sight of the eye and that all three of them are also used figuratively to denote the grasp of the intellect. . . . Every *mention of seeing*, when referring to God, may He be exalted, has . . . figurative meaning—as when Scripture says: . . . 'Oh, let me see Your *kavod*!' (Exod. 33: 18) . . . All this refers to intellectual apprehension and in no way to the eye's seeing . . .

The *kavod* that Moses seeks to 'see' in the Exodus text is thus nothing that can be seen with the eyes. The prophet seeks a deeper understanding of God, not a better view of God or of God's *kavod*. The emphasis in this passage is on the meaning of 'see'; in a subsequent discussion (*Guide* i. 59) Maimonides examines what it was that Moses sought to see.

The term 'place' (*makom*), Maimonides informs us in *Guide* i. 8 (pp. 33–4), originally signified a spatial location: 'Subsequently, language extended its meaning and made it a term denoting an individual's rank and situation. . . . It is in this figurative manner that it is said: "Blessed be the *kavod* of the Lord from His place" (Ezek. 3: 12), meaning, according to His rank and the greatness of his portion in existence.' Since God has no place, we should not expect God's *kavod* to occupy any place either. It is not the sort of thing that can be localized in space and time, and as such is not subject to any sensual apprehension.[33]

The point made here is emphasized again in the following chapter (i. 9; pp. 34–5), devoted to the term 'throne', where Maimonides writes:

The Sanctuary was called a throne, because of its indicating the grandeur of Him who manifested Himself therein and let His light and glory[34] descend upon it. Thus Scripture says: 'Thou throne of *kavod*, on high from the beginning, [Thou

[33] At a later point in this chapter Maimonides makes a methodological point worth noting: 'Know that with regard to every term whose equivocality we shall explain to you in this treatise that our purpose in such an explanation is not only to draw your attention to what we mention. Rather, do we open a gate and draw your attention to such meanings of that particular term as are useful for our purpose, not for the various purposes of whoever may speak the language of this or that people.' The same point is made again in *Guide* i. 10 (p. 35).　　　　[34] Both terms here are in Arabic.

place of our Sanctuary]' (Jer. 17: 12). On account of this sense, the heaven is called a throne, as indicating to those who have knowledge of them and reflect upon them the greatness of Him who caused them to exist and move, and who governs this lower world by means of the overflow of their bounty.

The term 'throne' indicates God's grandeur—it certainly does not denote a piece of furniture! It is in that sense that 'heaven' is called God's throne; heaven is not the site of God's throne, but an indication of God's grandeur. Thus, *kavod* as used in this verse denotes nothing which can be apprehended by the senses, but, rather, indicates God's grandeur.

In *Guide* i.18 (pp. 43–5) Maimonides teaches that the terms 'approach', 'touch', and 'come near' can mean

union in knowledge and drawing near through apprehension, not in space . . . Every mention of approaching and coming near that you find in the books of prophecy referring to a relation between God, may He be exalted, and a created being has this last meaning. . . . The same applies to its dicta: 'Nigh unto it' (Deut. 4: 7); 'approach thou and hear' (Deut. 5: 24); 'And Moses alone shall come near unto the Lord, but they shall not come near' (Exod. 24: 2). The verse is to be interpreted in this way, unless you wish to consider that the expression 'shall come near', used with reference to Moses, means that the latter shall approach the place on the mountain upon which the light, I mean the *kavod* of God, has descended. For you are free to do so.

For our purposes, two important points are implied here: approaching God's *kavod* means approaching God in knowledge, not in any spatial sense, and *kavod* and 'light' are synonymous terms in at least some contexts. These are implications, the second clearer than the first. What Maimonides teaches explicitly is that God's *kavod* (= light) manifested itself on the top of Mount Sinai. For Maimonides that means that it was on Mount Sinai that Moses achieved his highest understanding of God.

Our next passage (*Guide* i. 19; pp. 45–6) continues the themes just adumbrated. It teaches that the term 'to fill'

is also employed to signify the achievement of perfection in virtue and of the latter's ultimate end.[35] Thus: 'And full with the blessing of the Lord' (Deut. 33: 23); 'Them hath he filled with wisdom of heart' (Exod. 35: 35); 'He was filled with wisdom and understanding and skill' (1 Kgs. 7: 14). In this sense it is said: 'The whole earth is full of his *kavod*' (Isa. 6: 3); the meaning of this verse being that the whole earth bears witness to His perfection, that is, indicates it. Similar is its dictum:

---

[35] It is worth noting in passing that we see here an indirect expression of part of Maimonides' view that the fulfilment of the commandments subserves another end (intellectual fulfilment).

'And the *kavod* of the Lord filled the tabernacle' (Exod. 40: 34). Every mention of filling that you will find referring to God is used in this sense, and not in the sense of there being a body filling a place. However, if you wish to consider that the *kavod* of the Lord is the created light that is designated as *kavod* in every passage and that filled the tabernacle, there is no harm in it.

What does it mean to say that the whole earth is full of God's *kavod*? It means that the whole world bears witness to God's perfection. This is a theme that Maimonides emphasizes in the first four chapters of the *Mishneh torah* (to which we will turn below). *Kavod* is thus not something that fills spaces, be they the cosmos or the tabernacle. It is an expression denoting God's grandeur, visible (as Maimonides made clear in the *Mishneh torah*) through the wisdom evident in the workings of nature.[36]

So far so good; but then Maimonides tells us that if we choose to understand *kavod* as the created light which (actually) filled the tabernacle, we are free to do so. What does that mean? It turns out that he is making reference to a point he had made earlier, in *Guide* i. 5, where he had written:

Our whole purpose was to show that whenever the words seeing, vision, and looking occur in this sense, intellectual apprehension is meant and not the eye's sight, as God, may He be exalted, is not an existent that can be apprehended with the eyes. If, however, an individual of insufficient capacity should not wish to reach the rank to which we desire him to ascend and should he consider that all the words [figuring in the Torah] concerning this subject are indicative of sensual perception of created lights—be they angels or something else—why, there is no harm in his thinking this. (p. 31)

In this extremely important passage Maimonides informs his reader that God cannot be the object of sight, vision, or looking. If, however, one wants to believe that these expressions mean that a created light (of the sort associated with the tabernacle and the top of Mount Sinai) was actually visible, well, then, such a person is 'of insufficient capacity' and does not 'wish to reach the rank to which' Maimonides 'desires him to ascend', but he is really not such a bad sort, and there is no harm in his thinking these (wrongheaded, insufficiently sophisticated, lower-rank but withal ultimately harmless) thoughts. As we continue our survey of

---

[36] As Avram Montag pointed out to me, this point is indirectly expressed in *Guide* iii. 7: the prophet Ezekiel saw God's *kavod* (p. 430). As was made clear earlier in the chapter, the content of Ezekiel's vision of the *merkavah* was the structure of the universe. To have a vision of the *kavod*, in other words, is to understand the workings of nature. Note also should be made of Maimonides' claim in *Guide* iii. 25 (p. 506) that the whole Torah is founded on the opinion that the natural world expresses God's wisdom.

relevant texts it will become clearer and clearer that Maimonides identifies *kavod* and created light (and also, as we shall see, *shekhinah*). These three terms do not denote anything that can be the object of sight, vision, or looking: they refer to intellectual apprehension, not to sensual apprehension.[37]

Maimonides teaches (*Guide* i. 21; pp. 49–51) that Onkelos originated the interpretation according to which *kavod*, *shekhinah*, and created light refer to created entities that can be apprehended through the senses. I doubt that he meant to imply that Onkelos was a person of insufficient capacity; rather, it appears more likely to me, he thought that Onkelos' audience consisted of people of insufficient capacity.[38]

In this chapter Maimonides makes another important statement about the status of Onkelos' interpretation, one that bears citing in full:

You should not consider as blameworthy the fact that this profound subject, which is remote from our apprehension, should be subject to many different interpretations. For this does no harm toward that which we direct ourselves.[39] And you are free to choose whatever belief you wish. You may believe that the great station attained by [Moses] was indubitably, in its entirety, a vision of prophecy and that he solely desired intellectual apprehensions—everything, namely, that which he had demanded, that which was denied to him, and that which he apprehended, being intellectual and admitting of no recourse to the senses, as we had interpreted in the first place. Or you may believe that there was, in addition to this intellectual apprehension, an apprehension due to the sense of sight, which, however, had for its object a created thing, through seeing which the perfection of intellectual apprehension might be achieved. This would be the interpretation of this passage by Onqelos. . . . Choose whatever opinion you wish,

[37] Maimonides throws in free of charge an additional lesson: angels are not entities that can be seen. See below, Ch. 8.

[38] Maimonides knew very well, I am sure, that Sa'adiah made the same claim. Kreisel, *Prophecy*, 214, thinks that Maimonides cited Onkelos, and not Sa'adiah, since the former carried greater (tannaitic) authority among Maimonides' readers. That may be true, but it is simpler to suppose that Maimonides saw Onkelos (whom Maimonides believed lived in the 3rd century CE) as Sa'adiah's source. It is also true that Maimonides, for reasons he kept to himself, never cites earlier Jewish philosophers. But beyond these essentially technical points, there may be an issue of greater importance here: Maimonides may not have wanted to draw explicit attention to the fact that, according to his view, Sa'adiah and Halevi were individuals of 'insufficient capacity'. On Onkelos on the *shekhinah*, see Rappel, *Targum Onkelos*, 37–8.

[39] Which I take to be: achieving understanding of God's existence, unity, and incorporeality.

inasmuch as our only purpose is that you should not believe that [God is a body to which motion might be ascribed].[40]

Let no one be confused: Maimonides cites Onkelos' approach as acceptable, but hardly as the preferred option.[41]

Returning to our exposition of Maimonides' understanding of the biblical term *kavod*, we next find him mentioning it in i. 28 (pp. 59–60), where he says, as if in passing: 'Accordingly, [Onkelos] referred the term "throne" to His *kavod*, I mean to the *shekhinah*, which is a created light.' This is the first place in the *Guide* in which I have found Maimonides clearly making the equation: *kavod* = *shekhinah* = created light.[42]

Maimonides cites Exodus 33: 18 ('Oh, let me see Your *kavod*!') in *Guide* i. 54 (pp. 123–4). In i. 4 his discussion of the verse focused on the verb 'to see'; here the emphasis is on the *kavod* itself:

Know that the master of those who know, Moses our Master, peace be upon him, made two requests and received an answer to both of them. One request consisted in his asking Him, may He be exalted, to let him know His essence and true reality. The second request, which he put first, was that He should let him know His attributes. The answer to the two requests that He, may He be exalted, gave him consisted in His promising him to let him know all His attributes, making it known to him that they are His actions, and teaching him that His essence cannot be grasped as it really is. . . . Then he asked for the apprehension of His essence, may He be exalted. This is what he means when he says, 'Oh, let me see Your *kavod*!'; whereupon he received a [favourable] answer with regard to what he had asked for at first—namely, 'show me Thy ways'. For he was told: 'I will make all My goodness pass before you.' In answer to his second demand, he was told: 'You cannot see My face', and so on. This dictum—'all My goodness'—alludes to the display to him of all existing things . . .

[40] See the discussion in Kreisel, *Prophecy*, 214–15. To my surprise, H. A. Wolfson, *Crescas' Critique*, 459–62, interprets Maimonides as if he held Onkelos' interpretation to be normative, and not a concession to the weak-minded. For a close reading of this chapter of the *Guide*, see Schäfer, *Mirror of His Beauty*, 113–15.

[41] I once heard Lenn Evan Goodman summarize this point in a lecture as follows: to adopt this position (which turns out to be held by Onkelos and Sa'adiah), Maimonides holds, is not reprehensible, only unfortunate. Such a person misses an opportunity to see that the whole cosmos expresses and teaches God's glory.

[42] In *Guide* i. 25 (p. 55) Maimonides explains the verse 'And the *kavod* of the Lord dwelt' (Exod. 24: 16) as referring to the *shekhinah*, and in the same passage notes the identity of *shekhinah* and created light, but the three-way identity is implied, not explicit. In *Guide* i. 76 (p. 229), *shekhinah* is also presented as equivalent to created light.

Here *kavod* is made to mean God's essence. Moses had mistakenly thought it possible to understand the true nature of God and beseeched God to allow him to understand that essence. God explains to Moses that the request cannot be granted: it is beyond the power of human comprehension to know God as God truly is. The most that Moses can hope to attain is an understanding of how God acts in the world.[43] *Kavod* as understood here is in principle beyond human understanding, let alone sense experience. This use of the term comes up again in the very next chapter (i. 64) of the *Guide* in which Maimonides discusses the term.

The longest and most detailed of Maimonides' discussions of *kavod* is found in *Guide* i. 64 (pp. 156–7). In this chapter, he reiterates points already made, and makes some new ones, all in the context of describing the various meanings of the term *kavod*:

Similarly, the *kavod* of the Lord is sometimes intended to signify the created light that God causes to descend in a particular place in order to confer honour upon it in a miraculous way: 'And the *kavod* of the Lord abode upon Mount Sinai, and [the cloud] covered it', and so on (Exod. 24: 16); 'And the *kavod* of the Lord filled the tabernacle' (Exod. 40: 34).

One meaning of the term *kavod*, then, is created light. In this passage, Maimonides appears to adopt the approach of Onkelos, presenting the created light as something which actually shone on the top of Mount Sinai and which actually filled the tabernacle.[44] He continues:

The expression is sometimes intended to signify His essence and true reality, may He be exalted, as when he says, 'Oh, let me see Your *kavod*!' (Exod. 33: 18), and was answered: 'For man shall not see Me and live' (Exod. 33: 20). This answer indicates that the *kavod* that is spoken of here is His essence, and that [Moses'] saying 'Your *kavod*' is by way of honouring Him.

[43] Compare Maimonides' explanation of the term *aḥor* ('back') in *Guide* i. 38 (p. 87): 'The term also occurs in the meaning of following and imitating the conduct of some individual with respect to the conduct of life. Thus: "Ye shall walk at the back of the Lord your God" (Deut. 13: 5); "They shall walk at the back of the Lord" (Hos. 11: 10), which means following in obedience to Him and imitating His acts and conducting life in accordance with His conduct. Thus: "He walked at the back of a commandment" (Hos. 5: 11). In this sense it is said: "And thou shalt see My back", which means that thou shalt apprehend what follows Me, has come to be like Me, and follows necessarily from My will—that is, all the things created by Me, as I shall explain in a chapter of this treatise.'

[44] By describing this phenomenon as a miracle, Maimonides, I think, hints at its allegorical nature, but that is a quagmire best avoided at this point.

In asking to see God's *kavod*, Moses is not asking actually to see anything; he is asking better to understand the nature of God's existence.

Maimonides goes on, in effect playing on the ambiguity of the Hebrew word *kavod*, which generally means 'honour':

In fact, all that is other than God, may He be exalted, honours Him.[45] For the true way of honouring Him consists in apprehending His greatness. Thus everybody who apprehends His greatness and His perfection honours Him according to the extent of his apprehension. Man in particular honours Him by speeches so that he indicates thereby that which he has apprehended by his intellect and communicates it to others. Those beings that have no apprehension, as for instance the minerals, also as it were honour God through the fact that by their very nature they are indicative of the power and wisdom of Him who brought them into existence. For this induces him who considers[46] them to honour God, either by means of articulate utterance or without it if speech is not permitted him. . . . It is in view of this notion being named *kavod* that it is said, 'The whole earth is full of His *kavod*' (Isa. 6: 3), this being equivalent to the dictum, 'And the earth is full of His praise' (Hab. 3: 3), for praise is called *kavod*[47] . . . Understand then likewise the equivocality with reference to *kavod* and interpret the latter in every passage in accordance with the context. You shall thus be saved from great difficulty.[48]

This passage makes Moses' intent clear: he sought to understand God's *kavod* (understood as essence), so that he could have more *kavod* (understood as honour) for God, and thus better express *kavod* (understood as praise) for God. Hinted at here also is what I take to be the most important Maimonidean sense of the term *kavod*: the wisdom of God as manifested in creation.

---

[45] 'All that is other than God' means the entire cosmos, i.e. all that God created. Maimonides teaches in *MT* 'Laws of the Foundations of the Torah', 2: 1–2, that it is study of the cosmos that brings one to love and reverence God. The cosmos honours God by expressing God's wisdom through its workings; we honour God by studying those workings.

[46] On the nature of this consideration, with its important implications for the issue raised in the previous note, see W. Z. Harvey, 'Averroes and Maimonides'.

[47] Maimonides cites Jer. 13: 16 and Ps. 29: 6 as proof of this linguistic point.

[48] Schäfer, *Mirror of His Beauty*, 116, summarizes this passage as follows: 'According to Maimonides' highly sophisticated definition, the biblical Kavod ("Glory of God") can thus have three different meanings: following Targum Onkelos (but also Sa'adiah, Judah ben Barzillai, and Judah ha-Levi) it can refer to the created light; in the example of Moses, it can refer to God's essence; and a third and new aspect, it can refer to the praise of God.'

Maimonides discusses *kavod* again in *Guide* iii. 7 (p. 430), iii. 9 (p. 436–7), and iii. 13 (p. 453).[49] In the first of these, with reference to Ezekiel 1: 28, 'This was the appearance of the likeness of the *kavod* of the Lord', he says:

Now the *kavod* of the Lord is not the Lord, as we have made clear several times. Accordingly, everything to which the parables contained in these apprehensions [of Ezekiel's] refer is only the *kavod* of the Lord, I mean to say the chariot, not the Rider, as He, may He be exalted, may not be presented in a likeness in a parable.[50] Understand this.

Here Maimonides seems once again to be adopting the Onkelos/Sa'adiah position. The prophet Ezekiel saw something, but what he saw was not God, but, rather, God's *kavod*. When we examine below what it is that prophets see according to Maimonides, it will become clear that he is not actually adopting the Onkelos/Sa'adiah position here, and that the *kavod* which Ezekiel saw may better be understood along the lines of the way in which Moses' apprehension of the *kavod* of the Lord was presented above: as achieving a high understanding of truth about God.

Maimonides, as it were, approves this last suggestion in *Guide* iii. 9, writing:

Matter is a strong veil preventing the apprehension of that which is separate from matter as it truly is. It does this even if it is the noblest and purest matter, I mean to say even if it is the matter of the heavenly spheres. All the more is this true for the dark and turbid matter that is ours. Hence whenever our intellect aspires to apprehend the deity or one of the intellects, there subsists this great veil interposed between the two. . . . For everything that is apprehended in a vision of prophecy is only a parable for some notion . . . [Thus, God's manifestation] 'in a thick cloud' (Exod. 19: 9) . . . draws attention to the fact that the apprehension of His true reality is impossible for us because of the dark matter that encompasses us and not Him . . . This is also what is intended in its dictum: 'darkness, cloud, and thick darkness' (Deut. 4: 11), and not that He, may He be exalted, was encompassed by darkness; for near Him, may He be exalted, there is no darkness, but perpetual, dazzling light the overflow of which illumines all that is dark—in accordance with what is said in the prophetic parables: 'And the earth did shine with His *kavod*' (Ezek. 43: 2).

Our material nature makes it impossible for us to understand incorporeal entities (the separate intellects, and, even more so, God). This is true even

[49] For an interesting comment on Maimonides' use of Isa. 58: 8 (which contains the word *kavod*) in *Guide* iii. 51, see W. Z. Harvey, 'The Biblical Term "Kavod"'.

[50] For Maimonides' understanding of the term 'rider' when applied to God, see *Guide* i. 70.

of prophetic apprehension. Prophets do not actually see the heavenly realm, but, rather, representations of that realm in the form of parables. Thus God does not actually appear in a thick cloud, nor is He actually encompassed by darkness. These are metaphors for our inability to apprehend Him. In order to apprehend God to any extent, the darkness (of our material natures) must be driven away through the light (of the intellect); in that sense the prophet Ezekiel can say that the earth shines with the *kavod* of the Lord.

In *Guide* iii. 13 Maimonides reiterates in passing the point made in i. 59 and i. 64, that *kavod* can mean God's essence.

Maimonides' last reference to *kavod* in the *Guide* (iii. 52; p. 629) serves as a convenient transition to a discussion of *shekhinah*, since he deals with both terms in the same paragraph:

> You know already that they forbade walking about with an erect carriage because [of the biblical dictum,] 'The whole earth is full of His *kavod*' (Isa. 6:3); all this being intended firmly to establish the notion that I have mentioned to you, that we are always before Him, may He be exalted, and walk about to and fro while His *shekhinah* is with us. And the greatest among the Sages, may their memory be blessed, avoided uncovering their heads, because man is covered about by the *shekhinah*.[51]

Kavod and *shekhinah* are identified here and understood, I submit, as the evidence of God's wisdom manifest in the cosmos around us. I have not yet proved that this last claim is held by Maimonides, but our ensuing discussion will offer support for it.

Maimonides on *Shekhinah* in the *Guide of the Perplexed*

Turning now to *shekhinah*, we find the term first mentioned in the *Guide* (i. 10; pp. 35–7)[52] in connection with a discussion of the term *yarod* (descend), a term which can mean 'a lower state of speculation; when a

[51] It is worth noting in passing that this passage indicates that in Maimonides' day the custom of keeping one's head covered was a mark of special piety.

[52] In *Guide* i. 5 (p. 30), Maimonides makes reference to 'the divine holy presence' of God as something which can be looked upon (i.e. understood) only after many preparations. But in this passage he uses neither *shekhinah* in Hebrew nor *sakinah* in Arabic. Rather, he says: *al-ḥaḍrah al-qadisiyah al-ilahiyah*. The translators are far from unanimous in how to understand this expression. Friedlaender follows Ibn Tibbon, who has *hamaḥaneh hakadosh ha'elohi*. Al-Harizi, followed by Kafih, has *hama'amad hakadosh ha'elohi*. Schwartz agrees with Pines, translating: *lehabit banokheḥut hakedoshah ha'elohit*. My thanks to Raphael Jospe for his assistance here.

man directs his thoughts at a very mean object'. But, given the lowly state of human beings, descent can also mean

an overflow of prophetic inspiration, the alighting of the prophetic inspiration upon the prophet or the coming down of the *shekhinah*[53] to a certain place was termed descent; whereas the removal of this prophetic state from a particular individual or the cessation of the *shekhinah* was termed ascent. In every case where you find the terms descent and ascent applied to the Creator, may He be exalted, this last meaning is intended.

In every case, that is, where *shekhinah* is said to descend, the actual meaning is that a prophetic encounter has taken place.[54] Maimonides' analysis of prophecy focuses entirely on the 'ascent' of the prophet. To say that *shekhinah* rests on a prophet, or descends upon a prophet, then, says nothing about 'movement' on the part of God or *shekhinah*, and much about moral and spiritual/intellectual movement on the part of the prophet.

As with descent, so with ascent:

When, on the other hand, Scripture says, 'And Moses ascended to God' (Exod. 19: 3), the third meaning of the term [to ascend] is meant;[55] this in addition to the fact that [Moses] ascended to the top of the mountain[56] upon which the created light had descended. The verse does not mean that God, may He be exalted, has a place to which one may ascend or from which one may descend; He is exalted very high above the imaginings of the ignorant.

Just as God (and God's *shekhinah* and created light) do not actually descend, so, too, no one actually ascends to God.

In *Guide* i. 21 (pp. 47–51), as we saw above, Maimonides discussed the view of Onkelos, to which he gave condescending approval. In that chapter he also makes a number of points in passing which are important for our present purposes. He writes that the term 'to pass' (*avor*) 'was figuratively used to signify the descent of the light and of the *shekhinah* seen by the prophets in the vision of prophecy'. A reasonable way of reading this is that, in some contexts at least, the terms *shekhinah* and light point to the same thing. This is a point for which sufficient proof may and will be brought from other passages; more important, we learn here that *shekhinah* and

---

[53] Arabic *sakinah*; Pines translates this as 'Indwelling'.

[54] Compare *Guide* ii. 42 (pp. 389–90) on *shekhinah* as a term for prophecy.

[55] Pines explains in a note that this third meaning denotes 'the direction of thought to an exalted object'.

[56] Josh. 15: 8; Maimonides seems to be simply making use of the expression here, without meaning to interpret the verse in Joshua or even refer to it.

light, when 'seen' by prophets, are seen in a 'vision of prophecy'. We will examine below what Maimonides means by 'vision of prophecy'.

The term 'come' (*bo*) is discussed in *Guide* i. 22 (pp. 51–2). Of this term, Maimonides says,

[it] is also used figuratively to denote the coming about of something that is not at all corporeal. . . . Since the term had been thus figuratively applied to what is in no way a body, it was also figuratively applied to the Creator, may He be honoured and magnified, either to the descent of His decree or to that of His *shekhinah*. It is in view of this figurative use that it is said: 'Lo, I come unto thee in a thick cloud' (Exod. 19: 9); 'for the Lord, the God of Israel, comes through it' (Ezek. 44: 2). All passages similar to these signify the descent of the *shekhinah*.

Shekhinah, like God, descends, but only figuratively. Just as God does not actually come in a thick cloud, so also God's *shekhinah* does not actually descend, ascend, or move. All these expressions must be understood as figures of speech, examples of the Torah adopting human language.[57]

Just as God's coming is figurative, so also is His going, as we learn in *Guide* i. 23 (pp. 52–3): 'It says accordingly, "I will go and return to my place" (Hos. 5: 15), the signification of which is that the *shekhinah* that had been among us is removed. This removal is followed by a privation of providence, as far as we are concerned.' To say that God's *shekhinah* has been removed is another way of saying, at least in some contexts, that God's providential care has been withdrawn. But providence, as Maimonides takes great pains to make clear, is dependent upon intellectual perfection.[58] Removal of providence (= removal of *shekhinah*) means that one's intellectual bond with God has weakened. In other words, removal of *shekhinah* is the name given to the consequence of focusing one's mind on what is not God. It is entirely a consequence of what humans do, and connotes nothing whatsoever concerning God or any putative divine 'movements'.

Not surprisingly, Maimonides' most extended discussion of *shekhinah* is in the chapter devoted to the term *shakhon* (*Guide* i. 25; p. 55):

It is known that the meaning of this verb is, to dwell. . . . This verb is also figuratively applied to things that are not living beings and in fact to everything that is

---

[57] In *Guide* i. 26 (cited below) Maimonides cites the rabbinic dictum, 'the Torah speaks in the language of the sons of man'. On this expression in Maimonides, see Nuriel, '"Torah Speaks in the Language of Man"', 93–9. On the notion of divine accommodation to human weakness implied by it, see Funkenstein, '"Scripture Speaks the Language of Man"' and Benin, *Footprints of God*. For the use of this expression in the Talmud, see Harris, *How Do We Know This?*, 33–43.

[58] *Guide* iii. 17 (pp. 471–2).

permanent and is attached to another being. . . . It is on account of this latter figurative sense that the verb is applied figuratively to God, may He be exalted—I mean to the permanence of His Shekhinah or His providence in whatever place they may subsist in permanent fashion or toward whatever matter providence may be *permanently* directed.[59] Thus it is said: 'And the *kavod* of the Lord dwelt' (Exod. 24: 16); 'And I will dwell among the children of Israel' (Exod. 29: 45); 'And the good will of Him that dwelt in the bush' (Deut. 33: 16). In every case in which this occurs with reference to God, it is used in the sense of the permanence of his Shekhinah—I mean His created light—in a place, or the permanence of providence with regard to a certain matter. Each passage should be understood according to its context.

A number of extremely suggestive points are made in this paragraph. One of the important connotations of the term *shakhon* is permanence. Connecting that aspect of the term to the notion of providence (and here, once again, and more clearly than in the last passage, Maimonides makes *shekhinah* into a figurative term for divine providence) gives the impression that Maimonides here is hinting at the Aristotelian notion of providence, according to which providence is another way of saying that nature is permanent and natural forms are not subject to what we would today call evolutionary change, let alone extinction.[60] Maimonides also makes clear here that the three terms, *shekhinah*, *kavod*, and created light are synonyms, or may at least be used interchangeably, if the context allows.

According to Maimonides, God is transcendent, entirely and wholly unlike anything in the created cosmos. But, in principle, He is accessible in certain senses to those human beings who make heroic efforts to ascend, as it were, in His direction. The Torah expresses the possibility of this ascent by speaking figuratively of God's *shekhinah*, *kavod*, and created light. These terms are best understood as figures of speech, making known the possibility that human beings can approach God. They speak volumes about humans, but say next to nothing about God. This is the message of the texts we have studied so far, especially here in *Guide* i. 25.

Almost as if he were seeking to confirm my interpretation of his words, Maimonides writes in the very next chapter (i. 26; pp. 56–7):

You know their dictum that refers in inclusive fashion to all the kinds of interpretation connected with this subject, namely, their saying: 'The Torah speaketh in the language of the sons of man'. The meaning of this is that everything that all men are capable of understanding and representing to themselves at first thought

---

[59] Emphasis added; the significance of this comment will be explained below.

[60] I will explain this later in this chapter.

has been ascribed to Him as necessarily belonging to God, may He be exalted. . . . In a similar way one has ascribed to Him, may He be exalted, everything that in our opinion is a perfection in order to indicate that He is perfect in every manner of perfection and that no deficiency whatever mars Him. . . . All these terms indicative of various kinds of motions of living beings are predicated of God, may He be exalted, in the way that we have spoken of . . . There is no doubt that when corporeality is abolished, all these predicates are likewise abolished. I mean such terms as to descend, to ascend, to go, to stand erect, to stand, to go round, *to dwell*, to go out, to come, to pass, and terms similar to these.[61]

When applied to God, or to God's *kavod*, or to God's *shekhinah*, or to God's created light, all terms which refer to movement or posture must be abolished, so far as their literal sense goes. In effect, these terms say nothing at all about God, but much about the way in which we, as human beings, speak in connection with God. This paragraph, it should be further noted, confirms my claims above about Maimonides' attitude towards Onkelos' interpretation of these terms. When properly understood, these terms do not, *pace* Onkelos, denote entities actually perceived in the 'real world'; they are figures of speech, used to convey ideas in a graphic way.

But the interpretation of Onkelos, while not correct, is not blameworthy, as Maimonides indicates in the following chapter (i. 27; pp. 57–9):

Onqelos the Proselyte was very perfect in the Hebrew and Syrian languages and directed his effort toward the abolition of the belief in God's corporeality. Hence he interprets in accordance with its meaning every attribute that Scripture predicates of God and that might lead toward the belief in corporeality. Thus whenever he encounters one of the terms indicative of one of the kinds of motion, he makes motion to mean the manifestation and appearance of a created light, I mean the *shekhinah* or the action of providence.

Rather than attribute motion to God, Onkelos makes expressions that seem to indicate such motion mean 'the manifestation and appearance of a created light, I mean the *shekhinah* or the action of providence'. For Onkelos, if not for Maimonides, created lights are truly seen by human eyes, the presence of the *shekhinah* is in some fashion sensed. But God is not seen, nor is He present in any special sense. In this passage Maimonides further makes the important equivalence: created light = *shekhinah* = providence.

In *Guide* i. 28 (pp. 59–60), as we have seen above, Maimonides makes another equivalence: *kavod* = *shekhinah* = created light. Combining these two equivalences, we end up with: *kavod* = *shekhinah* = created light =

---

[61] Emphasis added.

providence. Four different terms are used, depending upon the context, to name one notion: the way in which we understand God's interaction with the cosmos.

Maimonides on Created Light in the *Guide of the Perplexed*

We can now turn to the notion of 'created light'. The term seems to have been introduced into Jewish texts by Sa'adiah Gaon and taken over by Halevi. Maimonides uses it as well, as we have already seen, and will see now in a more systematic fashion. Our discussion here can be brief, since almost all of the relevant texts have already been cited.

In *Guide* i. 5 (p. 29), Maimonides makes reference to a light manifesting itself that Moses feared to see ('And Moses hid his face, for he was afraid to look upon God'; Exod. 3: 6). He is careful to note that this is the external meaning of the verse. The important point, he makes clear, is that no one should think that Moses thought that the light in question was visible. From this chapter we have already cited Maimonides' statement: 'If, however, an individual of insufficient capacity should not wish to reach the rank to which we desire him to ascend and should he consider that all the words [figuring in the Torah] concerning this subject are indicative of sensual perception of created lights—be they angels or something else—why, there is no harm in his thinking this.' This certainly makes clear what he thinks of the notion of created light or lights.

In *Guide* i. 10 a created light was said to have been seen on top of Mount Sinai, at least according to the outward meaning of the biblical text. In i. 19 we learn that the terms *kavod* and 'created light' denote the same thing (which, as we have seen above, is nothing actually visible). Like *shekhinah*, Maimonides tells us in i. 21, the light is seen by prophets in prophetic visions. In i. 25, the terms *shekhinah* and created light are presented as meaning the same thing (so also in i. 76); in i. 28 these two terms are made to mean the same thing as *kavod*. In i. 64 *kavod* is again identified with created light, at least in some contexts.

Before attempting to synthesize our survey of *kavod*, *shekhinah*, and created light in the *Guide*, it is important to take note of something Maimonides teaches about the nature of prophecy. Prophecy, he says in *Guide* ii. 36, always involves the action of the imaginative faculty. Building on that claim, he glosses the verse, 'If there be a prophet among you, I the Lord do make Myself known unto him in a vision, I do speak with him in a dream' (Num. 12: 6) as follows:

prophecy ... is a perfection that comes in a dream or in a vision ... This signifies that the imaginative faculty achieves so great a perfection of action that it sees the thing as if it were outside, and the thing whose origin is due to it appears to have come to it by way of external sensation. In these two groups, I mean vision and dream, all the degrees of prophecy are included. (p. 370)

What the prophet sees, he or she sees alone, not because others are blind, but because the prophetic experience is internal to the prophet. There is simply nothing external to the prophet's consciousness for others to see. Presumably, according to Maimonides, if there were people with Ezekiel when he experienced the vision of the chariot, all that these people saw was Ezekiel in a trance or, perhaps, Ezekiel behaving oddly. What they certainly did not see was the heavenly chariot described in Ezekiel 1. This matter must be borne in mind whenever we read texts in which Maimonides says that *kavod, shekhinah*, or created light was seen in a vision of prophecy.

We may now summarize Maimonides' teachings concerning *kavod, shekhinah*, and created light in the *Guide*. The three terms, it turns out, mean the same thing, or, perhaps more precisely, share a common core of meaning. For Maimonides, unlike Onkelos, these terms do not denote anything that may actually be localizable in space or time, or apprehended by the senses. While it is permissible to teach weak-minded people that the terms denote special creations, visible to prophets and, on rare occasions, to the people of Israel as a whole, this is a concession to their intellectual frailty, and not actually the truth. That this is a concession is not only made clear by Maimonides' explicit statements to that effect, but by the fact that he repeatedly states that these phenomena are seen in prophetic visions. Thus, while the weak-minded may believe that the Torah speaks of a *kavod* that actually filled the tabernacle and Temple, of a light visible on top of Mount Sinai, and that talmudic rabbis speak of a localizable *shekhinah*, the careful student of Maimonides knows that these terms are all actually figurative expressions.

Kavod, shekhinah, and created light must therefore not be taken as entities in the world of shared experience. That being the case, to what do the terms refer? As we have seen above, when Moses seeks to see God's *kavod*, what he is actually seeking is to understand God. Ordinarily (for Maimonides, in any event), seeking to understand some notion means seeking to understand it in terms of Aristotle's four causes. This is obviously impossible in the case of God. It is also impossible to know God directly. The only way to learn anything at all about God (beyond the bare facts of His existence, unity, and incorporeality, which Maimonides thought were rationally provable) is to perceive His wisdom through the workings of that which He created, namely, the cosmos as a whole. This is precisely what Maimonides says in a number of the texts we have analysed above: to the extent that *kavod* (and, by implication, *shekhinah* and created light) can be apprehended by humans, it is only as the wisdom of God apparent to anyone who takes the trouble to examine nature carefully. This, it turns out, is the way in which Maimonides also explains the term *kavod* in one of the key texts in the *Mishneh torah* on our subject, as we will see immediately below. Before turning to that, however, it must be noted that the discussion here enables us to understand another point implied above. Our three terms, we have learned, are not only figurative expressions for the wisdom of God manifest in nature, they are also figurative expressions for the permanent nature of God's providence.

What aspect of divine providence is permanent? Clearly not the special providence extended to highly perfected individuals (as described in *Guide* iii. 17 and iii. 51); this connection is not permanent, since it must be achieved by the individual in question, can grow and deepen, and can, apparently, be snapped, or at least decisively weakened, by a moment's inattention. No, permanent providence is providence as understood by Aristotle, who holds that God 'takes care of the spheres and of what is in them and that for this reason their individuals remain permanently as they are' (*Guide* iii. 17; p. 465). Entities in the superlunary realm, although generated, never become corrupted, and are thus permanent and governed by providence. In the world below the sphere of the moon, on the other hand, divine emanation 'necessitates the durability and permanence of the species, though the durability of the latter's individuals be impossible'. But even individuals in the sublunar world are not entirely unprotected by providence, since they are given capacities and faculties through which they can prosper. These capacities and faculties are permanently found in the species in question (all horses can run, although this or that horse might do it better than others) and in that sense may be called providential (providence being God's wisdom expressed in nature).

When a prophet sees God's *kavod*, God's *shekhinah*, God's created light, what does he or she see? The prophet *sees* nothing; the prophet achieves some level or other of understanding of the wisdom manifest in the workings of the natural world.[62]

---

[62] After completing this chapter I read Esti Eisenmann's very perceptive study, 'The Term "Created Light"'. Eisenmann analyses many of the texts I examine here and concludes that Maimonides' esoteric teaching concerning *kavod*, *shekhinah*, and created

There are admittedly some texts in the *Guide of the Perplexed* in which Maimonides seems to be retreating from his conception of the *shekhinah* as analysed in this chapter. In each case closer examination shows that this is not the case. The first of these is *Guide* i. 5. The 'whole purpose' of this chapter, Maimonides writes, as we have already seen above,

was to show that whenever the words seeing, vision, and looking occur in this sense,[63] intellectual apprehension is meant and not the eye's sight, as God, may He be exalted, is not an existent that can be apprehended with the eyes. If, however, an individual of insufficient capacity should not wish to reach the rank to which we desire him to ascend and should he consider that all the words [figuring in the Torah] concerning this subject are indicative of sensual perception of created lights—be they angels or something else—why, there is no harm in his thinking this. (p. 31)

Leading up to this conclusion, Maimonides adduces the example of 'The nobles of the children of Israel' (Exod. 24: 11), who 'were overhasty, strained their thoughts, and achieved apprehension, but only an imperfect one' (p. 30). Rushing into metaphysical matters before they were properly prepared, the elders incurred God's wrath.[64] 'This having happened to these men', Maimonides advises,

it behooves us, all the more, as being inferior to them, and it behooves those who are inferior to us, to aim at and engage in perfecting our knowledge in preparatory matters and in achieving those premises that purify apprehension of its taint, which is error. It will then go forward to look upon the divine holy presence.[65]

Having made the appropriate preparations (i.e. having reached a high level of moral perfection which makes possible but does not guarantee the appropriate apprehension of physical and metaphysical matters), one can 'go forward to look upon the divine holy presence'. Given the context, there can be no doubt that the 'looking' spoken of here means intellectual apprehension 'and not the eye's sight'.

Guide iii. 39 (p. 552) also appears to present a problem for my interpretation of Maimonides. In his explanation of the commandment to read certain verses when the first fruits (*bikurim*) are brought, Maimonides writes:

light is that the terms refer to intellectual emanations from the Active Intellect. This is another way of referring to an understanding of the wisdom manifest in the workings of the natural world.

[63] i.e. when the object of sight, looking, or vision is God.

[64] On this passage in Maimonides, see Regev, 'Vision of the Nobles of Israel', and Levene, 'Maimonides' Philosophical Exegesis'.   [65] See above, n. 52.

As for the reading on the occasion of the offering of first fruits,[66] it also is conducive to the moral quality of humility, for it is carried out by him who carries the basket on his shoulders. It contains an acknowledgement of God's beneficence and bountifulness, so that man should know that it is a part of the divine worship that man should remember states of distress at a time when he prospers . . . For there was a fear of the moral qualities that are generally acquired by all those who are brought up in prosperity—I mean conceit, vanity, and neglect of the correct opinions . . . It is because of this apprehension that the commandment has been given to carry out a reading every year before Him, may He be exalted, and in presence of His *shekhinah*, on the occasion of the offering of first fruits.

Ought we take this literally, that one reads the verses from Deuteronomy in the actual spatio-temporal presence of God's *shekhinah*? That is, of course, what the text implies; must we admit that that is what Maimonides means? I think not. The point of the commandment to read Deuteronomy 26: 5–10 is to induce humility into people who might quite naturally be in a self-congratulatory mood. The harvest has been successful, Jerusalem is full of happy farmers bringing *bikurim* to the Temple, one sees prosperity all around; 'Jeshurun has waxed fat' and might therefore be tempted to kick.[67] This is surely an apposite time to remind the Jews that their forebears were nomads and slaves and that they owe their prosperity to God, and not to themselves.

Reciting these verses in the (metaphorical) presence of God's *shekhinah* (which is actually simply another way of saying in the Temple precincts)

---

[66] Deut. 26: 1–10: 'When you enter the land that the Lord your God is giving you as a heritage, and you possess it and settle in it, you shall take some of every first fruit of the soil, which you harvest from the land that the Lord your God is giving you, put it in a basket and go to the place where the Lord your God will choose to establish His name. You shall go to the priest in charge at that time and say to him, "I acknowledge this day before the Lord your God that I have entered the land that the Lord swore to our fathers to assign us." The priest shall take the basket from your hand and set it down in front of the altar of the Lord your God. You shall then recite as follows before the Lord your God: "My father was a fugitive Aramean. He went down to Egypt with meagre numbers and sojourned there; but there he became a great and very populous nation. The Egyptians dealt harshly with us and oppressed us; they imposed heavy labour upon us. We cried to the Lord, the God of our fathers, and the Lord heard our plea and saw our plight, our misery, and our oppression. The Lord freed us from Egypt by a mighty hand, by an outstretched arm and awesome power, and by signs and portents. He brought us to this place and gave us this land, a land flowing with milk and honey. Wherefore I now bring the first fruits of the soil which You, O Lord, have given me.'   [67] Deut. 32: 15, cited by Maimonides in one of the ellipses above.

certainly induces humility, one of the main points of the commandment. Another reason for the commandment is to correct the 'neglect of the correct opinions'—and what could be more incorrect for Maimonides than the opinion that the *shekhinah* can be localizable in space and time?

A third example, *Guide* iii. 41 (p. 566), strengthens this interpretation. In this passage Maimonides explains the commandment (Deut. 23: 14–15) to prepare latrines outside military camps in the following way:

> It has also included another notion, saying: 'That He see no unclean thing in thee, and turn away from thee' (Deut. 23: 15), this being against that which, as is well-known, is widespread among soldiers in a camp after they have stayed for a long time away from their homes. Accordingly, He, may He be exalted, has commanded us to perform actions that call to mind that the *shekhinah* has descended among us so that we be preserved from those actions.

It would appear from this that Maimonides holds that the *shekhinah* actually descends into the military camps of the Jewish nation. However, if we look at the sentences immediately preceding these, another picture emerges:

> This book ['Book of Judges' in the *Mishneh torah*] also includes the commandment to prepare a secluded place and a paddle.[68] For one of the purposes of this Law consists, as I have made known to you, in cleanliness and avoidance of excrements and of dirt and in man's not being like the beasts. And this commandment also fortifies, by the actions it enjoins, the certainty of the combatants that the *shekhinah* has descended among them—as is explained in the reason given for it: 'For the Lord thy God walketh in the midst of thy camp' (Deut. 23: 15).

We thus see that the point of the commandment is to make the soldiers *believe* that the *shekhinah* is among them and behave accordingly. Convincing soldiers that fastidious hygiene will enable the divine presence to be with them serves very practical ends: keeping Jewish army camps clean (certainly a challenge in the Israeli army today!) and fortifying the morale of the soldiers in those camps.[69] In these last two examples *shekhinah* is used as an educational tool, educating for both refined morality and correct doctrine. It is not a created entity which can properly be said to be located in some specific place and some specific time.

---

[68] See Deut. 25: 13–14.

[69] For a similar reading of this passage in Deuteronomy see the comment of R. Nissim of Marseilles on it. I cite from Kreisel's magnificent edition of *Ma'aseh nisim*, 470. While Nissim does not mention Maimonides in this context there is little doubt that this staunch Maimonidean was familiar with the Master's interpretation of these verses.

I take the understanding of *kavod*, *shekhinah*, and created light which we have here teased out of scattered texts in the *Guide* to be Maimonides' settled doctrine on the subject. Is there evidence of this metaphorical understanding of these terms in his earlier works as well? It is to that question that we now turn.

Shekhinah and *Kavod* in the *Mishneh torah* and *Commentary on the Mishnah*

W. Z. Harvey has recently argued that the *Mishneh torah* is a key to understanding the philosophical secrets of the *Guide of the Perplexed*.[70] Examining Maimonides' use of the terms *kavod* and *shekhinah* in the *Mishneh torah* certainly supports Harvey's thesis.[71]

'Laws of the Foundations of the Torah', 1: 10, reads as follows:

What was it that Moses sought to apprehend, when he said, 'Oh, let me see Your *kavod*!' (Exod. 33: 18)? He sought to know the truth of God's existence . . . God replied that it is beyond the mental capacity of a living man, composed of body and soul, to apprehend the complete truth in this matter. But the Holy One, blessed be He, caused Moses to know what no man knew before him and what no man will know after him: an apprehension of the truth of God's existence to the extent that God was distinct in his mind from all other existents, in the same way as an individual, whose back is seen, whose physical form and apparel are perceived, is distinguished in the observer's mind from the physical form of other individuals. And Scripture hints this in the text: ['Then I will take My hand away and] you will see My back; but My face must not be seen' (Exod. 33: 23).

This is the one passage that I have found in the *Mishneh torah* in which Maimonides uses the term *kavod* in the technical sense discussed in this chapter, and not in its simple sense of 'respect' or 'honour'. Maimonides reads the Exodus passage here (as he did later in the *Guide*) as meaning that Moses did not beseech God to allow him to *see* anything with his eyes; rather, he sought to *understand* something with his mind. God's *kavod* is not an entity to be seen, but an idea to be understood.

The term *shekhinah* occurs thirty-six times in the *Mishneh torah*. Most of these occurrences are unexceptional, and need not detain us;[72] a few of

---

[70] See W. Z. Harvey, 'The *Mishneh Torah* as a Key'.

[71] The term 'created light' does not appear in the *Mishneh torah*.

[72] Most of these involve: (*a*) prophecy or related phenomena; (*b*) conversion ('coming under the wings of the *shekhinah*'); (*c*) the term 'the encampment of the *shekhinah*'—the talmudic term for the tabernacle and its environs. But see *MT* 'Laws of Torah Study', 5: 1, where disrespect for one's teacher is presented as tantamount to disrespect for the

them, however, either confirm the thesis being defended in this chapter or, more interestingly, appear to refute it. I shall deal with the latter first.

'Laws of the Temple', 6: 16, reads in part[73] as follows:

Now why is it my contention that as far as the Sanctuary and Jerusalem were concerned the first sanctification hallowed them for all time to come, whereas the sanctification of the rest of the Land of Israel, which involved the laws of the sabbatical year and tithes and like matters, did not hallow the land for all time to come? Because the sanctity of the Sanctuary and of Jerusalem derives from the shekhinah, which could not be banished.[74]

'Banishment of the *shekhinah*' (*siluk hashekhinah*) is a rabbinic expression[75] ordinarily used in a clearly metaphorical sense.[76] But here, in a passage of some halakhic import, Maimonides seems to be using it in a more literal fashion: whereas the *shekhinah* can be banished from other locales, it never leaves the city of Jerusalem (which is rendered holy thereby). *Shekhinah* in this context appears to be something that can be localized in spatial terms, and as such must have some sort of ontological status; it cannot be interpreted as a metaphor for providence, prophecy, or the intellectual understanding of God.[77]

Is this indeed the case? If we compare Maimonides' statement here to the talmudic text to which he appears to be reacting, a different picture emerges.

In BT *Rosh hashanah* 31a we read:

Rabbi Judah ben Idi said in the name of Rabbi Johanan: The Divine Presence [so to speak][78] left Israel by ten stages[79]—this we know from references in Scripture—

shekhinah. However, one respects one's teacher for the Torah the teacher has learned and taught, not for anything intrinsic about him or her. Moreover, the verses cited by Maimonides in this passage show that he uses the term *shekhinah* as standing in for 'God'. It is fundamental to the entire Maimonidean project that God is neither a perceptible nor locatable entity.

[73] The entire passage is cited and discussed above in Ch. 3. See p. 108.

[74] Compare Maimonides' *Commentary on the Mishnah*, *Zev.* 14: 8, trans. and cited in Twersky, 'Maimonides on Eretz Yisrael', 286.

[75] See the chapter 'Siluk Ha-Shekhinah' in Klawans, *Impurity and Sin in Ancient Judaism*, 118–22.

[76] And used as such by Maimonides in the *Mishneh torah* (see e.g. 'Laws of Torah Study', 5: 8).

[77] All three of which reduce for Maimonides to more or less the same thing: human attempts to 'approach' God (and the consequences of these attempts).

[78] Added by the Soncino translation, clearly uncomfortable with the anthropomorphism of this text.

[79] Literally 'made ten journeys' when the Temple was destroyed.

and the Sanhedrin correspondingly wandered to ten places of banishment—this we know from tradition. 'The Divine Presence left Israel by ten stages—this we know from references in Scripture': [it went] from the Ark-cover to the Cherub and from the Cherub to the threshold [of the Holy of Holies], and from the threshold to the court, and from the court to the altar, and from the altar to the roof [of the Temple], and from the roof to the wall, and from the wall to the town, and from the town to the mountain, and from the mountain to the wilderness, and from the wilderness it ascended and abode in its own place, as it says, 'I will go and return to my place' (Hos. 5: 15).

By emphasizing in 'Laws of the Temple', 6: 16, that the *shekhinah* never left Jerusalem, Maimonides turns this passage from BT *Rosh hashanah* into an allegory instead of a travelogue. Rather than emphasizing the spatio-temporal character of the *shekhinah* as an entity, he succeeds in subtly de-emphasizing it.[80] To the best of my understanding, this is the only passage in the *Mishneh torah* in which the *shekhinah* is presented as an entity which can be located in space and time and which, presumably, can, under the right circumstances and by the right people, actually be perceived with the senses. Reading this text against the passage from BT *Rosh hashanah* seems to show that Maimonides was seeking to limit that understanding, for those Jews who, like Onkelos' audience, had not yet reached the stage of development which would enable them to understand that *shekhinah* (and *kavod*, and created light) is a metaphor for human striving to come close to God through understanding.[81]

Other passages in the *Mishneh torah* which, at first blush, might seem problematic actually turn out to support the reading of Maimonides offered here. In 'Laws of Repentance', 8: 2, for example, Maimonides describes the delights awaiting those who achieve a share in the world to come:

There is nothing corporeal or any bodies in the world to come; there are only the disembodied souls of the righteous which exist like the ministering angels . . . as the early Sages said: 'In the world to come there is no eating, or drinking, or sexual intercourse; rather, the righteous sit with crowns upon their heads, enjoying the splendour of the *shekhinah*.'[82]

---

[80] Maimonides had good historico-halakhic reasons to emphasize the superiority of Jerusalem over other locales; for an expression of this issue, see *MT* 'Laws of the Sanctification of the New Moon', 4: 12.

[81] For a similar case, see Maimonides' comment on Mishnah *BB* 2: 9 (with reference to BT *BB* 29a) as elucidated by H. A. Davidson, *Moses Maimonides*, 162–3.

[82] BT *Ber.* 17b.

One could dismiss this text as Maimonides' use of a standard rabbinic expression[83] for the splendours of paradise and leave it at that. I believe, however, that he actually meant this expression literally, after a fashion.

How does one achieve a share in the world to come? Anyone familiar with the Maimonidean corpus knows the answer immediately: the key to immortality is intellectual perfection.[84] The world to come is the name given to the experience of (egoless?[85]) intellects eternally contemplating (or, perhaps better, achieving some form of conjunction with) the eternal verities. In this context, using *shekhinah* as Maimonides understands it makes excellent sense. The outcome of a life devoted to intellectual striving (i.e. a life devoted to cultivating the 'presence' of the *shekhinah*) is an eternity of 'enjoying' the fruits of that striving without bodily distractions.

Let us remember too how Maimonides opens his discussion here: with an affirmation of the non-corporeal nature of existence in the world to come. If that in us that can survive death and reach the world to come is incorporeal, how much more so must the *shekhinah* be! In other words, even ignoring Maimonides' doctrine of immortality, we cannot possibly understand *shekhinah* here as something that can be localized in space and time, or that can be perceived through human senses.

A particularly interesting use of the term *shekhinah* appears in 'Laws of Prayer and the Priestly Blessing', 5: 3:

What does facing the sanctuary involve? Outside the Land of Israel, one should turn to face the Land of Israel and pray. In the Land, one faces towards Jerusalem. In Jerusalem, one faces the sanctuary. In the sanctuary, one faces the Holy of Holies. A blind person, or one who cannot determine the direction, or one travelling in a boat[86] directs his heart to the *shekhinah* and prays.

It is interesting that Maimonides' apparent talmudic source (*Berakhot* 30*a*) speaks of turning to one's father in heaven and does not mention *shekhinah* at all. There are two points of interest here. Who is supposed to face the *shekhinah* in prayer? A blind person. So much for the *shekhinah* as a visible entity! Second, one who does not know the direction of the Temple in Jerusalem 'directs his heart' to the *shekhinah* and prays. In biblical and medieval Hebrew, the heart is the seat of the intellect, not the seat of the

[83] The term occurs fifty-five times in midrashic texts and eight times in the Talmud.

[84] On this, see Ch. 7 below.

[85] For a discussion of what it is that survives death according to Maimonides, see Altmann, 'Maimonides on the Intellect and Metaphysics', 89–90.

[86] And thus presumably not sure in which direction to turn in order to face Jerusalem.

emotions. As Maimonides makes clear in *Guide* iii. 51, ideal prayer is intellectual meditation on God. These two points noted, it now becomes clear that his use of the term *shekhinah* in this paragraph, far from showing that he is using it in anything like the Onkelos/Sa'adiah/Halevi fashion, actually reveals him to be subtly indicating its metaphorical character.[87]

There is one more passage in the *Mishneh torah* relevant to our concerns. Maimonides ends 'Laws Concerning the Ritual Impurity of Foodstuffs' (16: 12) with a disquisition connecting ritual purity with moral purity:

Separation leads to the purifying of the body from evil deeds, and the purifying of the body leads to the sanctification of the soul from evil moral qualities, and the sanctification of the soul leads to the imitation of the *shekhinah*; for it is said, 'Sanctify yourselves therefore and be ye holy' (Lev. 11: 44), 'for I the Lord who sanctify you am holy' (Lev. 21: 8).[88]

The progression discussed here is interesting: good deeds lead to good moral habits (*de'ot*); good moral habits lead to the imitation of the *shekhinah*, i.e. to the imitation of God. In what way, according to Maimonides, is a person who has perfected his behaviour to imitate God? First and foremost, through the intellectual contemplation of God.[89] Once again, we see Maimonides using the term *shekhinah* to hint at his intellectualist conception of religion, and not in order to indicate that God's presence in the universe can in any fashion or in any place be apprehended through the senses.[90]

The foregoing discussion leads to the conclusion that Maimonides' ideas concerning *kavod* and *shekhinah* as expressed in the *Guide* were already present in the *Mishneh torah*.

I have found one other place in Maimonides' writings in which he uses some of these terms in a way relevant to our discussion here. This is in his famous comment on Mishnah Ḥagigah 2: 1. The Mishnah there states:

One does not expound upon forbidden sexual relations in the presence of three, nor upon *ma'aseh bereshit* in the presence of two, nor upon the *merkavah* in the

[87] James Diamond suggested to me that there may be an ascending hierarchy here: turning to the Land of Israel; turning to Jerusalem; turning to the sanctuary; and, finally, the blind person who 'directs [turns] his heart to the *shekhinah*'. This might be a subtle devaluation of sacred geography here in favour of an intellectualist understanding of prayer.

[88] *Book of Cleanness*, trans. Danby, 393. I discuss this passage above in Ch. 4.

[89] For the necessary explanations and qualifications, see Kellner, *Maimonides on Human Perfection*. [90] For more discussion of this passage, see p. 138 above.

presence of one, unless that one were wise and understood upon his own. All who look upon four things, it were better had they not come into the world: what is above, what is below, what is in front, and what is behind. All who are not protective of the honour of their master, it were better had they not come into the world.

The Hebrew here rendered as 'honour' is *kavod*. Anyone who is not protective of God's *kavod* would be better off not having been born. It would seem fairly obvious that the meaning of *kavod* here is 'honour' or 'respect'. It may be obvious to us, but it most assuredly was not obvious to Maimonides. He writes:

Examine this wonderful expression, said with divine help, 'all who are not protective of the *kavod* of their master', the meaning of this being, all who are not protective of their intellects, for the intellect is the *kavod* of the Lord. Since he does not know the value of this matter which was given him, he is abandoned into the hands of his desires, and becomes like an animal. Thus, they said, 'Who is he who is not protective of the honour of his Master? —he who transgresses secretly.' They said elsewhere, 'Adulterers do not commit adultery until the spirit of madness enters them.' This is the truth, for while one craves any of the desires, the intellect is not perfected.[91]

The expression, '*kavod* of the Lord' is crucial here. This is the standard biblical expression for *kavod* and occurs close to thirty times in the Bible. Maimonides here teaches that when the Torah speaks of the '*kavod* of the Lord' it actually means the human intellect, the tool through which, and only through which, humans can come close to God.[92]

The biblical *kavod*, as some sort of sensible manifestation of God's presence, and the post-biblical *shekhinah* and created light lend themselves to interpretations which undermine the severe notion of divine incorporeality which Maimonides placed at the heart of the Torah. Onkelos (followed by Sa'adiah and Halevi) had sought to draw the sting implicit in the dangerous notion of a sensible manifestation of God's presence. It fell to Maimonides to analyse many of the places where the three terms are used

---

[91] The complete text, with detailed explanatory notes, may be found in Kellner, 'Maimonides' Commentary'. For more on the use of *kavod* in this passage, see the illuminating comments of Diamond in 'Failed Theodicy', 369.

[92] Maimonides reiterates this understanding of '*kavod* of the Lord' in *Guide* i. 32 (p. 70) and i. 59 (p. 142).

in an attempt to show that the key meaning of the term *kavod* is the wisdom of God as expressed in the natural world, and that the way in which we best show *kavod* (= honour) to God, and express *kavod* (= praise) of God, is by seeking to understand divine wisdom as expressed in nature. In making these arguments Maimonides furthered his campaign against what we might call the re-mythologization of Judaism which is so prominent a feature of the world of Heikhalot texts.

SEVEN

Jews and Non-Jews

Introduction

MANY POST-RABBINIC TEXTS teach that there is some essential difference between Jews and non-Jews.[1] This teaching is not to be found in the Hebrew Bible at all, nor is it easy to find in post-biblical rabbinic writings. One of the first Jewish thinkers to emphasize that the distinction resides in a property shared by Jews and lacking in non-Jews is Judah Halevi.[2] He called this property the *amr al-ilahi*, a term we have come across in our earlier discussions of Halevi's thought.

Halevi makes passing reference to the distinction between Jew and non-Jew in several places in the *Kuzari*. Towards the beginning of the book (i. 26) the Khazar king enquiringly states to the Jewish sage, 'Your religious Law is a legacy for yourselves only.' To this the sage replies in the next paragraph:

[1] Of course, if the Zohar as we have it does not date from the 13th cent., but was written by the 2nd-cent. *tana* R. Simeon bar Yohai, this sentence would have to be dramatically modified. For more on this issue, see below in the Afterword, p. 288.

[2] On Halevi's view, see see Lasker, 'Proselyte Judaism'. The Halevian view was rejected by Abraham Ibn Ezra. Y. Tzvi Langermann notes: 'It is clear that the Jews possess no special anthropological or psychological standing in Ibn Ezra's philosophy. All of what has been said in the preceding section concerning astral destiny applies equally to all members of the human race. Ibn Ezra speaks only of the properties of the *human* soul; the notion of a *Jewish* soul which is in some meaningful, substantial sense different—an idea which bedevils some later Jewish thinkers—is totally foreign to his thought' ('Some Astrological Themes', 59). My late teacher Steven Schwarzschild tried to draw the sting of Halevi's 'biologicism', as he called it, in an unfinished article published after his untimely death: 'Proselytism and Ethnicism in R. Yehudah Halevy'. I leave it to the reader to decide how successful he was. It is important to emphasize: Halevi does not affirm that Jews differ biologically from non-Jews, that Jews have special souls, or that Jews are a species apart. He does not hold that non-Jews are any less created in the image of God than are Jews. He maintains that Jews have a special property (the potential to become prophets) lacking in non-Jews. This property is in some fashion (never explained by Halevi) transmitted through lineage.

Yes, that is so; but whoever joins us from among the nations especially will share in our good fortune although he will not be equal to us. Now, if the requirement of fulfilling the religious Law were due to the fact that God created us, then all people, the white and the black,[3] would indeed be equal in regard to that obligation because all of them are His creation, exalted be He. But the requirement of fulfilling the religious Law is in fact due to His having brought us out of Egypt and His becoming attached to us because we are the choicest of the descendants of Adam.

All humans are indeed descended from Adam. But some, the Jews, are more 'choice' than others. Halevi's protagonist is talking to a potential proselyte, a king no less, and tells him that if he, the king, were to convert he would share in the good fortune of the Jews, but not be equal to them. No one can accuse Halevi of beating about the bush![4]

At a later point (i. 96), following up on this claim, Halevi presents a history of the descent of the Jews, emphasizing their special character. The Khazar king admits the cogency of the theory, but pointedly asks: 'This is the true nobility that is passed down from Adam, inasmuch as Adam was the noblest creature on earth. Thus, it was necessary for you to have the same nobility, above and beyond every other existing thing on earth. But where was this nobility during this sin [of worshipping the golden calf]?'. It is obvious that the Khazar king asks this question in this way since he already accepts Halevi's claims about the superiority of the Jews as such.

Halevi understood that the Khazar king, as a potential convert, would have to find these claims about the innate superiority of born Jews troubling. He thus presents the following dialogue:

The sage said: Moses summoned only his own people and those who spoke his own language to accept his religious Law. Moreover, God promised them that He would confirm His revelation over the course of time by means of other prophets [Deut. 18: 15–18], and He did so during the entire time He was pleased with them and the Divine Presence dwelled among them.

The Khazar said: But wasn't this guidance meant for everyone? That would at least accord with God's wisdom.

The sage said: And wouldn't it also have been preferable for all animals to be rational? You must have forgotten in this connection what we discussed earlier

[3] On this, see Melamed, *Image of the Black*, 136–9.

[4] Kafih, in his edition and (Hebrew) translation of the *Kuzari*, notes: ' "although he will not be equal to us"—I do not know in what [the convert will not be equal to the born Jew], and do not [understand] R. Judah Halevi's intention'. I do not mean to accuse Rabbi Kafih of coyness, but I do not know how he could not understand Halevi here.

about the succession of Adam's progeny and how the prophetic divine order dwells within an individual who is the best of his brothers, and the choicest off-spring of his father, whereby one succeeds another continuously and receives that light. Others were like husks, who did not receive it until the children of Jacob came on the scene as the choicest offspring and best part of their father. They differ from the other children of Adam by virtue of a special divine distinctiveness, which made them as though they were a different species and a different, even angelic substance. (i. 101–3)

The implications of this passage are breathtaking in their chutzpah. As animals stand to humans, so humans, *simpliciter*, stand to Jews!

Painfully aware of the fact that the innate, angelic superiority of the Jews is rarely evident, Halevi has his sage say: 'Israel among the nations corresponds to the heart among the other organs of the body. It is more susceptible to diseases than they are, but also healthier than they are' (ii. 36). When the Jews are good, they are very, very good; when they are bad, they are horrid. Halevi reverts to this point in ii. 44:

The sage said: In addition, the divine order in relation to us corresponds to the soul in relation to the heart. Therefore, Scripture said, 'You only have I singled out of all the families of the earth—that is why I will call you to account for all your iniquities' (Amos 3: 2). These iniquities are the diseases of which I spoke.[5] ... Now, just as the heart is pure and endowed with a finely balanced constitution with respect to both its original nature and its developed substance so that the rational soul attaches itself to it, so, too, Israel is pure and endowed with a balanced constitution with respect to their original nature and their substance ...

Through our purity and our probity, therefore, the divine order attaches itself to this lower world, just as you have learned that the elements were arranged so that minerals might come into being from them, and then plants, and then the animals, and then human beings, and then, finally, the choicest offspring of Adam. Thus, everything is arranged for that choicest part so that the divine order might attach itself to it.[6] Now, that same choicest part exists in turn for the sake of the choicest part of the choicest, like the prophets and the pious friends of God ... the righteous are the choicest part of the choicest group.

Prophets are the choicest of the choice; given what we have seen here, is it any surprise that only Jews from birth can achieve that exalted state (ii. 50,

[5] In *Kuzari* ii. 36.
[6] Compare *Kuzari* iii. 17: 'the divine order, which is attached to the children of Israel, to the exclusion of the rest of the nations'.

iii. 1);[7] that only Jews were given the Torah (iv. 3);[8] that the choicest place on earth, the Land of Israel, was set aside for the Jews (ii. 50)?

[7] Harry A. Wolfson suggested that the differences between Halevi and Maimonides on the possibility of non-Jewish prophecy are smaller than usually suggested. See his 'Hallevi and Maimonides on Prophecy', where he writes (pp. 100–1): 'In view, however, of the fact that prophecy is considered in Judaism of being of various degrees, it is not impossible that, when Hallevi speaks of prophecy as being restricted to Jews, he has reference to a special kind of prophecy. In fact, Hallevi himself says that a non-Jew may become a *waliy*, which Arabic term, though translated into Hebrew *ḥasid, pious person*, is to be taken here to mean a prophet of a lower grade contrasted with a *nabiyy*, which means here a higher grade of prophet and hence a prophet in the true sense of the term.' About Maimonides he writes (pp. 111–12): 'If we should therefore assume, as suggested above, that Hallevi's restriction of prophecy to Jews refers only to a special higher degree of prophecy, and if we should also assume that Maimonides excludes non-Jews from the higher degrees of prophecy, then there really is no difference between them on this point.' Note that Wolfson has one 'it is not impossible' and two 'assumes'. To my mind, the apologetic nature of his writing about Halevi is blatant. In any event, Lasker's 'Proselyte Judaism' should be seen as a corrective to Wolfson here. Frank Talmage, it should be noted, follows Wolfson in this matter: see *Apples of Gold in Settings of Silver*, 14. Even if Wolfson is correct, by the way, it does not mean that Maimonides follows Halevi in putting prophecy beyond the reach of proselytes. It is worth noting that Wolfson's argument concerning Maimonides rests in great part upon the fact that in the *Guide* Maimonides never mentions any non-Jews who achieved any but the lowest level of prophecy. Given that Maimonides' data comes from the Hebrew Bible, a work uninterested, to put it mildly, in the question of non-Jewish prophecy, it is hardly surprising that Maimonides cites no examples of non-Jewish prophets of a high degree.

[8] Halevi's position on this boils down to the claim that the Jews were given the Torah because only they, of all the nations of the earth, were fit to receive it. In other words, the Jews received the Torah because they were antecedently the chosen people (see above, Ch. 2 n. 123). This reflects his view that God made the covenant between the pieces with Abraham, because, of all human beings then alive, only Abraham had the special divine spark which made such a covenant possible. Maimonides, on the other hand, as argued above in Ch. 2 (see especially the text from *Epistle to Yemen* cited there at n. 123), teaches that the descendants of Abraham, Isaac, and Jacob were constituted as the community of Israel by the receipt of the Torah. The Torah was given to Abraham's descendants because of God's promise to Abraham, which is a function of the historically contingent fact that Abraham chose God. Byron Sherwin contrasts Halevi's view to that of the talmudic rabbis, who, according to Sherwin, hold the view I here attribute to Maimonides: 'Underlying the modern of view of Hannukah is the assumption that without physical survival there can be no Judaism. As Judah Halevi already observed [*Kuzari* ii. 56], "If there were no Jews, there would be no Torah," that is, no Judaism. But underlying the rabbinic view of Hannukah is the assumption that the spiritual essence of Judaism ultimately holds the key to Jewish survival and continuity. In this view, there can be no Jews without Judaism' (Sherwin, 'Mai Hannukah', 22).

Judah Halevi may have been the first medieval Jew to teach the doctrine that Jews by birth are innately superior to non-Jews (and to proselytes[9]), but he was hardly the last. It is a teaching which permeates the Zohar and finds expression in the writings of Nahmanides. From these sources it slipped into the mainstream of Judaism and has become a basic axiom of most varieties of Jewish Orthodoxy today.[10]

Theory of the Acquired Intellect

Maimonides rejected Halevi's position. In his eyes human beings are human beings; there are not different species of human beings. He is, perhaps, the most consistent universalist in medieval Judaism. This universalism is, from a contemporary perspective, bought at a high price: profound intellectual elitism. Maimonides' universalism and elitism are grounded in a psychology and epistemology which he inherited from Aristotle via Avicenna. It is to a discussion of these matters that we must now turn.

Maimonides implicitly adopts a view (held afterwards explicitly by Gersonides) according to which that which makes us human, and in consequence that which survives our death,[11] is what we know.[12] According to

---

[9] On this, see the discussion in Lasker, 'Proselyte Judaism'.

[10] For a brief survey, see Kellner, *Maimonides on Judaism and the Jewish People*, 1–7. See further Abravanel, commentary on 1 Sam. 25, sixth 'root'. On the special character of the Jewish people in other Jewish thinkers, see Tirosh-Rothschild, 'Political Philosophy', 435–46. For more on the distinction between 'essentialist' and 'non-essentialist' interpretations of the Jewish people, see Jacobs, *God, Torah, Israel*, 57–8; for examples of essentialist interpretations, see ibid. 95–6. For more on the inferiority of non-Jewish souls in kabbalah, see the sources cited in Saperstein, 'Christians and Christianity', 238 n. 7. For some particularly hair-raising examples of Jewish particularism run amok in the writings of the Maharal of Prague (Judah Leib ben Bezalel Loewe, 1525–1609), see *Derekh haḥayim* iii.14 (end), *Gur aryeh* on Exod. 19: 22, *Netsaḥ yisra'el*, ch. 3 (p. 305; see p. 458 n. 1 for references to other particularist expressions in the writings of the Maharal), and *Tiferet yisra'el*, ch. 32. On this last, see L. Kaplan, 'Israel under the Mountain', 38. For a particularly odious example, see the comment of Maharsha (R. Solomon Edels, 1555–1631) on BT *San.* 37*a* on the mishnaic text (*San.* 4: 5) cited there.

[11] For, surely, what we share with animals (emotions, for example) is not going to survive our death.

[12] Gersonides held that what makes us human is our abstract knowledge. W. Z. Harvey has shown that, for Gersonides, any abstract knowledge 'counts', while for Maimonides it must be knowledge of metaphysical matters. See W. Z. Harvey, 'Rabbi Hasdai Crescas'. Gersonides' intellectualism led him to deprecate the importance of

this view, the human subject counts for nothing, the objects of knowledge, for everything. This Maimonidean–Gersonidean position follows from the adoption of the idea that human beings are rational animals. From this it follows that we share with animals all that is not rational in us.

What I will call Maimonides' 'hyper-intellectualist' (and hence elitist[13]) understanding of the nature of human nature is well known and need not be examined at length here.[14] There can be no doubt that he accepts Aristotle's definition of human beings as rational animals.[15] In terms of our genus, we are animals (as opposed to pieces of furniture or meteorological phenomena). Our specific difference, that which distinguishes us from all other members of the animal kingdom, is our rationality. Everything that is not a direct reflection of rational thought—hopes and fears, love and hates, desires, needs, passions—is a consequence of our animal nature.

In order to understand Maimonides' position on these matters we must glance at his theory of the soul. Maimonides adopted a variant of a fairly standard medieval Aristotelian account of the nature of the human soul. According to this approach humans are born with a potential to learn, which they may or may not actualize; it is in this capacity and its actualization that our humanity lies. We are born with differing capacities to learn and to know; to the extent that we actualize that capacity by learning abstract truths

human beings vis-à-vis the separate intellects. This aroused much anger against him, which could have been directed against Maimonides as well; see Kellner, 'Gersonides and his Cultured Despisers'. Interpreters of Maimonides are divided on the question of whether or not he thought that it was actually possible for anyone to achieve a share in the world to come. For the latest (and to my mind fully convincing) salvo in this discussion, and for references to relevant earlier studies, see H. A. Davidson, 'Maimonides on Metaphysical Knowledge'.

[13] Maimonides' intellectualist elitism is a prominent and well-known feature of his thought. See above, Ch. 1 n. 39.

[14] For a medieval thinker who interprets Maimonides in this way, see Kellner, 'Maimonides and Samuel ibn Tibbon'. Among the moderns, Isaac Husik reads Maimonides in this fashion; see his *History of Medieval Jewish Philosophy*, 299–300. If I understand him correctly, Leo Strauss also seems to adopt the hyperintellectualist view of Maimonides described here. See his *Philosophy and Law*, 105 (where Strauss gives a Gersonidean explanation of the role of the imagination in prophecy); compare also Eve Adler's introduction (ibid. 14), and Kellner, 'Strauss' Maimonides'. For reservations concerning this interpretation of Maimonides, see Kellner, 'Is Maimonides' Ideal Person Austerely Rationalist?'.

[15] On Maimonides' adoption of the definition of human beings as rational animals, see above, Ch. 2 n. 61.

we have actual intellects—we have thus actually *acquired* an intellect. If we
fail to actualize our intellectual potential, that capacity with which we were
born is wasted, and nothing survives the death of our body.[16]

Maimonides makes reference to the nature of human intellection in the
earliest of his major writings, his *Commentary on the Mishnah*. In the introduction to that work (addressed, it must be emphasized, to rabbinic scholars and not to philosophers) he writes: 'There is no doubt that the intellect
of one who understands something significant is not like the intellect of
one who does not grasp it. The former possesses actual intellect, and the
latter possesses only potential intellect.'[17] Human beings can grasp significant truths; that ability is called 'potential intellect'. Those who actually do
apprehend such truths convert their potential intellects into actual intellects. It is the actual intellect, Maimonides will make clear, and only the
actual intellect, which survives death.

The point is reiterated in another passage in the *Commentary on the
Mishnah*. We find the following statement in the first of the *Eight Chapters*
with which Maimonides prefaces his commentary on *Avot*:

Know that this single soul . . . is like matter, and the intellect is its form. If it does
not attain its form, the existence of its capacity to receive this form is for nought
and is, as it were, futile. This is the meaning of his [Solomon's] statement:
'Indeed, without knowledge, a soul is not good' [Prov. 19: 2]. He means that the
existence of a soul that does not attain its form, but is rather a soul without knowledge, is not good.[18]

With regard to intellect, the soul is like matter, while with regard to matter
it is a form; in the former respect, the soul is like matter (and matter, as students of Maimonides know well, exists potentially, not actually, so long as
it is not united with form[19]) and the intellect is its form (that which actually, and not only potentially, exists). If the soul remains in its material stage
(i.e. fails to attain the status of 'intellect'), then it will have wasted its capacity to achieve this level. A soul that remains material, never achieving the
status of intellect (which achievement depends upon knowledge), is not
good. This is a statement of the theory summarized above: we are born
with a capacity to know; to the extent that we actualize that capacity we

[16] A magisterial account of these matters may be found in H. A. Davidson, *Alfarabi,
Avicenna, and Averroes on Intellect*. Davidson discusses Maimonides on pp. 197–207.

[17] Trans. Kafih, i. 37.

[18] I quote from the text in Maimonides, *Ethical Writings*, trans. Weiss and
Butterworth, 64.   [19] See *Guide* iii. 8, esp. pp. 430–2.

become intellects *in actu*—we have *acquired* our intellects. If we fail to actualize our intellect, that capacity with which we are born is wasted and nothing survives the death of our body.

In the second of the *Eight Chapters* Maimonides states that the 'rational virtues' are wisdom and intelligence, the second including (*a*) 'the theoretical intellect', (*b*) 'the acquired intellect, but this is not the place for that'; and (*c*) 'brilliance'.[20] Especially significant here is the fact, noted by Herbert A. Davidson, that this term (i.e. the acquired intellect) does not appear in al-Farabi's *Fusul al-madani*, the text upon which Maimonides based his discussion. It was sufficiently important in his eyes for Maimonides to have added it on his own authority.[21]

A point similar to the one just adduced from the first of the *Eight Chapters* seems to come across in another text in the *Commentary on the Mishnah*, this from Maimonides' introduction to the tenth chapter of Mishnah *Sanhedrin*, the well-known 'Introduction to *Perek ḥelek*'. Commenting on the rabbinic statement, 'In the world to come there is no eating, drinking, washing, anointing, or sexual intercourse; but the righteous sit with their crowns on their heads enjoying the radiance of the *shekhinah*' (BT *Ber.* 17a), Maimonides writes, 'The intent of the statement, "their crowns on their heads", is the existence of the soul through the existence of that which it knows, in that they are the same thing, as the experts in philosophy have maintained.'[22] One achieves immortality, then, through that which one learns, 'as the experts in philosophy have maintained'.[23] In this text, Maimonides attributes to the talmudic rabbis a position held by 'the experts in philosophy'.[24] According to this position,

[20] Maimonides, *Ethical Writings*, 65.

[21] H. A. Davidson, 'Maimonides' *Shemonah Peraqim*'. Through detailed textual analysis, Davidson proves that Maimonides made extensive use of al-Farabi's *Fusul al-Madani* in the *Eight Chapters*. Our text here is based upon *Fusul al-Madani*, section 7 (ibid. 38 n. 16).   [22] Trans. Kafih, iv. 205.

[23] Barry Kogan suggests that the philosophical expert hinted at here is Avicenna: see ' "What Can We Know and When Can We Know It?" '.

[24] I am often surprised by how freely Maimonides allowed his rabbinic readers (we are dealing here with a text from his *Commentary on the Mishnah*) to see him using philosophical texts and ideas in his explanations of the authors of the Mishnah and Talmud. The *locus classicus* for this is his very brief introduction to the *Eight Chapters*, in which he announces to his readers that in order to explain the meaning of tractate *Avot* he had recourse to the writings of ancient and modern philosophers. As proved by H. A. Davidson in 'Maimonides' *Shemonah Peraqim*', these ancient and modern philosophers turn out to be Aristotle and al-Farabi.

one achieves immortality thanks and only thanks to the knowledge one has acquired.

Turning to Maimonides' next major work, his *Mishneh torah*, we find further indications that he had adopted a version of the theory of the acquired intellect. In 'Laws of the Foundations of the Torah', 4: 9, he explains why the soul can survive the death of the body: 'This form of the soul is not destroyed, as it does not require physical life for its activities. It knows and apprehends the intelligences that exist without material substance; it knows the Creator of all things; and it endures forever.'[25] If the last conjunction in this passage is construed to mean 'and therefore' (a construal certainly consistent with the Hebrew) we find Maimonides saying that one's soul endures forever thanks to the knowledge one has acquired of the Creator. Given the passage quoted from his 'Introduction to *Perek ḥelek*', and other passages to be considered later, this seems to be the best construal we can give this text.

Maimonides makes the point very clearly in the next passage to make some reference to our subject. Commenting again on the passage in BT *Berakhot* 17a to which he alluded in his commentary on *Perek ḥelek*, he says, 'The phrase "their crowns on their heads" refers to the knowledge they have acquired, and *on account of which* [*shebiglalah*] they have attained life in the world to come.'[26] Could he be any clearer? One attains life in the world to come thanks to the knowledge that one has acquired.

Turning to the *Guide*, we again find references and indications, but, as already noted, no clear-cut exposition of any psychological theory. In discussing the term 'to eat' in *Guide* i. 30 (p. 63), Maimonides notes that it is applied figuratively to 'knowledge, learning, and, in general, the intellectual apprehensions through which the permanence of the human form endures in the most perfect of states, just as the body endures through food in the finest of its states'. Perfection and 'permanent endurance' (i.e. immortality), then, are consequences of 'intellectual apprehensions'.

In his well-known discussion (in *Guide* i. 68; pp. 163–6) of the claim that God is 'the intellect, as well as the intellectually cognizing subject, and the intellectually cognized object', Maimonides makes use of many of the elements of the theory of the acquired intellect: 'that before a man intellectually cognizes a thing, he is potentially the intellectually cognizing subject', that if an intellect exists *in actu* 'it is identical with the apprehension of what has been intellectually cognized', and the identification of the 'hylic

[25] I quote from *Book of Knowledge*, trans. Hyamson, 39a.

[26] 'Laws of Repentance', 8: 3, in *Book of Knowledge*, trans. Hyamson, 90a–b.

intellect' with the 'potential intellect'. He further explains that he did not refer here to every aspect of his psychological theory, and explain every issue in it, because his book was intended for those 'who have philosophized and have acquired knowledge of what has become clear with reference to the soul and all its faculties'. Maimonides tells us here that he is working with what today we would call the standard or received theory of psychology of his day; and that can only be some variant of the theory of the acquired intellect.

Perhaps the clearest reference to the theory of the acquired intellect is found in *Guide* i. 70 (pp. 173–4):

For the souls that remain after death are not the soul that comes into being in man at the time he is generated. For that which comes into being at the time a man is generated is merely a faculty consisting in preparedness, whereas the thing that after death is separate from matter is the thing that has become actual and not the soul that also comes into being; the latter is identical with the spirit that comes into being.

Maimonides tells us here that the soul that survives death is not identical to the soul with which we are born. The soul with which we are born is merely a capacity. If we make it actual, it will then be transmogrified into an entity separate from (i.e. independent of) matter. We are told here that human beings are born with a capacity or potential to actualize their souls. To the extent that they do so, their soul will survive the death of their body. In this passage Maimonides does not say *how* we are to actualize our potential for immortality. Combining this text with those already quoted, however, yields a fairly complete picture of the theory of acquired intellect: we are born with a capacity to perfect ourselves intellectually. If we actualize that capacity we acquire intellects *in actu* and thereby achieve a measure of immortality.

In *Guide* i. 72 we find further, and clearer, evidence that Maimonides did indeed adopt some variant of the theory of the acquired intellect. First, in explaining why the human being, alone among all the denizens of the universe, is called a 'microcosm', he points out that 'this is because of that which is a proprium of man only, namely the rational faculty—I mean the intellect, which is the hylic intellect; something that is not to be found in any of the species of living beings other than man' (p. 190; compare also p. 192). Second, Maimonides comments, 'know that it behooved us to compare the relation obtaining between God, may He be exalted, and the world to that obtaining between the acquired intellect and man; this intellect is not a faculty in the body but is truly separate from the organic body and overflows towards it' (p. 193). Here we have a specific reference to the acquired intellect. Like the acquired intellect of the general theory, this acquired intellect is not a faculty in the body, and is separate from the body (compare the text cited from *Guide* i. 70).[27]

In *Guide* ii. 4 (p. 257), Maimonides, discussing the active intellect, says that its 'existence is indicated by the fact that our intellects pass from potentiality to actuality'. Here, then, we find him explicitly telling us that we are equipped from the factory, so to speak, with potential intellects, the actualization of which depends, in some fashion or other, on the activity of the active intellect.[28] This activity is what enables us to acquire an intellect *in actu*.

Further evidence in support of our thesis may be found towards the end of the *Guide*. In iii. 27 (p. 511) Maimonides tells us that man's 'ultimate perfection is to become rational *in actu*'. This means that we are born with the potential to become actually rational. Becoming rational, then, depends to one extent or another on our own efforts. Then, too,

the fourth kind [of perfection] is the true human perfection: it consists in the acquisition of the rational virtues—I refer to the conception of intelligibles, which teach true views concerning metaphysics. This is in true reality the ultimate end; this is what gives the individual true perfection, a perfection belonging to him alone; and it gives him permanent perdurance; through it man is man. (*Guide* iii. 54; p. 635)

It is the conception of intelligibles that perfects human beings as such, grants them immortality, and through which they actualize themselves as human beings.[29]

[27] The term 'overflow' (i.e. 'emanation'; *fayd* in Arabic and *shefa* in Hebrew) is defined by Maimonides as the activity peculiar to a being separate from matter. See *Guide* ii. 12 (p. 274) and Diamond, *Maimonides and the Hermeneutics of Concealment*, 193. Maimonides' source for this (mis)reading of Aristotle appears to have been Avicenna. See H. A. Davidson, 'Maimonides, Aristotle, and Avicenna'. Maimonides' statement here should not be read as if he meant that the acquired intellect exists independently of and antecedently to our intellectual activities. We *acquire*—in effect create—our acquired intellects. Once acquired, they do indeed affect our behaviour and thus 'overflow towards' us. Compare Altmann, 'Maimonides on the Intellect and Metaphysics', 75–80.

[28] Here Maimonides clearly disavows the Platonic theory (adopted explicitly by Sa'adiah and implicitly by Halevi) that humans are born with fully formed souls.

[29] It is worth noting that Abravanel, who had no interest in attributing to Maimonides a philosophical theory which he disliked, interprets the great eagle as I do here. See Abravanel's comment on *Guide* i. 1 and 41, his commentary on Genesis, p. 67,

The epistemology and psychology embodied in the theory of the acquired intellect find expression in a surprisingly large number of contexts. For example, humans are said to have been created in the image of God only because of 'the intellect that God made overflow unto man and that is the latter's ultimate perfection'.[30] What does it mean to have such an intellect in as perfect a fashion as possible? It consists in one's 'knowing everything concerning all beings that it is within the capacity of man to know in accordance with his ultimate perfection' (*Guide* iii. 27; p. 511). This perfection is purely intellectual. Maimonides continues: 'It is clear that to this ultimate perfection there do not belong either actions or moral qualities.' Thus, to be human, to actualize our potential for Godlikeness, is to know all that we can know. It is only this knowledge which makes us human: moral behaviour and moral virtues are, Maimonides holds, necessary propaedeutics to human (intellectual) perfection, but are not parts of it *per se*.[31]

Maimonides' radical intellectual elitism, noted above, is another example of a position forced upon him by the epistemology of the theory of the acquired intellect. Nor does he flinch from a necessary consequence of his view of humans as defined by their intellect: individuals born of human parents who have not achieved a minimum level of intellectual perfection are subhuman.[32] 'You know', Maimonides writes in *Guide* i. 7 (pp. 32–3),

and *Yeshuot meshiḥo*, Section (*iyun*) 1, ch. 5, p. 92. Abravanel sees Alexander of Aphrodisias as Maimonides' source and criticizes the latter heartily for following Alexander in this matter. It is amusing to note that in the Jerusalem, 1955 edition of Abravanel's commentary on the 'Earlier Prophets', 1 Sam. 25, sixth 'root' (where Abravanel also attributes the theory of the acquired intellect to Maimonides and points to Alexander as the source), the printer added a parenthetical note, identifying Alexander as 'Alexander [the Great] of Macedonia'. In this latter place, by the way, Abravanel explicitly adopts the view of the soul which I present as being derived from Plato, in opposition to the position of Maimonides. Like Abravanel, Shem Tov ibn Shem Tov clearly understood what Maimonides was teaching. See above, Ch. 2 n. 65. In the modern era, S. D. Luzzatto was also angered by Maimonides' adoption of an Aristotelian understanding of the soul. See Harris, 'Image of Maimonides', 119–20.

[30] *Guide* i. 2 (p. 24).

[31] For other relevant texts, and for discussion of interpretations other than that offered here, see Kellner, *Maimonides on Human Perfection*, 1–5, and the studies cited there. To these may be added Kreisel, *Maimonides' Political Thought*, 88–92, 128–41, and 164–75.

[32] For a valuable discussion of matters raised here, see S. Harvey, 'A New Islamic Source', 55–9.

'that whoever is not endowed with this form [of the intellect] . . . is not a man, but an animal having the shape and configuration of man.' Such human-appearing animals are actually more dangerous than simple beasts, since they can misuse their unrealized intellectual perfection for evil. So great is the danger of unrealized humans that 'it is a light thing to kill them, and has even been enjoined because of its utility' (*Guide* iii. 18; p. 475).[33] Such beings, Maimonides tells us near the end of the *Guide* (iii. 51; p. 618), 'do not have the rank of men, but have among the beings a rank lower than the rank of man but higher than the rank of apes'.[34]

All these positions flow from Maimonides' adoption of the theory of the acquired intellect. Human beings are all born with the potential to apprehend abstract truths. Those who do so become fully human and create for themselves a share in the world to come. Those who fail to do so die as they were born: potential human beings who have no share in the world to come. For our purposes, the most important consequence of the theory of the acquired intellect is that Maimonides has no mechanism by which he can distinguish Jews from non-Jews in any ontological fashion. Humans are humans, and Jewish humans are neither more nor less human than non-Jewish humans.[35] Just as the distinctions between permitted and forbidden,

[33] For examples of this 'utility' see *Book of Commandments*, positive commandments 186 ('apostate city'), 187 ('seven nations'), and 188 ('Amalek'), and negative commandment 49 ('seven nations' again) and the corresponding passages in the *Mishneh torah*. See also *Guide*, i. 37 and 54.

[34] See Melamed, *Image of the Black*, 139–48, for a discussion of the offensive examples Maimonides uses here. Compare further Maimonides' comment on Mishnah *Ḥag.* 2: 1, to the effect that it would have been better had unrealized humans not come into the world. For the text and discussion, see Kellner, 'Maimonides' Commentary'. This doctrine was strenuously criticized by Hasdai Crescas, who was particularly offended by the fact that, according to this doctrine, little children who had never sinned but who had also never had the chance to develop their intellects would have no share in the world to come. See his *Or hashem* ii. 6. i.

[35] At this point, we should note the following passage from *Guide* iii. 12 (p. 448): 'Through the two considerations that have been set forth, His beneficence, may He be exalted, with regard to His creatures will become clear to you, in that He brings into existence what is necessary according to its order of importance and in that He makes individuals of the same species equal at their creation. With a view to this true consideration, the Master of all who know [Moses] says: "For all His ways are judgement" (Deut. 32: 4). And David says: "All the paths of the Lord are mercy and truth," and so on (Ps. 25: 10), as we have made clear.' God 'makes individuals of the same species equal at their creation'. Unless one is willing to advance the absurd claim (supported by no text I have ever seen, and opposed by many) that Maimonides held that Jews and non-

holy and profane, and ritually pure and ritually impure relate only to halakhic status, so also, for Maimonides, the distinction between Jew and non-Jew is a function of halakhah, not of ontology. It is to a discussion of this matter, the point of this chapter, that we finally turn.

Jews and Non-Jews

As noted above, many medieval and post-medieval Jewish thinkers have been convinced that Jews as such have some quality or property whereby they are distinguished from non-Jews 'up front', as it were; in the terms I have been using in this study, Jews are said to be ontologically distinct from (and superior to) non-Jews. The theory of the acquired intellect renders such a position difficult to maintain. Unless it can be said that Jews as such are in some fashion better able to actualize their intellects than are non-Jews as such, there appears to be no way in which a thinker holding to the theory of the acquired intellect could maintain that Jews are distinct from (and superior to) non-Jews in the various ways that Halevi, the Zohar, etc. want to maintain. Maimonides consistently denies that Jews as such have any advantage over non-Jews as such in matters such as immortality, providence, prophecy, and so on.[36]

For reasons which will become clear below, let us focus on the question of immortality, and let me state Maimonides' position succinctly: Jews who actualize their intellect achieve a share in the world to come; the same is true of non-Jews. Similarly, Jews who fail to actualize their intellect cease to exist with their death; the same is true of non-Jews. While it is certainly true that Maimonides expected the world to come to be much more heavily 'populated' by the actualized intellects of Jews than of non-Jews, this is a consequence of obedience to the Torah, not of any inborn characteristic which Jews have and non-Jews lack. The Jews have an advantage over non-Jews because the Torah guides them more effectively than any other system of laws, first to moral perfection (a prerequisite for intellectual perfection[37]) and then to intellectual perfection. This advantage is relative, not absolute.

Jews belong to different species, we see here that he holds that all humans (Jews and non-Jews) are equal at their creation.

[36] I defend this claim in the following: *Maimonides on Judaism and the Jewish People*; 'On Universalism and Particularism in Judaism', 'Chosenness, Not Chauvinism', and 'Overcoming Chosenness'. At the end of the present chapter I deal with possible counter-examples to the thesis urged here.   [37] See Ch. 2 n. 71.

My point may be expressed in the following, admittedly extreme, terms: Maimonides distinguishes (or should have distinguished) between what may be called Israel of the commandments and Israel of the mind.[38] Israel of the commandments consists of all Jews by birth or conversion. Israel of the mind consists of all human beings who apprehend the truth and who achieve thereby a share in the world to come, whatever their ethnic background or confessional status. Maimonides, I will show here, is driven (or should be driven) to distinguish among three groups:

1. descendants of Abraham, Isaac, and Jacob, all of whom are obligated to fulfil the commandments of the Torah and to accept its doctrinal teachings, but many of whom do neither;

2. descendants of Abraham, Isaac, and Jacob who fulfil the commandments and correctly accept the Torah's doctrinal teachings;

3. individuals who are not descendants of Abraham, Isaac, and Jacob, who do not (and need not) observe the commandments of the Torah, but who do accept the doctrinal teachings of the Torah.[39]

The first group, to the extent that its members do not correctly accept the doctrinal teachings of Torah, is Israel of the commandments alone; the second group is Israel of the commandments and of the mind; the third group is Israel of the mind alone.

I write 'Israel of the mind' and not 'of the spirit' both in order to distinguish Maimonides from Christianity (the parallelism suggested by my language is only linguistic, not substantial) and in order to emphasize that the issue at hand is essentially philosophical: it is the correct understanding and

---

[38] I write 'or should have distinguished' since it is sufficient for my purposes here to show that this distinction is implict in Maimonides' writings, even if the latter was actually unaware of this implication of his views. It appears most likely to me, however, that Maimonides was aware of this implication and unperturbed by it. My understanding of Maimonides here was crucially influenced by my late teacher, Steven S. Schwarzschild.

[39] This in fact is the way that Maimonides' 'parable of the palace' in *Guide* iii. 51 is often interpreted (an interpretation which led the 15th-cent. Iberian commentator on the *Guide*, ibn Shem Tov, to comment: 'Many rabbinic scholars said that Maimonides did not write this chapter and if he did write it, it ought to be hidden away or, most appropriately, burned. For how could he say that those who know physics are on a higher level than those who engage in religion, and even more that they are with the ruler in the inner chamber, for on this basis the scholars who are engaged with physics and metaphysics have achieved a higher level than those engaged with Torah!'). For what it is worth, I do not believe that this interpretation of the parable is correct. See Kellner, *Maimonides on Human Perfection*, ch. 3.

acceptance of philosophically necessary statements which bring one into 'Israel of the mind'.

Maimonides never explicitly draws the tripartite distinction outlined here. It is even remotely possible that he was not consciously aware of it. It is, however, a distinction which grows out of his writings.

In general terms, it may be said that Sa'adiah Gaon and Rabbenu Bahya Ibn Pakuda (eleventh century) began the process of turning Judaism into a religion with a systematic theology. Sa'adiah offered his *Beliefs and Opinions* to those Jews who felt the need for the kind of certainty which only rational proof provides. Jews who did not feel that need had no need of his book.[40] Rabbenu Bahya took the process one step further, maintaining that Jews were religiously obligated to prove the truth of the tenets of their religion. He excused from this obligation only those Jews who were incapable of understanding such proofs.[41] In this he follows standard halakhic practice: no one is obligated to do what cannot be done.[42] Maimonides, in effect, took these matters two steps forward. First, he insisted that the obligation to understand (i.e. be able to prove rationally) the tenets of Torah falls upon all Jews. Those who do not or cannot do that fail to earn a share in the world to come.[43] Second, he maintained that some tenets of Torah are more fundamental than others; that is, he maintained that what we today call Judaism had dogmas.

The following text appears immediately after Maimonides' exposition of what came to be known as his Thirteen Principles of Faith:

When all these foundations are perfectly understood and believed in by a person he is within the community of Israel and one is obligated to love and pity him and to act towards him in all the ways in which the Creator has commanded that one should act towards his brother, with love and fraternity. Even were he to commit every possible transgression, because of lust and because of being overpowered by the evil inclination, he will be punished according to his rebelliousness, but he has a portion [of the world to come]; he is one of the sinners of Israel. But if a man doubts any of these foundations, he leaves the community [of Israel], denies the fundamental, and is called a sectarian, *epikoros*, and one who 'cuts among the

---

[40] See Sa'adiah Gaon, *Beliefs and Opinions*, introd., ch. 6.

[41] See Ibn Pakuda, *Duties of the Heart*, Treatise I, ch. 3.

[42] A man without a head, for example, is freed of the obligation of donning *tefilin* of the head; similarly, as Zev Harvey pointed out to me, a man without a head metaphorically does not have to prove the tenets of Judaism.

[43] 'Fail to earn'; not 'are not given'. Existence in the world to come is not a *reward* in the sense that God judges and grants; rather, it is something we *create* through our intellectual activity. For details, see H. Kasher, '"Torah for its Own Sake"'.

plantings'. One is required to hate him and destroy him. About such a person it was said, 'Do I not hate them, O Lord, who hate thee?' (Ps. 139: 21)

Maimonides makes no exceptions: all Jews must accept all the principles.[44] One who does not accept them excludes himself or herself from the community of Israel and from the world to come. Even more surprisingly, Maimonides makes acceptance of the principles the one criterion for joining the community of Israel.[45] This does not mean that Maimonides is redefining accepted halakhic norms, which establish that one joins the community of Israel through birth or conversion. Rather, I think that here he is redefining the notion of 'the community of Israel'. The community of Israel is no longer constituted by the descendants of Abraham, Isaac, and Jacob, but by all human beings who properly understand and accept the tenets of the Torah.

This point is hinted at by the eschatological context and nature of Maimonides' discussion.[46] He presents his Thirteen Principles as part of a commentary on a mishnaic text which opens with the words, 'All Israelites have a share in the world to come.'[47] In the text cited above, Maimonides makes it clear that acceptance of the principles guarantees one a share in the world to come and that rejection of them costs one his or her share in the world to come. He even goes so far as to drive an unprecedented wedge between theological orthodoxy and halakhic observance: 'Even were he to commit every possible transgression, because of lust and because of being overpowered by the evil inclination, he will be punished according to his rebelliousness, but he has a portion [of the world to come]; he is one of the sinners of Israel.'[48]

If we shift gears for a moment, and ask whom Maimonides expected to meet in the world to come, we can only answer: individuals who have achieved a sufficient level of intellectual perfection to have acquired actual

[44] For detailed analysis, see Kellner, *Dogma*, 10–65.

[45] By 'acceptance' Maimonides means 'understanding' (i.e. being able to prove rationally). On this, see the discussion in Kellner, *Must a Jew Believe Anything?*, 61–5.

[46] For a recent discussion, see A. Hyman, *Eschatological Themes*, 74–89.

[47] Abravanel was the first to point out that Maimonides presented his Principles by way of defining the term 'Israel'. See Abravanel, *Rosh amanah*, chs. 6 and 24.

[48] Norman Lamm is amazed by this: 'If we take [Maimonides] literally, we reach the astonishing conclusion that he who observes mitzvot but has not reflected upon their theological basis would also be excluded from the Children of Israel' ('Loving and Hating Jews', 115). Rabbi Lamm should actually have written: '. . . but has not *correctly* reflected upon their theological basis'.

intellects (which is another way of saying: understood—i.e. can rationally prove the truth of—the first five of the Thirteen Principles). I have no doubt that Maimonides fully expected that most of these disembodied intellects would have been earned by individuals who in this world were descendants of Abraham, Isaac, and Jacob, but that is a technical point. Intellectual perfection is impossible without antecedent moral perfection,[49] and the Torah is the best (but not the only!) guide to moral perfection. In the premessianic world, at least, descendants of Abraham, Isaac, and Jacob who wholeheartedly observe the commandments of the Torah thus have a tremendous advantage over non-Jews or descendants of Abraham, Isaac, and Jacob who do not observe the commandments of the Torah.[50]

Digression: Which of the Thirteen Principles Must Actually Be Accepted to Achieve a Share in the World to Come?

Before pursuing this matter it is crucial to flesh out a sentence in the preceding paragraph. I asserted that for Maimonides the key to immortality (i.e. to having a share in the world to come) is the intellectual acquiescence to the content of the first five principles of faith (God's existence, unity, incorporeality, and precedence, and that God is the only permissible object of worship).[51] In other words, I maintain that, when Maimonides claims that a person who even doubts any one of the other eight principles loses his or her share in the world to come, he is writing persuasively, and does not actually mean what he says.[52]

On what do I base this claim? In the first place, as we saw above, Maimonides repeatedly affirms or implicitly assumes the truth of the doctrine of the acquired intellect, according to which immortality depends upon the understanding, to one degree or another, of truths about God.[53]

[49] See above, Ch. 2 n. 71.

[50] For an analysis of Maimonides' universalist account of the messianic era, see my *Maimonides on Judaism and the Jewish People*, 33–47, and the sources cited there.

[51] By using the word 'content' here, I am not trying to weasel out of anything. Maimonides was not wedded to the language of his Thirteen Principles, and expressed them in different ways in different places (notably in *MT* 'Laws of Repentance', 3).

[52] In this Maimonides saw himself as following in God's footsteps. See e.g. the discussion of sacrifices at p. 140–8 above. One is tempted to write: *diber rambam kilshon elohim*—Maimonides spoke in the language of God.

[53] I once again refer the reader to W. Z. Harvey's very important discussion in 'R. Hasdai Crescas' Critique'.

In other words, he has no mechanism available to him whereby he could exclude from the world to come people who understand and accept the teachings included in Principles 1–5 while doubting or even rejecting Principles 6–13.

Second, there are a number of specific passages in the *Guide of the Perplexed* in which Maimonides distinguishes the 'salvific' character of the content of the first five principles from that of the content of the rest of the principles. By this I mean that he makes actualization of the intellect (and hence earning a share in the world to come) contingent upon knowledge concerning God. Even honest mistakes in these matters exclude one from the world to come. Honest mistakes about other matters cannot.

Thus, in *Guide* i. 35, Maimonides implicitly makes the distinction posited here; he then uses it to distinguish between acceptable and unacceptable mistakes in the following chapter. In i. 34 he had explained that many metaphysical matters must be kept hidden from the masses, who lack the tools to understand them. He then opens i. 35 with the following words (p. 79):

Do not think that all we have laid down in the preceding chapters regarding the greatness and the hidden nature of the matter, the difficulty of apprehending it, and its having to be withheld from the multitude, refers also to the denial of the corporeality of God and to the denial of His being subject to affections. It is not so.

Just as even children must be taught that God is one, Maimonides goes on and explains, so they must be taught that God has no body and is not subject to human emotions. The point is emphasized later in the chapter:

the negation of the doctrine of the corporeality of God and the denial of His having a likeness to created things and of His being subject to affections are matters that ought to be made clear and explained to everyone according to his capacity and ought to be inculcated in virtue of traditional authority upon children, women,[54] stupid ones, and those of a defective natural disposition, just as they adopt the notion that God is one, that He is eternal, and that none but he should be worshipped. (p. 81)

Maimonides goes on to explain that unity implies incorporeality, and concludes the chapter by strongly affirming that attributing corporeality to

---

[54] I hasten to note that, despite this and similar statements, Maimonides was one of the few medieval figures (in any Western religious tradition) to hold that women were no less created in the image of God than men. See the studies cited in Ch. 5 n. 13.

God is no better than atheism or idolatry:

> it is not meet that belief in the corporeality of God or in His being provided with any of the concomitant of the bodies[55] should be permitted to establish itself in anyone's mind any more than it is meet that belief should be established in the nonexistence of the deity, in the association of other gods with Him,[56] or in the worship of other than He.

In *Guide* i. 36 Maimonides uses the points made in i. 35 in order to distinguish what he calls inexcusable infidelity ('belief about a thing that is different from what the thing really is', p. 83),[57] from excusable ignorance ('ignorance of what it is possible to know'). Maimonides wants to show that, with respect to God's corporeality, there is no difference: ignorance is infidelity and both uniquely arouse God's wrath. The masses do not have to become philosophers, but they must find good teachers:

> Accordingly there is no excuse for one who does not accept the authority of men who inquire into the truth and are engaged in speculation if he himself is incapable of engaging in such speculation. I do not consider as an infidel one who cannot demonstrate that the corporeality of God should be negated. But I do consider as an infidel one who does not believe in its negation. (p. 85)

It is only errors about God which constitute infidelity. If Maimonides were serious in his claims about the salvific necessity of accepting all of the principles, no errors concerning them could be tolerated.

The distinction I am trying to demonstrate here in also hinted at in *Guide* iii. 28 (p. 512):

> Among the things to which your attention ought to be directed is that you should know that in regard to the correct opinions through which the ultimate perfection may be obtained, the Law has communicated only their end and made a call to believe in them in a summary way—that is, to believe in the existence of the Deity, may He be exalted, His unity, His knowledge, His power, His will, and His eternity. All these points are ultimate ends, which can be made clear in detail and through definitions only after one knows many opinions. In the same way the Law makes a call to adopt certain beliefs, belief in which is necessary for political welfare. Such, for instance, is our belief that He, may He be exalted, is violently angry with those who disobey Him and that it is therefore necessary to fear Him and to dread Him and to take care not to disobey.

[55] Such concomitants, it is worth noting, include emotions.

[56] Pines notes: 'the usual Arabic term for polytheism is employed'.

[57] Pines notes: 'The word rendered by "infidelity" is *kufr*, a term whose usual meaning is approximately: disbelief in one or several religious dogmas.'

As I read this passage, Maimonides maintains that the 'correct opinions through which the ultimate perfection may be obtained' are beliefs concerning God: existence, unity, knowledge, power, will, eternity. It is beliefs about God which are presented 'in a summary way' in the first five principles. The others, while true, are not necessary for the attainment of ultimate perfection but are 'necessary for political welfare'. By this I understand Maimonides to be claiming that the real point of the Torah, so to speak, is to teach truths about God. Individuals can achieve these truths only if they first live morally disciplined lives. Humans, as social animals (Aristotle's *zoon politikon*), need the fellowship of others. Morally disciplined communities are thus necessary if individuals are to reach their perfection.[58] Once again, the content of the first five principles is distinguished from that of the last eight.

There is a third point: in his statement at the end of the principles, Maimonides says that anyone who doubts any of the principles is called a God-hater. But in *Guide* i. 36 (p. 84) and i. 54 (p. 127) he specifies that it is only idolaters who are called haters of God, and idolatry is the subject of the first five principles. Reading the passage from the Thirteen Principles in light of these two texts from the *Guide*, we find Maimonides implicitly distinguishing once again the content of the first five principles from the content of the last eight.

Idolaters hate God. Whom does God, so to speak, hate? Who are the objects of His wrath? Maimonides answers these questions in *Guide* i. 36 (p. 82):

Know that if you consider the whole of the Torah and all the books of the prophets, you will find that the expressions, wrath [*ḥaron af*], anger [*ka'as*], and jealousy [*kinah*] are exclusively used with reference to idolatry. You will also find that the expressions, enemy of God [*oyev hashem*] or adversary [*tsar*] or hater [*sone*], are exclusively used to designate an idolater.

Once again, it makes sense to read the passage from the end of the Thirteen Principles in light of this text. Those who hate God, and are to be hated by those who love God, are those who deny the content of the first five principles, not those who deny (or make errors) about the last eight.

The following passage from *Guide* i. 54 (pp. 123–4) is particularly noteworthy:

[58] This is not the place to develop this point, but I further understand Maimonides to have held that God gave the Torah, not only to perfect individuals but, ultimately, to perfect all humanity. For background on this, see Hirshman, *Torah for the Entire World*. The central thesis of this important book is presented in English in Hirshman, 'Rabbinic Universalism'.

Furthermore his saying, 'That I may find grace in thy sight' (Exod. 33: 13), indicates that he who knows God finds grace in His sight and not he who merely fasts and prays, but everyone who has knowledge of Him. Accordingly those who know Him are those who are favoured by Him and permitted to come near Him, whereas those who do not know Him are objects of His wrath and are kept far away from Him. For His favour and wrath, His nearness and remoteness, correspond to the extent of a man's knowledge or ignorance.[59]

Knowledge of God is the key to nearness to God; those who do not know God, as opposed to those who fail to perform religious rituals such as fasting and praying, are the sole objects of God's wrath. It is very important to note in addition, in the context of our larger discussion here, that everyone who has knowledge of God 'finds grace in His sight'. There does not appear to be any way in which Maimonides can restrict (or wants to restrict) that knowledge to Jews alone.

There is a fourth way in which Maimonides indicates that he holds there to be a significant distinction between the content of the first five principles and that of the last eight. The distinction is reflected in some of his statements about the Karaites of his day. Karaites accepted the first five principles, but certainly rejected part of the eighth (about the normative character of the Oral Torah); despite that fact, Maimonides, in his later writings, insisted that they are not to be treated as heretics plain and simple, and that efforts must be made to draw them back into the fold.[60] Clearly, he did not treat them as people who hated God and who should be hated by those who love God.

Maimonides insisted that acceptance of the Thirteen Principles was the key to achieving a portion in the world to come, and that denial of them, or even errors about them, cost one her or his share in the world to come. This claim must now be seen as persuasive, or 'political' in contemporary parlance, not strictly true. Acceptance of the first five principles is the true key to achieving a share in the world to come; denial of those five, or errors concerning them, do cost one her or his share in the world to come. Such is not the case with the last eight. I hasten to add that I have no reason to think that Maimonides doubted the truth of any of the last eight. There are some true claims (about God) about which errors are fatal. There are other

[59] See also p. 127 in the same chapter: 'Know that His speech—"visiting the iniquity of the fathers upon the children" (Exod. 34: 7)—applies only to the sin of idolatry in particular and not any other sin.'

[60] On Maimonides' attitude towards Karaites, see Blidstein, 'The "Other" in Maimonidean Law', and the studies cited there.

true claims (about the Torah and reward and punishment) about which errors (or even outright denial) are not fatal.

Who is an 'Israelite'?

Applying all this back to the mishnaic text, 'All Israelites have a share in the world to come' we see that Maimonides may be read as hinting that the terms 'Israelite' and 'one who has a share in the world to come' are coextensive; after all, there are plenty of people whose identity cards, as it were, read 'Israelite' but who have no share in the world to come (because of errors about God). That being the case, the term 'Israelite' cannot be coextensive with the phrase 'descendants of Abraham, Isaac, and Jacob', since, as Maimonides explicitly teaches here, there are descendants of Abraham, Isaac, and Jacob who are excluded (better: exclude themselves) from the world to come.[61]

The point being made here may be better understood if we think in terms of Boolean diagrams. Maimonides the intellectual elitist is often understood as maintaining that there are two circles, one within the other. The larger circle consists of the descendants of Abraham, Isaac, and Jacob. The smaller circle, wholly contained in the first and thus a subset of it, consists of those descendants of Abraham, Isaac, and Jacob who correctly understand the Thirteen Principles (or, according to my understanding of Maimonides, those descendants of Abraham, Isaac, and Jacob who correctly understand the first five of the Thirteen Principles). As I understand him, Maimonides actually holds that there are two circles which partly overlap: one circle consists of the descendants of Abraham, Isaac, and Jacob and the second consists of individuals who correctly understand the first five of the Thirteen Principles. According to this picture, there are descendants of Abraham, Isaac, and Jacob who do not correctly understand the first five principles and thus have no share in the world to come (even if they accept the last eight principles and do their best to fulfil all the commandments), and there are individuals who are not descended from Abraham, Isaac, and Jacob (and who may not have even heard of Torah and its teachings) who correctly accept the content of the first five principles and do have a share in the world to come.

[61] Note also that in his comment on Mishnah *San.* 10: 2 (cited below), Maimonides explicitly notes that there are people who are not descendants of Abraham, Isaac, and Jacob who have shares in the world to come.

Given Maimonides' thoroughgoing universalism, it seems likely to me that he was aware of this implication of his thought.[62] There is another implication, however, of which he may have been unaware; if he had been aware of it, I am thoroughly convinced that he would have been unhappy with it. It follows from his positions as adumbrated here, when coupled with another notion, that a descendant of Abraham, Isaac, and Jacob who does not observe the commandments of the Torah, but who, despite that, achieves the requisite intellectual perfection, will have a share in the world to come. The rabbi in Maimonides could hardly have been happy with such a conclusion, but I do not see how it can be avoided.[63]

In order better to understand the point just made, a brief reminder of the discussion in Chapter 2 is necessary. For Maimonides 'halakhah' is the name given to a set of rules that create an institution called (in our language, but not, I realize, in that of Maimonides) 'Judaism'. These rules are contingent—in the sense that they could have been different—not because they

[62] I find support for the position being urged here in the passage just cited from *Guide* i. 54 (p. 123). Here Maimonides informs us that (presumably Jewish) religious rituals (fasting and praying) do not of themselves bring one close to God, but knowledge does. There does not appear to be any way in which he can restrict (or would want to restrict) that knowledge to Jews alone.

[63] My friend Daniel J. Lasker thinks it can be avoided. He maintains that, for Maimonides, it is inconceivable that a Jew could fail to see the wisdom in the commandments and yet still achieve enough intellectual perfection to warrant a share in the world to come. Lasker may be right about Maimonides the historical figure, but I do not see how Maimonides the philosopher could summarily reject the possibility that a (morally perfected) Jew could fail to obey the commandments without thereby losing his or her intellectual abilities. Indeed, another friend, Jerome Gellman, commented to me: 'I fail to see why, on Rambam's view, any Jew today should have an "obligation" to obey the mitzvot. After all, the mitzvot were intended for a very different cultural-historical setting that hardly exists today. In fact, it is hard for me to understand, given Rambam's view, what it might mean for a Jew to be "obligated" to keep the mitzvot. What is the source of this "obligation"? God? Moses? Rambam himself? The social-political needs of the Jewish people? When I think on the Rambam, I personally feel no obligation to keep the mitzvot.' Maimonides, I believe, would reply that an explanation of why commandments are given is not an explanation for why they ought to be obeyed. My thanks to Vint Cerf, the 'father of the internet', who made this exchange possible. For what is to my mind a very convincing account of how Maimonides could see the commandments as still binding even though they reflect ancient events and realities, see J. Stern, 'Maimonides on Education', 118. Kenneth Seeskin had earlier made a similar argument in *No Other Gods*, 13–49. For more on these matters, see above, Ch. 2 nn. 21 and 125, Ch. 4 n. 57.

do not express God's wisdom and benevolence, but because they reflect contingent historical circumstances. Violations of these rules can have serious consequences on the psychosocial level, leading up to and including the death penalty, but have no direct consequences on an ontological level. That this is indeed Maimonides' position may be seen from his treatment of the matter of sacrifices, which he presents as a divine concession to the primitive nature of the Israelites in Egypt and not part of some primordial, preordained divine plan. For Maimonides, obedience to the commandments is surely praiseworthy, but carries with it no actual earned reward; violation of the commandments is surely despicable, but carries with it no actual incurred punishment.[64]

The argument I am making here is stronger than the points urged in some of my earlier studies. In those studies I sought to prove that Maimonides saw the distinction between Jew and non-Jew to be a distinction of what Daniel J. Lasker has felicitiously called 'software', never of hardware.[65] Jews are distinguished from non-Jews by what they believe and what they do, not by what they are. In an earlier work I hesitantly distinguished 'those individuals constituted as a national group by their shared descent from Abraham' from 'that religious group constituted by its adherence to the Torah'.[66] I did not then realize that the logic of his position drove, or should have driven, Maimonides into recognizing a third group, philosophical adherents of the essential teachings of the Torah who are not descended from Abraham, Isaac, and Jacob. My late teacher Steven S. Schwarzschild called such individuals 'Jewish non-Jews'.[67]

But, to return—finally!—to the point of this chapter, if all, or even most, of what I have proposed here is true (and it is), then it is clear that Maimonides does not, indeed cannot, attribute to the Jew as such any ontological standing which sets him or her apart from non-Jews. For Maimonides, human beings are most importantly divided, not between Jews and non-Jews, but between those who actualize their human potential (and thus achieve a share in the world to come) and those who do not (and who simply cease to exist upon their death). By and large, Maimonides was convinced that in the pre-messianic era many more Jews than non-Jews would succeed in actualizing their human potential, thanks to adherence to the Torah, a God-given tool designed for that very purpose. But, in all seriousness, that is just a

[64] I defend these prima facie surprising claims in *Must a Jew Believe Anything?* (2nd edn.), Appendix 1, 149–63.   [65] For this distinction, see Lasker, 'Proselyte Judaism'.

[66] Kellner, *Maimonides on Judaism and the Jewish People*, 82.

[67] Schwarzschild, 'An Agenda', 116.

technicality. Non-Jews who achieve the necessary self-control and moral perfection to make intellectual perfection possible achieve the same level of human perfection as do Jews.[68]

Is this true? There is a famous text of Maimonides which seems to refute this claim.

Wise Non-Jews and the World to Come

Note must be taken of a well-known Maimonidean text which might be cited in opposition to all that I have written here. I refer to *MT* 'Laws of Kings and their Wars', 8: 11. The chapter in question opens with a discussion of how soldiers in a Jewish army are to comport themselves, and includes Maimonides' account of 'the beautiful captive' (Deut. 21: 10–14). This discussion focuses on the question of the beautiful captive's status vis-à-vis Judaism. This led Maimonides to continue with an account of other individuals whose status vis-à-vis Judaism needs clarification: the Noahide, the resident alien (*ger toshav*), and the righteous gentile (*ḥasid umot ha'olam*). Paragraph 11 reads:

Anyone who accepts the seven [Noahide] commandments and observes them scrupulously is one of the righteous of the nations of the earth and has a share in the world to come, on condition that he accept them and perform them because the Holy One, blessed be He, commanded them in the Torah and made known to us through Moses our Teacher that Noahides had been commanded to obey them before [the giving of the Torah]. But if he observed them because his reason compels him [*hekhre'a hada'at*], he is not a resident alien [*ger toshav*], nor one of the righteous gentiles [*meḥasidei umot ha'olam*], but one of their wise men.

This text has been exhaustively analysed and re-analysed since at least the time of Moses Mendelssohn, especially since it contains a notorious mistake in the printed editions of the *Mishneh torah*.[69] It is often read as if Maimonides is teaching that only those non-Jews who satisfy the criteria for being considered a *ḥasid umot ha'olam*, i.e. that they accept the Noahide

---

[68] Note should be taken of L. Kaplan, 'Maimonides on the Singularity'. On the basis of an analysis of Maimonides' *MT* 'Laws of Idolatry' Kaplan arrives at conclusions similar but not identical to those defended in this chapter.

[69] According to the corrupt editions, the last clause reads 'and not one of their wise men'. For an important and influential discussion, see Schwarzschild, 'Do Noachites Have to Believe in Revelation?'. Schwarzschild cites texts and studies up until 1962. Dienstag, 'Natural Law', brings the discussion up to 1987 and Korn, 'Gentiles, the World to Come, and Judaism', continues the discussion with insight.

commandments because they were taught in the Torah, have a share in the world to come.[70] If this is correct, then 'Jewish non-Jews' do not exist in the Maimonidean universe, and an important argument against the claim that Maimonides attributed no special ontological status to Jews as such loses some of its force.

Let us call this reading of our text here a minimalist interpretation of Maimonides' ideas on who enjoys a share in the world to come. This minimalist interpretation is supported by only one other Maimonidean text. In every other place where he alludes to the issue of 'life after death' the criterion that comes into play is intellectual perfection, pure and simple; matters of ethnicity,[71] confessional status, or even gender[72] are simply ignored. All these other texts reflect the fact, as shown above, that Maimonides has no mechanism that is philosophically acceptable to him by which to exclude from the world to come figures such as Aristotle, whom he certainly considered to be one of the wise men of the non-Jews, even as he equally certainly knew that the Stagirite did not qualify as a righteous gentile.

The other text which may be cited in support of the minimalist interpretation is *MT* 'Laws of Forbidden Intercourse', 14: 4.[73] There Maimonides discusses the procedures for conversion, and in that context writes that the court should say to the prospective convert:

Be it known unto you that the world to come is treasured up only for the righteous [*tsadikim*], who are Israel. As for what you see that Israel is in distress in this world, it is in reality a boon which is laid up for them, because it is not granted them to receive the abundance of good things in this world like other peoples, lest their hearts should wax haughty and they should go astray and squander the reward of the world to come, as it is said, 'But Jeshurun waxed fat and kicked' (Deut. 32: 15).

This text is clearly problematic, since it is even more minimalist than our

---

[70] Such a reading was presented recently in Gluck, 'The King in his Palace', and Korn, 'Gentiles'. See also Kraemer, 'Naturalism and Universalism', 58. Nehorai, 'A Portion in the World to Come', argues against this sort of interpretation of Maimonides as do I in *Maimonides on Judaism and the Jewish People*, 75–9. Nehorai and Hannah Kasher had earlier discussed the issue in an exchange in *Tarbits*, 64 (see below, n. 73).

[71] For the necessary qualifications to this statement, see Melamed, *Image of the Black*, 139–48.   [72] See above, n. 54.

[73] See H. Kasher, ' a Means'. Kasher cites this text in order to prove that Maimonides wanted his traditionalist readers to think that he held that obedience to the commandments was the sole key to entrance to the world to come. Her interpretation is disputed by Nehorai, 'How a Righteous Gentile can Merit'.

passage from 'Kings'; here, even righteous gentiles are excluded from the world to come, since the world to come is reserved for the righteous, 'who are Israel'. However, in addition to contradicting our passage from 'Kings', it also stands in direct contradiction to *MT* 'Laws of Repentance', 3: 1, 'Laws of Evidence', 11: 1, and *Commentary on the Mishnah, Sanhedrin* 10: 2. The first of these reads as follows:

Every human being has merits and iniquities. One whose merits exceed his iniquities is righteous [*tsadik*]. He whose iniquities exceed his merits is wicked. If the two balance in an individual, he belongs to the intermediate class.[74]

Maimonides continues his discussion of this matter in paragraph 5:

So, too all wicked persons whose iniquities exceed their merits are judged according to their sins and have a portion in the world to come; for all Israelites, notwithstanding that they have sinned, have a portion in the world to come . . . and so too, righteous gentiles have a portion in the world to come.[75]

MT 'Laws of Evidence', 11: 10 teaches:

As to informers, *epikorsim*, and apostates, the Rabbis did not deem it necessary to include them among those ineligible [for a share in the world to come] because they enumerated only the wicked among the Israelites. But these rebellious disbelievers are on a lower level than gentiles. In the case of heathens, we are bound neither to rescue them (from the pit) nor cast them (into it), and the righteous among them [*ḥasideihen*] are assured of a portion in the world to come.[76]

As he does in these texts in the *Mishneh torah*, so also in his earlier *Commentary on the Mishnah*: Maimonides takes it as a given that righteous gentiles have a share in the world to come. Explaining why the Mishnah excludes the prophet Balaam from the world to come, he writes: 'The Mishnah mentioned Balaam, even though he is not of Israel, since righteous gentiles have a share in the world to come, therefore the Mishnah taught that Balaam was a wicked gentile.'[77] 'Laws of Forbidden Intercourse', 14: 4 thus not only contradicts Maimonides' philosophical position that life in the world to come is open to all who have achieved the requisite level of intellectual perfection; it also contradicts several other clear-cut texts in his halakhic writings.

---

[74] Maimonides, *Book of Knowledge*, trans. Hyamson, 84*a*, with emendations.

[75] *Book of Knowledge*, trans. Hyamson, 84*b* (with emendations).

[76] Maimonides, *Book of Judges*, trans. Hershman, 107 (with emendations).

[77] *Commentary on the Mishnah*, San. 10: 2.

So far as I know, the first to draw attention to this problem was Tsevi Hirsch Chajes (1805–55) in his gloss on BT *Yev.* 47*a*.[78] The Talmud there discusses the procedure of conversion and comments:

As he [the candidate for conversion] is informed of the punishment for the [violation of] the commandments, so is he to be informed of the reward given [for their observance]. They [the members of the court] say to him: 'Be it known unto you that the world to come is made only for the righteous [*tsadikim*] and Israelites at the present time are unable to bear either too much prosperity or too much suffering.'

On this text Rabbi Chajes cites Maimonides, 'Laws of Forbidden Intercourse', 14: 4 ('Be it known unto you that the world to come is treasured up only for the righteous, who are Israel'), and comments: 'Not only does the Talmud not state this, but Maimonides himself in "[Laws of] Repentance" 3 and "[Laws of] Evidence" 21 writes that righteous gentiles will have a share in the world come; thus a copyist's error has occurred in the [text of] Maimonides [here].'[79]

Rabbi Chajes' supposition that there is a copyist's error in Maimonides' text becomes very convincing if we look at the talmudic text on which Maimonides was clearly basing himself in 'Laws of Forbidden Intercourse': 'Be it known unto you that the world to come is made only for the righteous and Israelites at the present time.' Maimonides' text reads as follows: 'Be it known unto you that the world to come is treasured up only for the righteous, who are Israel'. One can see how easy it would be for someone copying Maimonides' text to have 'corrected' it (deliberately or inadvertently) if they had the talmudic text in mind (but not in front of them).[80]

Rabbi Chajes' proposed emendation thus makes excellent sense; if he is right, the mistake fell into the text at a very early stage, since Frankel lists no manuscripts or editions which have what, according to Chajes, should

[78] I found this gloss thanks to the wonderful apparatus in the Shabse Frankel edition of the *Mishneh torah*.

[79] Rabbi Chajes' comments are printed in the back of the Vilna Talmud and many subsequent reprintings. A 'copyist's error' has occurred in Chajes' text, since the relevant passage in 'Laws of Evidence' is in ch. 11, not ch. 21.

[80] Avram Montag pointed out to me that the history of this passage in rabbinic literature supports R. Chajes' supposition. Alfasi and Rosh (on BT *Yev.* 47*a*) and the *Tur* ('Yoreh de'ah' 268) preserve the reading of the Talmud, while Karo, both in the *Beit yosef* and in the *Shulḥan arukh*, simply quotes Maimonides. Maimonides was a great admirer of Alfasi and it seems unlikely that on this matter he would consciously prefer a narrower and more particularist reading than that preferred by his great predecessor.

be the correct text. Another possibility is that Maimonides flatly contradicted himself. The first option is difficult: there is no manuscript evidence for it, and we know that the *Mishneh torah* was carefully read and transmitted. The second option is difficult: Maimonides was a careful writer, and should not be presumed to have contradicted himself in so obvious a fashion (and it is too obvious to be explained as a purposeful contradiction). I would like to propose a third option: the term 'Israel' in this context includes certain non-Jews. In other words, I am suggesting that when Maimonides says, 'Be it known unto you that the world to come is treasured up only for the righteous, who are Israel' he means to hint that the righteous are called Israel, whether or not they are descendants of Abraham, Isaac, and Jacob.[81]

This third option can be supported through the following (admittedly creative) exegesis. Anyone who has been convinced by my argument in this chapter will find it to be Maimonidean in spirit. My exegesis involves two verses:

'The righteous individual [*tsadik*] lives through [i.e. by virtue of] his faith' (Hab. 2: 4).[82]

Your people 'are all of them righteous [*tsadikim*]; they will inherit the land forever'. (Isa. 60: 21)

The first of these is never cited by Maimonides, while the second is cited by him only once (in 'Laws of Repentance', 3: 5),[83] where it is explained as follows: 'Land is an allegory; it means, "the land of the living", i.e. the world to come; and so too, righteous gentiles have a portion in the world

---

[81] R. Yehiel Ya'akov Weinberg (1885–1966) proposes another solution: by the phrase 'who are Israel' Maimonides means to say that the Jews are righteous by virtue of their obedience to the commandments without in any way prejudicing the case against the likelihood that (some) non-Jews will achieve a share in the world to come. Although R. Weinberg insists that he is not engaging in apologetics, it is hard to shake off the feeling that this is what he is actually doing. See Weinberg, *Writings*, i. 150–4. My thanks to Marc Shapiro for drawing my attention to this passage.

[82] Here is the immediate context of this partial verse (in the NJPS): 'Take up my station at the post, and wait to see what He will say to me, what He will reply to my complaint. The Lord answered me and said: Write the prophecy down, inscribe it clearly on tablets, so that it can be read easily. For there is yet a prophecy for a set term, a truthful witness for a time that will come. Even if it tarries, wait for it still; for it will surely come, without delay: lo, his spirit within him is puffed up, not upright, but the righteous man is rewarded with life for his fidelity.'

[83] I rely in these matters upon Kafih, *Maimonides on the Bible*.

to come.' This verse from Isaiah, of course, is cited in Mishnah *Sanhedrin* 10: 1, 'All Israelites have a share in the world to come.'[84] In my discussion of that text above I suggested that for Maimonides the terms 'Israelite' and 'have a share in the world to come' are coextensive.

We can now move that one step further. (True) Israelites, i.e. those descendants of Abraham, Isaac, and Jacob who have a share in the world to come, are the righteous, the *tsadikim*. As we have seen above, Maimonides, to Rabbi Norman Lamm's obvious distress, defines these *tsadikim* purely in terms of what they think, not what they do.[85]

Let us now connect the righteous person, the *tsadik* of Isaiah 60: 21, to the righteous person, the *tsadik* of Habakkuk 2: 4.[86] Maimonides believed that righteous individuals are both defined by their faith and achieve life in the world to come through it. He understands faith to be the affirmation of true claims (as opposed to an understanding of faith as trust in God expressed through behaviour). He was thus led to ask: which specific beliefs constitute the faith of the righteous Jew and grant that Jew access to the world to come? He phrased the answer to that question in his famous Thirteen Principles. Acceptance of these principles is the key to individual salvation. Rejecting any of the principles, or even doubting them, costs one his or her share in the world to come.

Maimonides' Habakkuk, as it were, defines righteousness as faith; Maimonides himself defines faith as assent to a set of propositions.[87] Such assent is not and cannot be restricted to descendants of Abraham, Isaac, and Jacob. Any human being who arrives at a correct understanding of the truths contained in the first five of the Thirteen Principles is thus a *tsadik*, will enjoy a share in the world to come, and, if not a descendant of Abraham, Isaac, and Jacob, is a Jewish non-Jew.[88]

---

[84] The source for Maimonides' statement here in 'Laws of Repentance' 3: 5.

[85] See n. 48 above. We must remember, of course, that for Maimonides one cannot achieve any significant level of intellectual perfection without first achieving (and maintaining) a high level of moral perfection.

[86] In making this move I basically follow Gersonides, who glossed Gen. 6: 9 ('Noah was a righteous man [*tsadik*]') as follows: '[the term] *tsadik* is used with respect to perfected moral virtues, or with respect to perfection of the intelligibilia [*shelemut hamusklalot*], as in "the righteous [*tsadik*] lives through his faith" [Hab. 2: 4]; it is in that second sense that it is used here.' For an expression of this view in the *Guide*, see i. 30 (p. 64), where Maimonides subtly leads the reader to equate righteousness with wisdom.

[87] Rosenberg, 'Concept of Emunah', and Manekin, 'Belief, Certainty, and Divine Attributes'.

[88] For a striking text easily read in this light, see *MT* 'Laws of Sabbatical Year and

We may now revert to 'Laws of Forbidden Intercourse', 14: 4, and its problematic assertion that the righteous are Israel. Perhaps Maimonides is hinting that the world to come is indeed treasured up only for the righteous (morally perfected individuals who go on to achieve a minimal level of intellectual perfection), who are indeed Israel, but Israel of the mind, not only Israel of descent.[89]

Having cleared away this apparent textual stumbling-block, we can now return to 'Laws of Kings', 8: 11. That text, it will be recalled, reads as follows:

Any who accept the seven [Noahide] commandments and observe them scrupulously is a righteous gentile and has a share in the world to come, on condition that he accept them and perform them because the Holy One, blessed be He,

Jubilee', 13: 13: 'Not only the Tribe of Levi, but each and every individual human being, whose spirit moves him and whose knowledge gives him understanding to set himself apart in order to stand before the Lord, to serve Him, to worship Him, and to know Him, who walks upright as God created him to do, and releases himself from the yoke of the many foolish considerations which trouble people—such an individual is as consecrated as the Holy of Holies, and his portion and inheritance shall be in the Lord forever and ever. The Lord grant him adequate sustenance in this world, the same as He had granted to the priests and to the Levites. Thus indeed did David, peace upon him, say, 'O Lord, the portion of mine inheritance and of my cup, Thou maintainest my lot' (Ps. 16: 5).' I cite Maimonides, *Book of Agriculture*, trans. Klein, 403.

[89] It is clearly no coincidence that Maimonides cites the verse, '[Abraham] planted a tamarisk at Beersheva, and invoked there the name of the Lord and Everlasting God' (Gen. 21: 33) at the beginning of the *Guide*, at the beginning of parts ii and iii of the *Guide*, at the beginning of the *Mishneh torah*, and at the beginning of close to a dozen of its parts. Perhaps he is hinting that he wants Jews to emulate Abraham, who sought to bring as many people as possible to join Israel of the mind (Abraham certainly was not trying to 'convert' them into becoming his descendants!). On Abraham, see 'Laws of Idolatry', 1: 3, and positive commandment 3 in the *Book of Commandments* (where Maimonides does not cite Gen. 21: 33, more's the pity), as well as *Guide* ii. 13 (p. 282) and iii. 29 (p. 516) (two other places where our verse is cited). On Maimonides' use of this verse see the comment in Michael Schwartz's new Hebrew translation of the *Guide*, vol. i, p. 4 (unpaginated); see also Spiegel, *Chapters*, 572–3, on the use of the verse not only by Maimonides himself, but by his descendants and followers, and above, Ch. 2 n. 115. In connection with Abraham, it ought to be noted that Yeshayahu Leibowitz finds a distinction in Maimonides between 'Abrahamic' and 'Mosaic' religion. Leibowitz and I agree in seeing Abrahamic religion as addressed to the world and Mosaic religion as addressed to the Jews, but we disagree on the nature of Abrahamic religion in Maimonides' thought (which, for Leibowitz, turns out to be identical with his own idiosyncratic version of Judaism). See Y. Leibowitz, 'Maimonides: The Abrahamic Man', and W. Z. Harvey, 'Leibowitz on Abrahamic Man'.

commanded them in the Torah and made known to us through Moses our
Teacher that Noahides had been commanded to obey them before [the giving of
the Torah]. But if he observed them because his reason compels him, he is not a
resident alien [*ger toshav*], nor one of the righteous gentiles [*meḥasidei umot
ha'olam*], but one of their wise men.

It appears evident to me that Maimonides is not setting up general criteria
here for who will and who will not have a share in the world to come. In
order to understand this, we must look at the previous two paragraphs:

9. . . . for any gentile who refuses to accept those seven [Noahide] commandments is put to death if he is under our control.

   10. Moses our teacher bequeathed the Torah and the commandments only to
Israel, as it is said 'an inheritance of the congregation of Jacob' (Deut. 33: 4), and
to those of other nations who wish to convert, as it is said: 'One law and one ordi-
nance shall be both for you and for the convert [*ger*]' (Num. 15: 16). But one who
does not wish to convert is not coerced to accept the Torah and the commandments. Moreover, Moses, our teacher, was commanded by God to compel all
human beings to accept the commandments enjoined upon the descendants of
Noah. Anyone who does not accept them is put to death.[90] He who does accept
them is the one styled in every place a resident alien [*ger toshav*]. He must declare
his acceptance in the presence of three associates.[91]

In paragraphs 9, 10, and 11, then, Maimonides distinguishes among several
classes of non-Jew:

1. non-Jews who refuse to accept the Noahide laws (and must be put to
   death);

2. full converts (*gerei tsedek*);

3. one who does not wish to convert and who is not coerced to do so (but
   must accept the Noahide laws);

4. Noahides (who formalize their status in the presence of a court);

5. Noahides who accept the seven laws and are scrupulous in their observance; these are called 'righteous gentiles', on condition that they accept
   the seven laws because they were given in the Torah; such invidiuals have
   a share in the world to come;

[90] Note well: Maimonides speaks here of killing a non-Jew who refuses to accept the
Noahide commandments; whatever we may think of that idea, the context of the discussion is obviously the Land of Israel under Jewish sovereignty.

[91] Heb. *ḥaverim*; in other words, in front of a court. This emphasizes that the
process of becoming a *ger toshav* is similar to the process of conversion; the term is thus
often translated as 'semi-convert'. I cite from *Book of Judges*, trans. Hershman, 230, with
emendations.

6. one who accepts the seven laws on the basis of rational considerations and is neither a *ger toshav*, nor a righteous gentile, but a wise gentile.[92]

Three questions immediately present themselves:

What is the difference between numbers 4 and 5?
Does number 4 have a share in the world to come?
Does number 6 have a share in the world to come?

For our present purposes, we can ignore the first two questions, however intriguing they are, and focus on the last. The text is silent on this subject; Nehorai argues that just as number 5 is superior to number 4, so number 6 is superior to number 5 and clearly has a share in the world to come.[93] We do not have to follow him in this extreme (if extremely interesting) interpretation in order to see that Maimonides says nothing explicit about our question. Had he believed that members of class 6 were not to enjoy a share in the world to come, there is no reason for him not to have stated it explicitly. Given that he does not say it, given that the text is ambiguous, and given that to exclude wise gentiles from the world to come we must ignore Maimonides' clearly enunciated opinions about how human beings do earn their place in the world to come, it seems clear that the burden of proof must rest on the minimalist interpreters of Maimonides, those who see him as excluding wise gentiles from the world to come.[94] In brief, 'Laws of Kings', 8: 11, does not stand in opposition to the claim advanced here, that in speaking of 'Jewish non-Jews' I, following Steven Schwarzschild, stand on firm Maimonidean ground.

There is another reason, noting in passing in Chapter 2, for accepting this reading of 'Laws of Kings', 8: 11. Abraham, as described by Maimonides, discovered God through *hekhre'a hada'at*, reasoned conviction. He also brought his contemporaries (Noahides in the most literal sense of the term) to acceptance of monotheism through *hekhre'a hada'at*. It is a safe assumption that, according to Maimonides' view, Abraham himself and

---

[92] For another division, see Korn, 'Gentiles, the World to Come, and Judaism', 274.

[93] Nehorai, 'A Portion of the World to Come'. In this Nehorai follows Kook, *Igerot hare'ayah*, 99–100. R. Kook's position here was earlier noted by W. Z. Harvey, 'Response', 90: 'It seems clear that [according to Maimonides in 'Kings', 8: 11] both the righteous Gentiles and the wise Gentiles have a portion in the world to come, and that the latter group, which would comprise such men as Aristotle and Alfarabi, has a securer portion (cf. Rav Kook, *Letters*, vol. i, pp. 99–100).' R. Kook's text is cited in English in Korn, 'Gentiles, the World to Come, and Judaism', 277.

[94] Levinger, *Maimonides as Philosopher and Codifier*, 23 n. 7, reads Maimonides in much the way I do, as does Henshke, 'On the Question of Unity', 48–50.

those whom he brought near to God achieved portions in the world to come. This, it appears to me, is a crushing refutation of all those who want to read our passage as excluding wise non-Jews from the world to come.

The upshot of the discussion to this point is that Maimonides does not distinguish Jews as such from non-Jews as such. The distinction between Jew and non-Jew is rooted in history, behaviour, and belief, not in ontology. Maimonides is a thoroughgoing universalist.

Was Maimonides Truly Universalist?

But was he really? There are about half a dozen passages in his writings from which it would appear that he does distinguish Jews from non-Jews in some intrinsic sense, from which one can deduce that in the final analysis he was indeed closer to Halevi than to the Maimonides described in this chapter.

Let us turn to the texts themselves: there is a variety of passages in the *Mishneh torah* in which he seems to impute to Jews qua Jews certain moral characteristics absent from non-Jews qua non-Jews. They are:

1. 'Laws of Repentance', 2: 10

It is forbidden to be obdurate and not allow oneself to be appeased [when a person asks forgiveness for some trespass]. On the contrary, one should be easily pacified and find it difficult to become angry. And, when asked by an offender for forgiveness, one should forgive with a sincere mind and willing spirit . . . Forgiveness is natural to the seed of Israel, characteristic of their upright heart. Not so are the gentiles[95] of uncircumcised heart [concerning whom it was said], 'his resentment keeps forever' (Amos 1: 11). Thus of the Gibeonites who did not forgive and refused to be appeased, it is said, 'Now the Gibeonites were not of the children of Israel' (2 Sam. 21: 2).[96]

---

[95] Hebrew: *goyim*; as Ya'akov Blidstein notes, this term often means 'idolaters' and not simply 'non-Jews'. See Blidstein, 'On the Status of the Resident Alien', 44–5. In several contexts Maimonides distinguishes between non-Jews who are idolaters, non-Jews who are monotheists but have not accepted the seven Noahide commandments *because* they were given by God through Moses, and non-Jews who are monotheists and have accepted the seven Noahide commandments *because* they were given by God through Moses. All of these are to be distinguished from proselytes. For sources, see 'Laws of Kings', 8: 10–11. In other contexts, Maimonides simply distinguishes between Jews and non-Jews, where the issue is obligations which Jews have to each other on a fraternal basis, or on the basis of their being fellows (*re'im* and *amitim*). For relevant texts and useful discussion, see Halbertal, *Between Torah and Wisdom*, 83 n.

[96] I cite Maimonides, *Book of Knowledge*, trans. Hyamson, 83*b*, with emendations.

2. 'Laws of Forbidden Intercourse', 19: 17

All families are presumed to be of valid descent and it is permitted to inter-marry with them in the first instance. Nevertheless, should you see two fam-ilies continually striving with one another, or a family which is constantly engaged in quarrels and altercations, or an individual who is exceedingly contentious with everyone, and is excessively impudent, apprehension should be felt concerning them, and it is advisable to keep one's distance from them, for these traits are indicative of invalid descent . . . Similarly, if a person exhibits impudence, cruelty, or misanthropy, and never performs an act of kindness, one should strongly suspect that he is of Gibeonite descent, since the distinctive traits of Israel, the holy nation [*ha'umah hakedoshah*], are modesty, mercy, and lovingkindness, while of the Gibeonites it is said, 'Now the Gibeonites were not of the children of Israel' (2 Sam. 21: 2), because they hardened their faces and refused to relent, show-ing no mercy to the sons of Saul, nor would they do a kindness unto the children of Israel, by forgiving the sons of their king, notwithstanding that Israel showed them grace at the beginning and spared their lives.[97]

3. 'Laws Concerning Gifts to the Poor', 10: 1–2

It is our duty to be more careful in the performance of the commandment of charity [*tsedakah*][98] than in that of any other positive commandment, for giving charity is the mark of righteous individuals who are of the seed of our father Abraham, as it is said, 'For I have known him, to the end that he may command his children . . . to do righteousness [*tsedakah*]' (Gen. 18: 19). The throne of Israel cannot be established, nor true faith made to stand up, except through charity, as it is said, 'In righteousness shalt thou be established' (Isa. 54: 14); nor will Israel be redeemed, except through the practice of charity, as it is said: 'Zion shall be redeemed with justice, and they that return of her with righteousness' (Isa. 1: 27). No man is ever impoverished by giving charity, nor does evil or harm befall anyone by rea-son of it, as it is said, 'And the work of righteousness shall be peace' (Isa. 32: 17). He who has compassion upon others, others will have compassion upon him, as it is said, 'That the Lord may . . . show thee mercy, and have compassion upon thee' (Deut. 13: 18). Whosoever is cruel and merciless lays himself open to suspicion as to his descent, for cruelty is found only among the gentiles [*goyim*], as it is said, 'They are cruel and have no compassion'

[97] Maimonides, *Book of Holiness*, trans. Rabinowitz and Grossman, 125.
[98] The words 'charity' and 'righteousness' in this passage are used to translate the sin-gle Hebrew term *tsedakah*.

(Jer. 50: 42). All Israelites and those who have attached themselves to them [*hanilvim aleihem*] are to each other like brothers, as it is said, 'Ye are the children of the Lord your God' (Deut. 14: 1). If brother will show no compassion to brother, who will? And unto whom shall the poor of Israel raise their eyes? Unto the gentiles who hate them and persecute them? Their eyes are therefore hanging solely upon their brethren.[99]

4. 'Laws Concerning Wounding and Damaging', 5: 10

The injured person, however, is forbidden to be harsh and to withhold forgiveness, for such behaviour does not become the seed of Israel.[100]

5. 'Laws Concerning Slaves', 9: 8

It is permitted to work a heathen slave with rigour. Though such is the rule, it is the quality of piety [*hasidut*] and the way of wisdom that a man be merciful and pursue justice and not make his yoke heavy upon the slave or distress him, but give him to eat and to drink of all foods and drinks. . . . Thus also the master should not disgrace them by hand or by word, because scriptural law has delivered them only unto slavery and not unto disgrace. Nor should he heap upon the slave oral abuse and anger, but should rather speak to him softly and listen to his claims. So it is also explained in the good paths of Job, in which he prided himself: 'If I did despise the cause of my manservant, or of my maidservant when they contended with me . . . Did not He that made me in the womb make him? And did not One fashion us in the womb?' (Job 31: 13, 15). Cruelty and effrontery are not frequent except with the uncircumcised gentiles.[101] The seed of our father Abraham, however, i.e. the Israelites, upon whom the Holy One, blessed be He, bestowed the favor of the Torah and laid upon them statutes and judgments, are merciful people who have mercy upon all. Thus also it is declared by the attributes of the Holy One, blessed be He, which we are enjoined to imitate: 'And His mercies are over all His works' (Ps. 145: 9). Furthermore, whoever has compassion will receive compassion, as it is said, 'And He will show thee mercy, and have compassion upon thee, and multiply thee' (Deut. 13: 18).[102]

---

[99] Maimonides, *Book of Agriculture*, trans. Klein, 89 (with slight emendations, following readings of the MSS cited in Shabse Frankel's edition of the *Mishneh torah*).

[100] Maimonides, *Book of Torts*, trans. Klein, 178 (with emendations).

[101] I follow the MSS and early editions here, and not the text found in most contemporary printed editions: 'except with the gentiles who worship idols'. This latter reading appears to have been an attempt to appease Christian censors.

[102] Maimonides, *Book of Acquisition*, trans. Klein, 281–2 (with emendations).

Before analysing these passages separately, I think it fair to assert that a reasonable way of reading them is as normative, not descriptive, claims. Maimonides is not describing how Jews actually behave here; rather, he is prescribing how Jews ought to behave. Telling people that certain kinds of behaviour casts doubt upon their pedigree is an effective way of getting them not to behave in that way. This seems particularly clear to me in the third, fourth, and fifth passages above, but I think a fair-minded reader could see it applying to all five passages.

Now, to the first passage; in it Maimonides says that 'forgiveness is natural to the seed of Israel, characteristic of their upright heart'. Jews are contrasted here with 'the gentiles of uncircumcised heart'. To read this text in a particularist fashion, one must make the following assumptions: the 'seed of Israel' as such is characterized by uprightness of heart, while non-Jews as such have uncircumcised hearts. But the text may be read in the following fashion just as easily: those Jews who have 'upright hearts' are superior to those non-Jews who have 'uncircumised hearts'. This reading allows for the possibility of there being Jews with uncircumcised hearts and non-Jews with upright hearts, or, at the very least, of there being non-Jews with upright hearts. One reason for preferring this reading is Maimonides' reference to Gibeonites here. The Gibeonites were said to embody the quality of cruelty.[103] But, as we learn in our second passage, Maimonides did not think that all non-Jews were cruel by nature. On this basis, I think it fair to read our first passage as referring to cruel non-Jews, not all non-Jews as such. There is another reason for reading our passage in this fashion. Maimonides clearly allowed for the possibility of wise non-Jews. Moral perfection is a prerequisite of wisdom.[104] Thus, not all non-Jews can be immoral.[105] Given Maimonides' often acerbic comments about his fellow Jews, it hardly needs saying that he did not think that all Jews had upright hearts.[106] Certainly worthy of note is the fact that the term 'uncircumcised hearts' derives from Jeremiah 9: 25, where the referent is Jews, not non-Jews.

In the second passage, Maimonides, following the Talmud, associates impudence, cruelty, misanthropy, and failure to perform acts of lovingkindness with Gibeonites specifically, not with non-Jews generally. Furthermore,

---

[103] JT *Kid*. 4: 1.   [104] See above, Ch. 2 n. 71.

[105] Given Maimonides' praise for Aristotle and other philosophers in his famous letter to Samuel ibn Tibbon, this point hardly needs to be made. For a valuable discussion of the letter, see S. Harvey, 'Maimonides' Letter to Samuel ibn Tibbon'.

[106] For one of many instances, see the parable of the palace in *Guide* iii. 51.

he associates modesty, mercy, and lovingkindness[107] with the 'holy nation' (*ha'umah hakedoshah*) of Israel. Just as Maimonides here speaks not of non-Jews generally, but of Gibeonites in particular, so also, I think, it is legitimate to read the first passage, with its emphasis on Gibeonites, as referring to only some non-Jews. In this passage, Israel is called 'the holy nation'. I have already shown that for Maimonides holiness is a matter of halakhic status, not an intrinsic characteristic. Thus, holiness is not a characteristic of Jews as such, but a status attained through consistent acts of 'modesty, mercy, and lovingkindness'.

In the third passage Maimonides associates charitableness with the 'righteous individuals who are of the seed of our father Abraham' (*tsadikei zera avraham avinu*) — not all of the seed of Abraham is righteous, but those individuals who are practise charity.[108] Being charitable, in other words, is not a matter of descent, but of righteousness, something Jews certainly should be, but are not necessarily.[109] Cruelty, Maimonides goes on, is found only among the non-Jews (*goyim*). Can this mean all non-Jews? In the first place the term 'non-Jew' in the *Mishneh torah*, as noted above, usually means idolater. Furthermore, we are told that those who attached themselves (*nilvim aleihem*[110]) to Israel 'are to each other like brothers' who are

---

[107] Modesty being the opposite of impudence, mercy the opposite of cruelty and misanthropy, and acting out of lovingkindness the opposite of never so acting.

[108] Note that Ishmael was also descended from Abraham; there is nothing in this passage which might lead to one impute to Maimonides the claim that Arabs generally and Muslims in particular do not practise charity. Indeed, since charity is one of the pillars of Islam, as Maimonides no doubt knew, it is likely that he was directly familiar with acts of charity on the part of the Muslims among whom he lived. On Maimonides' use of the term *zera avraham*, 'seed of Abraham', here, compare *MT* 'Laws of Kings', 10: 7: 'It follows that he alone is the offspring [*zera*] of Abraham, who adheres to his law and his straight path.' As Hannah Kasher notes, in this context Maimonides invests the word *zera* with 'religious and moral significance. The genetic singularity of Isaac is rooted in spiritual values' ('Maimonides' View of Circumcision', 105). I read this differently from Kasher: not that Isaac's descendants have 'genetic singularity', but that not all of Abraham's descendants (through Isaac) may truly and properly be called *zera avraham*.

[109] Compare the similar idea found in Maimonides' 'Letter to R. Ovadiah the Proselyte' in *Letters*, ed. Sheilat, i. 234. Holtzman, 'Rabbi Moshe Narboni', 289, reads the text there as if Maimonides held that only those of Abraham's descendants who follow in his ways may truly be called his descendants. Holtzman uses the text to distinguish Jews from Ishmaelites; I think Maimonides additionally meant to use it in order to distinguish righteous descendants of Abraham from unrighteous ones.

[110] The phrase derives from Isa. 56: 6 and Esther 9: 27; in both places the reference appears to be to 'fellow travellers' and not to converts. The use of the term by

merciful towards each other. Clearly, we are speaking here of 'Israel of the spirit' as opposed to 'Israel of the flesh', otherwise what sense does it make to include those who attach themselves to Israel among those who are merciful to each other?[111] To whom can poor Jews look for succour? Only to each other and to those who have attached themselves to the Torah; after all, non-Jews, i.e. idolaters, hate the Jews. What cannot be inferred from this passage, then, is that Maimonides holds all Jews as such to be merciful, all non-Jews as such to be cruel, and that all non-Jews as such hate the Jews. The persuasive, as opposed to descriptive, nature of this passage is clear. Maimonides cites seven verses in order to impress upon the reader the importance of giving charity as an expression of compassion. Were Jews as such truly charitable by nature, Maimonides would not have to work so hard to convince them to give charity.[112]

Beyond all this, comparing what Maimonides writes here with his apparent source (BT *Betsah* 32*b*) is most instructive. He writes: 'Giving charity is the mark [*siman*] of righteous individuals who are of the seed of our father Abraham.' The Talmud says: 'Whoever is merciful to his fellow-men is certainly of the children of our father Abraham.' Maimonides, as we have seen, connects *righteous* Jews to Abraham; the Talmud tells us that *anyone* who is merciful is certainly Jewish. Maimonides writes: 'Whosoever is cruel and merciless lays himself open to suspicion [*yesh laḥush*] as to his descent.' The Talmud says: 'and whosoever is not merciful to his fellow-men is certainly not [*beyadua she'eino*] of the children of our father Abraham'. The Talmud makes mercy a property of Jewishness and cruelty a proof of absence of Jewishness. Maimonides takes mercy as a sign of Jewishness and cruelty as a reason for suspecting the absence of Jewishness. The Talmud speaks in absolute terms, Maimonides in what might be called statistical terms.

Maimonides in *MT* 'Laws Concerning Idolatry', 1: 3, and 'Laws Concerning the Murderer', 13: 14, is ambiguous on this issue.

[111] I owe this point to Levinger, *Maimonides as Philosopher and Codifier*, 89.

[112] For another example of persuasive writing on the part of Maimonides, see *MT* 'Laws of Idolatry', 11: 16: 'These practices are all false and deceptive, and were means employed by the ancient idolaters to deceive the peoples of various countries and induce them to become their followers. It is not proper for Israelites who are highly intelligent [*ḥakhamim meḥukamim*] to suffer themselves to be deluded by such inanities or imagine that there is anything in them' (*Book of Knowledge*, trans. Hyamson, 80*a*). Maimonides certainly did not believe that all Jews were in fact highly intelligent! Anyone at all familiar with his writings can point to many places where he makes the opposite claim; for examples, see above, Ch. 1, 'Esotericism and Elitism'.

The fourth passage is the easiest for me to deal with, since it most clearly makes a normative, prescriptive claim, not a descriptive one. Forgiveness is certainly appropriate to the seed of Israel (*derekh zera yisra'el*). The very fact that Maimonides has to make this claim (and all the others analysed here) indicates that not all Jews behave as they should. Were all Jews qua Jews truly merciful, charitable, and forgiving, what would be the need for all these exhortations in what is allegedly a dry, halakhic compendium?

In the fifth passage Maimonides teaches that cruelty and effrontery are not frequent except among uncircumcised non-Jews. If we take him literally, he is exempting all Muslims from this charge. If we don't take him literally, then he is not drawing a literal distinction between Jews and non-Jews. And in this passage, from whom does Maimonides learn proper behaviour? From Job, a non-Jew![113] Maimonides goes on to teach that 'the seed of our father Abraham, however, i.e. the Israelites, upon whom the Holy One, blessed be He, bestowed the favour of the Torah and laid upon them statutes and judgements, are merciful people who have mercy upon all'. Let us examine this sentence very carefully. A literal translation would read as follows: 'But the seed of Abraham our father, they being that Israel upon whom the Holy One, blessed be He, emanated the boon of Torah and commanded them righteous statutes and judgements, have mercy upon all.' In this case Maimonides explicitly distinguishes those who have been given the Torah from among all the seed of Abraham. The second clause of the sentence can be read in a number of ways. One is to read it as if Maimonides said simply that Israelites have mercy upon all. A second way of reading it is that the Torah, which includes righteous statutes and judgements, brings its adherents to merciful behaviour. In the context of the clearly persuasive and prescriptive character of the whole paragraph (Maimonides is trying to wean his readers away from technically permissible behaviour, working heathen slaves with rigour), I think this second reading makes more sense.[114]

---

[113] According to Maimonides, Job was not Jewish. See the text cited below from the *Epistle to Yemen*. It is interesting to note that in *Guide* iii. 22 Maimonides mantains that Job was not a historical figure at all and that the whole story is a parable.

[114] On this passage, see Wurzburger, *Ethics of Responsibility*, 23: 'Maimonides pointed out that the deeply ingrained sense of pity and compassion and the resulting aversion to cruelty that [he thought] is characteristic of Jews can be traced back to the impact of the teachings of the Torah and of various historical experiences that engendered these character traits.'

Clearly, I have been reading these paragraphs in a tendentious fashion, but no more tendentiously than those who want to use them as proof that Maimonides held that Jews as such are kind, merciful, etc. while non-Jews as such are not. Given the readings offered here, none of which is unfair to the Hebrew and none of which demands uprooting isolated passages from their contexts, it seems fair to say that they do not represent counter-instances to Maimonides' generally universalist stance, according to which that which distinguishes Jews from non-Jews is the Torah, and nothing inherent, inborn, metaphysical, ontological, or in any other way essentialist.

There is a passage in Maimonides' *Epistle to Yemen* which has been offered as proof that (like Halevi, if for different reasons) he held prophecy to be available only to Jews.[115] In a learned and penetrating essay, Rabbi Yitshak Sheilat, the distinguished translator of many of Maimonides' writings into modern Hebrew, has argued that Maimonides held prophecy to be open to all in theory, but in practice (at least since the time of Moses[116]) to be found only among Jews, since God miraculously withholds prophecy from otherwise qualified non-Jews. Rabbi Sheilat is led to this (to my mind unacceptable[117]) interpretation by a text in the *Epistle to Yemen* which he reads as proving that Maimonides holds prophecy to be impossible for non-Jews.[118] The passage in question reads:

In order to comprehend the verse under discussion unequivocally: 'The Lord your God will raise up for you a prophet from among your own people like myself' [Deut. 18: 15], it is necessary to ascertain its context. . . . [Unlike the gentiles] you will arrive at a foreknowledge of the future from him [a true prophet like Moses], without recourse to augury, divination, astrology, and the like. . . . Moreover, He conveys another notion, namely, that in addition to being near you

[115] For an argument that Maimonides thought prophecy a perfection available in principle to all human beings, see my *Maimonides on Judaism and the Jewish People*, 26–9. As noted above, Harry Wolfson argues that the difference between Halevi and Maimonides on the question of the possibility of non-Jewish prophets is actually very small: see his 'Hallevi and Maimonides on Prophecy', 110–12, and my reply, above, n. 7.

[116] Sheilat, 'Uniqueness of Israel', 281, has Maimonides adopt the position found in the Talmud (*BB* 15*b*) that Moses beseeched God not to allow non-Jews to prophesy.

[117] If for no other reason than because it calls for God to perform otherwise unnecessary miracles. R. Sheilat presents no evidence that Maimonides actually held this view.

[118] To be entirely frank, I think it likely that R. Sheilat was also led to adopt this interpretation because of an antecedent conviction that Maimonides *had* to be closer to Halevi than he is ordinarily thought to be. I have no proof of this, and may simply be expressing my own prejudices here.

and living in your midst, he will also be one of you, an Israelite. The obvious deduction is that you shall be distinguished above all others by the sole possession of prophecy. The words 'like myself' were specifically added to indicate that only the descendants of Jacob are meant. . . . Our disbelief in the prophecies of Omar and Zeid is not due to the fact that they are non-Jews, as the unlettered folk imagine, and in consequence of it are compelled to establish their stand from the biblical phrase 'from among your own people'. For Job, Zophar, Bildad, Eliphaz, and Elihu are all considered prophets by us although they are not Israelites. . . . But we give credence to a prophet or we disbelieve him because of what he preaches, not because of his descent, as I shall explain.[119]

Rabbi Sheilat makes a great deal of the expression, 'you will be distinguished above all others by the sole possession of prophecy'. It is because of this phrase that he finds it necessary to find a way to maintain that Maimonides holds that non-Jews can prophesy in principle, but never in practice. I do not want to get involved in a philological discussion over whether Maimonides' words are best translated as above. I am willing to grant Rabbi Sheilat that they should be. But whatever Maimonides means here,[120] it boggles the mind to think that he would tell us that only Jews can prophesy and then, a few lines further on, explicitly say that non-Jews can prophesy.[121] Indeed, on the very next page of the *Epistle to Yemen* he writes:

Now, if a Jewish or gentile prophet urges and encourages people to follow the religion of Moses without adding thereto or diminishing therefrom, like Isaiah, Jeremiah, and the others, we demand a miracle from him. If he performs it we recognize him and bestow upon him the honor due to a prophet, but if he fails to do so he is put to death.[122]

---

[119] I cite the translation in Halkin and Hartman, *Epistles of Maimonides*, 110–11. For the Judaeo-Arabic source and modern Hebrew translation, see Maimonides, *Letters*, trans. Kafih, 36. For Sheilat's Hebrew translation, see Maimonides, *Letters*, trans. Sheilat, i. 135–6.

[120] Lenn Evan Goodman suggested the following to me in a private communication: 'The point of the distinction from the Gentiles here is that they, as a matter of culture, rely on divination, whereas Jews, as a matter of *mitsvah* [commandment] do not. The Rambam is glossing "from among you" and "like myself" as a reference to this cultural difference. He does so precisely in order to exclude ethnocentric readings of the passage, since it has a Halakhic bearing (on the treatment of future claimants to prophecy) and a political one in his contemporaries' immediate situation, the situation that prompted their inquiry.'

[121] The entire discussion is in the present tense; for R. Sheilat's position to make sense, the entire discussion would have to refer to the pre-Mosaic period.

[122] Translation cited from Halkin and Hartman, *Epistles of Maimonides*, 113.

Maimonides here explicitly allows for the possibility of non-Jewish prophecy after Moses. Rabbi Sheilat's interpretation, it seems abundantly clear, is unsupportable.[123]

There are two other passages in Maimonides' writings that have been proffered as proof of his assertion that Jews are in some innate way superior to non-Jews. In his *Commentary on the Mishnah* (*Bava kama* 4: 3) he writes:

I will explain to you how a case should be conducted if a Jew had a suit with a gentile. If, according to their laws, we are vindicated, we judge them according to their laws and say, 'this is your law'. But were it better for us to judge according to our laws, we judge them according to our laws and say, 'this is our law'. Let not this matter be hard in your eyes, nor be amazed at it, anymore than you are amazed at the slaughter of animals, even though they have done no wrong; for one in whom human characteristics have not been brought to perfection is not truly a human being and exists only to serve the purposes of the true human being. Explaining this matter would require a book of its own.

He repeats this law in two places in the *Mishneh torah*.

In 'Laws Concerning Damage by Chattels', 8: 5, Maimonides codifies the issue dealt with in his commentary on Mishnah *Bava kama*, but gives another reason for it:

If an ox belonging to a Jew gores an ox belonging to an alien [*nokhri*], the owner is exempt whether it is innocuous or forewarned. For gentiles do not hold one responsible for damage caused by one's animals, and their own law is applied to them. However, if an ox belonging to an alien gores an ox belonging to a Jew, the owner must pay for the full damage caused whether his ox is innocuous or forewarned. This is a fine imposed upon gentiles; being heedless of the scriptural commandments, they do not remove sources of damage. Accordingly, should they not

---

[123] R. Sheilat has a number of other texts in support of what I can only call his attempt to Halevi-ize Maimonides. With the exception of the text studied here, they are all either staples in the literature (and discussed in the present work) or are so forced as not to warrant detailed attention. I should add here that Maimonides' view that in principle all human beings are capable of achieving prophecy also finds expression in what might be called a negative fashion. There are biblical verses which can be construed as teaching that prophecy is restricted to Jews. Among them we find Deut. 18: 15, 'A prophet will the Lord thy God raise up unto thee, from the midst of thee, of thy brethren, like unto me; unto him ye shall hearken', and Deut. 18: 18, 'I will raise them up a prophet from among their brethren like unto thee'. Maimonides cites these verses some eleven times in his writings, according to Kafih, *Maimonides on the Bible*; in every instance he simply ignores the implication that only Jews will prophesy.

be held liable for damage caused by their animals, they would not take care of them and thus would inflict loss on other people's property.[124]

The law is the same as in the Mishnah commentary; Jews may take advantage of non-Jews in legal dealings, but the reason offered here is very different.

So, too, with the second place in which this law finds expression in the *Mishneh torah*, 'Laws Concerning Kings and their Wars', 10: 12:

In a suit involving a Jew and a gentile, if the Jew can be vindicated by the law of the gentiles, judgment is rendered according to the gentile law, and the [gentile] litigant is told: 'This is your law.' If the Jew can be vindicated by our law, the suit is decided according to Torah law and the [gentile] litigant is told: 'This is our law.' . . . Even with respect to gentiles,[125] the Rabbis bid us visit their sick, bury their dead along with the dead of Israel, and maintain their poor with the poor of Israel in the interests of peace, as it is written: 'The Lord is good to all; and His tender mercies are over all His works' (Ps. 145: 9). And it is also written, 'Her ways are ways of pleasantness, and all her paths are peace' (Prov. 3: 17).[126]

The law in question is repeated here with no reason given, but in a context which makes it clear that Maimonides sees non-Jews as worthy of the mercy and goodness of God, and as people towards whom Jews ought to behave as they are commanded to behave towards their brethren.

In the first place where this law appears (*Commentary* on BK 4: 3), Maimonides either holds that Jews are inherently distinct from and superior to non-Jews, maintaining that non-Jews are not human beings, or he is extremely elitist, holding the view that non-Jews 'in whom human characteristics have not been brought to perfection' may, in effect, be treated like animals. The reason for this is that such a person 'is not truly a human being and exists only to serve the purposes of the true human being'.

This second reading may 'save' Maimonides from the charge of proto-racism. But in so doing we have further confirmed that his definition of what it means to be a human is such that there are individuals born of human parents, raised among human beings, who look in many ways and act like human beings, who can give birth to human beings, but 'in whom human characteristics have not been brought to perfection', and who therefore are not truly human. Such individuals exist in order to serve true human beings, in the same way as animals exist in order to provide meat

---

[124] Maimonides, *Book of Torts*, trans. Klein, 29 (with emendations).

[125] As opposed to resident aliens, discussed in the passage skipped.

[126] Maimonides, *Book of Judges*, trans. Hershman, 237–8 (emended).

for the true human beings. Not a very attractive picture to us, of course, but one which was hardly unusual among the Aristotelians.[127]

Even if this interpretation is rejected, I have no trouble admitting that in his early *Commentary on the Mishnah* Maimonides made an isolated statement which no one today (be they universalist or particularist in their reading of the Jewish tradition) can fail to regret. Maimonides himself apparently came to regret having made the statement, since he took two opportunities to correct it. In the first he repeats the law and also feels the need to explain it (as he did in the Mishnah commentary), offering an explanation which does not offend non-Jews at all, and certainly does not present them as being in any sense subhuman or essentially distinct from Jews. He goes further in the second place, implicitly pointing to God's mercy towards non-Jews and their status as creatures of the Lord. Thus, if the juvenile Maimonides expressed the view that non-Jews are less than human, the mature thinker took two opportunities to correct himself.

The last passage which I would like to address is from the *Mishneh torah* and for me is the hardest of them all. Chapter 12 of 'Laws Concerning Forbidden Intercourse' deals with sexual congress between Jewish men and non-Jewish women. Paragraph 4 deals with the case of a Jewish man who has sexual relations with a non-Jewish woman (who is not the daughter of a resident alien) in public (in the presence of ten adult male Jews). Such a person may be attacked by zealots, and if brought before a court is to be flogged. In paragraph 6 we learn that if such a person escapes earthly punishment, he will suffer *karet*, 'excision', at the hands of God. Maimonides goes on to tell us that 'whosoever has intercourse with a gentile woman is considered as though he had intermarried with an idol . . . and he is called one who has profaned the holiness of the Lord'.[128] Paragraph 7 continues to emphasize the seriousness of the offence, while paragraph 8 explains why 'such conduct causes one to cleave to idolaters from whom the Holy One, blessed be He, has separated us, to turn away from God, and to break faith with Him'. Paragraph 9 discusses the fate of a non-Jewish man who cohabits with a Jewish woman. Paragraph 10 relates to the fate of a non-Jewish woman who has intercourse with a Jewish man, and teaches the following:

[127] Other treatments of these texts include Lifshitz, 'Rules Governing Conflict of Laws', 179–89, who thinks that Maimonides changed his mind. That is also the position of Lorberbaum, 'Maimonides on *Imago Dei*'. Sagi, *Judaism*, 170–1, reads Maimonides' comment in elitist terms. Sheilat, 'Uniqueness of Israel', 294, on the other hand, reads Maimonides as holding what today would be called racist views.

[128] Maimonides, *Book of Holiness*, trans. Rabinowitz and Grossman, 82.

If, however, an Israelite has intercourse with a gentile woman, whether she is a minor three years and one day old or an adult,[129] whether she is married or unmarried, even if the Israelite is only nine years and a day old, once he willfully has intercourse with her, she is liable to be put to death, because an offence has been committed by an Israelite through her, just as in the case of an animal.[130] This law is explicitly stated in the Torah,[131] 'Behold, these caused the children of Israel, through the counsel of Balaam, to revolt, so as to break faith with the Lord . . . therefore kill every woman that has known man by lying with him' (Num. 31: 16–17).[132]

I would feel immoral were I to try to defend Maimonides' decision and formulation in this paragraph.[133] Whatever motivated him, one thing should be clear: he is not saying that non-Jewish women are animals. In the case where a person has sexual relations with an animal, that animal is to be killed. The animal suffers death through no guilt of its own (obviously), but, apparently, because it was the tool through which a Jew performed a particularly odious transgression.[134] Similarly in a case the enormity of which Maimonides was at pains to emphasize (having intercourse with an idolater in the presence of ten adult male Jews), the person through whom a Jew is thus brought 'to marry' idolatry must be put to death, even if she is only a 3-year-old girl.[135] This may offend our sensibilities (it certainly offends mine), but it does not mean that Maimonides considers non-Jews as such to be on a par with animals.

The texts analysed here include all those I have found that might be cited as indicating that Maimonides held there to be some intrinsic difference

---

[129] In contrast to BT *Yev.* 60*b*, which restricts this law to an adult woman (as noted by Vidal Yom Tov (14th cent.), in his commentary *Magid mishneh* on this passage in the *Mishneh torah*).   [130] BT *San.* 55*b*.

[131] Maimonides has no known talmudic warrant for deducing this law from this verse.   [132] *Book of Holiness*, trans. Rabinowitz and Grossman, 82–3.

[133] In his comment on this passage, Kafih seeks to do so by reading the expression 'once he wilfully has intercourse with her' as applying to the woman as well; the only case in which she is executed is if she maliciously had intercourse with a Jew in public in an idolatrous context. He argues that this follows from Maimonides' citation of Num. 31: 16–17 and its reference to Midianite women who sought to entice the Jewish people into idolatry. But even Kafih has trouble explaining 'just as in the case of an animal'.

[134] Lev. 18: 23, 20: 15–16; *MT* 'Laws Concerning Forbidden Intercourse', 1: 4.

[135] It ought to be understood that this is a technicality; in Jewish law, a female under the age of 3 is considered incapable of intercourse.

between Jews and non-Jews, to the obvious advantage of the former. As I understand him, his true position is that Jews who obey the Torah are, because of that obedience and for no other reason, ethically superior to the general run of non-Jews. There is also no doubt that Maimonides held that the Torah is true and other purported revelations are false—he was no pluralist. It may even be the case (although I know of no text in which he makes this claim) that he held that generations of Torah obedience lead to a people who are on the whole finer than the descendants of corrupt idolaters. What he clearly did not believe is that there is some ontological distinction between Jews and non-Jews. People are people, all can be good, all can be bad, all can be righteous, all can be wicked.[136] It is God's Torah and nothing else which distinguishes Jews from non-Jews.[137]

Verus Israel thus turns out to be, not all the descendants of Abraham, Isaac, and Jacob, as Judah Halevi would have it, and not adherents of Jesus, as Christianity would have it, but all humans who sincerely and correctly attach themselves to God. The overwhelming majority of those are indeed descendants of Abraham, Isaac, and Jacob. But that is a temporary condition. Maimonides confidently expected that by the fruition of the messianic era, the terms 'Israel' and 'human being' would be coextensive.

---

[136] A point made explicitly by Maimonides about human beings (and not just Jews) in *MT* 'Laws of Repentance', 5: 5. That Maimonides is there referrring to human beings, and not just to Jews, is not only clear from the context, but from his use of Gen. 3: 22 (about Adam, progenitor of all human beings) as a prooftext.

[137] Acceptance of that Torah does not make Jews ontologically distinct from non-Jews. This is made clear from the way in which Maimonides 'defangs' a rabbinic passage which might otherwise be problematic for him. In *Guide* ii. 30 (pp. 356–7) he writes: 'Among the amazing dicta whose external meaning is exceedingly incongruous, but in which—when you obtain a true understanding of the chapters of this treatise—you will admire the wisdom of the parables and their correspondence to what exists, is their statement [BT *Shab.* 145*b*–146*a*]: 'When the serpent came to Eve, it cast pollution into her. The pollution of [the sons of] Israel, who had been present at Mount Sinai, has come to an end. [As for] the pollution of the nations who had not been present at Mount Sinai, their pollution has not come to an end. This too you should follow up in your thought.' Maimonides makes it clear in the chapter from which this passage is taken that the pollution of the non-Jews is their reliance upon imagination instead of intellect. This, indeed, is the way in which his medieval and modern commentators understand him. For details, see Kellner, *Maimonides on Human Perfection*, 76 n. 47, and cf. Ch. 3 n. 7.

As with all the other issues taken up in this book, we find Maimonides refusing to grant to Jews any special ontological status. Jews are human beings *tout court*. The key test for whether or not a person has achieved full human status is whether or not that person has earned for herself or himself a share in the world to come. All Israelites have a share in the world to come, and all who have a share in the world to come are, in this sense, Israelites.

In refusing to acknowledge any ontological distinction between Jew and non-Jew Maimonides undermines a key element in the world-view of proto-kabbalah. Despite his efforts, this view of the nature of Jews was to strike a responsive chord in subsequent generations of harassed and persecuted Jews and find repeated (if often subdued) expression in Jewish literature.

EIGHT

Angels

Introduction

ONE OF THE PROMINENT CHARACTERISTICS of the world that I
claim Maimonides consciously rejected is its angelology. There are a number of aspects of traditional beliefs about angels that Maimonides must
have found hard to accept: their independence, corporeality, vice-regency,
etc. However, while he could not have been happy with rabbinic personification of angels, with rabbinic doctrines of fallen angels,[1] and with some
talmudic texts which present the angel Metatron as a kind of vice-regent
to God, none of these presents more difficulties than biblical anthropomorphism. Why is he so troubled by the existence of intermediaries
between God and humans? It is the prominent place of angels in extra-
rabbinic literature that was probably the focal point of Maimonides' concern, but it is also likely that the ease with which talmudic rabbis saw angels
as intermediaries between humans and God also troubled him. Examining
a custom widespread throughout the Jewish world today will illustrate the
point.

Angels in Rabbinic Thought

Ashkenazi Jews the world over usher in the sabbath eve at home by singing
the hymn *Shalom aleikhem* before reciting kiddush. The third of the hymn's
four stanzas reads as follows: 'Bless me with peace, O angels of peace,
angels of the most high, from the King of kings, the holy One, blessed be
He.' The entire hymn appears to be based upon the following passage in the
Talmud:

Rabbi Hisda said in Mar Ukba's name: He who prays on the eve of the sabbath
and recites 'and [the heaven and the earth] were finished' (Gen. 2: 1), the two ministering angels who accompany man place their hands on his head and say to him,
'and your iniquity is taken away, and your sin purged' (Isa. 6: 7). It was taught,

[1] By the term 'rabbinic' here I mean texts and traditions that Maimonides had every
reason to attribute to the talmudic rabbis.

Rabbi Jose son of Rabbi Judah said: Two ministering angels accompany man on the eve of the sabbath from the synagogue to his home, one a good [angel] and one an evil [one]. And when he arrives home and finds the lamp burning, the table laid, and the couch [bed] covered with a spread, the good angel exclaims, 'May it be even thus on another Sabbath [too],' and the evil angel unwillingly responds 'Amen.' But if not, the evil angel exclaims, 'May it be even thus on another Sabbath [too],' and the good angel unwillingly responds, 'Amen.'[2]

This text teaches nothing about turning to angels in prayer, but since it talks of angels who can bless or curse returning home from the synagogue with a householder, it is not hard to see how the idea of turning to these angels in prayer would arise most naturally.[3] If we remember further that extra-mishnaic rabbinic literature[4] is replete with heavily anthropomorphized accounts of angels,[5] the move becomes even more understandable.

The hymn *Shalom aleikhem* is medieval[6] and I cite it here only because it is so well known. Angels show up in much earlier prayers as well, a sure sign of their normative status in classic Judaism. One common version of the first of the two benedictions that precede the recitation of the Shema in the morning service reads as follows:

[2] *Shab.* 119*b*; I cite the Soncino translation.

[3] On the issue of addressing angels in prayer in the period of the Mishnah, see Bar-Ilan, 'Prayers of Jews to Angels'; for geonic literature, see Brody, *Geonim of Babylonia*, 142. For a discussion of the issue in early modern Judaism, see Malkiel, 'Between Worldliness and Traditionalism'.

[4] Given the prominence of angels in rabbinic aggadah, it is quite remarkable to note that angels are not mentioned in the Mishnah at all. See Goldin, 'Magic of Magic', 375. In this connection, the following comment by David Halperin is apposite: 'Nothing in M Ḥag. II: 1 has anything to do with the Ḥagigah sacrifice. The passage stands where it does because of a tenuous chain of word associations. . . . the editors of the Mishnah . . . were eager to find a place for a hair-raising warning against the sort of studies in which they included the merkabah . . . I suspect, then, that we may find a consistent ideology behind the inclusion of both Meg. IV: 10 [not using the *merkavah* as a *haftorah*] and Ḥag. II: 1 in the Mishnah of Judah the Patriarch. It is perhaps the same ideology that led to the Mishnah's avoidance of angels, the next world, and apocalyptic or theosophic speculations' (Halperin, *Faces of the Chariot*, 24).

[5] For background on rabbinic anthropomorphization of angels, see Jung, *Fallen Angels*; Schultz, 'Angelic Opposition'; and Altmann, 'Gnostic Background'. For a general survey on angels in rabbinic texts, see E. Urbach, *Sages*, i. 134–83. For a study of 325 good angels and 131 destructive angels mentioned in what the author took to be rabbinic literature, see Margoliot, *Malakhei elyon*. For more on the personification of angels in rabbinic texts, see Bamberger, *Fallen Angels*, 89–111, 117–45, and Marmorstein, 'Discussion of the Angels'.   [6] See I. Davidson, *Thesaurus*, iii. 465, no. 1268.

Blessed are You, Lord our God, King of the universe, who forms light and creates darkness, who makes peace and creates all things. . . . The blessed God, great in knowledge, designed and made the brilliant sun. The Beneficent One created glory for His name. He placed luminaries round about His majesty. His chief hosts are holy beings that extol the Almighty. They constantly recount God's glory and holiness. . . . Be You blessed, our Stronghold, our King and Redeemer, Creator of holy beings; praised be Your name forever, our King, Creator of ministering angels,[7] all of whom stand in the heights of the universe and reverently proclaim in unison, aloud, the words of the living God and everlasting King. All of them are beloved, all of them are pure, all of them are mighty; they all perform with awe and reverence the will of their Creator; they all open their mouth with holiness and purity, with song and melody, while they bless and praise, glorify and reverence, sanctify and acclaim the name of the great, mighty, and revered God and King; holy is He. They all accept the rule of the kingdom of heaven, one from the other, granting permission to one another to hallow their Creator. In serene spirit, with pure speech and sacred melody, they all exclaim in unison and with reverence: 'Holy, holy, holy is the Lord of hosts; the whole earth is full of His glory' (Isa. 6: 3). Then the celestial *ofanim* and the holy beings,[8] rising with a loud sound towards the *serafim*, respond with praise and say: 'Blessed be the glory of the Lord from His abode' (Ezek. 3: 12). To the blessed God they offer melodies; to the King, the living and eternal God, they utter hymns and praises.[9]

Here biblical imagery of angels who minister to God, who are capable of awe and reverence, who fulfil God's will (freely?), who praise God, and who sing to and about God is presented in an apparently literal and straightforward fashion.[10]

The blessing just cited contains a version of the prayer known as Kedushah (literally 'sanctification'; often translated as 'doxology'). The Kedushah (quoted on page 183 above) focuses on the role of angels in the

---

[7] Hebrew: *mesharetim*, literally: 'servants'.

[8] Hebrew: *ḥayot hakodesh*. The *ofanim*, literally 'wheels', appear together with the 'holy beings' in Ezekiel's vision of the Chariot (Ezek. 1).

[9] Birnbaum (ed. and trans.), *Daily Prayer Book*, 71–4. For another example of the apparent infiltration of angels into the prayers, note the following from the Grace after Meals (ibid. 768): 'May they in heaven plead for all of us.'

[10] Maimonides includes the benediction before the Shema here quoted in the prayer-book that he appended to the second of the fourteen books of the *Mishneh torah*, the *Book of Love*. That should not surprise us: there is no reason to think that he believed that he had the right to change the accepted form of the prayers (much as he may have wanted to), and, in addition, there is good reason to think that the liturgy at the end of the *Book of Love* represents simply the accepted custom of Egyptian Jewry in Maimonides' day. For discussion, see Kadish, *Kavvana*, 317–20.

heavenly court and powerfully framed Jewish visions of the angelic hosts. There is no reason to believe that most Jews who recited this prayer over the generations understood it in any but literal terms. This is certainly the case for the authors and audience of the Heikhalot texts, in which the Kedushah is so central.[11]

Angels in *Piyutim*

It is a pretty safe bet that had Maimonides known *Shalom aleikhem* he would have refused to recite the third stanza. In the fifth of his Thirteen Principles he writes:

The fifth foundation is that He, may He be exalted, is He whom it is proper to worship and praise; and that it is also proper to promulgate praise of Him and obedience to Him. This may not be done for any being other than Him in reality, from among the angels, the spheres, the elements, and that which is composed of them, for all these have their activities imprinted upon them. They have no destiny [of their own] and no rootedness [of their own in reality] other than His love, may He be exalted, [of them]. Do not, furthermore, seize upon intermediaries in order to reach Him but direct your thoughts toward Him, may He be exalted, and turn away from that which is other than He. This fifth foundation is the prohibition against idolatry and there are many verses in the Torah prohibiting it.[12]

I am hardly the first person to point out the apparent contradiction between Maimonides' fifth principle of faith and the practice of addressing angels in prayer in general and the third stanza of *Shalom aleikhem* in particular.[13] Indeed, given the prominence of angels in the Torah and especially in rabbinic literature, it is surprising how little Maimonides was criticized for his statements in the fifth principle.

However, turning to angels in prayer (or even mentioning them in prayer[14]) is not the real issue here. One can see angels as addressees of prayer only if one believes them to exist as volitional entities with inde-

---

[11] On this, see Gruenwald, 'Song of the Angels'.

[12] I cite the translation of Blumenthal, *Commentary*, 107.

[13] See Shapiro, 'Last Word', 195–6 and id., *Limits of Orthodox Theology*, 78–86. My attention was first drawn to this matter when I had the privilege of having a sabbath evening meal in the home of a prominent rabbi in Queens, New York, who pointedly refused to sing the third stanza of *Shalom aleikhem* out of Maimonidean considerations.   [14] As in the first blessing before the recitation of Shema.

pendent powers. We will see Maimonides arguing mightily against this conception of angels.[15]

Angels in Heikhalot Literature

The role of angels as intermediaries between humans and God is one of the central features of Heikhalot literature.[16] Characteristic of this literature are the myriads of angels thought to exist, their power to help or hinder human beings, and a failure to draw sharp boundaries between the angels and God.[17] The blurring of distinctions between God and angels is particularly clear in the case of the angel Metatron, sometimes called the *sar hapanim* (minister of the countenance), who is often presented as a kind of assistant God.[18] Indeed, there are passages in which Metatron appears to

---

[15] For more on angels in the *piyutim*, see Dana, 'References to Angels'; on p. 76 Dana discusses anthropomorphic descriptions of angels in Moses ibn Ezra's synagogue poetry. On angels in the liturgy generally, see Elbogin, *Jewish Liturgy*, 19, 55–60, and 287–91.

[16] Rachel Elior maintains that 'The three primary characteristics, which together create the uniqueness of the Heikhalot tradition, are *mysticism, angelology*, and *magic*' ('Mysticism, Magic, and Angelology', 6; see also Swartz, *Scholastic Magic*, 20). Summarizing a huge body of research, Swartz identifies 'three prevailing elements of Jewish magical texts: 1. the emphasis on the power of the name of God; 2. the intermediacy of the angels in negotiating between divine providence and human needs; 3. the application of divine names and ritual practices for the needs of specific individuals.' The magical texts Swartz speaks of are all part of the Heikhalot literature.

[17] Apropos Merkavah texts, Gershom Scholem makes reference to 'the frequent use of secret or mystical names of God, the difficulties arising from such use, and the consequent blurring, in some instances, of the borderline between these names of God and the names of angels'. See id., *Jewish Gnosticism*, 10. See also Elior, 'Mysticism, Magic, and Angelology', 34: 'The abundance of angels and the appropriation of the uniqueness of the name of God indicate an essential change in religious conception . . . from a single God to a complex of divine forces, nullifying the uniqueness of the single divine entity.'

[18] For a survey of Metatron texts, see Margoliot, *Malakhei elyon*, 72–128. For an extended study of many Metatron texts, see Deutsch, *Guardians of the Gate*, and the important study by Idel, 'Enoch is Metatron'. Yehudah Liebes cites evidence of Jewish mystics who actually prayed to Metatron: see *Elisha's Sin*, 21. Other relevant studies include Dan, 'Seventy Names'; Abrams, 'Boundaries of Divine Ontology'; and Idel, 'Metatron'. The following two studies in particular contain references to the vast literature on Metatron: Bar-Ilan, 'Throne of God' and L. Kaplan, 'Adam, Enoch, and Metatron'. Metatron also became an important figure in Muslim literature. For a discussion of Metatron at the intersection of Jewish and Islamic texts, see Wasserstrom, *Between Muslim and Jew*, 181–205.

take the place of God altogether.[19] Since the angels are thought to have power to help or harm, much of Heikhalot literature is given over to adjurations addressed to the angels.[20]

Rachel Elior explains: 'Mysticism, magic, and angelology are founded upon a shared cosmological view which assumes continuity between the upper realms and the terrestrial world, allowing a reciprocal relationship between them.'[21] This confusion of boundaries must have been galling to someone like Maimonides, whose view of God is resolutely transcendent and who staunchly affirms the Aristotelian distinction between the nature of the sublunary and that of the superlunary world.[22]

Sa'adiah Gaon and Judah Halevi on Angels

For Sa'adiah, angels, more or less as traditionally understood, actually exist. He has no discussion of the subject *per se* in his *Beliefs and Opinions*, but he makes his position clear enough in a number of indirect ways. Thus, he writes: 'All existing things are namely divided into five principal groups:

[19] R. Abraham ben David of Posquières (Rabad), Maimonides' great controversialist, records traditions according to which it is Metatron, not God, who puts on *tefilin*, who appeared to Moses in the burning bush, and who appeared to Ezekiel in the chariot, and, most amazing of all, it is Metatron, not God, in whose image humankind is created. See Idel, 'Enoch is Metatron' (Hebrew, pp. 156–7; English, p. 232). L. Kaplan, 'Adam, Enoch and Metatron', 81, notes: 'Indeed, the Rabad's claim that it was Metatron in whose angelic image Adam was created would appear to have been anticipated by Abraham ibn Ezra, both in *Yesod mora* [ch. 12, p. 20] and in his comment on Genesis 1: 26, though ibn Ezra, as is his wont when treating esoteric matters, does not say so explicitly.'

[20] On this phenomenon, see Lesses, *Ritual Practices to Gain Power*. Compare also Elior, 'Mysticism, Magic, and Angelology', 39, who points out that in the Heikhalot literature angels 'are served, adored, praised, and worshipped'.

[21] Elior, 'Mysticism, Magic, and Angelology', 12; on p. 29 she goes so far as to see the 'perception of angels of the Hekhalot literature, [as] reflecting the continuation of the process of mythologization which began in post-Scriptural literature, [and which] was consolidated . . . in a period when polytheism, paganism, occult, and magical traditions were pre-eminent in the surrounding cultures'. Lesses agrees, characterizing the vision of Heikhalot literature as 'polytheistic' and as resembling 'the profusion of deities and angels whom the Graeco-Egyptian adjurations address' (*Ritual Practices to Gain Power*, 276). For more on angels in Heikhalot literature, see Gruenwald, 'Song of the Angels'.

[22] For a view of rabbinic literature which emphasizes those aspects from which Maimonides sought to purify Judaism, see Hayman, 'Monotheism'.

minerals, vegetables, animals, astral bodies, and angels, and the Scriptures exclude the idea that any of these five groups resembles the Creator or that He resembles them'.[23] Angels share actual physical existence, at the very least, in common with minerals, vegetables, animals, and astral bodies. It is their corporeal nature, it would seem, which makes these five groups so unlike God.

The fundamentally corporeal nature of angels is made clear in the following passage as well:

Furthermore, I wondered why, with all the distinction accorded to man, he came to have this feeble frame of a body composed of blood and phlegm and two galls. Why was it not constituted of pure elements resembling each other? But then I rejected this idea, saying [to myself] that for us to insist upon such a thing would only be equivalent to demanding that man should have been created as a star or an angel. For what is known as the human body is this thing, created of these mixtures, which is of all earthly things the purest. Anything purer would have to be one of the two, either an angel or a star.[24]

Angelic bodies are purer than human bodies, but are not any the less bodies.

For Sa'adiah, not only do angels actually exist, they exist pretty much as described in Scripture. Thus, Sa'adiah is led to ask: 'Are angels able to rebel against their Master or not?'[25] The question as posed makes it clear that for Sa'adiah angels are entities having self-awareness and continuity of existence. Otherwise, the question makes no sense. His answer to the question is reassuring: 'We must namely declare that, inasmuch as it seems plausible to reason that the Creator of all things knows what will happen to them before it comes to pass, we must needs assume that He would create as an angel only such a being as he knows will obey and not rebel against Him.' Angels in theory could rebel against God, but only such angels who will in fact not do so are brought into existence. It seems likely to me that in making this point Sa'adiah seeks to remain as true as he can to the simple sense of Scripture while undermining as much as he can of the angelology and demonology of Heikhalot literature and of contemporary Christianity and Islam.

The 'independent' character of angels is emphasized in Sa'adiah's gloss on Daniel 12: 5–7:

---

[23] *Book of Beliefs and Opinions*, ii. 9 (trans. Rosenblatt, 113).

[24] Ibid. iv. 2 (trans. Rosenblatt, 184); cf. ibid. vi. 9 (trans. Rosenblatt, 248).

[25] Ibid. vii. 9 (trans. Rosenblatt, 287).

Then I, Daniel, looked and saw two others standing, one on one bank of the river, the other on the other bank of the river. One said to the man clothed in linen, who was above the water of the river, 'How long until the end of these awful things?' Then I heard the man dressed in linen, who was above the water of the river, swear by the Ever-Living One as he lifted his right hand and his left hand to heaven: 'For a time, times, and half a time; and when the breaking of the power of the holy people comes to an end, then shall all these things be fulfilled.'

Sa'adiah writes: 'Then the angel that was suspended above the water *of his own accord* swore to him . . .'. And again, on the same page: 'Thereupon the angel *of his own accord*, before giving him the explicit answer, prefaced his remarks to him by mentioning the reason on account of which he had veiled this answer in obscure terms.'[26] Angels can clearly choose the way in which they fulfil the mandates given them by God. They may never be rebellious, but nor are they automata, having no will or freedom. This comment on Daniel is also important since it reminds us that angels serve as the conduit of prophecy between God and the prophet.[27] Sa'adiah's angels are surely 'demythologized' when compared to the angels of Scripture, rabbinic texts, and, especially, Heikhalot texts, but, as we shall see, they remain far too mythological for Maimonides.

Judah Halevi has very little to say about angels in the *Kuzari*. They are mentioned several times in iv. 3, and in one of those places he writes:

the *kavod* of the Lord is the entire ensemble of angels and spiritual instrumentalities [by means of which God acts, like] the Throne, the Chariot, the firmament, the Wheels, the Spheres, as well as other things that are stable and everlasting . . . [this is] something that [even] our own glances can withstand, like the 'cloud' (Exod. 24: 15) and the 'consuming fire' (Exod. 24: 17), for example, which belong to the class of things familiar to us.[28]

Angels are thus clearly entities that may actually be seen by normal (i.e. non-prophetic) human beings.[29]

Maimonides on Angels

Turning to Maimonides' account of angels, we find that while he gives the Hebrew term *malakh* many meanings, the one he refuses to attach to it is

[26] *Book of Beliefs and Opinions*, viii. 3 (trans. Rosenblatt, 296). Emphasis added.

[27] Kreisel, *Prophecy*, 57: 'Most prophecies in his view are transmitted via angels, which are treated by him as living creatures endowed with speech.'

[28] I examine this passage above in Ch. 6; see p. 186.

[29] Compare Silman, *Philosopher and Prophet*, 205, who also emphasizes the corporeal nature of angels in the *Kuzari*.

that of a being with independent, continued existence, sent on missions by God and visible to human beings.[30] Indeed, without ever confronting the matter directly, Maimonides reads out of Judaism altogether the anthropo-morphized conception of angels so prominent in Scripture and in rabbinic literature.[31] His depersonification of angels[32] seems to be a clear attempt to distance himself from the regnant Jewish culture of his day, i.e. the Judaism apparently taught as normative by many, perhaps all, of his rabbinic colleagues in North Africa and the Middle East.[33]

In the overwhelming majority of places where Maimonides has occasion to discuss the nature of angels, he understands the term to be the biblical-rabbinic way of naming those entities called 'separate intellects' in the tradition of Neoplatonized Aristotelianism to which he was heir.[34] Let us look

---

[30] In this, as in so many other issues, Maimonides' overall project may be understood as one of translation in the following sense: taking terms from classic texts, he empties them of all (or almost all) of their original meaning, and refills them, as it were, with new meaning. But Maimonides did not see it that way; he was convinced that he was expressing the original, pristine meaning of the terms.

[31] Howard Kreisel goes so far as to summarize Maimonides' position concerning angels in the following terms: 'The separate intellects, together with the celestial spheres and the natural existents and forces of the sublunar world are the "angels" spoken of in the Bible and in rabbinic literature according to Maimonides. The only existents not considered by him to be angels are the "angels" as they are literally depicted. Such creatures do not exist in his ontology. Maimonides considers the biblical and rabbinic descriptions of the angels to be imaginative representations, primarily of the separate intellects' (Kreisel, 'Moses Maimonides', 255). James A. Diamond provides close readings of several of Maimonides' passages on angels in the *Guide*; see his *Maimonides and the Hermeneutics of Concealment*, 49, 58–9, 107–13. I once heard Hannah Kasher point out in a lecture that Maimonides simply ignores the popular midrashic motif of angels as princes of the nations.

[32] A good example of which is his treatment of Satan; see *Guide* i. 2 (pp. 23–6), and iii. 22 (pp. 486–90).

[33] Given the importance of angels as intercessors between humans and God in Heikhalot literature, Maimonides' assertion in *Guide* iii. 23 (p. 493), that biblical passages which indicate that angels intercede to effect cures for sick persons ought to be taken as parables, is of special significance.

[34] For background on the notion of the separate intellects in general, see the studies of H. A. Wolfson, 'Problem of the Souls of the Spheres' and 'Plurality of Immovable Movers'. See also Grant, *Planets, Stars, and Orbs*, 471. For the Muslim background of the identity of angels with separate intellects, see Michael Schwarz's new Hebrew translation of the *Guide*, i. 49 n. 1 (p. 110). Maimonides' identification of the angels of Scripture with the separate intellects was not unprecedented in Judaism. Abraham ibn Daud (*c*.1110–80) made the same claim. See Eran, *From Simple Faith*, 187–206, and

at a pair of key texts, one from the *Mishneh torah* and one from the *Guide of the Perplexed*,[35] in which this becomes clear.

Maimonides devotes much of the second chapter of 'Laws of the Foundations of the Torah' to a discussion of angels. In paragraph 3 he writes:

All that the Holy One, blessed be He, created in His universe falls into three divisions. Some are creatures consisting of matter and form, continuously subject to generation and corruption . . . Others are creatures consisting of matter and form which do however . . . change from one body to another or from one form to another . . . Others again are creatures that consist of form without matter. These are the angels. For the angels are not material bodies, but only forms distinguished from each other.

Angels are creatures 'that consist of form without matter'. That being the case, they cannot be seen or grasped by any of the senses, and Maimonides devotes paragraph 4 to explaining that descriptions of angels in the Bible are parables.[36]

Only their matter distinguishes entities sharing the same form. But if angels are pure form, how can they be distinguished one from the other?[37] Paragraphs 5 and 6 answer that question:

T. A. M. Fontaine, *In Defence of Judaism*, 119–26. Maimonides' claims did not go unchallenged. Shem Tov ibn Shem Tov (above, Ch. 2 n. 65) acknowledges that Maimonides identified the angels of the Bible with the separate intellects of the philosophers, and goes on to criticize him mightily for it; see Ibn Shem Tov, *Sefer ha'emunot*, pt. (*sha'ar*) 4, ch. 1, pp. 24*b*–26*b*. For examples of more moderate criticism of Maimonides' identification of angels with the separate intellects in the 15th cent., see Kellner, 'Gersonides and his Cultured Despisers'.

[35] For studies on Maimonides' understanding of the nature of angels, see Blumberg, 'Separate Intelligences', and Goodman, 'Maimonidean Naturalism'. Also relevant to our theme are Heller, 'Essence and Purpose', and Langermann, 'Maimonides' Repudiation of Astrology'.

[36] Compare also the following from the *Guide* (i. 49; pp. 108–9): 'The Sages say in *Genesis Rabbah*: "The flaming sword which turns every way (Gen. 3: 24) is called thus with reference to the verse: 'His ministers a flaming fire' (Ps. 104: 4). [The expression] 'which turns every way' alludes to the fact that sometimes they turn into men, sometimes, into women, sometimes into spirits, and sometimes into angels." Through this dictum they have made it clear that the angels are not endowed with matter and that outside the mind they have no fixed corporeal shape, but that all such shapes are only to be perceived *in the vision of prophecy* in consequence of the action of the imaginative capacity, as will be mentioned in connection with the notion of the true reality of prophecy.' Compare also *Guide* ii. 6 (p. 265).

[37] *Guide* ii, introd. (p. 237): 'The sixteenth premise: In whatsoever is not a body, multiplicity cannot be cognized by the intellect, unless the thing in question is a force

In what way are these forms different from each other, seeing that they are incorporeal? The answer is that, they are not equal in the nature of their existence. Each of them is below another and exists by the other's force, and so, throughout, one angel being above the other. And all exist by the power and goodness of the Holy One, blessed be He . . . When we say that one angel is below another, this does not refer to position in space, as when we think of an individual who occupies a higher seat than another, but to superiority in rank, as when one says in reference to two scholars, one of whom has more wisdom than the other, that he is higher in degree, or when he says of the cause that it is higher than the effect.

This explanation makes the identity of biblical angel with the philosophical separate intellect complete, as we shall see below.

In paragraphs 7 and 8 Maimonides continues to describe angels in terms appropriate to the separate intellects, instantiations of emanation between God and the material world:[38]

The variety of names that the angels bear has reference to the difference in their rank.[39] . . . These ten names, by which the angels are called, correspond to their ten degrees.[40] . . . To the tenth degree, belongs the form called Ishim.[41] They are the angels that speak with the prophets[42] and appear to them in prophetic visions.

in a body, for then the multiplicity of the individual forces would subsist in virtue of the multiplicity of the matters or substances in which these forces are to be found. Hence no multiplicity at all can be cognized by the intellect in the separate things, which are neither a body nor a force in a body, except when they are causes and effects.'

[38] On the emanative relationship between God and the separate intellects, see *Guide* iii. 47 (p. 577): 'there are also other beings that are separate from matter and are not bodies, being toward whom His being, may He be exalted, overflows—namely the angels, as we have explained'.

[39] On the names given to these angels by Maimonides, see Blumenthal, 'Maimonides on Angel Names'.

[40] On these ten levels of angelic existence, see Idel, 'World of Angels', 62.

[41] Lit. 'men'. Moshe Idel reminds us that *ishim* = active intellect, which, in *Guide* ii. 6 (p. 264) = 'the Prince of the World', which in other contexts can refer to the angel Metatron. Assuming that there is more than an interesting coincidence here, I take this as another expression of Maimonides' effort to 'demythologize' Judaism. Metatron, far from being a pretender to God's throne, becomes a disembodied separate intellect, indeed, the 'lowest' of them all, having no will of its own, and existing only to transmit emanations it receives from on high. See Idel, 'Enoch is Metatron', 167 n. For more on possible hints referring to Metatron in Maimonides, and the latter's quiet attempt to defuse the situation, see below, in my discussion of *Guide* ii. 7.

[42] As is evident from Maimonides' account of prophecy in the *Guide* (i. 32–48), angels 'speak' to prophets in the sense that prophets learn truths from the intellectual emanations constantly and naturally produced by the separate intellects. For an

They are therefore called Ishim, because their rank is close to that of the intellect[43] of human beings. All these forms live, know the Creator and possess a knowledge of Him that is exceedingly great—a knowledge corresponding with the rank of each, but not [actually] in accord with the greatness of the Creator. Even the highest rank, cannot attain to a knowledge of the truth of the Creator as He truly is; for this, its capacity is insufficient. But it apprehends and knows more than the rank below it; and so on, through all the degrees, down to the tenth. This, too knows God with a knowledge, to the like of which human beings, consisting of matter and form, cannot attain. But none of them knows the Creator as He knows Himself.[44]

There are, it turns out, precisely ten angels.[45] These angels apprehend God, each to a different degree. That is the sum total of their 'job' as described in this passage of the *Mishneh torah*.[46]

In the *Guide of the Perplexed* Maimonides continues to identify angels with the separate intellects. He also explicitly takes up the relationship of biblical angels to philosophic separate intellects: 'Now a chapter making it

illuminating and very useful discussion of this, see Samuelson, *Gersonides on God's Knowledge*, 284–6. Samuelson explains that the active intellect functions like a radio transmitter, broadcasting ('emanating') to all and sundry, while prophets are like individuals with highly tuned radio receivers. See also *Guide* iii. 45 (p. 577), where Maimonides makes the existence of angels as conduits of prophecy a matter of great importance. Angels (i.e. separate intellects) are conduits of prophecy, not its originators. For a full discussion, see the chapter on Maimonides in Kreisel, *Prophecy*.

[43] Hebrew: *da'at*. See Septimus, 'What Did Maimonides Mean by *Madda*?', 90.

[44] Maimonides, *Book of Knowledge*, trans. Hyamson, 35*b*–36*a*.

[45] By limiting the number of angels (separate intellects) to ten, Maimonides quietly polemicizes against the traditional claim that heaven was full of numberless myriads of angels.

[46] Michael Fishbane argues that these passages betray familiarity with Heikhalot literature. In the language so dear to contemporary Departments of English Literature, we might say that if Fishbane is correct, then Maimonides subverts the Heikhalot texts for his own, philosophical, purposes. Fishbane goes so far as to say: 'It is therefore not the least of the paradoxes of the history of ideas that the language of religious philosophy, so keen to purify anthropomorphic thought, should also derive from mystical theosophy—in which knowledge of the "Form(s) of God" is the highest wisdom. Any chapter on the historical relationships between the philosophers and their sources must bear this in mind. Maimonides' remark that all divine manifestations are "created forms" (*tsurot nivraot*) should therefore be viewed in this light. And this is also the context in which we should understand his statement that the angels are "created of form" (*beru'im tsurah*), but without any substance or body (cf. Book of Knowledge, ['Laws of the Foundations of the Torah', 2: 3])' (Fishbane, 'Some Forms', 270).

clear that the angels are not bodies occurs previously in this Treatise.[47] This is also what Aristotle says. But there is a difference in the terms; for he speaks of separate intellects, and we speak of angels.'[48] Maimonides could hardly be clearer; what Aristotle (as he was understood in Maimonides' time) called separate intellects, Jewish texts called angels—the two terms denote the same entities.[49] But how can that be? Separate intellects do not do anything; they simply exist, apprehending God in different degrees of changeless perfection. What idea could the Torah have been trying to get across in describing the separate intellects as angels? Maimonides devotes considerable attention to this problem.

He continues: 'As for his saying that these separate intellects are also intermediaries between God, may He be exalted, and the existents, and that it is through their intermediation that the spheres are in motion, which motion is the cause of the generation of things subject to generation: this too is the textual teaching of all the books' (ii. 6; p. 262). Aristotle (as Maimonides understood him) teaches that the separate intellects are intermediaries between God and the rest of the created world. It is thanks to them that the spheres revolve, and it is revolution of the spheres that brings about all change in the sublunar world.[50] Not only does Aristotle teach this, it is also 'the textual teaching [i.e. actual meaning of] of all the [biblical] books'. Maimonides goes on:

For you never find therein that an act was performed by God otherwise than through an angel. Now you already know that the meaning of angel is messenger. Accordingly, everyone who carries out an order is an angel; so that the

---

[47] *Guide* i. 49 (pp. 108–10).

[48] *Guide* ii. 6 (p. 262); cf. ii. 2 (p. 253) and ii. 18 (p. 302).

[49] For a comprehensive discussion of medieval Muslim philosophers and their teachings concerning separate intellects, see H. A. Davidson, *Alfarabi, Avicenna, and Averroes on Intellect*.

[50] The angels (separate intellects) are related to the spheres and the heavenly bodies in the way souls are related to bodies in the sublunar world. On this, see *MT* 'Laws of the Foundations of the Torah', 3: 9. It is important to remember that the angels, spheres, and heavenly bodies do not function as efficient causes, but as final causes. They generate change in entities beneath them, not as mechanical agents (as we would expect in a Newtonian universe), but as objects of adoration on the part of the entities beneath them. The heavenly spheres do not know God in some coldly dispassionate, 'scientific' way only, but are brought by that knowledge to the love of God. That love in turn makes them strive to be like God. The outermost sphere 'is moved by its love for God, and, being moved, communicates motion to the rest of the universe'. Love literally makes the world go round. I quote here from Lewis, *Discarded Image*, 113.

movements of animals, even when these beings are not rational, are stated in the text of the Scripture to have been accomplished through an angel, if the motion was produced in accordance with the intention of the deity, who put a force in the living being that moved him according to that motion.

The Torah seeks to teach the doctrine that God is the ultimate (but never the proximate) cause of all that occurs. It does so by describing Him as working through angels. In this way, Maimonides goes on to explain, the term 'angel' can mean the elements (earth, water, air, fire), human messengers, prophets,[51] even the forces that govern animal physiology.[52] Further on in this same chapter, the term 'angel' is said occasionally to stand for the intellect and occasionally for the imagination (ii. 6; p. 264).[53]

But does not the Torah describe God as conversing with the angels and even consulting with them? One can sense Maimonides' anger with those who take such things literally when he writes:

In all these texts the intention is not, as thought by the ignorant, to assert that there is speech on the part of [God], may He be exalted, or deliberation or sight or consultation and recourse for help to the opinion of someone else. For how could the Creator seek help from that which He has created? Rather do all these texts state plainly that all this—including the various parts of that which exists and even the creation of limbs of animals as they are—has been brought about through the intermediation of angels. For all forces are angels. How great is the blindness of ignorance and how harmful! If you told a man who is one of those who deem themselves the Sages of Israel that the deity sends an angel who enters the womb of a woman and forms the fetus there, he would be pleased with this assertion and would accept it and would regard it as a manifestation of greatness and power on the part of the deity, and also of His wisdom, may He be exalted. Nevertheless he would also believe at the same time that the angel is a body formed of burning fire and that his size is equal to that of a third part of the whole world. He would regard this as possible with respect to God. But if you tell him that God has placed in the sperm a formative force shaping the limbs and giving them their configuration and that this force is the angel, or that all the forms derive from the act of the

[51] See also *Guide* i. 15 (p. 41) and ii. 42 (p. 390).

[52] Including even the ability to reach orgasm, as James Diamond pointed out to me (see *Guide*, ii. 6; p. 264). For possible Karaite background for Maimonides' view of angels as (natural) forces, see Pines, 'God, the Divine Glory, and the Angels', 9.

[53] For more on the equivocal nature of the term 'angel' see *Guide* i. 64 (p. 156). In iii. 22 (pp. 486–90) the good and evil inclinations are also called angels. *Guide* ii. 7 (p. 266)—'We have explained the equivocality of the term angel and that it includes the intellects, the spheres, and the elements, inasmuch as all of them carry out orders'—will be discussed below.

Active Intellect and that the latter is the angel and prince of the world[54] constantly mentioned by the Sages, the man would shrink from this opinion. (ii. 6; p. 263)

Maimonides' point here relates to one of his fundamental orientations: he thinks more highly of a Creator who creates a cosmos that functions well without tinkering than of one who must constantly 'pull strings and push buttons' (in one of the late Yeshayahu Leibowitz's more memorable lines) to make it work.[55] The Torah expresses the idea of natural forces (what we would call today laws of nature) as explaining all that happens in the cosmos in terms of anthropomorphized entities called angels. This is one of many ways in which the Torah accommodates itself to the weaknesses of its audience.

Maimonides' apparent anger here may be better understood in the following terms: most of his interlocutors had no problem accepting the idea that God has no body and no human affections. When the Torah describes God in human terms, that is understood as an example of *dibrah torah kilshon benei adam* ('the Torah adopts human language').[56] Why are people willing to accept this and not that the Torah speaks in the same, human, metaphorical way, when it describes angels?

Summing up his discussion, Maimonides writes:

There is then nothing in what Aristotle for his part has said about this subject [i.e. angels] that is not in agreement with the Law. However, a point on which he disagrees with us in all this is constituted by his belief that all these things are eternal and that they proceed necessarily from Him, may He be exalted, in that way. (ii. 6; p. 265)

The only difference between the Aristotelian separate intellect and the biblical angel is that the former (like the rest of the cosmos) is uncreated, and the latter (like the rest of the cosmos) is created.[57]

---

[54] If this 'angel and prince of the world' is Metatron (see n. 41 above), then here we have a text in which Maimonides teaches that Metatron is simply a name for the Active Intellect. The Active Intellect, of course, has none of the characteristics traditionally associated with angels. Once again we may be seeing Maimonides working subtly and without fanfare to 'demythologize' the Judaism dominant in his day.

[55] He makes this point explicitly in his *Treatise on Resurrection*. See Halkin and Hartman, *Epistles of Maimonides*, 224: 'It is recognized that I shun as best I can changes in the physical order.' For a discussion of Maimonides on miracles, and references to other scholarly studies, see Kellner, *Maimonides on the 'Decline of the Generations'*, 30–6.

[56] See above, Ch. 6 n. 57.

[57] For other relevant texts, see ch. 14 in Maimonides' *Treatise on Logic*, trans. Efros, 63, and the first of his Thirteen Principles, where he writes: 'Everything other than He of the Intelligences, *meaning the angels*, and the matter of the spheres, is dependent upon Him for its existence' (emphasis added). See Blumenthal, *Commentary*, 142–3.

The next chapter both serves to sum up the discussion to this point and to add suggestive new elements:

We have explained the equivocality of the term angel and that it includes the intellects, the spheres, and the elements, inasmuch as all of them carry out orders. Do not think, however, that the spheres or the intellects have the same rank as the other corporeal forces which are a thing of nature and do not apprehend their acts. For the spheres and the intellects apprehend their acts, choose freely, and govern, but in a way that is not like free choice and our governance, which deal wholly with things that are produced anew.[58] The Torah has by its letter expressed several notions that drew our attention to this. Thus the angel says to Lot: 'For I cannot do anything' and so on (Gen. 19: 22); and again in order to deliver him, he says to him: 'Behold, I have accepted thee concerning this thing also' (Gen. 19: 21). Scripture also says: 'Take heed of him, and hearken unto his voice; be not rebellious against him; for he will not pardon your transgression; for My name[59] is in him' (Exod. 23: 21).[60] All this indicates to you that they[61] apprehend their acts and have will and free choice with regard to the governance committed to them, just as we have will with regard to that which from the foundation of our existence has been committed to us and given over to our power. Only we sometimes do things that are more defective than other things, and our governance and our action are preceded by privations; whereas the intellects and the spheres are not like that, but always do that which is good, and only that which is good is with them, as we shall explain in several chapters; and all that they have exists always in perfection and in actu since they have come into existence.[62]

The main point of this passage seems to be that angels (when construed as the spheres and the separate intellects[63]) enjoy a form of freedom similar to that enjoyed by human beings and superior to it. That issue, and the related question of whether this claim contradicts what Maimonides wrote in his fifth principle ('for all these have their activities imprinted upon them') need not detain us here. It is more important for our purposes to focus on a point that is only hinted at here. Maimonides' use of Exodus 23: 21 is well worth examining. The full passage (verses 20–6) reads as follows (in the NJPS translation):

[58] In the fifth of his Thirteen Principles Maimonides explicitly states that the separate intellects have no free will. For a discussion of this apparent contradiction, see Shapiro, *Limits of Orthodox Theology*, 57, 78, and 85.

[59] See *Guide* i. 64 (p. 156). [60] Compare *Guide* ii. 34 (p. 366).

[61] Pines notes: 'the spheres and intellects'.

[62] *Guide* ii. 7; p. 266. On this text, see Kreisel, *Prophecy*, 236.

[63] On angels as spheres and separate intellects (and their superiority over humans), see also *Guide* iii. 13 (p. 455).

I am sending an angel before you to guard you on the way and to bring you to the place that I have made ready. Pay heed to him and obey him. Do not defy him, for he will not pardon your offences, since My Name is in him; but if you obey him and do all that I say, I will be an enemy to your enemies and a foe to your foes. When My angel goes before you and brings you to the Amorites, the Hittites, the Perizzites, the Canaanites, the Hivites, and the Jebusites, and I annihilate them, you shall not bow down to their gods in worship or follow their practices, but shall tear them down and smash their pillars to bits. You shall serve the Lord your God, and He will bless your bread and your water. And I will remove sickness from your midst. No woman in your land shall miscarry or be barren. I will let you enjoy the full count of your days.

Who is the angel, in whom God's name is found, and who was sent by God to guard the people of Israel on their way to the Holy Land? A passage in the Talmud (*San.* 38*b*) offers an answer:

Once a sectarian said to Rabbi Idith: It is written, 'Then God said to Moses: "Come up to the Lord, [with Aaron, Nadab and Abihu, and seventy elders of Israel, and bow low from afar. Moses alone shall come near the Lord; but the others shall not come near, nor shall the people come up with him]"' (Exod. 24: 1–2). Surely it should have said, 'Come up to Me'!

Rabbi Idith replied: This[64] is Metatron, whose name is like that of his master,[65] for it is written: '[I am sending an angel before you to guard you on the way and to bring you to the place that I have made ready. Pay heed to him and obey him. Do not defy him, for he will not pardon your offenses] since My Name is in him; [but if you obey him and do all that I say, I will be an enemy to your enemies and a foe to your foes]' (Exod. 23: 20–2).

But, if so, [the sectarian replied] we should worship him![66]

Rabbi Idith replied: The same verse, however, says, 'Do not defy [*tamer*] him', i.e. Do not exchange him for Me [*temireni*].

But, if so, [countered the sectarian] why is it stated: 'he will not pardon your offences' (Exod. 23: 21)?[67]

---

[64] i.e. the expression 'the Lord' in Exod. 24: 1 refers to Metatron.

[65] *Sefer zerubavel* (a text which predates Sa'adiah Gaon and which the latter took seriously enough to use in his account of the messianic era) notes that the name Metatron in *gematriyah* (314) equals Shaddai (314). According to this text, Metatron, also known as Michael, is not only the angel who led the Jews through the wilderness, but is also the angel who led Abraham through the land of Israel, destroyed Sodom and Gomorrah, saved Isaac from being sacrificed by his father, wrestled with Jacob, led Israel through the wilderness, and revealed himself to Joshua at Gilgal. See Martha Himmelfarb's translation of *Sefer zerubavel* in D. Stern and Mirsky (eds.), *Rabbinic Fantasies*, 71–90, esp. p. 73.

[66] Instead of God.   [67] i.e. Metatron has the power to pardon offences.

He [Rabbi Idith] answered: Indeed we would not accept him even as a messenger, for it is written: '[Moses said to the Lord, "See, You say to me, 'Lead this people forward,' but You have not made known to me whom You will send with me. Further, You have said, 'I have singled you out by name, and you have, indeed, gained My favour.' Now, if I have truly gained Your favour, pray let me know Your ways, that I may know You and continue in Your favour. Consider, too, that this nation is Your people." And He said, "I will go in the lead and will lighten your burden." And he said to Him,] "Unless You go in the lead, [do not make us leave this place. For how shall it be known that Your people have gained Your favour unless You go with us, so that we may be distinguished, Your people and I, from every people on the face of the earth?"]' (Exod. 33: 12–16).[68]

This is one of the few places in the Talmud where Metatron is mentioned by name.[69] The text here seems to indicate clearly that some of the rabbis, at least, understood the danger of Metatron worship and sought to combat it. But for our purposes the text is important for another reason; it allows us to see Maimonides quietly and unobtrusively replacing a dangerous view with one more to his liking. The biblical text is troubling enough: God places His name in an angel,[70] gives that angel the power to pardon or not pardon offences, and delegates to that angel the job of ushering the Jews through the wilderness and into the Land of Israel! The Talmud takes this one step further, telling us that this angel is Metatron, the same Metatron whom the *tana* Elisha ben Abuyah thought to be a second God.

Maimonides uses the Exodus passage in order to remind us that the essential definition of an angel is an (impersonal) entity that carries out divine orders (such as 'the intellects, the spheres, and the elements'). To the extent that Metatron can be said to exist, he is not a vice-regent to God, but part of the natural array through which God wisely orders the cosmos. The

---

[68] R. Idith's answer seems to be that the Jews rejected God's offer of Metatron as guide and it is only the Lord to whom Jews pray and who can forgive the offences of the Jews.

[69] The other is BT *Ḥag*. 15*a*: Elisha ben Abuyah sees Metatron seated (in the presence of God) and mistakenly concludes that there are 'two powers in heaven'. Moshe Idel pointed out to me that some (esp. Karaite) MSS of BT *San*. 38*b* have 'Yahoel' instead of 'Metatron'. See Scholem's discussion in *Major Trends*, 67–70. There is no way of knowing which text was available to Maimonides, although it seems unlikely to me that he would have favoured Karaite over Rabbanite MSS. The standard reading is further supported by the play on the words 'Metatron' and '*temireni*'.

[70] Most angels have names that end in the suffix '-el' (God), but here is an angel whose name is equivalent to one of the special names of God (*el*, after all, can also mean 'god' in the generic sense), Shaddai.

point is emphasized in another chapter of the *Guide* (i. 64; p. 156), where Maimonides explains 'My name is in him' as meaning 'that he is an instrument of my will and volition'.[71]

Maimonides uses the Exodus passage in another place in the *Guide* (ii. 34; p. 366). Here, too, we see him quietly undermining the standard picture of angels in general and of Metatron in particular:

Regarding the text that is in the Torah, namely, 'Behold, I will send an angel before thee', and so on (Exod. 23: 20)—the meaning of that text is the one explained in Deuteronomy,[72] namely that God said to Moses at the Gathering at Mount Sinai: 'I will raise up a prophet' and so on (Exod. 23: 21).[73] A proof for this is his saying concerning this angel: 'Take heed of him, and hearken unto his voice', and so on (Exod. 23: 21). Now there is no doubt that this injunction is addressed only to the multitude. An angel, however, does not manifest himself to the multitude and does not give them orders and prohibitions; consequently they could not be ordered not to disobey him. Accordingly, the meaning of this dictum is that He, may He be exalted, gave them knowledge that there would be a prophet among them to whom an angel would come and who would speak to him and give him orders and prohibitions. Thus God forbade us to disobey that angel whose words the prophet would transmit to us. It makes that clear in Deuteronomy, saying: 'Unto him shall ye hearken' (Deut. 18: 15). And it also says: 'And it shall come to pass, that whosoever shall not hearken unto My words which he shall speak in My name', and so on (Deut. 18: 19)—this being the explanation of the dictum: 'For My name is in him' (Exod. 23: 21). All this merely taught them this: this great gathering that you saw—I mean to say the Gathering at Mount Sinai—will not be a thing subsisting permanently with you, and in the future there will not be anything like it; and there will not permanently be fire and a cloud, such as those that are now always on the tabernacle.[74] However, an angel whom I shall send to your prophets will conquer the country for you, will smooth out the land before you, and will let you know what you should do. He will let you know what you should approach and what you ought to avoid. Thereby the fundamental principle was given, which I have never ceased explaining, namely, that to every prophet except Moses our Master prophetic revelation comes through an angel. Know this.

The point of this passage is tolerably clear. In the Exodus 23 passage, the term angel actually means 'prophet'. The passage can hardly be speaking

---

[71] Schwartz's note on his translation here (p. 130) repays study, but does not bear directly upon our issue.   [72] Deut. 18: 18.

[73] i.e. the angel in Exodus is like the angel in Deuteronomy, namely, a 'normal' angel, not a special, Metatron-like angel, which might be confused with God.

[74] Pines cites Exod. 40: 38 and Num. 9: 15–16.

about an angelic vice-regent like Metatron, since it is not speaking about angels at all. Maimonides adds another point here worth emphasizing: angels are only seen by prophets. But, as we know, prophets do not actually 'see' things that actually exist outside of their visions, dreams, or trances.[75]

In another chapter of this book we saw that Maimonides was willing to tolerate mistaken views about the nature of God's *kavod* and *shekhinah*. So, too, in the case of angels, he points out in his *Treatise on Resurrection* that the ignorant may be excused their views:

Hence, I believe that the angels are not bodies. . . . If one of the simpletons does not care to accept this, and prefers to believe that the angels are bodies and even eat . . . I do not mind. I would this were the extent of the ignorance of any of them. . . . If a boor . . . damns me for thinking that the angels . . . are separated from matter and free of it, I hold no grievance against him.[76]

Persons who believe in the corporeal nature of angels are ignorant simpletons and boors. Taking Maimonides at his word here, and there is no apparent reason not to, anyone who reads biblical and rabbinic accounts of angels literally, the authors of many prayers and *piyutim* (and those who take them literally when they recite them), the authors of many Heikhalot texts, and even Sa'adiah Gaon and Judah Halevi, are all ignorant simpletons and boors.[77]

[75] *Guide* ii. 36 (p. 370); see above, Ch. 6 on *kavod*, p. 204. For more on Maimonides on Metatron, see Diamond, *Maimonides and the Hermeneutics of Concealment*, 60.

[76] Maimonides, *Essay on Resurrection*, trans. Halkin, in Halkin and Hartman, *Epistles of Maimonides*, 215–16.

[77] If Maimonides was unenthusiastic about angels as traditionally understood, he was downright antagonistic to demons. See his comment on Mishnah *AZ* 4: 6; *MT*, 'Laws of Idolatry', 11: 20, *Guide* i. 7, iii. 29 and 46, and the discussions in Kafih, 'Aspects of Maimonides' Philosophy'; Shapiro, 'Maimonidean Halakhah and Superstition', 69–70; Safran, 'Maimonides' Attitude to Magic'; and Langermann, 'A New Source'. While Maimonides may have never explicitly denied the existence of demons, he was certainly understood to have done so. R. Elijah b. Solomon Zalman, the Gaon of Vilna (1720–97), as is well known, attacked him fiercely for having denied the existence of demons; see his gloss on *Shulḥan arukh*, 'Yoreh de'ah', 179.13, and the discussion in Dienstag, 'Relation of R. Elijah Gaon'. For further background, see Lamm, *Torah Lishmah*, 45 n. 98. An amusing sidelight on this issue is the position attributed to R. Menahem Mendel of Kotsk (1787–1859), who, it is said, tried to reconcile Maimonides' denial of the existence of demons with the many rabbinic texts that accept

Maimonides lived in a world in which there were only two 'things': God and all creation.[78] Creation 'works' by virtue of impersonal forces, none of which has a will of its own. Maimonides' contemporaries, on the other hand, lived in a world full of personal forces: demonic, angelic, magical, and astrological. Maimonides' insistence that the separate intellects have no will should also be understood against this background, as should his uncompromising opposition to all intermediaries between humans and God (as expressed in the fifth of his Thirteen Principles). A view which imputes will to all sorts of agents between God and humans invites the propitiation of those agents. The step thence to full-fledged idolatry is short indeed. However, in addition to these weighty considerations there is another issue: repopulating the heavens leads to metaphysical clutter, a clutter deeply at odds with Maimonides' austere Ockhamite desire for an elegant and simple universe.

Of all the notions taken up in this book, Maimonides' subversion[79] of the traditional notion of angels may be the most radical. Maimonides reduces angels to every single causal force in nature. He thus transforms a prominent aspect of otherworldliness into one that simply means 'nature'. A term which was taken in ordinary discourse to mean the supernatural takes on the exact opposite meaning in Maimonides' hands: the world of nature and natural processes. Maimonides' world, relative to that of many of his rabbinic contemporaries, was demythologized, de-ontologized—in a word, de-paganized.[80]

their existence as factual. When Maimonides declared that demons did not exist, the Kotsker is said to have maintained, 'Heaven accepted his position, and demons ceased to exist.' I found this in Bransdorfer, *Hasidic Anthology*, 22. For insight into why Maimonides' attitude to demons aroused so much ire, see Faur, 'Anti-Maimonidean Demons', 50–2.

[78] See *Guide*, i. 34 (p. 74) and i. 71 (p. 183).

[79] Ordinarily, I would suffer immolation before using this term, so beloved of our literary-critical establishment, but here I use it in its literal, not trendy metaphorical, sense.

[80] I thank James Diamond for drawing my attention to this point. Here, as in many other places, he helped me to see the implications of the claims I make.

AFTERWORD

Contemporary Resistance to the Maimonidean Reform

❦

ANYONE FAMILIAR WITH contemporary Jewish life, especially within Orthodoxy, will see immediately that the Maimonidean reform described in this book has failed to take hold. In addition to the seven specific issues addressed here—the nature of halakhah; distinctions between holy and profane and ritually pure and ritually impure; the character of the Hebrew language; the notion of *kavod/shekhinah/*created light; the distinction between Jew and non-Jew; and the existence of angels as popularly understood—Maimonides also sought to reform the curriculum of Jewish learning.[1] In each of these areas he sought to transform the Judaism of his day, and in each of these areas Judaism continued to develop as if Maimonides had never existed and never written.

However, in contrast to the items in this list, there are areas in which Maimonides' influence has been decisive. He succeeded in convincing almost all Jews that the God of Judaism is entirely incorporeal. Given the dramatic anthropomorphism and anthropaphism of the Bible and rabbinic literature this is no mean feat. He also convinced subsequent generations of Jews that the Jewish religion has a firm dogmatic base.[2] But his own set of dogmas was never as widely accepted as many Jews today think it was,[3] and the dogmas were never accepted in the form in which he laid them down.[4] The project of creating comprehensive and logically organized codes of

---

[1] Maimonides sought to lessen the emphasis on talmudic give and take and make room for 'scientific' studies. I discuss the relevant texts and studies in 'Mishneh Torah: Why?'. See also above, Ch. 2 n. 37.

[2] My thanks to Jolene S. Kellner for pointing this out to me; it is a point concerning which I, of all people, should not have needed reminding!

[3] For the first two centuries after his death, see Kellner, *Dogma*; for the later medieval and early modern period, see Shapiro, *Limits of Orthodox Theology*.

[4] On this, see Kellner, *Must a Jew Believe Anything?*.

law, culminating in the publication of the *Shulḥan arukh*, must also be seen as at least a partial success of Maimonides.[5]

However, despite these achievements, his overall reform cannot be considered a success. Indeed, if Graetz, Scholem, and Idel are all correct, Maimonides' attempted reform boomeranged badly: his attempt to 'demythologize' post-talmudic Judaism, to bring about the 'fall of myth in ritual', in the perceptive words of Josef Stern,[6] led to the enthusiastic 'remythologization' of Judaism through kabbalah.[7] Whether or not the need to counter Maimonides was indeed a catalyst for the composition and publication of kabbalistic literature, there can be no doubt that its acceptance as normative by the rabbinic elite and by the rank and file of the Jewish people sounded the death knell for his projected reforms. Of course, if Maimonides did indeed 'create an opposition'[8] that might be construed as a form of success, since only a foolish general mobilizes his or her forces in the face of an inconsequential threat. Maimonides was not construed as being an inconsequential threat.

In the body of this book I have shown that many of Maimonides' writings are best understood as an attempt not only to harmonize Torah and what he considered to be science, but also to counteract the influence of what I have called 'proto-kabbalistic' elements in pre-Maimonidean Judaism. In this, I believe (but cannot prove), Maimonides followed in the footsteps of those editors of the normative rabbinic writings who kept the Heikhalot texts and allied literature out of the canon of Judaism. The widespread acceptance of the Zohar as the work of the second-century *tana* Rabbi Simeon bar Yohai doomed this millennium-long attempt to failure.

---

[5] His success in this was only partial since his motivation for codification (above, n. 1) was so unlike that of subsequent codifiers.

[6] *Problems and Parables*, 109–60.

[7] It is important to emphasize that Maimonides was convinced that the Judaism of Bible, Mishnah, Talmud, and midrash, when properly understood, did not need demythologizing. The authors and editors of these texts, he was certain, were as motivated as he was to keep 'proto-kabbalistic' texts out of the canon of normative Judaism. For whatever it is worth, I think that he was by and large right about this. In general, it ought to be noted that my interest in this book is in the historical question, 'What did Maimonides say?', not in the Jewish question, 'Was he right?'. Very few readers will be surprised, I am sure, to discover that I also believe that he captured what might be called (in Jewish, not historical terms) the essential thrust of normative rabbinic teaching. Support for this thesis may be found in Hartman, *Israelis and the Jewish Tradition*. See also Ch. 4 n. 17 above.   [8] This was pointed out to me by Alan Yuter.

For traditionally oriented Jews, an important religious issue rests upon what might be called a bibliographical question: who wrote the Zohar? If the Zohar represents the work of Rabbi Simeon bar Yohai and a circle of colleagues and students, then the teachings of the Zohar must be seen as part of the body of normative rabbinic Judaism, carrying at least as much authority as other midrashic compilations. No Jew today, believer or scholar, would think of claiming that the ideas and values of, say, midrashic compilations such as *Sifra* and *Sifrei* do not represent ideas and values at the heart of rabbinic Judaism. There may be questions about how to express these ideas and values in a modern idiom, how to understand them, and, for the most traditional, how to apply them, but there can be no doubt that they constitute an integral part of 'classical Judaism'.

If the Zohar, on the other hand, is the brilliant work of Moses de Leon (*c*.1240–1305) and his friends, if the *Sefer habahir* is a clumsy forgery, then the ideas and values embodied in these works have much less normative import for subsequent Judaism. Moses de Leon did indeed live during the period of the *rishonim* (early authorities), but had no particular credentials as halakhist or exegete that we know of. If the Zohar is his, and not Rabbi Simeon bar Yohai's, then it should be no more normative, say, than his contemporary Gersonides' *Wars of the Lord* (indeed, less, since Gersonides at least had solid rabbinic credentials).

Even if we agree with those scholars who see the Zohar and allied literature as the written and public expression of centuries of oral and esoteric teaching, its normative nature in the eyes of the traditionalist Jew is still weakened.

So, putting the question rather tendentiously, is Judaism the sort of religion found in the Bible, Mishnah, Talmud, and Maimonides, or is Judaism the sort of religion found in the Bible, Mishnah, Talmud, and Zohar? These are very different sorts of religions (as should be clear to anyone who has read this book) and the answer to the question depends on the answers to the question, who wrote the Zohar and when?

To all intents and purposes the question has been settled in Jewish history, if not by Jewish scholarship: in Orthodox circles, the Zohar is almost universally seen as the work of Rabbi Simeon bar Yohai, with all that this implies. That being the case, it is no surprise that what might be called, anachronistically, Maimonides' anti-zoharic reform had little chance of success. In the rest of this chapter I want to indicate, in most cases very briefly, how very little of Maimonidean Judaism can be found in the contemporary Orthodox world.[9]

This is probably clearest with respect to the first issue I take up in this book, the nature of halakhah. Let me approach this indirectly. If one follows 'Jewish politics', both in Israel and abroad, it is easy to come to the conclusion that Orthodox Judaism recognizes the authority of rabbis as such to make policy determinations. It is a staple of *ḥaredi* (separatist Orthodox) politics, both hasidic and mitnagdic, that rabbinic leaders decide all matters. Indeed, one of the hallmarks of *ḥaredi* parties is that each has a council of sages which determines all matters of policy for the party's representatives in the Knesset and government. Until recently, it was this reliance upon the *da'at torah*[10] of prominent rabbis which distinguished *ḥaredi* from Zionist Orthodox politics. In the old Mizrahi movement, and to an ever-diminishing extent in its offshoot, the religious Zionist party Mafdal, rabbis were respected and occasionally consulted, but on matters of policy the party leadership made its own decisions. In the 1970s young Turks in the party took advantage of the prominence of the late Rabbi Shlomo Goren (and of his own apparent desire for power and prestige) to involve rabbinic authorities in internal political disputes. Debates within

---

[9] Berel Dov Lerner suggested another reason to me for resistance to Maimonides. In very general terms, Judaism has focused on social and interpersonal issues. In a real sense, the individual Jew's relationship to God is mediated through *kelal yisra'el*, the generality of Israel. Maimonides, however, largely ignores the people of Israel in order to focus on the strivings of the individual towards personal intellectual perfection and hence salvation. The closing chapter of the *Guide*, it is true, broadens the focus from the individual to his or her obligations to the rest of Israel (and humanity), but for most traditionalist readers, this is probably too little, too late.

[10] There appear to be two distinct ways in which this term has been used by those who propound it as Jewish doctrine. There are those who hold that all matters are subject to halakhic determination. On this view, every issue is a halakhic issue and ought properly to be submitted to competent halakhic authorities for determination. A second position admits that some matters are not covered by halakhah *per se*, but that some extraordinary individuals who have devoted their lives to Torah (called *gedolim*, 'great ones', by their followers) are granted a kind of insight into the Torah and into the world denied all others and thus have the right (and obligation) to express the binding position of the Torah on all matters. While these two views have been held separately, they can, of course, be held together, and often are. See A. Cohen, 'Daat Torah', for a discussion of many of these issues, for a survey of many relevant texts, and for a nuanced defence of what can be called a weak version of the doctrine of *da'at torah*.

the religious Zionist community over the Oslo peace process were often phrased in terms of acceptance or rejection of this or that *da'at torah*.

All observers agree that this phenomenon is gaining strength with each passing year. There must therefore be strong forces within Jewish Orthodoxy pushing in this direction. After all, an objective examination of the actual political record of rabbis is hardly encouraging. From the first rabbi whom we know to have actively involved himself in politics (Rabbi Akiva vis-à-vis Bar Kokhba) to the rabbis who counselled Jews not to flee Europe before the Holocaust,[11] prominent rabbis as a class do not appear to have distinguished themselves by their political acumen.[12]

Those elements in what is often called Modern Orthodoxy that seek to resist what they see as the 'creeping haredization' of Orthodoxy regard this issue as crucial. It is often phrased in terms of whether what *haredi* Orthodoxy calls *da'at torah* is a modern innovation or a venerable tradition.[13] For years I have been convinced that the notion of *da'at torah* was a *haredi* innovation, a politically expedient if Jewishly questionable response to the challenges of modernity. In conducting the research for this book, however, I have been forced to change some of my cherished opinions. While it is clear that the term *da'at torah* is a late nineteenth-century innovation,[14] the notion actually reflects forces which existed earlier in Judaism.

In Chapter 2 I analysed two opposed philosophies of halakhah, that of Halevi and his successors, which tends towards the expansion of rabbinic authority into political spheres, and that of Maimonides, which tends to limit the authority of rabbis to what may be called technical matters of halakhah. In its narrowest form, the debate revolves around the question: what role do prophets as such have in the halakhic process? This issue has been studied at length, both within the tradition and by academic scholarship.[15] I will argue here, however, that this debate reflects a much deeper

---

[11] This is, not surprisingly, a hotly debated issue in *haredi* circles, giving rise to heated polemics. For a recent article which gives examples of rabbinic pronouncements against moving to Palestine just before the Holocaust, see Finkelman, 'Haredi Isolation'. For references to discussions of the most notorious case, see Pick, 'Concerning *Da'at Torah*'.

[12] For a recent critique of the political leadership of rabbis in the world of Zionist Orthodoxy, see Bin-Nun, 'Religious Zionism Presents'.

[13] See L. Kaplan, *Daas Torah*.

[14] See Katz, '"Da'at Torah"', and Bacon, *Politics of Tradition*.

[15] See E. Urbach, 'Halakhah and Prophecy', and Arieli, 'Rabbi Judah Halevi and the Halakhah'.

and more profound difference of opinion. For religious thinkers like Halevi, the issue is not only that prophets have a role to play in the halakhic process, but that the very nature of halakhah makes it necessary that prophecy play a role in its determination. For religious thinkers like Maimonides, on the other hand, the nature of halakhah is such that prophets as prophets are irrelevant to the process.

This debate itself reflects an even deeper one, about the nature of God's relationship to the created cosmos. In many ways, the God of Halevi is more present in the world as we know it than is the God of Maimonides. The immanent God of Halevi acts more directly on the world than does the transcendent God of Maimonides and is acted upon by inhabitants of that world in ways which would have scandalized Maimonides.[16]

These fundamental debates lead to other, subsidiary debates: can and ought there to be a 'separation of powers' in Judaism? Are there areas of life which are by definition outside the reach of rabbinic authority?

For Halevi, fulfilling the commandments actually does something in the world and accomplishes something which cannot be accomplished in any other fashion. I do not want to get into the question of whether or not Halevi's position constitutes full-blown theurgy, as found in kabbalah. This issue has been debated by Shlomo Pines and Diana Lobel.[17] For our purposes, it is enough to note that, for Halevi, proper fulfilment of the commandments has actual consequences: when sacrifices are brought in the proper manner, the person bringing the sacrifice is brought closer to God. A sacrifice improperly brought brings no religious benefit to the person bringing the sacrifices.

How and why does this work? For Halevi, the commandments of the Torah reflect an antecedent reality. For him, halakhic distinctions reflect a reality which is really 'out there', an actual facet of the cosmos, even if it is a reality not accessible to our senses. Holiness, for example, is something which actually inheres in holy places, objects, people, and times. Were we able to invent a 'holiness counter' it would click every time its wand came near something holy, just as a Geiger counter clicks in the

---

[16] Zev Harvey pointed out to me that there is no logical connection between the halakhah/prophecy issue on the one hand and the God/cosmos issue on the other hand. Indeed, as he points out, Rabbenu Nissim Gerondi agreed with Maimonides on the first and with Halevi on the second. Harvey admits that Gerondi is an unusual case, and that most authorities line up with either Maimonides or Halevi in both cases. For more on Gerondi, see the opening paragraphs of Ch. 2.

[17] See Lobel, *Between Mysticism and Philosophy*, 85–7.

presence of radioactivity. Radioactivity, of course, is present in the physical universe, while holiness is present only in the metaphysical universe, as it were. Just as radioactivity can have effects, even though it is not apprehended by the senses, so also holiness can have effects, even though it cannot be apprehended by the senses—there really is something there, but not on the plane of existence accessible to people who lack contact with the *inyan ha'elohi*.

Maimonides, as we have seen, saw the commandments of the Torah as creating a social reality, not as reflecting anything actually existing in the universe. Maimonides, as opposed to Halevi (and Nahmanides), sees halakhah as constituting institutional, social reality, not as reflecting an antecedent ontological reality. In further opposition to Halevi and Nahmanides, he distinguishes between mistakes in halakhic contexts, which have relatively modest consequences, and errors in scientific and dogmatic contexts, which have profound consequences. This reflects his perception of halakhah as a system of rules imposed upon reality. In further opposition to what I have been calling the Halevi–Nahmanides stance, Maimonides maintains that ritual purity and impurity are not states of objects in the 'real world', but descriptions of legal status only.

If halakhah reflects an antecedent reality, a reality which cannot be apprehended through normal tools of apprehension but only through an 'inner eye', enriched in some fashion by contact with the divine in some fashion, then people who can properly make halakhic decisions are people endowed with a power of apprehension which rises above the natural. That being the case, it makes sense to accept their leadership even in matters which many might think lie outside the four cubits of the law. Halevi's insistence on blurring the boundaries between halakhah and prophecy is thus seen as an outgrowth of his philosophy of halakhah. Deciding halakhic matters is not simply a matter of erudition, training, insight, and skill; it demands the ability to see things invisible to others.

Maimonides, on the other hand, sees halakhah as a social institution, ordained by God, of course, but an institution which creates social reality, not one which reflects antecedent metaphysical reality. Since he holds that so much of halakhah is historically contingent (i.e. it could have been otherwise), he could not have held otherwise. For Maimonides, halakhah does not 'work' in the way in which it 'works' for Halevi. Obedience to the commandments is, for Maimonides, immensely important on all sorts of levels—personal, educational, moral, social—but accomplishes nothing outside the psycho-social realm.

A good way to see the difference between Halevi and Maimonides is to focus on the following question. Can a non-Jew (or, for that matter, a future computer) determine halakhah? For Halevi the question is ridiculous. In order to determine the law a person must be a Jew who has perfected his contact with the *inyan ha'elohi* to the greatest extent possible. For Maimonides, the question is not ridiculous. I assume that for many reasons he would not want to see the halakhic decision of a non-Jew as authoritative,[18] but he would have to invoke arguments which do not reject the theoretical possibility of a non-Jew achieving sufficient familiarity with halakhic texts and canons of reasoning to formulate decisions which stand up to the most rigorous halakhic examination.[19]

The doctrine of *da'at torah* is thus clearly Halevian and not Maimonidean. For Halevi, in order properly to determine halakhah one must tap into a kind of quasi-prophecy; for Maimonides, one must learn how to handle halakhic texts and procedures properly. If halakhah *creates* institutional reality, then, beyond technical competence (and, one hopes, personal integrity), the charismatic or other qualities of the individual halakhist are really irrelevant to questions of authority; if, on the other hand, halakhah *reflects* antecedent ontological reality, then the only competent halakhist is the one who can tap into that reality, a function of divine inspiration, not personal ability or institutional standing.

No observer familiar with Jewish Orthodoxy today can doubt that Halevi's view of halakhah is paramount. It was adopted by the Zohar and its related literature and spread from there into almost every nook and cranny of halakhic thinking. Maimonides' attempt to move halakhah from

---

[18] Beyond the obvious issues of social cohesion, communal authority and standing, etc., most of us would agree that when seeking a plumber or car mechanic, questions of technical competence are paramount; but in seeking a physician, considerations of judgement, wisdom, insight, and humanity often trump considerations of technical competence. Maimonides was very much aware of this issue when it came to physicians and, as indicated by many of his criticisms of his rabbinic colleagues, no less sensitive to it in matters of halakhah.

[19] This point may help us understand part of Maimonides' motivation in writing the *Mishneh torah*. If halakhic decision-making is fundamentally an issue of technical competence (and individual talent), then the creation of a logically organized compendium like the *Mishneh torah* makes excellent sense: it is a tool to make the work of the halakhic decisor more effective. If, on the other hand, the importance of technical competence in halakhic decision-making is a secondary consideration and access to divine inspiration of some sort is primary, the nature of the tools one uses becomes less pressing. I owe this interesting insight to Jolene S. Kellner.

the realm of prophetic inspiration to the realm of institutions has not yet succeeded.

There is another point to be made here. Maimonides tells us what a law is, and how one determines what a law is. There is a real sense in which he wants to 'rationalize' the whole process, excluding from it appeals to *seyata deshemayah* ('help of heaven') or to *ruaḥ hakodesh* ('holy spirit'). This, of course, is threatening to people whose authority rests upon their access to such sources. I do not mean to accuse anti-Maimonideans of playing Machiavellian power politics, but it would be naive to ignore this aspect of the matter.

Having made these points in some detail, the other issues dealt with in this book can be treated here in a more summary fashion.

Issues of sanctity and of ritual purity and impurity, the subjects of Chapters 3 and 4, obviously relate to halakhah, but also, at least in the eyes of Maimonides' opponents, to the nature of the universe itself. Much of the discourse in contemporary Orthodoxy (both Zionist and *ḥaredi*) about the Land of Israel relates to its ontological status as a land significantly unlike all other lands. I literally have no idea how Maimonides, were he to walk among us today, would react to the State of Israel, and to questions concerning territorial compromise. But I am certain that he would not phrase the question in terms of the ontological status of the Land of Israel.

With respect to the issue of ritual purity and impurity, one example taken from contemporary discourse will show how far Maimonides is from being representative today. Newly observant Jews in the *ḥaredi* world invariably marry other newly observant Jews. One of the reasons for this is that such people were born to unobservant parents. That means that at the moment of conception their mothers were tainted by menstrual impurity, so that their offspring are in some sense also tainted. This taint in no way impinges upon their character, their chances of a share in the world to come, or the esteem in which they are held. But it is a taint nonetheless, a defect in *yiḥus*, or lineage. As should be evident from the discussion in Chapter 4, this whole approach is dramatically anti-Maimonidean.

Matters of holiness and ritual purity relate to the kind of world in which Maimonides wants us to live. It is a 'disenchanted' world, a world which can be understood and, so to speak, applied. It is a world which demands maturity of those who live in it, since nothing, not their humanity, not their Jewishness, is presented to them on a silver platter; everything must be earned. It is a world in which Jews are called upon to fulfil the commandments, not because failure to do so is metaphysically harmful, but because fulfilling them is the right thing to do. By making demands, imposing challenges, Maimonidean Judaism empowers Jews. Their fate is in their own hands, not in the hands of semi-divine intermediaries or in the hands of a rabbinic elite.

The world favoured by Maimonides' opponents, on the other hand, is an 'enchanted' world. Many of Maimonides' opponents, in his day and ours, do indeed accept the efficacy of charms and amulets, and fear the harm of demons and the evil eye. But it is not in that sense that I maintain that they live in an enchanted world. Theirs is not a world which can be explained in terms of the unvarying workings of divinely ordained laws of nature; it is not a world which can be rationally understood. It is a world in which the notion of miracle loses all meaning, since everything that happens is a miracle. In such a world instructions from God, and contact with the divine in general, must be mediated by a religious elite who alone can see the true reality masked by nature. This is the opposite of an empowering religion, since it takes their fate out of the hands of Jews, and, in effect, puts it into the hands of rabbis.

However, and this must be admitted, a disenchanted world may be empowering, but it is also frightening; in such a world, God can be approached, but rarely approaches. It is a world fit for a philosopher like Maimonides, but hard on a frightened person, who does not want the challenge of living by his or her wits (literally), but the comfort of God's love and the instructions of God's agents. We may admire those who think for themselves, but many are just as happy to have their thinking done for them. An enchanted world has many attractions. This indeed may be one of the reasons why Maimonides' attempted reforms aroused so much opposition.

One does not need the nonsense associated with the singer Madonna to know that many contemporary Jews treat the Hebrew language as mystically significant and ontologically distinct from other languages. Here, too, the world of contemporary Orthodoxy is far from Maimonidean.

The hypostasization of *kavod* and *shekhinah* in kabbalah, and the fact that all contemporary Orthodoxy, hasidic and mitnagdic, is infused with kabbalistic motifs makes it clear beyond the need of demonstration that Maimonides' 'de-hypostasization' of these notions (the subject of Chapter 6) has few echoes in contemporary Judaism. In this case, as in the case of Hebrew, there seems to be no substantial distinction between Orthodoxy, on the one hand, and Conservative, Reform, Reconstructionist, and New Age Judaism on the other; all have enthusiastically adopted kabbalistic motifs.

Chapter 7 deals with the nature of Jews as individuals and, by implication, with the nature of Israel as a collective entity. Here Maimonides is deeply at variance with the spirit of (to my mind) much too much of contemporary Orthodoxy. The easy acceptance of the idea that Jews as such are in some important way (spiritually and morally) superior to non-Jews as such permeates much of Orthodox discourse. Prudential considerations often lead to attempts to downplay or hide these notions, but no honest observer can deny their prevalence. Maimonides' failure here is particularly pronounced.

Maimonides, as I pointed out in an earlier chapter, sought to 'depopulate' the heavens. Angels do not appear to play much of a role in religious life these days, whether in Judaism, Christianity, or Islam. But there can be little doubt that Maimonides' denial of the existence of angels as traditionally construed would strike few responsive chords in the hearts of many contemporary Jews.

Maimonides' Judaism demands much, offers little. More precisely, it offers much, but few can take advantage of it. Even more precisely, Maimonides' Judaism offers much, but few can take advantage of it in the pre-messianic age. Seeking to help the few who could immediately benefit from his teachings and to minimize the damage to those who could not, he presented his views gingerly. The rage provoked by these views when they were understood proves the wisdom of his approach. Those, like me, who find in his views a vision of Judaism which is both attractive in its own right and true to Torah, can only regret that he has as yet not succeeded in winning over the vast bulk of Jews who study his writings with devotion. But, with Maimonides, I am optimistic that the day will come when 'the earth will be full with the knowledge of the Lord as the waters cover the sea'.[20]

---

[20] Isa. 11: 9.

Glossary

al-amr al-ilahi the divine order (Arabic); = *inyan elohi*

beit din rabbinic court

da'at torah authoritative rabbinic position

de'ot moral habits

epikorsim heretics (sing. *epikoros*)

gematriyah Hebrew-language numerology, in which words are assigned
    numerical values (often for the purpose of kabbalistic interpretation)

ger toshav non-Jew permitted to reside in the Land of Israel (BT *AZ* 64*b*)

ger tsedek convert to Judaism

halakhah Jewish law

ḥaredi separatist, strictly Orthodox

ḥasidei umot ha'olam righteous gentiles who are guaranteed a place in the
    world to come

heikhalot heavenly palaces

hekhre'a hada'at reasoned conviction

ḥokhmah lit. 'wisdom'; for Maimonides it often signifies science (in the
    premodern sense of the term)

ḥukim divine statutes

inyan elohi the divine order; = *al-amr al-ilahi*

kavod the divine glory

ma'aseh bereshit lit. 'the work of Creation'; for Maimonides: physics

ma'aseh merkavah lit. 'the work of the Chariot'; for Maimonides: the divine
    science, metaphysics

mezuzah parchment inscribed with texts from Numbers and Deuteronomy
    and enclosed in a protective case, attached to the doorpost of a Jewish house
    in fulfilment of a biblical commandment

notarikon a technique widely applied in kabbalistic literature through which
    standard Hebrew words are understood as acronyms, thereby allowing
    dramatic expansion of meaning

perishut separation, keeping apart

perush commentary, interpretation

piyut liturgical poem

sefirot in kabbalah, the ten hypostasized attributes or emanations by means of which the Infinite enters into relationship with the finite

segulah special characteristic, property

sha'atnez fabric made of wool and linen, a halakhically forbidden combination (Lev. 19: 19)

shekhinah the divine presence

shem (pl. *shemot*) [divine] name

ta'amei hamitsvot reasons for the commandments

tana sage of the mishnaic period

tefilin small leather boxes containing scrolls inscribed with biblical passages, worn on the head and arm during morning prayer (Deut. 6: 8; 11: 18)

toharah ritual purity

tsadik righteous person

tsitsit ritual fringes, attached to the corners of garments (Exod. 15: 38)

tsora'at skin condition mentioned in the Bible (Lev. 13–14), not to be confused with Hansen's Disease ('leprosy')

tumah ritual impurity

zaken mamre rebellious elder

Bibliography

Works by Maimonides

Book of Commandments [Sefer hamitsvot], trans. C. Chavel, 2 vols. (London: Soncino, 1967).

Commentary on the Mishnah [Mishnah im perush rabenu mosheh ben maimon], ed. and trans. from the Arabic by Joseph Kafih, 6 vols. (Jerusalem: Mosad Harav Kuk, 1963–7).

Commentary to Mishnah Aboth, trans. Arthur David (New York: Bloch, 1968).

Eight Chapters, [introd. to commentary on Mishnah *Avot*], trans. in Raymond L. Weiss and Charles Butterworth (eds.), *Ethical Writings of Maimonides* (New York: Dover, 1983), 60–104.

Epistle to Yemen, trans. in Abraham Halkin and David Hartman, *Epistles of Maimonides: Crisis and Leadership* (Philadelphia, Pa.: Jewish Publication Society, 1985), 91–131.

Essay on Resurrection, trans. in Abraham Halkin and David Hartman, *Epistles of Maimonides: Crisis and Leadership* (Philadelphia, Pa.: Jewish Publication Society, 1985), 209–33.

Ethical Writings of Maimonides, trans. Raymond Weiss and Charles Butterworth (New York: Dover, 1983).

Guide of the Perplexed [Arabic: Dalalat al-ḥa'irin; Heb.: Moreh nevukhim], English trans. from the Arabic by Shlomo Pines (Chicago: University of Chicago Press, 1963); Hebrew trans., J. Kafih (Jerusalem: Mosad Harav Kuk, 1972); Hebrew trans., Michael Schwartz, 2 vols. (Ramat Aviv: Tel Aviv University Press, 2002).

Letters of Maimonides [Igerot harambam], Hebrew trans. J. Kafih (Jerusalem: Mosad Harav Kuk, 1972); Hebrew trans. Y. Sheilat, 2 vols. (Jerusalem: Ma'aliyot, 1987); English trans. L. Stitskin (New York: Yeshiva University Press, 1977).

Medical Aphorisms of Maimonides, trans. Fred Rosner and Suessman Muntner, 2 vols. (New York: Yeshiva University Press, 1970).

Mishneh torah, 12 vols. (Benei Berak: Hotsa'at Shabse Frankel Ltd, 1975–2001).

Mishneh torah, trans. into English as *The Code of Maimonides* (Yale Judaica Series) (New Haven, Conn.: Yale University Press): *The Book of Acquisition*, trans. Isaac Klein (1951); *The Book of Agriculture*, trans. Isaac Klein (1979); *The Book of*

Cleanness, trans. Herbert Danby (1954); *The Book of Holiness*, trans. Louis I.
     Rabinowitz and Phillip Grossman (1965); *The Book of Judges*, trans.
     A. M. Hershman (1949); *The Book of Love*, trans. Menachem Kellner (2004);
     The Book of Temple Service, trans. Mendel Lewittes (1957); *The Book of Torts*,
     trans. Hyman Klein (1954).

Mishneh torah: The Book of Knowledge, trans. Moses Hyamson (Jerusalem:
     Feldheim, 1974).

Mishneh torah: The Book of Love, trans. Eliyahu Touger (New York: Moznaim, 1990).

Responsa of Maimonides [She'elot uteshuvot rabenu mosheh ben maimon], ed.
     David Yosef (Jerusalem: Makhon Or Hamizrah, 1984); Hebrew trans. J. Blau,
     3 vols. (Jerusalem: Mekize Nirdamim, 1960).

Treatise on Logic, trans. I. Efros (New York: American Academy for Jewish
     Research, 1938).

Other Works

ABELSON, JOSHUA, *The Immanence of God in Rabbinical Literature* (New York:
     Hermon Press, 1969).

ABRAMS, DANIEL, 'The Boundaries of Divine Ontology: The Inclusion and
     Exclusion of Metatron in the Godhead', *Harvard Theological Review*, 87
     (1994), 291–321.

—— ' "The Secret of Secrets": The Concept of the Divine Glory and the Intention
     of Prayer in the Writings of R. Eleazar of Worms' (Heb.), *Da'at*, 34 (1995),
     61–81.

ABRAVANEL, ISAAC, *Perush bereshit* [Commentary on Genesis] (Jerusalem:
     Benei Arabel, 1964).

—— *Perush moreh nevukhim* [Commentary on Maimonides, *Guide of the Perplexed*]
     (Warsaw: Goldman, 1872).

—— *Perush nevi'im aḥaronim* [Commentary on the Latter Prophets] (Jerusalem:
     Torah Vada'at, 1957).

—— *Perush nevi'im rishonim* [Commentary on the Earlier Prophets] (Jerusalem,
     1955).

—— *Rosh amanah* [Principles of Faith], ed. Menachem Kellner (Ramat Gan: Bar
     Ilan University Press, 1993); trans. Menachem Kellner, *Principles of Faith*
     (London: Littman Library of Jewish Civilization, 1982).

—— *Yeshu'ot meshiḥo* [Salvations of His Anointed] (Benei Berak: Me'orei Sefarad,
     1993).

ALEXANDER, P. S., 'Incantations and Books of Magic', in Emil Schuerer, *The
     History of the Jewish People in the Age of Jesus Christ (175 BC–AD 135)*, ed. Fergus
     Millar, Martin Goodman, and Geza Vermes (Edinburgh: T. & T. Clark, 1986),
     342–79.

ALHARIZI, JUDAH, *The Book of Tahkemoni*, ed. and trans. David S. Segal (London: Littman Library of Jewish Civilization, 2001).

ALLONI, NEHEMIAH, 'The Date of the Composition of *Sefer Yetsirah*' (Heb.), *Temirin*, 2 (1981), 41–50.

—— '*Kuzari*: Book of the Jewish War of Independence from the "Arabiyya"' (Heb.), *Eshel be'ersheva*, 2 (1980), 119–37.

ALTER, ROBERT, 'Jewish Mysticism in Dispute', *Commentary* (Sept. 1989), 53–9.

ALTMANN, ALEXANDER, 'The Climatological Factor in Judah Halevi's Theory of Prophecy' (Heb.), *Melilah*, 1 (1944), 1–17.

—— 'The Gnostic Background of the Rabbinic Adam Legends', in id. (ed.), *Essays in Jewish Intellectual History* (Hanover, NH: University Press of New England, 1981), 1–16.

—— 'Maimonides' Attitude towards Jewish Mysticism', in Alfred Jospe (ed.), *Studies in Jewish Thought: An Anthology of German Jewish Scholarship* (Detroit: Wayne State University Press, 1981), 200–19.

—— 'Maimonides on the Intellect and Metaphysics', *Von der mittelalterlichen zur modernen Aufklaerung* (Tübingen: Mohr, 1987), 60–91.

—— 'Moses Narboni's "Epistle on *Shi'ur Qoma*"', in id. (ed.), *Jewish Medieval and Renaissance Studies* (Cambridge, Mass.: Harvard University Press, 1967), 225–88.

—— 'Saadya's Theory of Revelation: Its Origin and Background', in E. I. J. Rosenthal (ed.), *Saadya Studies* (Manchester: Manchester University Press, 1943), 4–25.

AMITAI, SHMUEL, 'Maimonides on Hebrew as a Sacred Language' (Heb.), *Shema'atin*, 27/101 (1989–90), 80–1.

ARIELI, NACHUM, 'Rabbi Judah Halevi and the Halakhah' (Heb.), *Da'at*, 1 (1978), 43–52.

ARUSSI, RATSON, 'Unity and Separatism in the Teaching of Maimonides' (Heb.), *Tehumin*, 8 (1987), 462–87.

BACHER, WILHELM (Ze'ev), 'The Views of Jehudah Halevi Concerning the Hebrew Language', *Hebraica*, 8 (1892), 136–49.

—— *Maimonides as Biblical Commentator* [Harambam parshan hamikra], trans. from the German by A. Z. Rabinovitch (Tel Aviv, 1932).

BACON, GERSHON C., *The Politics of Tradition: Agudat Yisrael in Poland, 1916–1939* (Jerusalem: Magnes Press, 1996).

BAER, YITSHAK, 'The Land of Israel and Exile in the Eyes of Medieval Generations' (Heb.), in *Mehkarim umasot betoldot am yisra'el*, vol. ii (Jerusalem: Israel Historical Society, 1986), 37–59.

BAER, YITSHAK, 'Towards a Clarification of Second Temple Eschatology' (Heb), in *Meḥkarim umasot betoldot am yisra'el*, vol. i (Jerusalem: Israel Historical Society, 1986), 78–134.

BAMBERGER, BERNARD J., *Fallen Angels* (Philadelphia, Pa.: Jewish Publication Society, 1952).

BANETH, DAVID Z., 'Maimonides' Philosophical Terminology' (Heb.), *Tarbits*, 6 (1935), 10–40.

BAR-ILAN, MEIR, 'The Idea of Crowning God in Heikhalot Mysticism and the Karaitic Polemic' (Heb.), *Jerusalem Studies in Jewish Thought*, 7 (1987), 221–33.

—— 'Major Trends in the Formation and Crystallization of the Kedushah' (Heb.), *Da'at*, 25 (1990), 5–20.

—— 'Prayers of Jews to Angels and Other Mediators in the First Centuries CE', in Marcel Poorthuis and Joshua Schwartz (eds.), *Saints and Role Models in Judaism and Christianity* (Leiden: Brill, 2004), 79–95.

—— Review of Yuval Harari, *Ḥarva demosheh: mahadurah ḥadashah umeḥkar*, *Da'at*, 43 (1999), 125–40.

—— 'The Throne of God: What Is Under It, What Is Opposite It, What Is Near It' (Heb.), *Da'at*, 15 (1985), 21–36.

BAR-LEVAV, AVRIEL, 'We Are What We Are Not: The Cemetery in Jewish Culture', *Jewish Studies*, 42 (2002), 15*–46*.

BARON, SALO WITTMAYER, 'Yehudah Halevi: An Answer to an Historical Challenge', in Leon A. Feldman, *Ancient and Medieval Jewish History: Essays by Salo Wittmayer Baron* (New Brunswick, NJ: Rutgers University Press, 1972), 128–48.

BENIN, STEPHEN D., *The Footprints of God: Divine Accommodation in Jewish and Christian Thought* (Albany, NY: SUNY Press, 1993).

BENOR, EHUD, *Worship of the Heart* (Albany, NY: SUNY Press, 1995).

BEN-SHAMMAI, HAGGAI, 'Saadya's Goal in his *Commentary on Sefer Yezira*', in Ruth Link-Salinger (ed.), *A Straight Path: Studies in Medieval Philosophy and Culture. Essays in Honor of Arthur Hyman* (Washington, DC: Catholic University of America Press, 1988), 1–9.

BERGER, DAVID, 'On Some Ironic Consequences of Maimonides' Rationalist Messianism' (Heb.), *Maimonidean Studies*, 2 (1991), 1–8.

BERMAN, LAWRENCE V., 'Maimonides, the Disciple of Alfarabi', *Israel Oriental Studies*, 4 (1974), 154–78.

—— 'Maimonides on the Fall of Man', *AJS Review*, 5 (1980), 1–15.

BIN-NUN, YOEL, 'Religious Zionism Presents: This Is How We Lost Everything' (Heb.), *Mosaf hatsofeh* (9 Apr. 2003), 4–5.

BIRNBAUM, PHILIP (ed. and trans.), *Daily Prayer Book* (New York: Hebrew Publishing Company, 1949).

BLAU, JOSHUA, ' "At Our Place in al-Andalus", "At Our Place in the Maghreb" ', in Joel Kraemer (ed.), *Perspectives on Maimonides: Philosophical and Historical Studies* (Oxford: Littman Library of Jewish Civilization, 1991), 293–4.

—— 'Maimonides, al-Andalus, and the Influence of the Spanish-Arabic Dialect on his Language', in Yedida K. Stillman and George K. Zucker (eds.), *New Horizons in Sephardic Studies* (Albany, NY: SUNY Press, 1993), 203–10.

BLIDSTEIN, YA'AKOV (Gerald), *Authority and Dissent in Maimonidean Law* [Samkhut umeri behalakhat harambam] (Tel Aviv: Hakibuts Hame'uhad, 2002).

—— ' "Even if He Tells You Right Is Left": The Validity of Institutional Authority in the Halakha and its Limitations' (Heb.), in Moshe Beer (ed.), *Studies in Halakha and Jewish Thought Presented to Rabbi Professor Menachem Emanuel Rackman* (Ramat Gan: Bar-Ilan University Press, 1994), 221–42.

—— 'Living in the Land of Israel According to Maimonides, "Laws of Kings" 5: 9–12' (Heb.), in Blidstein et al. (eds.), *Me'ah She'arim: Studies in Medieval Jewish Spiritual Life in Memory of Isadore Twersky* (Jerusalem: Magnes Press, 2001), 171–90.

—— 'Maimonidean Structures of Institutional Authority: Sefer ha-Mizvot Aseh 172–177', *Dine Yisrael*, 17 (1993–4), 103–26.

—— 'On the Status of the Resident Alien in Maimonides' Thought' (Heb.), *Sinai*, 101 (1988), 44–52.

—— 'Oral Law as Institution in Maimonides', in Ira Robinson, Lawrence Kaplan, and Julien Bauer (eds.), *The Thought of Moses Maimonides: Philosophical and Legal Studies* (Lewiston, NY: Edwin Mellen Press, 1990), 167–82.

—— 'The "Other" in Maimonidean Law', *Jewish History*, 18 (2004), 173–95.

—— *Prayer in Maimonidean Halakhah* [Hatefilah bemishnato hehilkhatit shel harambam] (Jerusalem: Mosad Bialik, 1994).

—— 'Tradition and Institutional Authority: On Oral Law in Maimonides' (Heb.), *Da'at*, 16 (1986), 11–28.

BLUMBERG, TSEVI (Harry), 'The Separate Intelligences in Maimonides' Philosophy' (Heb.), *Tarbits*, 40 (1971), 216–25.

BLUMENTHAL, DAVID, *The Commentary of R. Ḥoter Ben Shelomo to the Thirteen Principles of Maimonides* (Leiden: Brill, 1974).

—— 'Maimonides on Angel Names', in A. Caquot et al. (eds.), *Hellenica et Judaica: Hommage à Valentin Nikiprowetzky* (Louvain: Peeters, 1986), 357–69.

—— 'Maimonides: Prayer, Worship, and Mysticism', in R. Goetschel (ed.), *Prière, mystique et Judaisme* (Paris: Presses Universitaires de France, 1984), 89–106.

BORODOWSKI, ALFREDO FABIO, *Isaac Abravanel on Miracles, Creation, Prophecy, and Evil: The Tension between Medieval Jewish Philosophy and Biblical Commentary* (New York: Peter Lang, 2003).

BORTZ, JAIME ELIAS, 'El mas insignificante de los sabios de España: Notas sobre la identidad Sefardi de Maimonides', *Sefardica*, 12 (2001), 15–51.

BOTWINICK, ARYEH, *Skepticism, Belief, and the Modern: Maimonides to Nietzsche* (Ithaca, NY: Cornell University Press, 1997).

BRANN, ROSS, 'The Arabized Jews', in R. F. Scheindlin, Maria Rosa Menocal, and Michael Sells (eds.), *The Literatue of Al-Andalus* (Cambridge: Cambridge University Press, 2000), 435–54.

—— *The Compunctious Poet: Cultural Ambiguity and Hebrew Poetry in Muslim Spain* (Baltimore: Johns Hopkins University Press, 1991).

BRANSDORFER, YEHEZKEL, *Hasidic Anthology* [Leket me'otsar haḥasidut] (Jerusalem, 1976).

BRODY, ROBERT, *The Geonim of Babylonia and the Shaping of Medieval Jewish Culture* (New Haven: Yale University Press, 1998).

BRUCKSTEIN, ALMUT S., 'How Can Ethics Be Taught? "Socratic" and "Post-Socratic" Methods in Maimonides' Theory of Emulation', *Jewish Studies Quarterly*, 4 (1997), 268–84.

Chapters of Rabbi Eliezer, see *Pirkei derabi eli'ezer*

COHEN, ALFRED, 'Daat Torah', *Journal of Halacha and Contemporary Society*, 40 (2003), 65–104.

COHEN, BOAZ, 'The Responsum of Maimonides Concerning Music', in id. (ed.), *Law and Tradition in Judaism* (New York: Ktav, 1969), 167–81.

COHEN, MARTIN SAMUEL, *The Shi'ur Qomah: Liturgy and Theurgy in Pre-Kabbalistic Jewish Mysticism* (Lanham, Md.: University Press of America, 1983).

—— *The Shi'ur Qomah: Texts and Recensions* (Tübingen: Mohr, 1985).

COHEN, MORDECAI Z., 'Logic to Interpretation: Maimonides' Use of Al-Farabi's Model of Metaphor', *Zutot*, 2 (2002), 104–13.

COHEN, NAOMI G., 'Context and Connotation: Greek Words for Jewish Concepts in Philo', in James L. Kugel (ed.), *Shem in the Tents of Japhet: Essays on the Encounter of Judaism and Hellenism* (Leiden: Brill, 2002), 31–61.

COHEN, SHAYE J. D., 'Purity and Piety: The Separation of Menstruants from the Sancta', in Susan Grossman and Rivka Haut (eds.), *Daughters of the King: Women and the Synagogue* (Philadelphia, Pa.: Jewish Publication Society, 1992), 103–15.

CORBIN, HENRY, 'Sabian Temple and Ismailism', in id. (ed.), *Temple and Contemplation* (London: KPI and Islamic Publications, 1986), 132–82.

CRESCAS, HASDAI, *Or hashem* [Light of the Lord], ed. Shelomoh Fisher (Jerusalem: Ramot, 1990).

DAN, JOSEPH, *The Esoteric Theology of Ashkenazi Hasidism* [Torat hasod shel ḥasidut ashkenaz] (Jerusalem: Mosad Bialik, 1968).

—— 'Margolioth's Edition of *Sefer harazim*' (Heb.), *Tarbits*, 37 (1968), 208–14.

—— 'Nachmanides and the Development of the Concept of Evil in the Kabbalah', in id., *Jewish Mysticism*, vol. iii (Northvale, NJ: Jason Aronson, 1999), 391–414.

—— *On Holiness* [Al hakedushah] (Jerusalem: Magnes Press, 1997).

—— 'The Religious Meaning of *Sefer Yetsirah*' (Heb.), *Jerusalem Studies in Jewish Thought*, 11 (1993), 7–36.

—— 'The Seventy Names of Metatron' (Heb.), *Proceedings of the Eighth World Congress of Jewish Studies*, vol. C (1981), 19–24; English trans. in id., *Jewish Mysticism in Late Antiquity* (Northvale, NJ: Jason Aronson, 1988), 229–34.

—— 'Three Phases of the History of Sefer Yetzira', in id., *Jewish Mysticism in Late Antiquity* (Northvale, NJ: Jason Aronson, 1998), 155–87.

DANA, JOSEPH, 'References to Angels in the *Piyutim* [of Moses ibn Ezra]' (Heb.), *Daruna: Pedagogy and Literature*, 13 (1997), 73–84.

DAVIDSON, HERBERT A., *Alfarabi, Avicenna, and Averroes on Intellect: Their Cosmologies, Theories of the Active Intellect, and Theories of Human Intellect* (New York: Oxford University Press, 1992).

—— 'The Authenticity of Works Attributed to Maimonides', in G. Blidstein et al. (eds.), *Me'ah She'arim: Studies in Medieval Jewish Spiritual Life in Memory of Isadore Twersky* (Jerusalem: Magnes Press, 2001), 111–33.

—— 'Maimonides on Metaphysical Knowledge', *Maimonidean Studies*, 3 (1992–3), 49–103.

—— 'Maimonides, Aristotle, and Avicenna', in Regis Morelon and Ahmad Hasnawi (eds.), *De Zénon d'Elée à Poincaré: Recueil d'études en hommage à Roshdi Rashed* (Louvain: Peeters, 2004), 719–34.

—— 'Maimonides' *Shemonah Peraqim* and Alfarabi's *Fusul al-Madani*', *Proceedings of the American Academy for Jewish Research*, 31 (1963), 33–50.

—— *Moses Maimonides: The Man and his Works* (Oxford: Oxford University Press, 2004).

DAVIDSON, ISRAEL, *Thesaurus of Medieval Hebrew Poetry* [Otsar hashirah vehapiyut], 4 vols. (New York: Jewish Theological Seminary, 1924–33; repr. New York: Ktav, 1970).

DE BLOIS, FRANÇOIS, 'The "Sabians" (Sabiun) in Pre-Islamic Arabia', *Acta Orientalia*, 56 (1995), 39–61.

DEUTSCH, NATHANIEL, *The Gnostic Imagination: Gnosticism, Mandaeism, and Merkabah Mysticism* (Leiden: Brill, 1995).

DEUTSCH, NATHANIEL, *Guardians of the Gate: Angelic Vice-Regency in Late Antiquity* (Leiden: Brill, 1999).

DIAMOND, JAMES A., 'The Failed Theodicy of a Rabbinic Pariah: A Maimonidean Recasting of Elisha ben Abuyah', *Jewish Studies Quarterly*, 9 (2002), 353–80.

—— *Maimonides and the Hermeneutics of Concealment: Deciphering Scripture and Midrash in* The Guide of the Perplexed (Albany, NY: SUNY Press, 2002).

—— 'Maimonides on Leprosy: Illness as Contemplative Metaphor', *Jewish Quarterly Review*, 96 (2006), 95–122.

DIENSTAG, JACOB I., 'Art, Science, and Technology in Maimonidean Thought: A Preliminary Classified Bibliography', *Torah u-Madda Journal*, 5 (1994), 1–100; 6 (1995), 138–204.

—— 'Binyamin Ze'ev Bacher as Scholar of Maimonides' (Heb.), *Sinai*, 55 (1964), 65–82.

—— 'Nachman Krochmal's Defence of Maimonides in the Light of the Critique of S. D. Luzzatto' (Heb.), *Bitsaron*, 55 (1967), 34–7.

—— 'Natural Law in Maimonidean Thought (on *Mishneh Torah*, Kings, VIII.11)', *Jewish Law Annual*, 6 (1987), 64–77.

—— 'The Relation of R. Elijah Gaon to the Philosophy of Maimonides' (Heb.), *Talpiot*, 4 (1949), 253–68.

DINARI, YEDIDYA, 'Customs Relating to Impurity of Menstruants: Sources and Development' (Heb.), *Tarbits*, 49 (1980), 302–24.

—— 'The Profanation of the Holy by the Menstruant Woman and "Takanat Ezra"' (Heb.), *Te'udah*, 3 (1983), 17–37.

DODDS, E. R., *The Greeks and the Irrational* (Berkeley, Calif.: University of California Press, 1964).

DOTAN, ARON, *The Dawn of Hebrew Linguistics: The Book of Elegance of the Language of the Hebrews by Sa'adiah Gaon* [Or rishon beḥokhmat halashon: sefer tsaḥut leshon ha'ivrim lerabi sa'adyah gaon] (Jerusalem: World Union of Jewish Studies, 1997).

DOUGLAS, MARY, *Leviticus as Literature* (Oxford: Oxford University Press, 1999).

—— *Purity and Danger: An Analysis of the Concepts of Pollution and Taboo* (London: Routledge, 1984).

DURKHEIM, ÉMILE, *The Elementary Forms of Religious Life*, trans. Karen E. Fields (New York: Free Press, 1995).

EDELS, SOLOMON (Maharsha), *Ḥidushei halakhot*. Printed in standard editions of the Talmud.

EINBINDER, SUSAN L., *Beautiful Death: Jewish Poetry and Martyrdom in Medieval France* (Princeton, NJ: Princeton University Press, 2002).

EISENMANN, ESTI, 'The Term "Created Light" in Maimonides' Philosophy' (Heb.), *Da'at*, 55 (2005), 41–7.

ELBOGIN, ISMAR, *Jewish Liturgy: A Comprehensive History*, ed. and trans. Raymond P. Scheindlin (Philadelphia, Pa.: Jewish Publication Society, 1993).

ELIOR, RACHEL, 'The Concept of God in Hekhalot Literature', in Joseph Dan (ed.), *Binah: Studies in Jewish History, Thought, and Culture*, vol. ii (New York: Praeger, 1989), 97–120.

—— 'Mysticism, Magic, and Angelology: The Perception of Angels in Hekhalot Literature', *Jewish Studies Quarterly*, 1 (1993), 3–53.

—— *The Three Temples: On the Emergence of Jewish Mysticism*, trans. from the Hebrew by David Louvish (Oxford: Littman Library of Jewish Civilization, 2004).

ELUKIN, JONATHAN, 'Maimonides on the Rise and the Fall of the Sabians: Explaining Mosaic Laws and the Limits of Scholarship', *Journal of the History of Ideas*, 63 (2002), 619–37.

EPSTEIN, J. N., *Introduction to the Mishnah* [Mavo lenusaḥ hamishnah], 2 vols. (Jerusalem, 1948; repr. Jerusalem: Magnes Press, 2000).

ERAN, AMIRA, *From Simple Faith to Sublime Faith* [Me'emunah tamah le'emunah ramah] (Tel Aviv: Hakibuts Hame'uhad, 1998).

FAIERSTEIN, MORRIS, ' "God's Need for the Commandments" in Medieval Kabbalah', *Conservative Judaism*, 36 (1982), 45–59.

FARBER-GINAT, ASI, 'Studies in *Sefer Shiur Komah*' (Heb.), in Michal Oron and Amos Goldreich (eds.), *Masuot: meḥkarim basifrut hakabalah uvemaḥshevet yisra'el mukdashim lezikhro shel profesor efrayim gotlieb* (Jerusalem: Mosad Bialik, 1994), 361–94.

FAUR, JOSÉ, 'Anti-Maimonidean Demons', *Review of Rabbinic Judaism: Ancient, Medieval, and Modern*, 6 (2003), 3–52.

—— *Golden Doves with Silver Dots: Semiotics and Textuality in Rabbinic Tradition* (Bloomington: Indiana University Press, 1986).

—— *In the Shadow of History: Jews and Conversos at the Dawn of Modernity* (Albany, NY: SUNY Press, 1992).

FEINSTEIN, NURIT, 'Reflections of Jewish and General Philosophy and of Kabbalah in the Commentary of Don Isaac Abravanel on the Passover Haggadah, *Zevaḥ Pesaḥ*' [Histakyufoteihen shel hafilosofiyah hayehudit vehakelalit veshel hakabalah beferusho shel don yitsḥak abravanel lehagadah shel pesaḥ - zevaḥ pesaḥ], MA diss., University of Haifa, 2005.

FEINTUCH, ABRAHAM, *Pikudei yesharim* [Just Precepts] (Jerusalem: Ma'aliyot, 2000).

FENTON, PAUL B., *Sefer Yesirah: Le Livre de la Création* (Paris: Payot & Rivages, 2002).

FINKELMAN, YOEL, 'Haredi Isolation in Changing Environments: A Case Study in Yeshiva Immigration', *Modern Judaism*, 22 (2002), 61–84.

FISHBANE, MICHAEL, 'The "Measures" of God's Glory in the Ancient Midrash', in S. Shaked, Ithamar Gruenwald, and G. Stroumsa (eds.), *Messiah and Christos: Studies in the Jewish Origins of Christianity Presented to David Flusser on the Occasion of his 75th Birthday* (Tübingen: Mohr, 1992), 53–74; repr. in Michael Fishbane, *The Exegetical Imagination: On Jewish Thought and Theology* (Cambridge, Mass.: Harvard University Press, 1998), 56–72.

—— 'Some Forms of Divine Appearance in Ancient Jewish Thought', in Jacob Neusner (ed.), *From Ancient Israel to Modern Judaism—Intellect in Quest of Understanding: Essays in Honor of Marvin Fox*, vol. iii (Atlanta, Ga.: Scholars Press, 1989), 261–70.

FLEISCHER, EZRA, 'The Kedushah of the Amidah (and Other Kedushot): Historical, Liturgical, and Ideological Aspects' (Heb.), *Tarbits*, 67 (1998), 301–50.

—— 'On the Antiquity of Sefer Yetsirah: The Qilirian Testimony Revisited' (Heb.), *Tarbits*, 71 (2002), 405–32.

—— 'Towards a Clarification of the Expression *Pores al Shema*' (Heb.), *Tarbits*, 41 (1971), 133–44.

FONTAINE, RESIANNE, 'Between Scorching Heat and Freezing Cold: Medieval Jewish Authors on the Inhabited and Uninhabited Parts of the Earth', *Arabic Sciences and Philosophy*, 10 (2000), 101–38.

—— 'The Inhabited Parts of the Earth According to Medieval Hebrew Texts', in Ulf Haxen (ed.), *Jewish Studies in a New Europe: Proceedings of the Fifth Congress of Jewish Studies* (Copenhagen: C. A. Reitzel, 1998), 254–61.

FONTAINE, T. A. M., *In Defence of Judaism: Abraham ibn Daud—Sources and Structures of ha-Emunah ha-Ramah*, Studia Semitica Neerlandica (Assen: Van Gorcum, 1990).

FREUDENTHAL, GAD, 'Jerusalem ville sainte? La Perspective maimonidienne', *Revue de l'histoire des religions*, 217 (2000), 689–705.

—— 'Stoic Physics in the Writings of R. Saadia Ga'on al-Fayyumi and its Aftermath in Medieval Jewish Mysticism', *Arabic Sciences and Philosophy*, 6 (1996), 113–36.

FRIEDLAENDER, M., 'Jehudah ha-Levi on the Hebrew Language, Kuzari II: 67–80', in George Alexander Kohut (ed.), *Semitic Studies in Memory of Rev. Dr. Alexander Kohut* (Berlin: S. Calvary, 1897), 139–51.

FRIEDMAN, MORDECHAI A., *Maimonides, the Yemenite Messiah, and Apostasy* [Harambam, hamashiaḥ beteiman, vehashemad] (Jerusalem: Yad Ben-Tsevi, 2002).

—— 'Social Realities in Egypt and Maimonides' Rulings on Family Law', in Nahum Rakover (ed.), *Maimonides as Codifier of Jewish Law* (Jerusalem: Library of Jewish Law, 1987), 225–36.

—— 'Tamar: A Symbol of Life: The "Killer Wife" Superstition in the Bible and Jewish Tradition', *AJS Review*, 15 (1990), 23–61.

FUNKENSTEIN, AMOS, *Perceptions of Jewish History* (Berkeley, Calif.: University of California Press, 1993).

—— '"Scripture Speaks the Language of Man": The Uses and Abuses of the Medieval Principle of Accommodation', *Philosophes Médiévaux*, 26 (1986), 92–101.

—— *Theology and the Scientific Imagination* (Princeton, NJ: Princeton University Press, 1986).

GASTER, MOSES, *Studies and Texts in Folklore, Magic, Mediaeval Romance, Hebrew Apocrypha, and Samaritan Archaeology*, 2 vols. (London: Maggs, 1925; repr. New York: Ktav, 1971).

GERSONIDES (Levi ben Gershom), *Perush vayikra* [Commentary on Leviticus], ed. Ya'akov Levi (Jerusalem: Mosad Harav Kuk, 1997).

GIL, MOSHE, and EZRA FLEISCHER, *Judah Halevi and his Circle* [Yehudah halevi uvenei ḥugo] (Jerusalem: World Union of Jewish Studies, 2001).

GILLER, PINCHAS, *Reading the Zohar: The Sacred Text of the Kabbalah* (New York: Oxford University Press, 2001).

GINSBURG, ELLIOT K., 'The Sabbath in the Classical Kabbalah', Ph.D. diss., University of Pennsylvania, 1984.

GLUCK, ANDREW L., 'The King in his Palace: Ibn Gabirol and Maimonides', *Jewish Quarterly Review*, 91 (2001), 337–57.

GOETSCHEL, ROLAND, 'Le Sacrifice d'Isaac dans le Gebia Kesef de Joseph ibn Kaspi d'Argentières (1279–1340)', *Pardes*, 22 (1996), 69–82.

GOLDENBERG, DAVID, 'The Development of the Idea of Race: Classical Paradigms and Medieval Elaborations', *International Journal of the Classical Tradition*, 5 (1999), 561–70.

GOLDIN, JUDAH, 'The Magic of Magic and Superstition', in Barry L. Eichler and Jeffrey H. Tigay (eds.), *Studies in Midrash and Related Literature* (Philadelphia, Pa.: Jewish Publication Society, 1988), 337–57.

GOLDMAN, ELIEZER, *Researches and Studies* [Meḥkarim ve'iyunim] (Jerusalem: Magnes Press, 1996).

GOLDSTEIN, NAFTALI, 'Sacrifice and Worship of God in Rabbinic Thought after the Destruction of the Temple' (Heb.), *Da'at*, 8 (1982), 29–51.

GOODMAN, LENN EVAN, 'Jewish and Islamic Philosophy of Language', in Marcelo Dascal et al. (eds.), *Philosophy of Language*, vol. i (Berlin: Walter de Gruyter, 1992), 34–55.

GOODMAN, LENN EVAN, 'Maimonidean Naturalism', in R. S. Cohen and H. Levine (eds.), *Maimonides and the Sciences* (Dordrecht: Kluwer, 2000), 57–85.

GORDON, MARTIN L., '*Mezuzah*: Protective Amulet or Religious Symbol?', *Tradition*, 16 (1977), 7–40.

GRANT, EDWARD, *Planets, Stars, and Orbs: The Medieval Cosmos, 1200–1687* (Cambridge: Cambridge University Press, 1994).

GREEN, ARTHUR, *Keter: The Crown of God in Early Jewish Mysticism* (Princeton, NJ: Princeton University Press, 1997).

GREEN, TAMARA, *City of the Moon God: Religious Traditions of Harran* (Leiden: Brill, 1992).

GREEN, WILLIAM SCOTT, 'Writing with Scripture: The Rabbinic Uses of the Hebrew Bible', in Jacob Neusner and William Scott Green (eds.), *Writing with Scripture: The Authority and Uses of the Hebrew Bible in the Torah of Formative Judaism* (Minneapolis, Minn.: Fortress Press, 1989), 7–23.

GROEZINGER, KARL ERICH, 'The Names of God and the Celestial Powers: Their Function and Meaning in the Hekhalot Literature', *Jerusalem Studies in Jewish Thought*, 6 (1987), 53–70.

GRUENWALD, ITAMAR, *Apocalyptic and Merkavah Mysticism* (Leiden: Brill, 1980).

—— '*Haketav, Hamikhtav*, and the Articulated Name: Magic, Spirituality, and Mysticism' (Heb.), in Michal Oron and Amos Goldreich (eds.), *Masuot: meḥkarim basifrut hakabalah uvemaḥshevet yisra'el mukdashim lezikhro shel profesor efrayim gotlieb* (Jerusalem: Mosad Bialik, 1994), 75–98.

—— 'Maimonides' Quest Beyond Philosophy and Prophecy', in Joel L. Kraemer (ed.), *Perspectives on Maimonides: Philosophical and Historical Studies* (Oxford: Littman Library of Jewish Civilization, 1991), 141–57.

—— 'A Preliminary Critical Edition of *Sefer Yeẓira*', *Israel Oriental Studies*, 1 (1971), 132–77.

—— 'The Song of the Angels, the Kedushah, and the Composition of the Heikhalot Literature' (Heb.), in A. Oppenheimer et al. (eds.), *Perakim betoledot yerushalayim biyemei bayit sheni: sefer zikaron le'avraham shalit* (Jerusalem: Yad Yitshak Ben-Tsevi, 1981), 459–81.

HAACK, SUSAN, 'Staying for an Answer: The Untidy Process of Groping for Truth', *Times Literary Supplement* (9 July 1999), 12–14.

HALBERTAL, MOSHE, *Between Torah and Wisdom* [Bein torah leḥokhmah] (Jerusalem: Magnes Press, 2000).

HALKIN, ABRAHAM, and DAVID HARTMAN, *Epistles of Maimonides: Crisis and Leadership* (Philadelphia, Pa.: Jewish Publication Society, 1985).

HALLAMISH, MOSHE, 'The Sabbath in Kabbalistic Thought' (Heb.), *Da'at*, 54 (2004), 5–28.

HALPERIN, DAVID, *The Faces of the Chariot* (Tübingen: Mohr, 1988).

HARARI, YUVAL, *The Ḥarva demosheh: New Edition and Study* [Ḥarva demosheh: mahadurah ḥadashah umeḥkar] (Jerusalem: Akademon, 1997).

—— 'Religion, Magic, and Adjurations: Methodological Reflections Aimed at a New Definition of Early Magic' (Heb.), *Da'at*, 48 (2002), 33–56.

HARRIS, JAY M., *How Do We Know This? Midrash and the Fragmentation of Modern Judaism* (Albany, NY: SUNY Press; 1995).

—— 'The Image of Maimonides in Nineteenth Century Jewish Historiography', *Proceedings of the American Academy for Jewish Research*, 54 (1987), 117–39.

HARTMAN, DAVID, *Israelis and the Jewish Tradition: An Ancient People Debating its Future* (New Haven, Conn.: Yale University Press, 2000).

HARVEY, STEVEN, 'Did Maimonides' Letter to Samuel ibn Tibbon Determine which Philosophers Would Be Studied by Later Jewish Thinkers?', *Jewish Quarterly Review*, 83 (1992), 51–70.

—— 'Maimonides in the Sultan's Palace', in Joel L. Kraemer (ed.), *Perspectives on Maimonides: Philosophical and Historical Studies* (Oxford: Littman Library of Jewish Civilization, 1991), 47–75.

—— 'The Meaning of Terms Designating Love in Judaeo-Arabic Thought and Some Remarks on the Judaeo-Arabic Interpretation of Maimonides', in N. Golb (ed.), *Judaeo-Arabic Studies* (Amsterdam: Harwood, 1997), 175–96.

—— 'A New Islamic Source of the *Guide of the Perplexed*', *Maimonidean Studies*, 2 (1991), 31–59.

HARVEY, WARREN ZEV, 'Averroes and Maimonides on the Obligation of Philosophical Contemplation (*i'tibar*)' (Heb.), *Tarbits*, 58 (1989), 75–83.

—— 'The Biblical Term "Kavod" in Spinoza's *Ethics*', *Iyyun*, 48 (1999), 447–9.

—— 'Holiness: A Command to Imitatio Dei', *Tradition*, 16 (1977), 7–28.

—— 'How to Begin to Study the *Guide of the Perplexed*, i. 1' (Heb.), *Da'at*, 21 (1988), 5–24.

—— 'Leibowitz on Abrahamic Man, Faith, and Nihilism' (Heb.), in H. Kasher, M. Hallamish, and Y. Silman (eds.), *Avraham, avi hama'aminim* (Ramat Gan: Bar Ilan University Press, 2002), 347–52.

—— 'Les Sacrifices, la prière, et l'étude chez Maimonide', *Revue des Etudes Juives*, 154 (1995), 97–103.

—— 'Levi ben Abraham of Villefranche's Controversial Encyclopedia', in S. Harvey (ed.), *The Medieval Hebrew Encyclopedia of Science and Philosophy* (Dordrecht: Kluwer, 2000), 171–88.

HARVEY, WARREN ZEV, 'The *Mishneh Torah* as a Key to the Secrets of the *Guide*', in Gerald Blidstein et al. (eds.), *Me'ah She'arim: Studies in Medieval Jewish Spiritual Life in Memory of Isadore Twersky* (Jerusalem: Magnes Press, 2001), 11–28.

—— *Physics and Metaphysics in Ḥasdai Crescas* (Amsterdam: Gieben, 1998).

—— 'Political Philosophy and Halakhah in Maimonides', in Joseph Dan (ed.), *Binah 3: Jewish Intellectual History in the Middle Ages* (Westport, Conn.: Praeger, 1994), 47–64.

—— 'Rabbi Hasdai Crescas' Critique of Philosophical Happiness' (Heb.), *Proceedings of the Sixth World Congress of Jewish Studies*, vol. 3 (Jerusalem: World Union of Jewish Studies, 1977), 143–9.

—— 'Response [to Marvin Fox]', in Jacob Katz (ed.), *The Role of Religion in Modern Jewish History* (Cambridge, Mass.: Association for Jewish Studies, 1975), 87–90.

HASNAWI, AHMAD, 'Réflexions sur la terminologie logique de Maimonide et son contexte farabien: Le *Guide des perplexes* et le *Traité de logique*', in Tony Levy and Roshdi Rashed (eds.), *Maimonide: Philosophe et savant* (Louvain: Peeters, 2004), 39–78.

HAYMAN, PETER, 'Monotheism: A Misused Word in Jewish Studies?', *Journal of Jewish Studies*, 42 (1991), 1–15.

—— 'The "Original Text": A Scholarly Illusion?', in G. Harvey, Jon Davies, and W. Watson (eds.), *Words Remembered, Texts Renewed: Essays in Honour of John F. A. Sawyer* (Sheffield: Sheffield Academic Press, 1995), 434–49.

HELLER, JOSEPH ELIAS, 'The Essence and Purpose of the Active Intellect According to Maimonides' (Heb.), in S. Bernstein and G. Churgin (eds.), *Sefer yovel lishmuel kalman mirski* (New York: Mirsky Jubilee Committee, 1958), 26–42.

HENSHKE, DAVID, 'The Basis of Maimonides' Concept of Halakhah' (Heb.), *Hebrew Law Annual*, 20 (1997), 103–49.

—— 'On Judicial Reality in the Teachings of Maimonides' (Heb.), *Sinai*, 92 (1982–3), 228–39.

—— 'The Legal Source of the Concept "Nation": Between Maimonides and Nahmanides' (Heb.), *Hebrew Law Annual*, 18–19 (1995), 177–98.

—— 'On the Question of Unity in Maimonides' Thought' (Heb.), *Da'at*, 37 (1996), 37–52.

HERRING, BASIL, *Joseph ibn Kaspi's Gevia Kesef: A Study in Medieval Jewish Philosophic Bible Commentary* (New York: Ktav, 1982).

HIGGER, MICHAEL, *Masekhet semaḥot* (Jerusalem: Makor, 1970).

HIRSHMAN, MENACHEM, 'Rabbinic Universalism in the Second and Third Centuries', *Harvard Theological Review*, 93 (2000), 101–15.

—— *Torah for the Entire World* [Torah lekhol ba'ei olam: zerem universali besifrut hatana'im veyaḥaso leḥokhmat he'amim] (Tel Aviv: Hakibuts Hame'uḥad, 1999).

HOFFMANN, DAVID TSEVI, *Leviticus* [Sefer vayikra] (Jerusalem: Mosad Harav Kuk, 1953).

HOLTZMAN, GITIT, 'Rabbi Moshe Narboni on the Relation Between Judaism and Islam' (Heb.), *Tarbits*, 64 (1995), 277–99.

HON, GIORA, 'Going Wrong: To Make a Mistake, to Fall into Error', *Review of Metaphysics*, 49 (1995), 3–20.

HOROWITZ, ELLIOTT, 'Speaking to the Dead: Cemetery Prayer in Medieval and Early Modern Jewry', *Journal of Jewish Thought and Philosophy*, 8 (1999), 303–17.

HUSIK, ISAAC, *A History of Medieval Jewish Philosophy* (New York: MacMillan, 1930).

HUSS, BOAZ, 'Sefer ha-Zohar as Canonical, Sacred, and Holy Text: Changing Perspectives of the Book of Splendor between the 13th and 18th Centuries', *Journal of Jewish Thought and Philosophy*, 7 (1998), 257–307.

HYMAN, ARTHUR, *Eschatological Themes in Medieval Jewish Philosophy* (Milwaukee, Wis.: Marquette University Press, 2002).

HYMAN, PAULA, 'Was God a Magician? *Sefer Yesira* and Jewish Magic', *Journal of Jewish Studies*, 40 (1989), 225–37.

IBN EZRA, ABRAHAM, *Yesod mora* [Foundation of Awe] (Jerusalem, 1955).

IBN KASPI, JOSEPH, *Asarah kelei kesef* (Pressburg, 1903).

IBN PAKUDA, BAHYA, *Duties of the Heart* [Ḥovot halevavot], Bar-Ilan University Responsa Project, CD-ROM, version 13.

IBN SHEM TOV, SHEM TOV BEN SHEM TOV, *Sefer ha'emunot* (Ferrara, 1556; photo edition, 1969).

IBN TIBBON, SAMUEL, *Perush hamilot hazarot*, printed in most editions of Ibn Tibbon's translation of the *Guide of the Perplexed*.

IDEL, MOSHE, *Absorbing Perfections: Kabbalah and Interpretation* (New Haven, Conn.: Yale University Press, 2002).

—— 'Abulafia's Secrets of the Guide: A Linguistic Turn', *Revue de Metaphysique et de Morale*, 4 (1998), 495–528.

—— 'Enoch is Metatron' (Heb.), *Jerusalem Studies in Jewish Thought*, 6 (1987), 151–70; English trans. in *Immanuel*, 24 (1990), 220–40 (= *The New Testament and Christian–Jewish Dialogue: Studies in Honor of David Flusser*).

—— *Golem: Jewish Magical and Mystical Traditions on the Artificial Anthropoid* (Albany, NY: SUNY Press, 1990).

IDEL, MOSHE, 'Infinities of Torah in Kabbalah', in Geoffrey H. Hartman and Sanford Budick (eds.), *Midrash and Literature* (New Haven, Conn.: Yale University Press, 1986), 141–57.

—— 'Jewish Thought in Medieval Spain', in Haim Beinart (ed.), *Moreshet Sepharad: The Sephardi Legacy* (Jerusalem: Magnes Press, 1992), 261–81.

—— 'Judaism, Jewish Mysticism, and Magic' (Heb.), *Jewish Studies*, 36 (1996), 25–40.

—— *Kabbalah: New Perspectives* (New Haven, Conn.: Yale University Press, 1988).

—— *Language, Torah, and Hermenutics in Abraham Abulafia*, trans. Menahem Kallus (Albany, NY: SUNY Press, 1989).

—— 'Maimonides' *Guide of the Perplexed* and the Kabbalah', *Jewish History*, 18 (2004), 197–226.

—— 'Maimonides and Kabbalah', in Isadore Twersky (ed.), *Studies in Maimonides* (Cambridge, Mass.: Harvard University Press, 1990), 31–81.

—— 'Metatron: Comments on the Development of Myth in Judaism' (Heb.), in Haviva Pedayah (ed.), *Myth in Judaism* [Hamitos bayahadut] (= Eshel Be'ersheva, 4) (Be'ersheva: Ben-Gurion University Press, 1996), 29–44.

—— 'Midrashic versus Other Forms of Jewish Hermeneutics: Some Comparative Reflections', in Michael Fishbane (ed.), *The Midrashic Imagination: Jewish Exegesis, Thought, and History* (Albany, NY: SUNY Press, 1993), 45–58.

—— 'On the Significances of the Term "Kabbalah"' (Heb.), *Pe'amim*, 93 (2003), 39–76.

—— 'On Some Forms of Order in Kabbalah', *Da'at*, 50–2 (2003), pp. xxxi–lviii.

—— ' "The Reasons for Unkosher Birds" According to Rabbi David Hehasid and their Significance' (Heb.), in Moshe Hallamish (ed.), *Alei Shefer: Studies in the Literature of Jewish Thought Presented to Rabbi Dr Alexandre Safran* (Ramat Gan: Bar Ilan University Press, 1990), 11–27.

—— 'Reification of Language in Jewish Mysticism', in Steven Katz (ed.), *Mysticism and Language* (New York: Oxford University Press, 1992), 42–79.

—— 'Sabbath: On Concepts of Time in Jewish Mysticism', in Gerald J. Blidstein (ed.), *Sabbath: Idea, History, Reality* (Be'ersheva: Ben Gurion University Press, 2004), 57–93.

—— 'Rabbinism versus Kabbalism: On G. Scholem's Phenomenology of Judaism', *Modern Judaism*, 11 (1991), 281–96.

—— '*Sitre 'Arayot* in Maimonides' Thought', in Shlomo Pines and Yirmiyahu Yovel (eds.), *Maimonides and Philosophy* (Dordrecht: Kluwer, 1986), 79–91.

—— 'Some Conceptions of the Land of Israel in Medieval Jewish Thought', in Ruth Link-Salinger (ed.), *A Straight Path: Studies in Medieval Philosophy and*

Culture. Essays in Honor of Arthur Hyman (Washington, DC: Catholic University of America Press, 1988), 124–41.

—— 'The World of Angels in Human Form' (Heb.), *Jerusalem Studies in Jewish Thought*, 3 (1984), 1–66.

IVRY, ALFRED, 'Isma'ili Theology and Maimonides' Philosophy', in Daniel Frank (ed.), *The Jews of Medieval Islam: Community, Society, and Identity* (Leiden: Brill, 1995), 271–99.

—— 'Strategies of Interpretation in Maimonides' *Guide of the Perplexed*', *Jewish History*, 6 (1992), 113–30.

JACOBS, LOUIS, *God, Torah, Israel: Traditionalism Without Fundamentalism* (Cincinnati, Ohio: Hebrew Union College Press, 1990).

—— 'Holy Places', *Conservative Judaism*, 37/3 (1984), 4–16.

JANOWITZ, NAOMI, *The Poetics of Ascent: Theories of Language in a Rabbinic Ascent Text* (Albany, NY: SUNY Press, 1989).

JANSSON, EVA-MARIA, 'The Magic of the Mezuzah in Rabbinic Literature', in Ulf Haxen (ed.), *Jewish Studies in a New Europe: Proceedings of the Fifth Congress of Jewish Studies* (Copenhagen: C. A. Reitzel, 1998), 413–25.

JOHNSON, GEORGE, *In the Palaces of Memory* (New York: Vintage, 1992).

JOSPE, RAPHAEL, 'Early Philosophical Commentaries on the *Sefer Yeẓirah*: Some Comments', *Revue des Études Juives*, 149 (1990), 369–415.

—— 'Maimonides and *Shiur Komah*' (Heb.), in Devora Dimant, Moshe Idel, and Shalom Rosenberg (eds.), *Minḥah lesarah: meḥkarim befilosofiyah yehudit vekabalah*, Sarah Heller Wilensky Jubilee Volume (Jerusalem: Magnes Press, 1994), 195–209.

—— *Torah and Sophia: The Life and Thought of Shem Tov ibn Falaquera* (Cincinnati, Ohio: Hebrew Union College Press, 1988).

JUDAH HALEVI, *The Book of Refutation and Proof on Behalf of the Despised Religion (The Book of the Khazars) Known as* The Kuzari, trans. Barry S. Kogan and Lawrence V. Berman (New Haven, Conn.: Yale University Press, forthcoming).

—— *Sefer hakuzari* [The Kuzari], trans. from Arabic by Joseph Kafih (Kiryat Ono: Makhon Mishnat Harambam, 1996).

JULIUS, ANTHONY, *Idolizing Pictures: Idolatry, Iconoclasm and Jewish Art* (London: Thames & Hudson, 2000).

JUNG, LEO, *Fallen Angels in Jewish, Christian, and Mohammedan Literature* (New York: Ktav, 1974).

KADISH, SETH, *Kavvana: Directing the Heart in Jewish Prayer* (Northvale, NJ: Jason Aronson, 1997).

KAFIH, JOSEPH, 'Aspects of Maimonides' Philosophy' (Heb.), *Teḥumin*, 8 (1987), 511–20.

KAFIH, JOSEPH, 'Fragment from an Ancient Yemenite Composition Concerning *Shiur Komah*' (Heb.), in id., *Writings* [Ketavim], ed. J. Tobi, vol. i (Jerusalem: General Council of Yemenite Communities in Israel, 1989), 475–8.

—— *Maimonides on the Bible* [Hamikra barambam] (Jerusalem: Mosad Harav Kuk, 1972).

—— *Writings* [Ketavim], 3 vols., ed. J. Tobi (Jerusalem: General Council of the Yemenite Communities in Israel, 1989–2002).

KANARFOGEL, EPHRAIM, 'On the Assessment of R. Moses ben Nahman (Naḥmanides) and his Literary Oeuvre', *Jewish Book Annual*, 54 (1997), 66–80.

—— *'Peering Through the Lattices': Mystical, Magical, and Pietistic Dimensions in the Tosafist Period* (Detroit: Wayne State University Press, 2000).

KANYEVSKY, HAYIM, *Kiryat melekh* [City of the King] (Benei Berak, 1983).

KAPLAN, ARYEH, *Sefer Yezirah: The Book of Creation in Theory and Practice* (York Beach, Maine: Weiser, 1997).

KAPLAN, LAWRENCE, 'Adam, Enoch, and Metatron Revisited: A Critical Analysis of Moshe Idel's Method of Reconstruction', *Kabbalah*, 6 (2001), 73–119.

—— '*Daas Torah*: A Modern Conception of Rabbinic Authority', in Moshe Sokol (ed.), *Rabbinic Authority and Personal Autonomy* (Northvale, NJ: Jason Aronson, 1992), 1–60.

—— 'Israel Under the Mountain: Emmanuel Levinas on Freedom and Constraint in the Revelation of the Torah', *Modern Judaism*, 18 (1998), 35–46.

—— 'Maimonides on the Singularity of the Jewish People', *Da'at*, 15 (1985), pp. v–xxvii.

—— 'Maimonides and Soloveitchik on the Knowledge and Imitation of God', in Goerg K. Hasselhoff and Oftried Fraise (eds.), *Moses Maimonides (1138–1204): His Religious, Scientific, and Philosophical Wirkungsgeschichte in Different Cultural Contexts* (Würzburg: Ergon, 2004), 491–523.

—— and David Berger, 'On Freedom of Inquiry in the Rambam and Today', *Torah u-Madda Journal*, 2 (1990), 37–50.

KASHER, HANNAH, '"How Could God Command Us to Perform Such an Abomination?" Rabbi Joseph Ibn Kaspi's Critique of the Binding of Isaac' (Heb.), *Et hada'at*, 1 (1997), 38–47.

—— 'Maimonides' Interpretation of the Story of the Divine Revelation in the Cleft of the Rock' (Heb.), *Da'at*, 35 (1995), 29–66.

—— 'Maimonides' View of Circumcision as a Factor Uniting the Jewish and Muslim Communities', in R. Nettler (ed.), *Studies in Muslim–Jewish Relations* (Luxembourg: Harwood Academic, 1995), 103–8.

—— 'Talmud Torah as a Means of Apprehending God in Maimonides' Teachings' (Heb.), *Jerusalem Studies in Jewish Thought*, 5 (1986), 71–81.

—— 'Three Punishments which Are One, According to Maimonides' (Heb.), *Sidra*, 14 (1988), 39–58.

—— 'The Torah as a Means of Achieving the World to Come' (Heb.), *Tarbits*, 64 (1995), 301–6.

—— ' "Torah for its Own Sake", Torah Not for its Own Sake, and the Third Way', *Jewish Quarterly Review*, 79 (1988–9), 153–63.

KASHER, MENACHEM, 'The Meaning of the Phrase *Barukh shem kevod malkhuto le'olam va'ed*' (Heb.), *No'am*, 22 (1979–80), 49–54.

KATZ, JACOB, ' "Da'at Torah": The Unqualified Authority Claimed for Halachists', *Jewish History*, 11 (1997), 41–50.

—— *Tradition and Crisis: Jewish Society at the End of the Middle Ages*, trans. Bernard Dov Cooperman, 2nd edn. (New York: New York University Press, 1993).

KELLNER, MENACHEM, 'Chosenness, Not Chauvinism: Maimonides on the Chosen People', in Daniel H. Frank (ed.), *A People Apart: Chosenness and Ritual in Jewish Philosophical Thought* (Albany, NY: SUNY Press, 1993), 51–76, 85–9.

—— 'Could Maimonides Get into Rambam's Heaven?', *Journal of Jewish Thought and Philosophy*, 8 (1999), 231–42.

—— *Dogma in Medieval Jewish Thought* (Oxford: Littman Library of Jewish Civilization, 1986).

—— ' "Farteitsht un Farbessert": Tendentious "Corrections" in Maimonides' Writings' (Heb.), in Benjamin Ish-Shalom (ed.), *Sefer hayovel likhvod shalom rosenberg* (Jerusalem: Beit Morashah and Eliner Library, forthcoming).

—— 'Gersonides and his Cultured Despisers: Arama and Abravanel', *Journal of Medieval and Renaissance Studies*, 6 (1976), 269–96.

—— 'Is Maimonides' Ideal Person Austerely Rationalist?', *American Catholic Philosophical Quarterly*, 76 (2002), 125–43.

—— 'The Literary Character of the *Mishneh Torah*: On the Art of Writing in Maimonides' Halakhic Works', in Gerald Blidstein et al. (eds.) *Me'ah She'arim: Studies in Medieval Jewish Spiritual Life in Memory of Isadore Twersky* (Jerusalem: Magnes Press, 2001), 29–45.

—— 'Maimonides' Allegiances to Torah and Science', *Torah u-Madda Journal*, 7 (1997), 88–104.

—— 'Maimonides' Commentary on *Mishnah Hagigah* II.1: Translation and Commentary', in Marc D. Angel (ed.), *From Strength to Strength: Lectures from Shearith Israel* (New York: Sepher-Hermon Press, 1998), 101–11.

KELLNER, MENACHEM, *Maimonides on the 'Decline of the Generations' and the Nature of Rabbinic Authority* (Albany, NY: SUNY Press, 1996).

—— *Maimonides on Human Perfection* (Atlanta, Ga.: Scholars Press, 1990).

—— *Maimonides on Judaism and the Jewish People* (Albany, NY: SUNY Press, 1991).

—— 'Maimonides and Samuel ibn Tibbon on Jer. 9: 22–23 and Human Perfection', in M. Beer (ed.), *Studies in Halakha and Jewish Thought Presented to Rabbi Proferssor Menachem Emanuel Rackman* (Ramat Gan: Bar Ilan University Press, 1994), 49–57.

—— 'Messianic Postures in Israel Today', *Modern Judaism*, 6 (1986), 197–209; repr. in Marc Saperstein (ed.), *Essential Papers on Messianic Movements in Jewish History* (New York: New York University Press, 1992), 504–19.

—— 'Mishneh Torah: Why?' (Heb.), *Mesorah leyosef*, 4 (2005), 316–29.

—— *Must a Jew Believe Anything?* (Oxford: Littman Library of Jewish Civilization, 1999; 2nd edn. 2005).

—— 'On Universalism and Particularism in Judaism', *Da'at*, 36 (1996), pp. v–xv.

—— 'Overcoming Chosenness', in Raphael Jospe and Seth Ward (eds.), *Revelation and Redemption in Judaism and Mormonism* (Madison, Wis.: Farleigh Dickinson University Press, 2001), 147–72.

—— 'Philosophical Misogyny in Medieval Jewish Thought: Gersonides vs. Maimonides' (Heb.), in A. Ravitzky (ed.), *Meromi leyerushalayim: sefer zikaron leyosef baruch sermoneta*, Joseph Baruch Sermonetta Memorial Volume (Jerusalem: Magnes Press, 1998), 113–28.

—— 'Rabbis in Politics: A Study in Medieval and Modern Jewish Political Theory' (Heb.), *Ḥevrah umedinah*, 3 (2003), 673–98.

—— 'Revelation and Messianism: A Maimonidean Study', in Dan Cohn-Sherbok (ed.), *Torah and Revelation* (New York: Edwin Mellen Press, 1992), 117–33.

—— 'Strauss' Maimonides vs. Maimonides' Maimonides: Could Maimonides have been *Both* Enlightened and Orthodox?', *Le'ela* (Dec. 2000), 29–36.

—— 'Was Maimonides Truly Universalist?', *Trumah. Beitraege zur juedischen Philosophie*, 11 (Festgabe zum 80. Geburtstag von Ze'ev Levy) (2001), 3–15.

KIENER, RONALD C., 'Astrology in Jewish Mysticism from the *Sefer Yesira* to the *Zohar*', *Jerusalem Studies in Jewish Thought*, 6 (1987), 1*–42*.

—— 'The Hebrew Paraphrase of Saadiah Gaon's *Kitab al-amanat wa'l-i'tiqadat*', *AJS Review*, 11 (1986), 1–25.

KIMELMAN, REUVEN, 'The Shema' Liturgy: From Covenant Ceremony to Coronation', in Joseph Tabory (ed.), *Kenishta: Studies of the Synagogue World* (Ramat Gan: Bar Ilan University Press, 2001), 9–105.

KLAWANS, JONATHAN, *Impurity and Sin in Ancient Judaism* (Oxford: Oxford University Press, 2000).

—— 'Ritual Purity, Moral Purity, and Sacrifice in Jacob Milgrom's *Leviticus*', *Religious Studies Review*, 29 (2003), 19–28.

KLEIN, MICHAEL L., 'The Translation of Anthropomorphisms and Anthropopathism in the Targumim', *Congress Volume: Vienna 1980*, supplement to *Vetus Testamentum*, 32 (Leiden: Brill, 1981); Hebrew trans. in id., *Anthropomorphisms and Anthropopathisms in the Targum of the Pentateuch* [Hagshamat ha'el betargumim arami'im latorah] (Jerusalem: Makor, 1982).

KLEIN-BRASLAVI, SARA, *King Solomon and Philosophical Esotericism in Maimonides* [Shelomoh hamelekh veha'ezoterizm hafilosofi bemishnat harambam] (Jerusalem: Magnes Press, 1996).

KOGAN, BARRY, ' "What Can We Know and When Can We Know It?" Maimonides on the Active Intelligence and Human Cognition', *Studies in Philosophy and the History of Philosophy*, 19 (1989) (= *Moses Maimonides and his Time*, ed. Eric L. Ormsby), 121–37.

KOOK, ABRAHAM ISAAC, *Igerot hare'ayah* [Correspondence] (Jerusalem: Mosad Harav Kuk, 1943).

KOREN, SHARON FAYE, ' "The Woman from whom God Wanders" : The Menstruant in Medieval Jewish Mysticism', Ph.D. diss., Yale University, 1999.

KORN, EUGENE, 'Gentiles, the World to Come, and Judaism: The Odyssey of a Rabbinic Text', *Modern Judaism*, 14 (1994), 265–87.

KOZODOY, NEIL, 'Reading Medieval Hebrew Love Poetry', *AJS Review*, 2 (1977), 111–29.

KRAEMER, JOEL, *Humanism in the Renaissance of Islam: The Cultural Revival During the Buyid Age* (Leiden: Brill, 1986).

—— 'The Influence of Islamic Law on Maimonides' (Heb.), *Te'udah*, 19 (1996), 225–44.

—— 'The Life of Moses ben Maimon', in Lawrence Fine (ed.), *Judaism in Practice From the Middle Ages through the Early Modern Period* (Princeton, NJ: Princeton University Press, 2001), 413–28

—— 'Maimonides and the Spanish Aristotelian School', in Mark D. Meyerson and Edward D. English (eds.), *Christians, Muslims, and Jews in Medieval and Early Modern Spain: Interaction and Cultural Exchange* (Notre Dame, Ind.: University of Notre Dame Press, 1999), 40–68.

—— 'Naturalism and Universalism in Maimonides' Political and Religious Thought', in G. Blidstein et al. (eds.), *Me'ah She'arim: Studies in Medieval Jewish Spiritual Life in Memory of Isadore Twersky* (Jerusalem: Magnes Press, 2001), 47–81.

—— 'Six Unpublished Maimonides Letters from the Cairo Genizah', *Maimonidean Studies*, 2 (1991), 61–94.

KREISEL, HOWARD (Hayim), 'Judah Halevi's Influence on Maimonides: A Preliminary Appraisal', *Maimonidean Studies*, 2 (1991), 95–122.

—— 'The Land of Israel and Prophecy in Medieval Jewish Philosophy' (Heb.), in M. Hallamish and A. Ravitzky (eds.), *Erets yisra'el behagut hayehudit biyemei habeinayim* (Jerusalem: Yad Yitshak Ben-Tsevi, 1991), 40–51.

—— *Maimonides' Political Thought* (Albany, NY: SUNY Press, 1999).

—— 'Moses Maimonides', in Daniel H. Frank and Oliver Leaman (eds.), *History of Jewish Philosophy* (London: Routledge, 1997), 245–80.

—— *Prophecy: The History of an Idea in Medieval Jewish Philosophy* (Dordrecht: Kluwer, 2001).

—— 'The Torah Commentary of R. Nissim ben Mosheh of Marseilles: On a Medieval Approach to Torah u-Madda', *Torah u-Madda Journal*, 10 (2001), 20–36.

—— ' "The Voice of God" in Medieval Jewish Philosophical Exegesis' (Heb.), *Da'at*, 16 (1986), 29–38.

LAMM, NORMAN, 'Loving and Hating Jews as Halakhic Categories', *Tradition*, 24 (1989), 98–122.

—— *Torah Lishmah: Torah for Torah's Sake in the Works of Rabbi Hayyim of Volozhin and his Contemporaries* (New York: Yeshiva University Press, 1989).

LANGERMANN, Y. TZVI, 'Cosmology and Cosmogony in *Doresh Reshumoth*, a Thirteenth-Century Commentary on the Torah', *Harvard Theological Review*, 97 (2004), 199–227.

—— 'Hebrew Astronomy: Deep Soundings from a Rich Tradition', in Helaine Selin (ed.), *Astronomy Across Cultures: The History of Non-Western Astronomy* (Dordrecht: Kluwer, 2000), 555–84.

—— 'The Letter of Rabbi Shemuel ben Eli on Resurrection' (Heb.), *Kovets al yad*, 15 (2000), 41–92.

—— 'Maimonides and Miracles: The Growth of a (Dis)belief', *Jewish History*, 18 (2004), 147–72.

—— 'Maimonides' Repudiation of Astrology', *Maimonidean Studies*, 2 (1991), 123–58.

—— 'A New Redaction of Sefer Yeşira?', *Kabbalah*, 2 (1997), 49–64.

—— 'A New Source Concerning Samuel ibn Tibbon's Translation of the *Guide of the Perplexed* and his Comments On It' (Heb.), *Pe'amim*, 72 (1997), 51–74.

—— 'On the Beginnings of Hebrew Scientific Literature and on Studying History Through "Maqbilot" (Parallels)', *Aleph*, 2 (2002), 169–89.

—— 'On Some Passages Attributed to Maimonides', in G. Blidstein (ed.), *Me'ah She'arim: Studies in Medieval Jewish Spiritual Life in Memory of Isadore Twersky* (Jerusalem: Magnes Press, 2001), 223–40.

—— 'Saving the Soul by Knowing the Soul: A Medieval Yemeni Interpretation of Song of Songs', *Journal of Jewish Thought and Philosophy*, 12 (2003), 147–66.

—— 'Science and the *Kuzari*', *Science in Context*, 10 (1997), 495–522.

—— 'Some Astrological Themes in the Thought of Abraham ibn Ezra', in I. Twersky and J. Harris (eds.), *Rabbi Abraham ibn Ezra: Studies in the Writings of a Twelfth-Century Jewish Polymath* (Cambridge, Mass.: Harvard University Press, 1993), 28–85.

LASKER, DANIEL J., 'Judah Halevi and Karaism', in Jacob Neusner (ed.), *From Ancient Israel to Modern Judaism: Essays in Honor of Marvin Fox*, vol. iii (Atlanta, Ga.: Scholars Press, 1989), 111–25.

—— 'Proselyte Judaism, Christianity, and Islam in the Thought of Judah Halevi', *Jewish Quarterly Review*, 81 (1990), 75–91.

LEIBOWITZ, NEHAMA, *Studies in Vayikra*, trans. Aryeh Newman (Jerusalem: World Zionist Organization, 1980).

LEIBOWITZ, YESHAYAHU, 'Maimonides: The Abrahamic Man', *Judaism*, 6 (1957), 148–54.

LERNER, RALPH, 'Winged Words to Yemen', *Revue de Métaphysique et de Morale*, 4 (1998), 479–93.

—— *Maimonides' Empire of Light: Popular Enlightenment in an Age of Belief* (Chicago: University of Chicago Press, 2000).

LESSES, REBECCA M., *Ritual Practices to Gain Power: Angels, Incantations, and Revelation in Early Jewish Mysticism* (Harrisburg, Pa.: Trinity Press International, 1998).

LEVENE, MICHELLE, 'Maimonides' Philosophical Exegesis of the Nobles' Vision (Exodus 24): A Guide for the Pursuit of Knowledge', *Torah u-Madda Journal*, 11 (2003), 61–106.

LEVI BEN GERSHOM *see* Gersonides

LEVINE, BARUCH, 'Appendix: The Language of the Magical Bowls', in Jacob Neusner, *A History of the Jews in Babylonia* (Leiden: Brill, 1970), 343–75.

LEVINE, LEE I., *Judaism and Hellenism in Antiquity: Conflict or Confluence?* (Seattle, Wash.: University of Washington Press, 1998).

LEVINGER, JACOB, *Maimonides as Philosopher and Codifier* [Harambam kefilosof ukefosek] (Jerusalem: Mosad Bialik, 1989).

—— *Maimonides' Techniques of Codification* [Darkhei hamaḥshavah hahilkhatit shel harambam] (Jerusalem: Magnes Press, 1965).

LEVY, B. BARRY, *Fixing God's Torah: The Accuracy of the Hebrew Bible Text in Jewish Law* (New York: Oxford University Press, 2001).

LEWIS, C. S., *The Discarded Image* (Cambridge: Cambridge University Press, 1964).

LICHTENSTEIN, YEHEZKEL SHRAGA, 'The Mezuzah as an Amulet' (Heb.), *Teḥumin*, 10 (1988/9), 417–26.

—— 'The Rambam's Approach Regarding Prayer, Holy Objects, and Visiting the Cemetery' (Heb.), *Hebrew Union College Annual*, 72 (2001), 1–34 (Hebrew pagination).

LIEBERMAN, SAUL, 'Appendix D', in Gershom Scholem, *Jewish Gnosticism, Merkabah Mysticism, and Talmudic Tradition* (New York: Jewish Theological Seminary, 1960), 124–5.

—— 'The Knowledge of the Halakhah by the Author (or Authors) of the Heikhaloth', in Ithamar Gruenwald, *Apocalyptic and Merkavah Mysticism* (Leiden: Brill, 1980), 241–4.

—— *Tosefta kifshutah*, 10 vols. (New York: Jewish Theological Seminary of America, 1973).

LIEBES, YEHUDAH, *Ars Poetica in* Sefer Yetsirah [Torat hayetsirah shel sefer yetsirah] (Jerusalem: Schocken, 2000).

—— *Elisha's Sin* [Ḥeto shel elisha] (Jerusalem: Academon, 1990).

LIFSHITZ, BERACHYAHU, 'The Rules Governing Conflict of Laws between a Jew and a Gentile According to Maimonides', in *Mélanges à la mémoire de Marcel-Henri Prevost* (Paris: Presses Universitaires de France, 1982), 179–89.

LOBEL, DIANA, *Between Mysticism and Philosophy: Sufi Language of Religious Experience in Judah Ha-Levi's Kuzari* (Albany, NY: SUNY Press, 2000).

—— 'A Dwelling Place for the Shekhinah', *Jewish Quarterly Review*, 90 (1999), 103–25.

LOEWE, JUDAH LEIB BEN BEZALEL (Maharal of Prague), *Derekh ha-ḥayim*, Taklitor hatorani, CD-ROM, version 2.4.

—— *Gur aryeh*, Taklitor hatorani, CD-ROM, version 2.4.

—— *Netsaḥ yisra'el* (Jerusalem: Makhon Yerushalayim, 1997).

—— *Tiferet yisra'el*, Taklitor hatorani, CD-ROM, version 2.4.

LOEWE, RAPHAEL, 'The Divine Garment and Shi'ur Komah', *Harvard Theological Review*, 58 (1965), 153–60.

LORBERBAUM, YAIR, 'Maimonides on *Imago Dei*: Philosophy and Law—The Felony of Murder, the Criminal Procedure, and Capital Punishment' (Heb.), *Tarbits*, 68 (1999), 533–56.

LUCK, GÖRG, 'Theurgy and Forms of Worship in Neoplatonism', in E. Frerichs, Jacob Neusner, and P. Flesher (eds.), *Religion, Science, and Magic: In Concert and in Conflict* (New York: Oxford University Press, 1989), 185–225.

MACCOBY, HYAM, *Ritual and Morality: The Ritual Purity System and its Place in Judaism* (Cambridge: Cambridge University Press, 1999).

MALKIEL, DAVID, 'Between Worldliness and Traditionalism: Eighteenth Century Jews Debate Intercessionary Prayer', *Jewish Studies Internet Journal*, 2 (2003), 169–98.

MANEKIN, CHARLES H., 'Belief, Certainty, and Divine Attributes in the *Guide of the Perplexed*', *Maimonidean Studies*, 1 (1990), 117–41.

—— 'Conservative Tendencies in Gersonides' Religious Philosophy', in Daniel H. Frank and Oliver Leaman (eds.), *The Cambridge Companion to Medieval Jewish Thought* (Cambridge: Cambridge University Press, 2003), 304–44.

MARGOLIOT, REUVEN, *Malakhei elyon* [Angels on High] (Jerusalem: Mosad Harav Kuk, 1945).

MARGOLIOTH, MORDECAI, *Sefer harazim* (Jerusalem: American Academy for Jewish Research, 1967).

MARIENBERG, EVYATAR, 'Niddah: Études sur la Baraita de Niddah et sur la conceptualisation de la menstruation dans le monde juif et son écho dans le monde chrétien de l'époque médiévale à nos jours', Ph.D. diss., Paris: Écoles des Hautes Études en Sciences Sociales, 2002.

MARMORSTEIN, ABRAHAM, 'The Discussion of the Angels with God' (Heb.), *Melilah*, 3–4 (1950), 93–102.

MARX, ALEXANDER, 'A List of Poems on the Articles of the Creed', *Jewish Quarterly Review*, OS 9 (1919), 305–36.

MATT, DANIEL C., 'The Mystic and the *Mizwot*', in Arthur Green (ed.), *Jewish Spirituality*, i: *From the Bible through the Middle Ages* (New York: Crossroads, 1986), 367–404.

Mekhilta de-rabbi ishmael, ed. and trans. Jacob Z. Lauterbach, 3 vols. (Philadelphia, Pa.: Jewish Publication Society, 1933–5).

MELAMED, ABRAHAM, '*Al yithalel*: Philosophical Commentaries on Jeremiah 9: 22–23 in Medieval and Renaissance Jewish Thought' (Heb.), *Jerusalem Studies in Jewish Thought*, 4 (1985), 31–82.

—— *The Image of the Black in Jewish Culture: A History of the Other* (London: Routledge Curzon, 2003).

—— 'The Land of Israel and Climatology in Jewish Thought' (Heb.), in M. Hallamish and A. Ravitzky (eds.), *Erets yisra'el behagut hayehudit biyemei habeinayim* (Jerusalem: Yad Yitshak Ben-Tsevi, 1991), 52–79.

—— 'Maimonides on Women: Formless Matter or Potential Prophet?', in E. Wolfson et al. (eds.), *Perspectives on Jewish Thought and Mysticism. Proceedings of the International Conference Held by the Institute of Jewish Studies, University College London, 1994, in Celebration of its Fortieth Anniversary: Dedicated to the Memory and Academic Legacy of its Founder Alexander Altmann* (Amsterdam: Harwood Academic, 1998), 99–134.

MENOCAL, MARIA ROSA, *The Ornament of the World: How Muslims, Christians, and Jews Created a Culture of Tolerance in Medieval Spain* (New York: Little, Brown, 2002).

Midrash tehilim [Midrash on Psalms], Bar-Ilan University Responsa Project, CD-ROM, version 13.

Midrash vayikra rabah, ed. Mordecai Margulies, 2nd edn. (New York: Jewish Theological Seminary, 1993).

MILGROM, JACOB, *JPS Torah Commentary, Numbers* (Philadelphia, Pa.: Jewish Publication Society, 1990).

MORGAN, MICHAEL, *Sepher ha-Razim: The Book of the Mysteries* (Chico, Calif.: Scholars Press, 1983).

NAHMANIDES, MOSES, *Commentary on the Torah*, trans. Charles B. Chavel: *Genesis* (New York: Shilo, 1971); *Leviticus* (New York: Shilo, 1974).

—— *Writings* [Kitvei ramban], ed. Charles B. Chavel, 2 vols. (Jerusalem: Mosad Harav Kuk, 1964).

NEHORAI, MICHAEL Z., 'The Land of Israel in Maimonides and Nahmanides', in M. Hallamish and A. Ravitzky (eds.), *Erets yisra'el behagut hayehudit biyemei habeinayim* (Jerusalem: Yad Yitshak Ben-Tsevi, 1991), 123–37.

—— 'How a Righteous Gentile Can Merit the World to Come' (Heb.), *Tarbits*, 64 (1995), 307–8.

—— 'A Portion in the World to Come for the Righteous/Sages of the Nations' (Heb.), *Da'at*, 50–2 (2003), 97–105.

NEUSNER, JACOB, *The Idea of Purity in Ancient Judaism* (Leiden: Brill, 1973).

NISSIM OF MARSEILLES, *Ma'aseh nisim: perush letorah* [Commentary on Torah], ed. H. Kreisel (Jerusalem: Mekize Nirdamim, 2000).

NISSIM BEN REUVEN GERONDI, *Derashot haran* [Sermons], ed. Aryeh Leib Feldman (Jerusalem: Mosad Harav Kuk, 2003).

NOVAK, DAVID, *The Theology of Nahmanides Systematically Presented* (Atlanta, Ga.: Scholars Press, 1992).

NURIEL, ABRAHAM, 'Are There Really Maimonidean Elements in the Philosophy of Leibowitz?' (Heb.), in id., *Galui vesamui bafilosofiyah hayehudit biyemei habeinayim* (Jerusalem: Magnes Press, 2000), 172–8.

—— '"Torah Speaks in the Language of Man" in Maimonides' *Guide*' (Heb.), in id., *Galui vesamui bafilosofiyah hayehudit biyemei habeinayim* (Jerusalem: Magnes Press, 2000), 93–9.

OATES, JOYCE CAROL, 'Depth-Sightings', *New York Review of Books*, 44/14 (24 Sept. 1998), 4.

OTTO, RUDOLPH, *The Idea of the Holy*, trans. John W. Harvey (Oxford: Oxford University Press, 1950).

PEARL, CHAIM, *Rashi* (New York: Grove Press, 1988).

PELEG, EREZ, 'Between Philosophy and Kabbalah: Criticism of Jewish Philosophy in the Thought of Rabbi Shem-Tov ben Shem-Tov' [Bein filosofiyah lekabalah: bikoret hasekhaltanut hayehudit bahaguto shel r. shem tov ibn shem tov], Ph.D. diss., University of Haifa, 2003.

PETERS, F. E., 'Hermes and Harran: The Roots of Arabic-Islamic Occultism', in Michael M. Mazzaoui and Vera B. Moreen (eds.), *Intellectual Studies on Islam: Essays Written in Honor of Martin B. Dickson* (Salt Lake City, Utah: University of Utah Press, 1990), 185–215.

—— *Jerusalem and Mecca: The Typology of the Holy City in the Near East* (New York: New York University Press, 1986).

PETUCHOWSKI, JAKOB, *Theology and Poetry: Studies in the Medieval Piyyut* (London: Routledge & Kegan Paul, for the Littman Library of Jewish Civilization, 1978).

PICK, SHLOMO, 'Concerning *Da'at Torah*' (Heb.), *Da'at*, 46 (2001), 139–43.

PINCHOT, ROY, 'The Deeper Conflict between Maimonides and Ramban over the Sacrifices', *Tradition*, 33 (1999), 24–33.

PINES, SHLOMO, 'God, the Divine Glory, and the Angels According to Second-Century Theology' (Heb.), *Jerusalem Studies in Jewish Thought*, 6 (1987), 1–14.

—— 'On the Term *Ruḥaniyut* and its Origin, and on Judah Halevi's Doctrine' (Heb.), *Tarbits*, 57 (1988), 511–34.

—— 'Parallels Between the *Kuzari* and the Non-Philosophical Treatises of Maimonides' [Appendix VII to 'Shi'ite Terms and Conceptions in Judah Halevi's *Kuzari*'], in Warren Zev Harvey and Moshe Idel (eds.), *Studies in the History of Jewish Thought by Shlomo Pines*, vol. v (Jerusalem: Magnes Press, 1997), 248–51.

—— 'Quotations from Saadya's Commentary on Sefer Yeẓirah in Maimonides' *Guide of the Perplexed*' [Appendix III to 'Points of Similarity between the Exposition of the Doctrine of the Sefirot in the *Sefer Yeẓirah* and a Text of the Pseudo-Clementine *Homilies*: The Implications of This Resemblance'], in Warren Zev Harvey and Moshe Idel (eds.), *Studies in the History of Jewish Thought by Shlomo Pines*, vol. v (Jerusalem: Magnes Press, 1997), 158–63.

—— 'Translator's Introduction: The Philosophic Sources of the *Guide of the Perplexed*', in Maimonides, *Guide of the Perplexed*, trans. Shlomo Pines (Chicago: University of Chicago Press, 1963), pp. lvii–cxxxiv.

Pirkei de rabi eliezer, ed. and trans. Gerald Friedlander (London, 1916; repr. New York: Hermon Press, 1965).

POSEN, RAPHAEL, 'Targum Onkelos in Maimonides' Writings' (Heb.), in Zohar Amar and Hananel Seri (eds.), *Sefer zikaron lerav yosef ben david kafih* (Ramat Gan: Office of the Bar Ilan University Rabbi, 2001), 236–56.

POSEN, RAPHAEL, *Translation Consistency in Targum Onkelos* [He'akivut hatargumit betargum onkelos] (Jerusalem: Magnes Press, 2004).

RABINOVITCH, NACHUM L., 'Maimonides, Science, and *Ta'amei ha-Mitzvot*', in Ya'akov Elman and Jeffrey Gurock (eds.) *Hazon Nahum: Studies Presented to Norman Lamm* (New York: Yeshiva University Press, 1977), 187–206.

RAPPEL, DOV, *Targum Onkelos as a Commentary on the Torah* [Targum onkelos keferush latorah] (Tel Aviv: Hakibuts Hame'uhad, 1985).

RAVITZKY, AVIEZER, 'Awe and Fear of the Holy Land in Jewish Thought' (Heb.), in id. (ed.), *Erets yisra'el behagut hayehudit ba'et hahadashah* (Jerusalem: Yad Yitshak Ben-Tsevi, 1998), 1–41.

—— 'Introduction—The Binding of Isaac and the Covenant: Abraham and his Descendants in Jewish Thought' (Heb.), in Hannah Kasher, Moshe Hallamish, and Yohanan Silman (eds.), *Avraham, avi hama'aminim: demuto bere'i hehagut ledoroteha* (Ramat Gan: Bar Ilan University Press, 2003), 11–38.

—— 'Maimonides and his Students on Linguistic Magic and the "Lunacy of Amulet Writers"' (Heb.), in Avi Sagi and Nahem Ilan (eds.), *Tarbut yehudit be'ein hase'arah: sefer yovel . . . yosef ahituv* (Ein Tsurim: Hakibuts Hame'uhad and Merkaz Ya'akov Herzog, 2002), 431–58.

—— 'On the Image of the Leader in Jewish Thought' (Heb.), *Pirsumei hug beit hanasi letanakh ulemekorot yisra'el*, 1 (1998), 33–46.

REGEV, SHAUL, 'The Land of Israel in Sixteenth-Century Jewish Thought: Climatology vs Centre' (Heb.), in Warren Zev Harvey (ed.), *Tsiyon utsiyonut bekerev yehudei sefarad vehamizrah* (Jerusalem: Misgav Yerushalayim, 2002), 115–37.

—— 'The Vision of the Nobles of Israel in the Jewish Philosophy of the Middle Ages' (Heb.), *Jerusalem Studies in Jewish Thought*, 4 (1984–5), 281–302.

ROSENBERG, SHALOM, 'Bible Exegesis in the *Guide*' (Heb.), *Jerusalem Studies in Jewish Thought*, 1 (1981), 85–157.

—— 'The Concept of Emunah in Post-Maimonidean Jewish Philosophy', in I. Twersky (ed.), *Studies in Medieval Jewish History and Literature*, vol. ii (Cambridge, Mass.: Harvard University Press, 1984), 273–308.

—— 'The Link to the Land of Israel in Jewish Thought: A Clash of Perspectives', in Lawrence Hoffman (ed.), *The Land of Israel: Jewish Perspectives* (Notre Dame, Ind.: Notre Dame University Press, 1986), 139–69.

—— 'You Shall Walk in his Ways' (Heb.), in Asa Kasher and Moshe Hallamish (eds.), *Filosofiyah yisra'elit* (Tel Aviv: 1983), 72–92.

ROSNER, FRED, 'Moses Maimonides on Music Therapy and his Responsum on Music', *Journal of Jewish Music and Liturgy*, 16 (1993), 1–16.

RUBIN, MILKA, 'The Language of Creation or the Primordial Language: A Case of Cultural Polemics in Antiquity', *Journal of Jewish Studies*, 49 (1998), 306–33.

RYNHOLD, DANIEL, 'Good and Evil, Truth and Falsity: Maimonides and Moral Cognitivism', *Trumah*, 12 (2002), 163–82.

SA'ADIAH GAON, *The Book of Beliefs and Opinions* [Hanivḥar be'emunot vede'ot], Hebrew trans. Joseph Kafih (New York: Sura, 1970); English trans. Samuel Rosenblatt (New Haven, Conn.: Yale University Press, 1948).

SAFRAN, BEZALEL, 'Maimonides' Attitude to Magic and to Related Types of Thinking', in B. Safran and E. Safran (eds.), *Porat Yosef: Studies Presented to Rabbi Dr Joseph Safran* (New York: Ktav, 1992), 92–110.

SAGI, AVI, *Judaism: Between Religion and Morality* [Yahadut: bein dat lemusar] (Tel Aviv: Hakibuts Hame'uhad, 1998).

SAMUELSON, NORBERT, *Gersonides on God's Knowledge* (Toronto: Pontifical Institute of Medieval Studies, 1977).

SAPERSTEIN, MARC, 'Christians and Christianity in the Sermons of Jacob Anatoli', *Jewish History*, 6 (1992), 225–42.

SCHÄFER, PETER, *The Hidden and Manifest God: Some Major Themes in Early Jewish Mysticism*, trans. Aubrey Pomerance (Albany, NY: SUNY Press, 1992).

—— 'The Idea of Piety of the Ashkenazi Hasidim and its Roots in Jewish Tradition', *Jewish History*, 4 (1990), 9–23.

—— 'Jewish Magic Literature in Late Antiquity and Early Middle Ages', *Journal of Jewish Studies*, 41 (1990), 75–91.

—— 'The Magic of the Golem: The Early Development of the Golem Legend', *Journal of Jewish Studies*, 46 (1995), 259–61.

—— 'Magic and Religion in Ancient Judaism', in P. Schäfer and Hans G. Kippenberg (eds.), *Envisioning Magic: A Princeton Seminar and Symposium* (Leiden: Brill, 1997), 19–43.

—— *Mirror of His Beauty: Feminine Images of God from the Bible to the Early Kabbalah* (Princeton, NJ: Princeton University Press, 2002).

—— *Synopse zur Hekhalot-Literatur* (Tübingen: J. C. B. Mohr [Paul Siebeck], 1981).

SCHEINDLIN, RAYMOND, 'Merchants and Intellectuals, Rabbis and Poets: Judeo-Arabic Culture in the Golden Age of Islam', in David Biale (ed.), *Cultures of the Jews: A New History* (New York: Schocken, 2002), 313–86.

—— *Wine, Women, and Death: Medieval Hebrew Poems on the Good Life* (Philadelphia, Pa.: Jewish Publication Society, 1986).

SCHIFFMAN, LAWRENCE, 'The Recall of Rabbi Nehuniah ben ha-Qanah from Ecstasy in the *Hekhalot Rabbati*', *AJS Review*, 1 (1976), 269–81.

SCHIRMANN, JEFIM HAYIM, 'Maimonides and Hebrew Poetry' (Heb.), *Moznayim*, 3 (1933–4), 433–6.

SCHOLEM, GERSHOM, *Jewish Gnosticism, Merkabah Mysticism, and Talmudic Tradition* (New York: Jewish Theological Seminary, 1960).

—— *Major Trends in Jewish Mysticism* (New York: Schocken, 1954).

—— 'The Name of God and the Linguistic Theory of the Kabbala', *Diogenes*, 79 (1972), 59–80.

—— *On the Kabbalah and its Symbolism* (New York: Schocken, 1996).

—— *On the Mystical Shape of the Godhead: Basic Concepts in the Kabbalah* (New York: Schocken, 1991).

—— *Origins of the Kabbalah* (Princeton, NJ: Princeton University Press, 1987).

SCHULTZ, JOSEPH, 'Angelic Opposition to the Ascension of Moses and the Revelation of the Law', *Jewish Quarterly Review*, 61 (1970/1), 282–307.

SCHWARTZ, DOV, *Amulets, Properties, and Rationalism in Medieval Jewish Thought* [Kame'ot, segulot, usekhaltanut behagut hayehudit biyemei habeinayim] (Ramat Gan: Bar Ilan University Press, 2004).

—— *Astrology and Magic in Jewish Thought* [Astrologiyah vemagiyah behagut yehudit] (Ramat Gan: Bar Ilan University Press, 1999).

—— 'From Theurgy to Magic: The Evolution of the Magical-Talismanic Justification of Sacrifice in the Circle of Nahmanides and his Interpreters', *Aleph*, 1 (2001), 165–213.

—— 'Rationalism and Conservatism' (Heb.), *Da'at*, 32–3 (1994), 143–82.

SCHWARZSCHILD, STEVEN S., 'An Agenda for Jewish Philosophy in the 1980s', in Norbert Samuelson (ed.), *Studies in Jewish Philosophy: Collected Essays of the Academy for Jewish Philosophy, 1980–5* (Lanham, Md.: University Press of America, 1987), 101–25.

—— 'Do Noachites Have to Believe in Revelation? (A Passage in Dispute Between Maimonides, Spinoza, Mendelssohn, and Herman Cohen): A Contribution to a Jewish View of Natural Law', *Jewish Quarterly Review*, 52 (1962), 297–308; 54 (1962), 30–65; repr. in Menachem Kellner (ed.), *The Pursuit of the Ideal: Jewish Writings of Steven Schwarzschild* (Albany, NY: SUNY Press, 1990), 29–59.

—— 'Proselytism and Ethnicism in R. Yehudah Halevy', in Bernard Lewis and Friedrich Niewoehner (eds.), *Religionsgespräche im Mittelalter* (Wiesbaden: O. Harrasowitz, 1992), 27–41.

—— 'Shekhinah and Eschatology', in Menachem Kellner (ed.), *The Pursuit of the Ideal: Jewish Writings of Steven Schwarzschild* (Albany, NY: SUNY Press, 1990), 235–50.

SCHWEID, ELIEZER, *The Land of Israel: National Home or Land of Destiny* (Rutherford: Farleigh Dickinson University Press, 1985).

—— 'Prayer in the Thought of Yehudah Halevi', in Gabriel H. Cohn and Harold Fisch (eds.), *Prayer in Judaism: Continuity and Change* (Northvale, NJ: Jason Aronson, 1996), 109–17.

SEESKIN, KENNETH, 'Holiness as an Ethical Ideal', *Journal of Jewish Thought and Philosophy*, 5 (1996), 191–203.

—— 'Maimonides, Spinoza, and the Problem of Creation', in Heidi M. Ravven and Lenn E. Goodman (eds.), *Jewish Themes in Spinoza's Philosophy* (Albany, NY: SUNY Press, 2002), 115–30.

—— *No Other Gods: The Modern Struggle against Idolatry* (New York: Behrman House, 1995).

—— 'Sanctity and Silence: The Religious Significance of Maimonides' Negative Theology', *American Catholic Philosophical Quarterly*, 76 (2002), 7–24.

—— *Searching for a Distant God: The Legacy of Maimonides* (New York: Oxford University Press, 2000).

Sefer haḥinukh (Jerusalem: Eshkol, 1961).

SEPTIMUS, BERNARD, *Hispano-Jewish Culture in Transition: The Career and Controversies of Ramah* (Cambridge, Mass.: Harvard University Press, 1982).

—— 'Maimonides on Language', in Aviva Doron (ed.), *The Heritage of the Jews of Spain* (Tel Aviv: Levinsky College of Education Publishing House, 1994), 35–54.

—— 'What Did Maimonides Mean by *Madda*?', in G. Blidstein et al. (eds.), *Me'ah She'arim: Studies in Medieval Jewish Spiritual Life in Memory of Isadore Twersky* (Jerusalem: Magnes Press, 2001), 83–110.

SHAKED, SHAUL, ' "Peace Be Upon You, Exalted Angels": On Hekhalot, Liturgy, and Incantation Bowls', *Jewish Studies Quarterly*, 2 (1995), 197–219.

SHAPIRO, MARC, 'The Last Word in Jewish Theology? Maimonides' Thirteen Principles', *Torah u-Madda Journal*, 4 (1993), 187–242.

—— *The Limits of Orthodox Theology: Maimonides' Thirteen Principles Reappraised* (Oxford: Littman Library of Jewish Civilization, 2004).

—— 'Maimonidean Halakhah and Superstition', *Maimonidean Studies*, 4 (2000), 61–108.

SHATZ, DAVID, 'Worship, Corporeality and Human Perfection: A Reading of the Guide of the Perplexed III. 51–54', in Ira Robinson, Lawrence Kaplan, and Julien Bauer (eds.), *The Thought of Moses Maimonides: Philosophical and Legal Studies* (Lewiston, NY: Edwin Mellen Press, 1990), 77–129.

SHEAR, ADAM, 'The Later History of a Medieval Hebrew Book: Studies in the Reception of Judah Halevi's *Sefer Ha-Kuzari*', Ph.D. diss., University of Pennsylvania, 2003.

SHEILAT, YITSHAK, 'The Uniqueness of Israel: Comparing the Kuzari and Maimonides' (Heb.), in E. Samet and E. Fishler (eds.), *Me'aliyot 20: Essays and Studies on Maimonides* (Ma'aleh Adumim: Ma'aliyot, 1999), 271–302.

SHERWIN, BYRON, 'Mai Hannukah: What is Hannukah?', *CCAR Journal* (Fall 2003), 19–28.

SILMAN, YOCHANAN, 'Commandments and Transgressions in Halakhah: Obedience and Rebellion, or Repair and Destruction?' (Heb.), *Dine Israel*, 16 (1991), 183–201.

—— 'Halakhic Determinations of a Nominalistic and Realistic Nature: Legal and Philosophical Considerations' (Heb.), *Dine Israel*, 12 (1986), 249–66.

—— 'Introduction to the Philosophical Analysis of the Normative–Ontological Tension in the Halakha', *Da'at*, 31 (1993), pp. v–xx.

—— *Philosopher and Prophet: Judah Halevi, the Kuzari, and the Evolution of his Thought* (Albany, NY: SUNY Press, 1995).

—— *The Voice Heard at Sinai: Once or Ongoing* [Kol gadol velo yasaf] (Jerusalem: Magnes Press, 1999).

SIMON, URIEL, *Four Approaches to the Book of Psalms* (Albany, NY: SUNY Press, 1991).

SINCLAIR, DANIEL, 'Legal Thinking in the Teachings of Maimonides and Nachmanides' (Heb.), in Itamar Wahrhaftig (ed.), *Sefer yovel minhah le'ish: kovets ma'amarim mugash lerav simon dolgin* (Jerusalem: Congregation Beth David and Ariel United Israel Institutes, 1991), 349–55.

SIRAT, COLETTE, *A History of Jewish Philosophy in the Middle Ages* (Cambridge: Cambridge University Press, 1985).

—— 'The Study of *Ma'aseh Bereshit* in the Thought of Maimonides and his Students' (Heb.), *Hagut umikra* (Jerusalem: Ministry of Education, 1977), 4–11.

SOCHER, ABRAHAM, 'Of Divine Cunning and Prolonged Madness: Amos Funkenstein on Maimonides' Historical Reasoning', *Jewish Social Studies*, 6 (1999), 6–29.

SPIEGEL, YA'AKOV, *Chapters in the History of the Jewish Book: Writing and Transmission* [Amudim betoledot hasefer ha'ivri: ketivah veha'atakah] (Ramat Gan: Bar Ilan University Press, 2005).

STEINSCHNEIDER, MORITZ, 'Indications of Maimonides' Status' (Heb.), *Kovets al yad*, 1 (1885), 1–32.

STERN, DAVID, and MARK MIRSKY (eds.), *Rabbinic Fantasies: Imaginative Narratives from Classical Hebrew Literature* (New Haven, Conn.: Yale University Press, 1998).

STERN, JOSEF, 'The Fall and Rise of Myth in Ritual: Maimonides vs. Nahmanides on the Huqqim, Astrology, and the War against Idolatry', *Journal of Jewish Thought and Philosophy*, 6 (1997), 185–263.

—— 'Language', in Arthur A. Cohen and Paul Mendes-Flohr (eds.), *Contemporary Jewish Religious Thought* (New York: Scribners, 1987), 543–52.

—— 'Maimonides on Education', in Amelie Rorty (ed.), *Philosophers on Education* (London: Routledge, 1998), 109–23.

—— 'Maimonides on Language and the Science of Language', in Robert S. Cohen and Hillel Levine (eds.), *Maimonides and the Sciences* (Dordrecht: Kluwer, 2000), 173–226.

—— *Problems and Parables of Law: Maimonides and Nahmanides on Reasons for the Commandments (Ta'amei Ha-Mitzvot)* (Albany, NY: SUNY Press, 1998).

STRAUSS, LEO, *Philosophy and Law: Contributions to the Understanding of Maimonides and his Predecessors*, trans. Eve Adler (Albany, NY: SUNY Press, 1995).

STROUMSA, SARA, 'Elisha ben Abuyah and Muslim Heretics in Maimonides' Writings', *Maimonidean Studies*, 3 (1992–3), 173–94.

—— 'Entre Harran et al-Maghreb: La Théorie maimonidienne de l'histoire des religions et ses sources arabes', in Maria Isabel Fierro (ed.), *Judíos y musulmanes en al-Andalus y el Magreb* (Madrid: Casa de Velásquez, 2002), 153–64.

—— *On the Beginnings of the Maimonidean Controversy in the East: Yosef ibn Shimon's Silencing Epistle Concerning the Resurrection of the Dead* [Reshito shel pulmus harambam bemizraḥ] (Jerusalem: Makhon Ben-Tsevi, 1999).

—— 'The Sabians of Haran and the Sabians According to Maimonides: On the Development of Religion According to Maimonides' (Heb.), *Sefunot*, 7 (1999), 277–95; trans. into French as 'Sabéens de harran et Sabéens de Maïmonide', in Tony Levy and Roshdi Rashed (eds.), *Maimonide: Philosophe et savant* (Louvain: Peeters, 2004), 335–52.

SWARTZ, MICHAEL D., 'Book and Tradition in Hekhalot and Magical Literatures', *Journal of Jewish Thought and Philosophy*, 3 (1994), 189–229.

—— 'Magical Piety in Ancient and Medieval Judaism', in Marvin Meyer and Paul Mirecki (eds.), *Ancient Magic and Ritual Power* (Leiden: Brill, 1995), 167–84.

—— *Mystical Prayer in Ancient Judaism* (Tübingen: Mohr, 1992).

—— *Place and Person in Ancient Judaism: Describing the Yom Kippur Sacrifice* (Ramat Gan: Bar Ilan University Faculty of Jewish Studies, 2001).

—— 'Ritual about Myth about Ritual: Towards an Understanding of the Avodah in the Rabbinic Period', *Journal of Jewish Thought and Philosophy*, 6 (1997), 135–55.

—— *Scholastic Magic: Ritual and Revelation in Early Jewish Mysticism* (Princeton, NJ: Princeton University Press, 1996).

TALMAGE, FRANK, *Apples of Gold in Settings of Silver: Studies in Medieval Jewish Exegesis and Polemics* (Toronto: Pontifical Institute of Medieval Studies, 1999).

TA-SHEMA, ISRAEL, 'The Library of the Ashkenaz Sages in the
Eleventh–Twelfth Centuries' (Heb.), *Kiryat Sefer*, 60 (1985), 298–309; English
trans. in Gabrielle Sed-Rajna (ed.), *Rashi, 1040–1990: Hommages à Ephraim E.
Urbach*, Congrès Européen des Études Juives (Paris: Cerf, 1993), 635–40.

TIROSH-ROTHSCHILD, Hava, 'The Political Philosophy of Rabbi Abraham
Shalom: The Platonic Tradition', *Shlomo Pines Jubilee Volume*, pt. 2
(= *Jerusalem Studies in Jewish Thought*, 9) (Jerusalem: Jewish National and
University Library, 1990), 409–40.

TISHBY, ISAIAH, *The Wisdom of the Zohar: An Anthology of Texts*, trans. David
Goldstein, 3 vols. (Oxford: Littman Library of Jewish Civilization, 1989).

TWERSKY, ISADORE (Yitshak), 'Did Rabbi Abraham Ibn Ezra Influence
Maimonides?' (Heb.), in I. Twersky and Jay Harris (eds.), *Rabbi Abraham Ibn
Ezra: Studies in the Writings of a Twelfth-Century Jewish Polymath* (Cambridge,
Mass.: Harvard University Press, 1993), 21–48.

—— *Introduction to the Code of Maimonides* (New Haven, Conn.: Yale University
Press, 1980).

—— 'Maimonides on Eretz Israel: Halakhic, Philosophic, and Historical
Perspectives', in Joel Kraemer (ed.), *Perspectives on Maimonides* (Oxford:
Littman Library of Jewish Civilization, 1991), 257–90.

—— 'Maimonides' Image: An Essay on His Unique Stature in Jewish History'
(Heb.), *Asufot*, 10 (1997), 9–35.

—— *A Maimonides Reader* (New York: Behrman House, 1972).

—— 'Martyrdom and Sanctity of Life: Aspects of Holiness in Maimonides'
Teachings' (Heb.), in Isaiah Gafni and Aviezer Ravitzky (eds.), *Sanctity of Life
and Martyrdom: Studies in Memory of Amir Yekutiel* (Jerusalem: Merkaz
Zalman Shazar, 1992), 167–90.

UNTERMAN, ALAN, 'Shekhinah', *Encyclopaedia Judaica* (Jerusalem: Keter, 1972),
xiv. 1349–54.

URBACH, EPHRAIM, 'Fragments of *Tanhuma-Yelamdenu*' (Heb.), *Kovets al
yad*, NS 14/6, pt 1 (1966), 1–54.

—— 'Halakhah and Prophecy' (Heb.), *Tarbits*, 18 (1947), 1–27; repr. with additions
in id., *Me'olaman shel hakhamim* (Jerusalem: Magnes Press, 1988), 21–49.

—— *The Sages: Their Concepts and Beliefs*, 2 vols., trans. Israel Abrahams
(Jerusalem: Magnes Press, 1975).

—— (ed.), *Sefer arugat habosem* (Jerusalem: Mekize Nirdamim, 1939).

URBACH, YA'AKOV, 'Concerning the Secret of the Recitation of the Shema
(The Matter of *Barukh shem kevod malkhuto le'olam va'ed*)' (Heb.), *Sinai*, 92
(1982–3), 86–90.

VERMAN, MARK, 'Reincarnation and Theodicy: Traversing Philosophy,
Psychology, and Mysticism', in Jay Harris (ed.), *Be'erot Yitzhak: Studies in

Memory of Isadore Twersky (Cambridge, Mass.: Harvard University Press, 2005), 399–426.

VICKERS, BRIAN, 'Analogy vs Identity: The Rejection of Occult Symbolism, 1580–1680', in id. (ed.), *Occult and Scientific Mentalities in the Renaissance* (Cambridge: Cambridge University Press, 1984), 95–164.

WASSERSTROM, STEVEN, *Between Muslim and Jew: The Problem of Symbiosis under Early Islam* (Princeton, NJ: Princeton University Press, 1995).

—— 'Further Thoughts on the Origin of *Sefer Yesirah*', *Aleph*, 2 (2002), 201–20.

—— 'Sefer Yesira and Early Islam: A Reappraisal', *Journal of Jewish Thought and Philosophy*, 3 (1993), 1–30.

WEINBERG, YECHIEL YA'AKOV, *Writings* [Kitvei harav veinberg], vol. i, ed. Melekh (Marc) Shapiro (Scranton, Pa., 1988).

WEINBERGER, LEON J., *Jewish Hymnography: A Literary History* (Oxford: Littman Library of Jewish Civilization, 1998).

WEINFELD, MOSHE, ' "We Will Sanctify Your Name in the World" ' (Heb.), *Sinai*, 108 (1991), 69–76.

WEISS, ROSLYN, 'See No Evil: Maimonides' on Onqelos' Translation of the Biblical Expression "And the Lord Saw" ', *Maimonidean Studies*, 4 (2000), 135–62.

WHITE, NICHOLAS P., *Plato on Knowledge and Reality* (Indianapolis, Ind.: Hackett, 1976).

WOLFSON, ELLIOT R., 'Merkavah Traditions in Philosophical Garb: Judah Halevi Reconsidered', *Proceedings of the American Academy for Jewish Research*, 57 (1990/1), 179–242.

—— 'The Theosophy of Shabbetai Donnolo, with Special Emphasis on the Doctrine of *Sefirot* in *Sefer Hakhmoni*', *Jewish History*, 6 (1992) (= Frank Talmage Memorial Volume), 281–316.

—— *Through a Speculum that Shines: Vision and Imagination in Medieval Jewish Mysticism* (Princeton, NJ: Princeton University Press, 1995).

WOLFSON, HARRY A., *Crescas' Critique of Aristotle* (Cambridge, Mass.: Harvard University Press, 1929).

—— 'Hallevi and Maimonides on Prophecy', in Isadore Twersky and George H. Williams (eds.), *Studies in the History and Philosophy of Religion*, vol. ii (Cambridge, Mass.: Harvard University Press, 1977), 60–119.

—— 'Maimonides and Halevi: A Study in Typical Jewish Attitudes Towards Greek Philosophy in the Middle Ages', in Isadore Twersky and George H. Williams (eds.), *Studies in the History of Philosophy and Religion*, vol. i (Cambridge, Mass.: Harvard University Press, 1973), 120–61.

—— 'The Plurality of Immovable Movers in Aristotle, Averroes, and St. Thomas', in Isadore Twersky and George H. Williams (eds.), *Studies in the History and*

Philosophy of Religion, vol. i (Cambridge, Mass.: Harvard University Press, 1973), 1–21.

WOLFSON, HARRY A., 'The Problem of the Souls of the Spheres, from the Byzantine Commentaries on Aristotle through the Arabs and St. Thomas to Kepler', in Isadore Twersky and George H. Williams (eds.), *Studies in the History and Philosophy of Religion*, vol. i (Cambridge, Mass.: Harvard University Press, 1973), 22–59.

—— *Repercussions of the Kalam in Jewish Philosophy* (Cambridge, Mass.: Harvard University Press, 1979).

—— 'The Veracity of Scripture from Philo to Spinoza', in *Religious Philosophy: A Group of Essays* (Cambridge, Mass.: Harvard University Press, 1961), 217–45.

WOOLF, JEFFREY, 'Medieval Models of Purity and Sanctity: Ashkenazic Women in the Synagogue', in M. J. H. M. Poorthuis and J. Schwartz (eds.), *Purity and Holiness: The Heritage of Leviticus* (Leiden: Brill, 2000), 263–80.

WURZBURGER, WALTER S., *Ethics of Responsibility: Pluralistic Approaches to Covenantal Ethic* (Philadelphia, Pa.: Jewish Publication Society, 1994).

YAHALOM, JOSEPH, 'The Journey Inward: Judah Halevi between Christians and Muslims in Spain, Egypt, and Palestine', in Nicholas de Lange (ed.), *Hebrew Scholarship and the Medieval World* (Cambridge: Cambridge University Press, 2001), 138–48.

—— 'Maimonides and Hebrew Poetry' (Heb.), *Pe'amim*, 81 (1999), 4–14.

—— ' "Sayeth Tuviyah ben Tsidkiyah": The *Maqama* of Joseph ben Simeon in Honour of Maimonides' (Heb.), *Tarbits*, 65 (1997), 544–77.

YOM TOV BEN ABRAHAM OF SEVILLE, *Sefer hazikaron*, ed. Kalman Kahane (Jerusalem: Mosad Harav Kuk, 1982).

YUTER, ALAN J., 'Positivist Rhetoric and its Functions in Haredi Orthodoxy', *Jewish Political Studies Review*, 8 (1996), 127–88.

ZWIEP, IRENE, *Mother of Reason and Revelation: A Short History of Medieval Jewish Linguistic Thought* (Amsterdam: Gieben, 1997).

Index of Citations from Moses Maimonides and Judah Halevi

General Index